ACHIEVING PERMANENCE
FOR OLDER CHILDREN
AND YOUTH IN FOSTER CARE

Achieving Permanence for Older Children and Youth in Foster Care

Edited by
Benjamin Kerman, Madelyn Freundlich,
and *Anthony N. Maluccio*

COLUMBIA UNIVERSITY PRESS New York

Columbia University Press
Publishers Since 1893
New York   Chichester, West Sussex
Copyright © 2009 Columbia University Press

Library of Congress Cataloging-in-Publication Data
Achieving permanence for older children and youth in foster care / edited by
Benjamin Kerman, Madelyn Freundlich, and Anthony M. Maluccio.
p.   cm.
Includes bibliographical references and index.
ISBN 978-0-231-14688-3 (cloth : alk. paper) — ISBN 978-0-231-14689-0
(pbk. : alk. paper) — ISBN 978-0-231-51932-8 (ebook)
1. Foster children—United States. 2. Foster home care—United States.
I. Kerman, Benjamin. II. Freundlich, Madelyn. III. Maluccio, Anthony N. IV. Title.

HV881.A62 2009
362.73'30973—dc22
2008054450

Columbia University Press books are printed on permanent and durable acid-free paper.
This book is printed on paper with recycled content.
Printed in the United States of America

c 10 9 8 7 6 5 4 3 2 1

Contents

Acknowledgments

In April 2005, the organizers of the fourth National Convening on Youth Permanency facilitated a discussion among researchers concerning the state of research about permanency services to promote family relationships and connections and the needs of older youth served by the child welfare system. A general consensus emerged that there is a troubling lack of systematic empirical insight into the dynamics of the child welfare population, the needs of older youth, the impact of policy and the effectiveness of the services provided, and even the definition of "youth permanency." It also became apparent that, while a variety of investigators might be working to address these shortcomings in the research base, their individual efforts were disparate, too insular, and often unknown to one another.

Planners of the fifth National Convening quickly recognized this need with a sense of urgency, initiating the development of a Research Roundtable to coincide with the meeting in September 2006. With input from Rosemary Avery and Ruth McRoy, Anthony Maluccio and Benjamin Kerman designed a format of presentation and discussion and assembled a diverse group of researchers well positioned to summarize the state of research on the needs and outcomes for older youth involved in child welfare, as well as research on policy and practice initiatives to address these concerns. The invited panelists responded enthusiastically, eagerly engaging in their respective tasks as reviewers, presenters, respondents, and authors. We deeply appreciate the panelists' commitment to the children and families served in child welfare, made abundantly manifest in their contributions to this volume.

We also greatly appreciate the generous support provided to the participants in the Research Roundtable by the Annie E. Casey Foundation and its direct services agency, Casey Family Services. At the same time, it should be noted that all opinions expressed in this volume are those of the respective authors and do not necessarily reflect the positions of the funders or our home institutions.

This volume would not have made it to paper without the essential and able logistical and clerical assistance of Sharon Pitman and Pamela Harrison. Ms. Pitman's ever-present common sense often came in handy in the face of momentary shortages. Other Casey Family Services colleagues contributed in myriad ways to make the Roundtable and editing enterprise a success: Raymond Torres, Joy Duva, Sarah Greenblatt, Lee Mullane, and Lauren Frey, as well as Gretta Cushing, Ellen Ross, and Karen Jointer. Likewise, Columbia University Press's Lauren Dockett has been steadfast and patient in her support, enabling this work to make it to the done section of our to-do list.

While the volume would be literally empty without the contributions of our professional colleagues, our understanding of the true meaning and impact of family connections would be hollow had we not benefited so deeply from two groups of families. We are humbled before the collective commitment, guidance, wisdom, perseverance, and example personified by the families with whom we have had the honor of working and learning over the years. Finally, we are each most permanently indebted to the abiding and sustaining connections with our own families—our parents, spouses, children, and grandchildren. Their day-to-day patience, and weekly willingness to share our burdens and joys, juxtaposed alongside our life-long connections, provides permanence's greatest tribute and most compelling evidence.

ACHIEVING PERMANENCE
FOR OLDER CHILDREN
AND YOUTH IN FOSTER CARE

Introduction

Older children and youth in recent years have come to comprise an increasingly larger proportion of the foster care population in the United States. Their needs differ in significant ways from those of younger children for whom permanency has long been a primary goal. Traditionally, child welfare systems have focused on preparing older children and youth for adulthood—with far less attention directed to efforts to reunify them with their birth families, find new families for them through adoption or guardianship, or help them forge lifelong connections with caring, committed adults who will "be there" for them as they transition to the adult world and beyond. Although permanency planning is certainly not new to those familiar with foster care, efforts to achieve enduring connections to families for older children and youth too often have been sacrificed in the service of concentrating on preparation for independent living.

In this volume, we explore the challenges that child welfare systems confront in meeting the permanency needs of older children and youth in foster care. We examine the potentially conflicting goals that can lead to the development of policies and practices that fail to support efforts to achieve and sustain enduring family relationships, and we propose practice and policy approaches that can guide effective permanency work with these children and youth. We recognize that although states are charged with acting in loco parentis when children and youth enter foster care, bureaucracies cannot provide them with the nurturing, guidance, cheerleading, safety net in times of trouble, and ongoing supports into adulthood that "good" parents provide.

The volume is based on a belief that child welfare systems will better serve children and youth by redefining their role, changing it from substitute parenting to ensuring that children and youth are connected to safe, nurturing, and forever families. With a commitment to achieving and sustaining family permanence for these youth, child welfare agencies can ensure that when they leave care and their cases are closed, they will have the benefit of caring, supportive families that young people require as they move into adulthood and beyond.

PERMANENCE AND LIFELONG FAMILY CONNECTIONS

From both a practice and a legal perspective, family-based permanence is the preferred outcome for children and youth in foster care. Families provide them not only with shelter and financial supports but also with a set of relationships with consistent and supportive adults that are intended to last indefinitely—individuals to whom a child can return for support even as an adult. For these young persons, permanence means lifelong family connections and can take a variety of forms: reunification with parents; permanent placement with relatives; guardianship with relatives or other committed adults; adoption; or, when legal permanence is not possible, life-long connections with caring adults who, though not in a legal relationship, are committed to the child into adulthood. The objective of achieving permanence is to reach the optimal balance of physical, emotional/relational, legal, and cultural dimension within every child's and youth's array of family relationships.

As defined by Casey Family Services, the direct services agency of the Annie E. Casey Foundation (2005), permanence means having an enduring family relationship that

- is safe and meant to last a lifetime
- offers the legal right and social status of full family membership
- provides for physical, emotional, social, cognitive, and spiritual well-being

- assures lifelong connections to extended family, siblings, and other significant adults, along with family history and traditions, race, ethnicity, culture, religion, and language

Despite the diversity of shapes that families take across cultures, the protective and nurturing social bonds are omnipresent (Erera, 2002). Families locate children in the social order and play a major role in the enculturation and socialization of children and youth. Contemporary society generally views "family" as a haven from the world, encouraging "intimacy, love and trust where individuals may escape the competition of dehumanising forces in modern society" (Zinn and Eitzen, 1987:18). The family provides love and protection from the outside world and is seen ideally as a place where parents provide warmth, tenderness, understanding, and protection. Some have argued, however, that personal or family fulfillment—that is, the role of the family in supplying what is "vitally needed but missing from other social arrangements"—has replaced protection as the major role of the family (Zinn and Eitzen, 1987:29).

The first teacher of life skills has always been the family. While the notions of childhood and adolescence have changed over time, there is remarkable cross-cultural consistency regarding the progressive assumption of adult roles within the context of protective family and supportive community, punctuated by a variety of rituals that recognize the emerging independent adult, connected to family and community in a different, more autonomous, and more responsible manner. Within families, children and youth have opportunities to practice the skills that they will need when they take their place as adults in their communities.

Western literature reflects the centrality of—and dependence on—the family for helping youth through the difficult adjustment to adulthood. Case histories ranging from Shakespeare's *Romeo and Juliet*, to Dickens's orphaned Oliver Twist and Pip of *Great Expectations*, to *Star Wars*' Luke and Leia Skywalker, highlight the potential destructive influence of missing or dysfunctional family on adolescents, as well as the power of a loving family to rescue and rehabilitate. These universal themes are particularly salient to young people in foster care, given their earlier experiences within troubled families of origin; their often mixed experiences within foster families who may or may not provide them with meaningful relationships; and uncertainties about the future as they set about navigating the adult world without the clear support and assistance of parents or extended family.

OLDER YOUTH AND PREPARATION FOR ADULTHOOD

Older youth in foster care may be launched into adulthood directly from their placements with foster families, in group homes, or in institutional settings. Like all youth, they need a variety of preparatory training and experiential learning opportunities in order to transition successfully to adulthood (Georgiades, 2005). For youth in foster care, these training experiences and learning opportunities are particularly vital. They leave the relatively protected shelter of life in foster care to live on their own, and they generally have not had the benefit of progressive preparation for adulthood that families normatively provide to their children over the course of pre-adolescence and adolescence. Child welfare systems have long recognized the urgent need to provide youth with a range of social and life skills that can assist them in navigating the adult world.

Although there has been a mobilization of a variety of resources to train youth in concrete independent living skills, primarily in classroom environments, less attention has been given to the critical role of relationships in preparing them for adulthood and sustaining them as they transition to adult roles and beyond. Criticism of independent living programs has focused on the absence of efforts to connect youth with family members or other caring, committed adults who can offer them the benefits of a *family* relationship that will sustain them as they transition to adulthood and beyond.

For some years, permanency specialist Lauren Frey has asked her workshop audiences to write down "the things that your family did for you, gave to you, taught you or passed on to you that helped you to become a successful, productive adult" (Frey, 2005:6). She then asks participants to select the top three "must-haves if you have to choose." She notes that people consistently prioritize qualities such as unconditional love, a sense of belonging, family traditions, a strong work ethic, a chance to make mistakes, the value of spirituality, a home, emotional support, and belief in one's self. In contrast, items on a sample standardized pre-discharge checklist from child welfare agencies seem to miss the mark: youth will have an alarm clock, a high school diploma or GED, a source of income, a hobby, a library card, and a driver's license.

Ensuring that youth in foster care are connected with families through legal relationships or family-like relationships with caring, committed adults presents a complicated challenge to researchers, policymakers, and social service practitioners. This volume represents an effort to assemble research from disparate fields to shed light on the integration of the two primary and potentially complementary goals of the child welfare system: connecting youth with families for life and providing youth with the skills and assets they will need to survive and prosper in their adulthood.

ORGANIZATION OF THIS BOOK

The authors contributing to this volume answered an invitation from the editors to consider what their research meant for efforts to promote permanence for older children and youth in foster care. As participants in a Research Roundtable in September 2006, the authors brought differing perspectives, engaged in a rich exchange with other researchers and practitioners, and contributed to the evidence base. The Roundtable was held in conjunction with the 2006 National Convening on Youth Permanence, sponsored by the Annie E. Casey Foundation/Casey Family Services. Specifically, they addressed the following questions:

- What is the current state of child welfare practice and research in the United States?
- Which questions have been addressed?
- Which new questions need to be addressed?
- What are the child and family characteristics that predict enduring outcomes in family relationships and effective life skills?
- What are the implications for recruitment and retention of foster families?
- What are the implications for work with special populations, such as:
  Eliminating disproportionality in service provision and outcomes?
  Addressing the special needs of children of color; newer immigrant families; gay, lesbian, bisexual, transgender, and questioning youth; and other historically underserved groups?
- What are the policies and practices that have been found to promote success in building enduring family relationships for youth in foster care?
  With whom? Under what conditions? How?
  How do these efforts relate to previous policy or practice reform (e.g., concurrent planning)?
- What are the implications for shaping future practices and policies that will promote permanency for youth in foster care?
  What is needed to implement and achieve this outcome?
  What must organizations provide to support this work?
  What preventive and early intervention efforts are needed?

The participants discussed critical issues; explored emerging policy and practice responses; and offered recommendations to policymakers, service providers, and researchers to increase the likelihood that each youth in foster care will exit the system with an enduring family relationship that he or she can count on for life. Their presentations were organized into three panels, which parallel this volume: describing the problem, policy responses, and practice responses.

Describing the Problem

To craft an effective and efficient response, the problem has to be well understood. In the first section of this volume, the focus is on describing the challenges associated with meeting the permanency needs of youth in foster care. How many youth leave foster care without families? What are the characteristics of these youth and their experiences before leaving care? What are the outcomes for youth who leave foster care through "aging out"? To what extent do these youth have family relationships on which they can depend? When youth leave foster care to families, how "permanent" are these arrangements? To what extent do placement-related factors influence the permanence of these family relationships? Do the research findings make the case for urgency with regard to new policy and practice responses?

In the chapters in this section, researchers—both those who presented at the Roundtable and the respondents to those presentations—explore what is known from national data about youth who age out of foster care and those who leave care to family. They also examine the dynamics associated with "impermanence" when youth leave foster care.

Policy Responses

Federal, state, and local policies play a key role in defining permanence as a priority and in directing resources to permanency efforts and to preparation of youth in foster care for adulthood. It is essential that the strengths and challenges of the current policy framework be carefully examined:

- What are the key federal laws that impact permanency planning for youth and preparation for adulthood?

- Are federal and state policy goals regarding permanence and preparation for adulthood consistent with one another?
- To what extent are certain permanence outcomes given incentives and others are not?
- What is the role of kinship care in providing expanded permanency opportunities for youth in foster care?
- How can existing resources through federal, state, and local funding streams be maximized to achieve the best outcomes for youth and support for their families?
- How effective are the relationships among different service systems, particularly child welfare agencies and the courts?
- What is the role of the courts in ensuring that youth in foster care achieve permanence?
- To what extent do courts and child welfare agencies coordinate efforts to ensure that youth have lifelong family connections?

In this section, the authors examine the policy framework created by federal law and state policies as they support and create challenges to achieving permanence for youth in care and preparing them for adulthood, consider the policy framework for kinship care as an important avenue for permanence and preparation of youth for adulthood, and examine the research regarding the court's role in ensuring that youth have the benefit of permanence and preparation for adulthood.

Practice Responses

Practitioners who work with *real* youths and *real* families creatively respond to a range of vexing challenges as they attempt to ensure that each young person has lifelong family connections and is well prepared to transition to adulthood. Their perspectives, their training, and their personal and professional histories may pull them in different directions: some practitioners may place primary emphasis on permanence, whereas others may see the task as preparing youth as fully as possible for life on their own. Practitioners often struggle with balancing the urgency of a youth's immediate needs and their recognition that the youth's long-term needs will best be met by family members who understand and are committed to "being there" for her or him. The limited body of evidence-based practice in child welfare adds to the challenges that practitioners face.

In this section, the authors focus on practices aimed at optimizing the two primary paths to legal permanence: reunification and adoption. They explore key strategies that can promote permanence: services that support youth in remaining safely with their families, family-involvement meetings to promote the engagement of family when youth enter foster care, the community as a resource for preventive services and ongoing support for youth and their families, and youth's development of life skills within a family context. The final chapter in this section presents a series of case vignettes illustrating the application of many of these practices.

This volume concludes with a chapter that synthesizes current evidence-based policies and practices that support family permanence for youth and outlines the need for additional research in several critical areas. It advocates for a deeper understanding of "what works" and the implementation of evidence-based policies and practices to ensure that when child welfare systems close youth's cases, they leave foster care to permanent families.

REFERENCES

Casey Family Services, the Direct Service Agency of the Annie E. Casey Foundation (2005). *A Call to Action: An Integrated Approach to Youth Permanency and Preparation for Adulthood*. New Haven, Conn.: Author.

Erera, P. I. (2002). *Family Diversity: Continuity and Change in the Contemporary Family*. Thousand Oaks, Calif.: Sage.

Frey, L. (2005). A time for change: Permanency and preparation for adulthood. *Connection* (Winter/Spring): 5–7.

Georgiades, S. D. (2005). Emancipated young adults' perspectives on independent living programs. *Families in Society* 86(4): 503–10.

Zinn, M., and D. Eitzen (1987). *Diversity in American Families*. New York: Harper and Row.

Describing the Problem | **PART I**

A necessary foundation for the development of a successful policy and practice response to the permanence needs of youth in foster care is an accurate and detailed description of the challenges. It is essential to clearly frame the problem, specify the questions that must be answered in order to develop sound policy and practice, and use data to address those questions as fully as possible. Only through clarifying what is known and what needs to be known is it possible to set priorities within policy and practice and identify the needed levers for change.

Historically, national child welfare data have been limited. Until the mid-1990s, states were asked to voluntarily provide child welfare data through the Voluntary Cooperative Information System (VCIS). There were limited outcome studies regarding youth in foster care, and in few studies were the voices of youth sought as a source of information about youth's experiences and outcomes in foster care. Foster care and adoption data, however, have become more available since the mid-1990s with implementation of the Chapin Hall Multi-State Foster Care Data Archive and the federal Adoption and Foster Care Analysis and Reporting System (AFCARS). At the same time, certain broad-based studies seeking the perspectives of youth have examined the outcomes for youth who age out of foster care.

Fred Wulcyzn and Penelope Maza use two major sources of child welfare data to help clarify the challenges associated with youth permanence and to describe some of the dynamics that shape the experiences and outcomes of youth in foster care. In chapter 1, Wulcyzn uses data from the Chapin Hall archive to answer several questions: Who grows up in foster care, and what portion of their childhood was spent in a foster home or some other placement setting? Where do adolescents fall within the broader context of children entering foster care for the first time? Are there entry rate disparities for white children and black children when age is taken into account? How do youth leave foster care: that is, what portion of youth leave through reunification, adoption, aging out, and running away? In chapter 2, Maza uses AFCARS data to identify the similarities and differences between youth who achieved and who did not achieve permanence. She examines various factors that are associated with permanence, including gender, race/ethnicity, placement history, length of stay, and age at time of removal. Using a different data repository, her findings triangulate on similar themes and lend credence to the conclusions, despite the limitations of looking across states' administrative data.

The growing body of outcome research has contributed to a fuller understanding of the poor outcomes for many youth who leave foster care to live on their own. The research contributes to the great sense of urgency that policy and practice respond more effectively to the needs of youth in foster care, particularly those who age out to "independent living." In chapter 3, Mark Courtney provides a concise but comprehensive review of the findings from twenty-two studies with samples of youth who had aged out of foster care. These findings make clear that, on average, young people who age out of foster care are significantly disadvantaged across a number of domains as they approach and later negotiate the transition to adulthood. The studies also demonstrate that youth in foster care are much less likely than their peers to be able to rely on family for support to compensate for their disadvantages during the transition. In chapter 4, Peter Pecora responds, discussing two additional, recently completed studies and highlighting some of the most pressing needs facing youth who have exited foster care. Both Courtney and Pecora discuss the implications of the research findings for policy, program, and practice improvements.

Progress in child welfare research is impeded by lack of conceptual models that can be tested. In chapter 5, Richard Barth and Laura Chintapalli suggest one such model. They propose a model for understanding the relationships among placement instability, youth's emotional and behavioral problems, administrative decisions, disconnection from family, and placement into residential care. In particular, they examine instability in care and the use of congregate care facilities as impediments to permanence, and they describe the challenges of "impermanent" permanence when reunifications are not successful and when termination of parental rights does not lead to adoption.

In response, in chapter 6, Gretta Cushing and Benjamin Kerman spotlight the need for clarity around the dimensions of permanence that further reflect on the ultimate goal of family connections. They urge that the discourse regarding research, interventions, and policy extend beyond legal permanence and incorporate a recognition of the vital role that nurturing parental connections plays in youth development, irrespective of whether the relationships are formally recognized with legal sanction. With a focus on emotional security and belonging, they explore the practice, policy, and research implications of viewing permanency as a "state of security and attachment."

Foster Youth in Context ONE

FRED WULCZYN

According to national statistics, upward of twenty thousand children left foster care in 2002 after their eighteenth birthday; among children in care, emancipation was listed as the case goal for more than thirty-four thousand children (U.S. Department of Health and Human Services, 2007). Not surprisingly, the issue of foster youth has attracted considerable attention, particularly over the past decade since the beginning of the twenty-first century. For the most part, that attention has focused on the transition to adulthood by children who reach the age of majority while still in foster care (that is, while in state custody). Policymakers at the federal level have addressed the problem at least twice. The Independent Living Act of 1985 established a pool of federal resources for youth leaving foster care. More recently, the Foster Care Independence Act of 1999 (the Chafee Act) renewed the focus on children leaving foster care and their preparation for adulthood.

Despite the policy attention, relatively little empirical work has been done to place foster youth (children age thirteen and above) in the broader context of the foster care system. Discussions of foster youth often begin with an image of children who grow up in foster care only to face the transition to adulthood without the benefit of any social connections. Although that is a powerful image, the pathways that adolescents take through the foster care system are often more complex. This chapter addresses a set of basic questions designed to broaden our understanding of adolescents within the foster care system. The first question deals directly with the issue of who grows up in foster care and the portion of childhood that they spent in foster care. The second question relates to the entry of children into foster care, with specific attention to where adolescents fall within the broader context of children entering foster care for the first time and entry rate disparities for white children and black children that take age into account. The third question relates to youth's exits from foster care. Youth placed in foster care leave care for a variety of reasons that include reunification, adoption, aging out, and running away.

Foster youth, as described in this chapter, generally refers to children between the ages of thirteen and seventeen. The definition, however, is flexible, depending on the context. From an admission perspective, a definition of foster youth as children between the ages of thirteen and seventeen is workable; from a discharge perspective, it is better to expand the definition to include individuals leaving care at eighteen and older. For other questions, it is useful to consider the experience of children admitted before they turned thirteen.

GROWING UP IN FOSTER CARE

The issue of youth aging out of foster care has gained salience for the reason that the state has an obligation to shape successful transitions to adulthood for these youth. Because the state has care and custody of the child, it must, as any parent is expected to do, see to it that foster youth have the requisite assets needed to complete a successful transition to adulthood.

Although who grows up in foster care is a straightforward question, very few empirical data are available to answer it. Moreover, from the data that are available, it is difficult to say whether growing up in foster care has become more or less likely over time. The paucity of data is attributable to the fact that, in all but a few states, there are no administrative data that allow the tracking of outcomes for children who entered foster care as young children. As an example, most states do not have data that answer a question such as the following: Of children admitted as babies in 1986, how many spent their childhood through age eighteen in foster care, leaving care in

2004? The same challenges remain in answering questions about children who were admitted to foster care in 1987 at one year of age or older and who may have spent what was "left" of their childhood in foster care once they were placed. Time spent in foster care for these children, however, would represent a declining portion of their childhood, if childhood were measured from birth through age eighteen. Moreover, with each passing year from 1987 through 2004, less and less would be known about how much time was spent in foster care relative to childhood in its entirety because the group of children whose eighteenth birthday has been observed is smaller as time moves closer to the present.

Fortunately, a handful of states have data from 1986 that provide a preliminary answer to this important question. Even with these data, it is difficult to identify trends as from 1986 to the present. There have been a number of policy initiatives designed to influence outcomes for children in foster care. Some children placed in foster care in 1986 were in care when each of these policies was put into place by law. For other children, only some of the policy changes would have affected their placement experiences and outcomes.

For this analysis, we look at all children admitted to foster care for the first time from 1986 through 2004. The total number of children is 701,233; the number of children who aged out of placement (that is, were in foster care on their eighteenth birthday and left foster care at that time) is 35,979, or about 5 percent of the total. It is possible to know whether a child aged out of foster care only if we observe the child's eighteenth birthday. For other children admitted since 1986, we will not observe their eighteenth birthdays as of 2004. As these birthdays are observed, the 5 percent will grow over time.

For children admitted as babies, we look at 1986–1987 data to answer the question of how likely it is that a child will spend his or her entire childhood in foster care. The question of how many babies age out of foster care is important because babies make up the largest group of children admitted since 1986. Of the total 701,233 children admitted to foster care, babies accounted for 150,000, or about 20 percent. Unfortunately, relatively little is known about these babies. As noted earlier, only babies from the 1986 entry cohort have been alive long enough to determine whether they were still in foster care upon reaching their eighteenth birthday. The number of babies who aged out is very small. Notwithstanding sources of error in the data (e.g., children who moved to other states or were otherwise lost to the tracking system), only twenty-five children stayed in

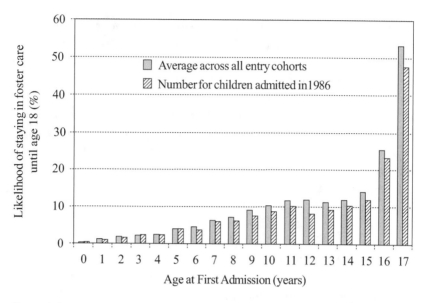

Figure 1.1 Percentage of children aging out of foster care by age at admission, 1986–2004 admissions

foster care for their entire childhoods, a figure that represents about one-half of 1 percent of the five thousand infants admitted in 1986.

In Figure 1.1, data representing the likelihood of entering care and staying in foster care until age eighteen by age at first admission are given for all children between the ages of birth and seventeen. Two sets of data are displayed: the average across all entry cohorts and the specific figures for children admitted in 1986. When viewing the data, it is important to bear in mind that the sample used to compute the average grows by one year with each age group. The figure for babies represents the experience of babies admitted in 1986, the only year for which data are available. For one year olds, there are two years of data available: 1986 and 1987. For seventeen year olds, there are seventeen years of experience to consider, given that any child who entered foster care at seventeen would have been observed to age out if, in fact, they did.

The data show that through age six, fewer than 5 percent of the children in each age group admitted remained in their first placement spell through their eighteenth birthday. Among children between the ages of one and ten, the comparable figure was between 6 and 10 percent. For children between the ages of eleven and fifteen, the percentage of children who aged out was between 11 and 14 percent. The percentage of children who aged out was highest among children admitted between the ages of sixteen and seventeen. About one in four children placed in foster care at age sixteen aged out; among seventeen year olds, the figure was above 50 percent.

Because a child may move in and out of foster care over the course of childhood, capturing only the time spent in the first placement spell understates how much time is spent in care relative to childhood. To correct for this downward bias, we calculated total time in care across all placement spells and expressed the result as the percent of childhood. These data, presented in Figure 1.2, are somewhat complicated, again because the level of incomplete data limits what can be said. To resolve these issues, we computed the following:

- Childhood: the number of days between birth and the eighteenth birthday
- Total time in care: the number of days spent in foster care through age eighteen if the eighteenth birthday was observed or the end of observation, whichever came first; for a child placed on the day he or she was born and stayed in foster care through his or her eighteenth birthday, childhood and total time in care would be the same
- Possible observed days: the number of days from the date of first entry into placement through age eighteen; this refers simply to the maximum number of days a child can be in care if he or she were to spend the rest of his or her childhood in care
- Observed days: the total number of days from placement to age eighteen or the end of observation, whichever comes first; the use of the term "observed days" is meant to capture the idea that from the date of placement, the child welfare system has the opportunity to observe what happens to the child through age 18; if the eighteenth birthday is observed, then possible observed days and observed days are one and the same

Figure 1.2 addresses two broad notions of childhood. The first is the proportion of childhood (birth to age eighteen) spent in foster care on average. The second is, given the starting date of placement and the time left before a child turns age eighteen, how much of a child's remaining childhood is spent in foster care, given the age at placement. With regard to the proportion of childhood spent in foster care, Figure 1.2 shows that children admitted to foster care between the ages of birth and nine years spent between 20 and 24 percent of their childhood in foster care. Among

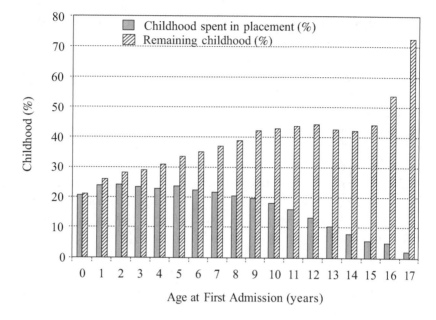

Figure 1.2 Foster care in the context of childhood, 1986–2004 admissions

older children, the proportion of their childhood spent in foster care declines through age seventeen because days in care are counted from the point of first entry. Children placed after age nine have already lived half their childhood outside the foster care system. With each passing year, the percentage of time a child could spend in care goes down as they reach their eighteenth birthday. Understandably, children who enter placement as seventeen year olds spend the least of amount of time in care relative to childhood.

Figure 1.2 also shows the time spent in foster care as a percentage of how much childhood is left, given a placement in foster care. Viewed in this way, foster care becomes an increasingly important context for growing up. For example, among children age twelve at the time of placement, 45 percent of their remaining childhood is spent in one or more placements. With each additional year, foster care plays an increasingly important role in the life of a child. For children who enter care at age seventeen, more than 70 percent of their remaining childhood is spent in foster care. In other words, foster care represents a small fraction of their childhood, but it is the context that defines the months and days leading up to their eighteenth birthday.

FOSTER CARE ENTRY

Three issues are important to consider in relation to foster care entry: the risk of entering foster care, entry rate disparities, and placement types.

Risk of Entry into Foster Care

The risk of entry into foster care refers to the probability a child will enter foster care. The risk can be computed in any one of several ways. As a rate per one thousand children in the population, the rate of entry measures the risk of entry within a given population. Figure 1.3 illustrates the admission rates per one thousand children in the general population in 2004. Admissions are counted as first ever admissions in 2004 from a collection of fourteen states that provided data to Chapin Hall and the Center for Foster Care and Adoption at the University of Chicago. The data are presented by single year of age and race in order to place the risk of placement among adolescents within the population of all children.

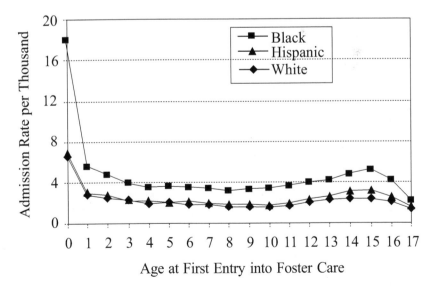

Figure 1.3 Admission rate per 1,000 children by race or ethnicity, 2004

As reported in previously published work (Wulczyn et al., 2005), the data point to persistent risk patterns regardless of race. Among black children, the likelihood of placement is greatest among infants and adolescents, especially adolescents who are age fourteen and fifteen. For these children, the rate of placement is just above five per thousand. Only black babies face a substantially higher risk of placement.

Although uniformly lower than placement rates for black children, the placement rates for white and Hispanic children follow the same general pattern in relation to age. Among whites, fifteen year olds have the highest rate of placement except for white babies; for Hispanics, placement rates are highest for babies and fifteen year olds.

Entry Rate Disparity

Disproportionality occurs when one population (e.g., black foster children) is out of proportion with respect to an appropriate reference population (e.g., black children in the general population). Differences in the likelihood of entry into foster care are an important component of racial disproportionality.

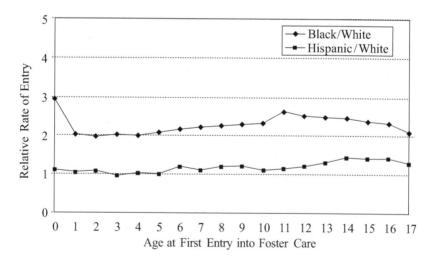

Figure 1.4 Entry rate disparities by age and race or ethnicity, 2004

In Figure 1.4, the data point to the fact that, across all age groups, black children are more likely to enter foster care. The data also suggest that disparity varies across childhood. Figure 1.4 highlights entry rate disparities by age at entry and race or ethnicity. In this figure, two comparisons are offered. The first compares the rate of black placement to the rate of white placement, by age; the second draws the same comparison for Hispanics and whites. In each case, the relative rate of entry is determined by dividing the age-specific rate of entry for white children into the corresponding rate for either black or Hispanic children.

Although significant disparities exist for black children of all ages, the data also point to the fact that disparity is not constant across childhood. For black children, disparity is greatest among young babies. Among children between the ages one and four (preschool years), disparity is approximately one-third lower than it is for babies. Once black children reach school, the disparity rates grow through age eleven, but they never reach the level reported for babies. Among adolescents, disparity rates decline, with the lowest level reached at age seventeen.

Among Hispanics, the general pattern holds, with important exceptions. First, disparity rates are generally lower. Second, disparity among the youngest children is absent. Notwithstanding problems with the coding of race or ethnicity in the source data, Hispanic children are placed into foster care at about the same rate as white children. That said, disparity rates are slightly higher among children in elementary and junior high school. For adolescents, entry disparities grow smaller, although the differences are not as distinct as those observed for whites and blacks.

Placement Type

The placement into different care types also varies by age at admission. As Figure 1.5 shows, adolescents are the children least likely to be placed in family-based care. More than one-half the children below the age of twelve spent most of their time in foster care in the home of a family. Another 25 percent or more spent the majority of their placement time in the care of a relative. For children aged twelve and above, group care became the predominant care type. For fifteen year olds, one-half the youth spent the majority of their time in care in a group setting.

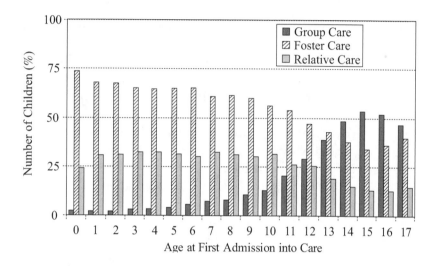

Figure 1.5 Predominant placement type by age at admission, 2004

LEAVING FOSTER CARE

As a developmental construct, age is a useful way to organize data about who enters foster care and how long any given group of children spends in foster care. The same is true for how children leave foster care. Age-structured data reveal patterns that reflect transcendent developmental processes.

Discharge reasons by the child's age at admission are presented in Figure 1.6 (for black children) and Figure 1.7 (for white children). The data, drawn from a collection of states, show by age the likelihood of each of three exit types. The exit types are family exits (which include reunification, discharge to relatives, and guardianship); adoption; and all other exit types, including running away and aging out. Figure 1.6 and Figure 1.7 also show whether children in the sample were still in care.

Patterns in the data show a remarkable consistency. Babies from this collection of states, whether black or white, are the children most likely to be adopted and the least likely to be reunified. For children generally, adoption rates fall as the age at admission rises. At age thirteen, the likelihood of adoption falls below 5 percent, regardless of whether the children are black or white.

Among all black children, children between the ages of one and nine have the highest reunification rates. At age ten, reunification rates start to

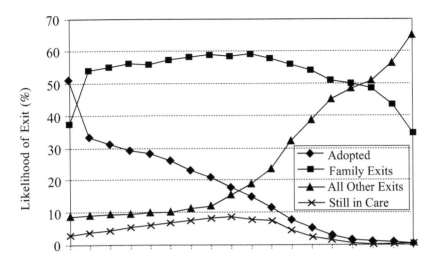

Figure 1.6 Likelihood of exit by exit reason, black children, 1990–1999

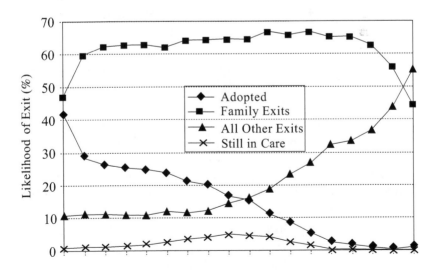

Figure 1.7 Likelihood of exit by exit reason, white children, 1990–1999

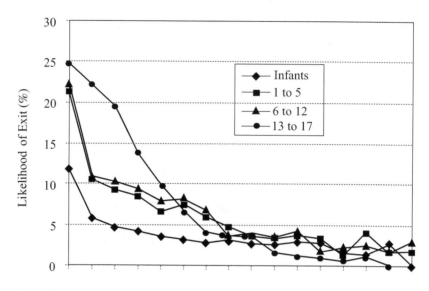

Figure 1.8 Likelihood of exit to reunification by time since admission to foster care and age, 1990–1999

decline, and at admission ages sixteen and seventeen, the likelihood of reunification is below 50 percent for black children. The pattern for white children is generally the same with important differences. Overall, reunification rates are slightly higher for white children. Reunification rates for white children drop with age, but the decline starts later in adolescence.

Other exit types grow as the reason that children leave foster care starting around age nine. From a base of about 10 percent of all exits for all children under the age of nine, regardless of race or ethnicity, other exits rise persistently as the age at admission grows from ten to seventeen. Although black youth, when compared with white youth, are more likely to leave placement for other reasons, the basic patterns underscore the importance of the similarities in the developmental processes.

The timing of exit, expressed as a conditional probability in relation to placement duration, is presented in Figures 1.8 and 1.9. Figure 1.8 shows when children are reunified; Figure 1.9 shows the same data for adoption. In each figure, the data are displayed for separate age groups, so that the experience of foster youth is more readily discerned.

These data reveal well-established facts about both the reunification and adoption processes. In the initial six-month period after admission, reunifi-

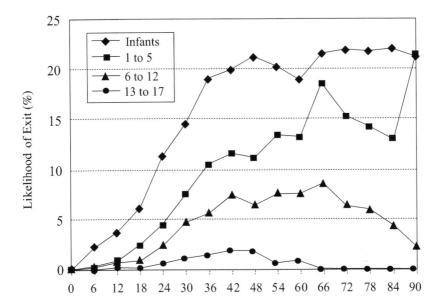

Figure 1.9 Likelihood of exit to adoption by time since admission to foster care and age, 1990–1999

cation rates are relatively high, regardless of age. Thereafter, the likelihood of reunification declines rapidly, particularly for children between the ages of birth and twelve at admission. For example, when children are still in foster care six months after admission, the likelihood of reunification during the second six-month period falls by 50 percent. Adolescents have the highest initial rate of reunification, and the change in reunification rates is smaller during the first twelve months. However, by thirty-six months, adolescent reunification rates are below those recorded for children of other ages.

Adoption rates follow a notably different pattern, although the age differences are no less noteworthy. In essence, the adoption process is the mirror image of reunification, with the likelihood of adoption holding at a low rate during the weeks and months immediately after admission. The passage of time (placement duration) brings higher adoption rates for all children, regardless of their age at admission.

What differs is the rate at which the adoption rate changes, given age at admission. Among infants, the rate of adoption rises more quickly and reaches a higher level than is the case for other age groups. For adolescents, the pattern is much less pronounced. The adoption rate for children between the ages of thirteen and seventeen rises as placement duration increases, but the rate of increase is slower and the peak adoption rates are much lower.

CHILDREN IN CARE AT AGE SIXTEEN

The data presented thus far give what might be called a long-term view of children placed in foster care. Data from 1986–1987 suggest that although older children tend to spend a smaller portion of their total childhood in foster care, a good portion of what remains of their childhood is spent in foster care after they are admitted to care. These data also describe what happens to children once they enter foster care, a point of view that further highlights the importance of basic age differences.

In this section, we use data to address the question of what happens to children who were in care at some point during the year they were sixteen. Using data on children who spent one day as a sixteen year old in foster care during 2002, we determined where they were on their eighteenth birthdays. Did they reach the age of majority while still in care, or were they

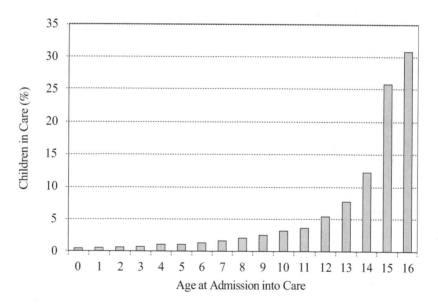

Figure 1.10 Children in care at age sixteen by age at admission, 2002

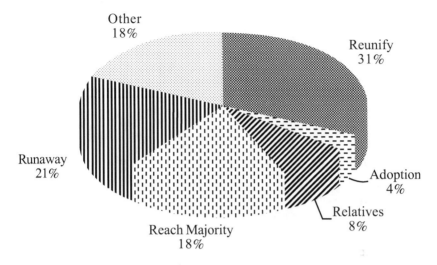

Figure 1.11 Children in care at age sixteen by exit type, 2002

discharged and, if so, how? This more compressed view offers a somewhat more realistic picture of states' planning processes with older youth.

The initial question is when children in care at age sixteen entered foster care for the first time. As Figure 1.10 shows, not surprisingly, most children in care at age sixteen (56 percent) entered care as either fifteen or sixteen year olds. Children who entered care before their twelfth birthday represent about 25 percent of the children in care at age sixteen, a nontrivial figure. Few of the sixteen year olds entered foster care before their fifth birthdays, although for those children who did, foster care was a significant component of their lives.

Exit data for this population are presented in Figures 1.11 and 1.12. Figure 1.11 shows exits for children in care at age sixteen through their eighteenth birthdays. Permanency rates (adoption, reunification, and discharges to relatives) account for about 43 percent of exits involving youth in care at age sixteen, regardless of age at admission. Nonpermanent exits (other exits not listed separately and running away) account for another 39 percent of the exits. Children who were in foster care at age sixteen and who reached the age of eighteen still in care are listed as having reached majority and represent about 18 percent of all exits.

Exit data are also presented in Figure 1.12. These data differ from those in Figure 1.11 in two ways. First, Figure 1.12 takes age at admission into

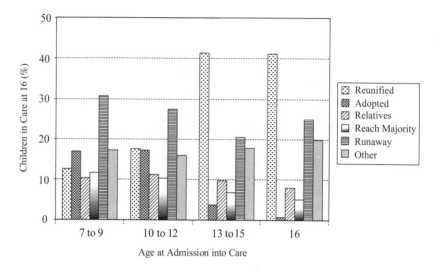

Figure 1.12 Children in care at age sixteen by age at admission and exit status, 2002

consideration. Second, the data show what happened to children in care at age sixteen up to and including their eighteenth birthday. To be counted, youth had to be in care during their sixteenth year and discharged before turning age eighteen. If youth were in care on their eighteenth birthdays, they are listed as having reached majority.

Four distinct groups are portrayed: children admitted between the ages of seven and nine, children admitted between the ages of ten and twelve, children admitted between the ages of thirteen and fifteen, and sixteen year olds. Among the groups admitted between the ages of seven and twelve, running away is the most common exit reason (more than 25 percent). Family exits, as a group, account for about 40 percent of the exits, whereas youth who reached majority make up about 10 percent of the children who were under the age of twelve at admission.

Children in care at age sixteen who entered as older children (above the age of twelve) are much more likely to be reunified than are younger children. Indeed, reunification is the outcome most often achieved with children who entered care later in their childhood. Adoption rates for older children, however, are very low, and exits to relatives are not common outcomes. The likelihood of reaching age eighteen while still in care is smaller for children who were older at admission.

SUMMARY AND IMPLICATIONS

Although foster youth have attracted a great deal of interest on the part of policymakers and practitioners of late, the focus of that interest has tended to emphasize the transition of foster youth to adulthood. In this chapter, the goal was to broaden our understanding of youth within the foster care system. Two simple questions served as the point of departure: How likely is it that a child will grow up in foster care? How much of childhood is spent in foster care? In addition, in this chapter I consider risk of entry into foster care for older youth compared with children of other ages. Finally, the issue of aging out is examined alongside the other ways children leave placement.

The data presented speak to a need to see the placement of youth in broader terms. First, the data indicate that very few children spend their entire childhood in foster care. Notwithstanding problems tracking children over a long period of time, the likelihood of spending an entire childhood in foster care (from birth to age eighteen) was less than 1 percent of the five thousand infants admitted in 1986. The data did show that that aging out of foster care was most common among children who entered foster care for the first time late in adolescence. On average, slightly more than one-half the children admitted as seventeen year olds were still in care at age eighteen. However, of the children admitted as sixteen year olds, slightly more than 20 percent remained in foster care long enough to reach age eighteen. For children between the ages of nine and fifteen, the likelihood of leaving care at age eighteen fell to between 8 and 14 percent. In short, the likelihood of reaching age eighteen while still in care is relatively rare, except for the children who enter care late in adolescence.

To place these data into fuller perspective, I also examined the portion of childhood spent in foster care. Again, childhood was treated as the period from birth to age eighteen. The data indicate that teenagers (children admitted to foster care for the first time as teens) spend a relatively small portion of their entire childhood in foster care. For example, among children age thirteen and above, less than 10 percent of their entire childhood is spent in placement. That said, among children placed as teens, about 40 percent of what remains of childhood is spent in care.

In sum, the data point to groups of children with distinct placement experiences. Younger children spend a greater portion of their childhood in foster care than older children do. When children enter placement for the first time as teens, they may spend a large portion of what remains of their childhood in care, but foster care represents a smaller portion of their total childhood.

Given the desire to improve outcomes for foster youth, these data imply a need to think carefully about program models. Among older youth, work with families falls in the midst of a unique developmental stage. The data suggest that when compared with children between the ages of two and ten, the likelihood of placement rises through adolescence, regardless of whether the children are white, black, or Hispanic. In 2007, Richard Barth (personal communication) argued that older children enter the child welfare system for reasons that revolve around their behavior problems, such as mental health issues, and the ability of their parents to manage those behaviors as opposed to child abuse and neglect more narrowly defined. Simply put, these data suggest that the transition into adolescence may be just as important from a service design and delivery perspective as the transition out of adolescence.

The data also suggest that older youth are more likely to leave foster care for reasons other than aging out of care. For example, children who enter care as adolescents return home more quickly than do younger children. Among children in care during the year they were age sixteen, aging out was the least common exit type. Exits to permanency, a category of exit types that includes reunification, adoption, and guardianship, accounted for about 43 percent of the exits compared with just 18 percent for children who aged out. Running away from placement was actually more common than aging out.

Again, these data make it clear that a much broader range of service choices for youth have to be offered. More pointedly, all youth have to negotiate the transition to adulthood. Among youth who have had some experience in the foster care system, youth in care at age eighteen may represent an important target group, but the data indicate that the larger group is composed of those teens who enter foster care close to their sixteenth birthday and exit within the next twelve to eighteen months (before they turn eighteen). For this larger group of youth, services designed to facilitate the transition to adulthood may be best viewed not as an extension of their foster care placement but as family-based and community-based services that connect youth with their families.

In closing, the emphasis on foster youth and their preparation for adulthood within the context of the foster care system acknowledges the important obligations child welfare agencies assume when they place children away from their parents and families. Nevertheless, aging out is but one point in the life course of children. The data presented in this chapter highlight the need to plan interventions with the full span of childhood in view, from birth through the transition to adulthood.

NOTE

I thank Kristen Hislop for her help preparing the analysis.

REFERENCES

U.S. Department of Health and Human Services, Administration for Children and Families (2007). *The AFCARS Report*. Washington, D.C.: Author. At www.acf.hhs .gov/programs/cb/stats_research/afcars/tar/report12.htm (accessed June 7, 2007).

Wulczyn, F. H., R. Barth, Y. Yuan, B. Jones Harden, and J. Landsverk (2005). *Beyond Common Sense: Child Welfare, Child Well-Being and the Evidence for Policy Reform*. New Brunswick, N.J.: Aldine Transaction.

A Comparative Examination of
Foster Youth Who Did and
Did Not Achieve Permanency

TWO

PENELOPE L. MAZA

Between federal fiscal years 2000 and 2005, there were approximately 1.66 million exits of children from the public foster care system.[1] The number of youth aged fifteen and older[2] who exited care during this period was approximately 473,000, equally distributed over the five fiscal years.[3] The achievement of permanency for these youth is a primary goal of the child welfare system because permanency is critical for well-being. The identification of youth at greatest risk for not achieving permanency can assist child welfare agencies in targeting limited resources. Using national data, in this chapter I provide an analysis of the relationship of certain child and case characteristics—gender, race or ethnicity, age at removal, circumstances associated with the removal, and length of stay in care—with the achievement of permanence.

PERMANENCE ACHIEVED AND NOT ACHIEVED

To identify the similarities and differences between youth who achieved and those who did not achieve permanency, a variable called "Permanency

Table 2.1   Categorization of Reasons for Discharge from Foster Care for Youth 15–20 Years Old by Whether or Not Permanence Was Achieved

	RESPONSES (%)	SAMPLE (N)
Achieved		
Reunification	49	233,000
Live with other relatives	6	27,000
Adoption	3	13,000
Guardianship	3	12,000
Not Achieved		
Emancipation/age out	25	120,000
Runaway	5	24,000
Excluded		
Transfer to another agency	5	23,000
Death	<1	<1,000
Missing data	4	20,000å

Achieved" was created, containing two categories: "yes" and "no." Before I discuss this variable, limitations of the data used in this analysis must be noted. The data do not track children after they exit foster care unless they return to care, generally before their eighteenth birthdays. Given the age range of the group being analyzed, the number of reentries is very small because there is very little time remaining for these youth to formally reenter the foster care system. As a result, permanency outcome data are not available on the majority of youth because they do not return to foster care. It is not possible to determine whether permanency, if achieved, was lasting or temporary. It cannot be determined, for example, whether youth who reunified with their parents subsequently ran away from their parent(s) or caregiver(s), and it cannot be determined whether youth who were legally emancipated remained connected to a relative after discharge from foster care. Some of these issues will be addressed by the new national data system, the National Youth in Transition Database (NYTD), under development by the U.S. Department of Health and Human Services.[4]

Table 2.1 shows the classifications of various discharge reasons in the "Permanency Achieved" variable. Almost one-half (49 percent) of the youth exiting foster care ages fifteen to twenty were reunified with the caregiver with whom they were living before removal and their entry into foster care. An additional 12 percent achieved permanence through other means, including living with relatives, adoption, and guardianship. The percentages associated with these permanency-related discharge reasons are lower for youth ages fifteen to twenty than they are in the general foster care population. More than one-half (54 percent) of the general foster care population exited to reunification, and another 33 percent exited to other permanency outcomes in FY 2005 (U.S. Department of Health and Human Services, 2006). Most of the difference between youth ages fifteen and twenty and the general foster care population can be explained by the higher rates of running away, formal emancipation at the age of majority, and aging out for this age group. These outcomes are rare in younger age groups. For this analysis, the following categories were excluded from the variable: transfer to another agency, death, and missing data.

FACTORS ASSOCIATED WITH PERMANENCE

The achievement of permanence for youth is related to both gender and race or ethnicity. Females are slightly less likely to achieve permanence than males (66 percent versus 70 percent). Hispanic and African American youths are less likely to achieve permanence than white youth (64 percent, 61 percent, and 73 percent, respectively) (Table 2.2).

Youth who achieved permanence differed in some notable ways from youth who did not (Table 2.3). For over one-half (52 percent) of the youth who achieved permanence, a child behavior problem was identified as a circumstance of removal, compared with less than one-third (32 percent) of youth who did not achieve permanence. Youth who did not achieve

Table 2.2   Demographic Characteristics of Youth 15–20 Who Were Discharged from Foster Care by Whether or Not They Achieved Permanence

	ACHIEVED (%)	NOT ACHIEVED (%)
Gender		
Male	70	30
Female	66	34
Race/Ethnicity		
African American Nonhispanic	61	39
Hispanic	64	36
White Nonhispanic	73	27

Table 2.3   Case Characteristics of Youth 15–20 Who Were Discharged from Foster Care by Whether or Not They Achieved Permanence

	ACHIEVED (%)	NOT ACHIEVED (%)
Circumstances of Removal[a]		
Child behavior problem	52	32
Neglect	28	39
Caretaker inability to cope	16	21
Physical abuse	13	15
Sexual abuse	7	10
Total Removals		
One	72	67
More than one	28	33
Total Placement Settings		
One	48	22
More than one	52	78
Last Placement Setting		
Institution	26	14
Foster family home (nonrelative)	20	32
Group home	20	15
Trial home visit	16	0
Foster family home (relative)	11	12
Preadoptive home	3	0
Runaway	2	16
Supervised independent living	1	12
AVERAGE NO. OF MONTHS IN LAST PLACEMENT SETTING	N	N
Foster family home (relative)	15	38
Foster family home (nonrelative)	9	24
Group home	6	14
Institution	6	12

[a] This is a multiple response set. Therefore, the columns do not total 100%. The columns for the other three table segments that include percentages total 100% or nearly 100% if there is rounding error.

permanency were more likely than those who achieved permanence to have entered foster care because of neglect (39 percent versus 28 percent), caregiver inability to cope (21 percent versus 16 percent), physical abuse (15 percent versus 13 percent), and sexual abuse (7 percent versus 10 percent).

Almost three-fourths (72 percent) of youth who achieved permanency, compared with about two-thirds (67 percent) of youth who did not, experienced only one removal and placement into foster care. Almost one-half (48 percent) of youth who achieved permanence compared with less than one-fourth (22 percent) of youth who did not achieve permanence had one placement before exiting care.

An institution was the last placement setting for over one-fourth (26 percent) of youth who achieved permanence compared with 14 percent of youth who did not achieve permanence. A group home was the last placement setting for one-fifth (20 percent) of youth who achieved permanence compared with 15 percent of the youth who did not achieve permanence. A nonrelative foster family home was the last placement setting for one-fifth (20 percent) of the youth who achieved permanence compared with almost one-third (32 percent) of youths who did not.

Further examination of the relationship between last placement setting for both length of stay and age at time of removal suggests that the more recent the removal, the more likely that permanence will be achieved regardless of the placement setting (Table 2.4). Two patterns emerge. First, youth who did not achieve permanence spent a considerably longer period of time in their last placement setting than youth who did achieve permanency. The average length of time that youth who did not achieve permanence spent in a relative foster family home, for example, was over three years (thirty-eight months) compared with fifteen months for youth who achieved permanency. Among youths in nonrelative foster family homes, the average time for youth who did not achieve permanence was two years

Table 2.4   Length of Stay and Age at Removal by Last Placement Setting

	ACHIEVED	NOT ACHIEVED
Length of Stay (months)		
Foster family home (relative)	15	38
Foster family home (nonrelative)	9	24
Group home	6	14
Institution	6	12
Average Age at Removal (years)		
Foster family home (relative)	13.9	12.3
Foster family home (nonrelative)	14.5	13.0
Group home	15.3	13.9
Institution	15.2	14.0

(twenty-four months) compared with nine months for youth who achieved permanence. For youth in group homes, the average stay was fourteen months for youth who did not achieve permanence compared with six months for youth who did so. For youth in institutions, the average stay was one year (twelve months) for youth who did not achieve permanence compared with six months for youth who achieved permanence.

A similar pattern holds for age at time of removal. For all major placement settings for youth, those who achieved permanence were older at time of removal than youth who did not achieve permanence. For all placement types, there was more than one year's difference in the age of youth at time of removal. For youth in relative foster homes, the average age was 13.9 years for youth who achieved permanence versus 12.3 years for youth who did not achieve permanence; for youth in nonrelative foster homes, it was 14.5 years versus 13.0 years; for youth in group homes, it was 15.3 years versus 13.9 years; and for youth in institutions, it was 15.2 years versus 14.0 years.

Finally, provisions of the Adoption and Safe Families Act of 1997 have had some effect on achieving permanence for youth ages fifteen to twenty years. Of the 473,000 youths who exited foster care between FY 2000 and FY 2005, approximately thirty thousand were free for adoption: that is, the rights of both parents had been terminated. Of these youth, thirteen thousand did not achieve permanence. Table 2.5 shows the trend in the achievement of permanence for youth compared with all children who exited foster care during this period. For all children and, specifically, for the youth population, the percentage achieving permanence declined slightly over recent years. For all children, the percentage declined from 96 percent in FY 2000 to 92 percent in FY 2005. For youth, the percentage declined from 58 percent in FY 2000 to 48 percent in FY 2005. These data suggest that although the slice of the total population leaving foster care without any kind of legal parent is modest, this group still represents

Table 2.5 Trends in the Percentage of Freed Children Who Achieved Permanence, by Fiscal Year

	2000	2001	2002	2003	2004	2005
All children	96	96	96	95	94	93
Fifteen and older	58	55	55	54	51	48

a sizable proportion of the youth exiting foster care each year. The percentage of youth freed for adoption who do not achieve permanence may be increasing. Recent analyses suggest that the increase is likely a function of the increasing average age of children at time of removal who are on the road to adoption (Maza, 2007).

IMPLICATIONS

Most youth who exit foster care achieve permanence, particularly through reunification. Demographically, white males are most likely to achieve permanence. The case characteristics most closely associated with permanence are stable placements and one removal that occurred at an older age and therefore resulted in a shorter length of stay in foster care. The association of permanence with late, older removals may be related to youth maintaining contact with parent(s) or caregivers after, in many cases, having lived with them most of their lives. The findings further suggest that special attention should be paid to youth who are removed at younger ages and have spent much of their lives in foster care. These youth appear to be at highest risk for not achieving permanence.

Readers should take care in interpreting some of the findings from this analysis, particularly in regard to the relationship between the last placement setting for youth and the achievement of permanence. As with all child welfare phenomena, the reported relationships are likely more complex than discussed in this chapter. More complex multivariate analyses need to be conducted to tease out the interrelationships among a number of variables (such as age at removal, length of stay, and child demographic characteristics) that possibly affect these relationships.

NOTES

1. The data used in this chapter are from the Adoption and Foster Care Analysis and Reporting System (AFCARS) available as of June 30, 2006. For information about AFCARS, see www.acf.hhs.gov/programs/cb/systems/index.htm.
2. This analysis uses age fifteen as the minimum age because that is the age in the AFCARS database at which emancipations occur frequently enough to inform the analysis. The analysis uses age twenty as the maximum age because a substantial number of children are emancipated after their eighteenth birthday.

3. Unless specifically identified as a trend analysis, the total number of youth exits during these years is combined in the tables.

4. Information on the National Youth in Transition Database can be found at www .a257.g.akamaitech.net/7/257/2422/01jan20061800/edocket.access.gpo.gov/2006 /pdf/06–6005.pdf.

REFERENCES

Maza, P. L. (2007). Children who fall through the cracks. *Roundtable* 21(1): 4.

U.S. Department of Health and Human Services, Administration for Children and Families (2006). *The AFCARS Report: Preliminary FY 2005 Estimates as of September 2006*. Washington, D.C.: Author.

Outcomes for Older Youth
Exiting the Foster Care
System in the United States

THREE

MARK E. COURTNEY

Interest in the transition of foster children to adulthood is not new. Over eighty years ago, the State Charities Aid Association of New York commissioned Sophie van Senden Theis (1924) to attempt to find 910 of their former wards who, by that time, were adults. Working with a thoughtfully selected sample and achieving a respectable follow-up rate, Theis provided a rich description of the post–foster care well-being of the association's former wards. Although some were doing well, many of the former foster children experienced problems that troubled the leaders of the State Charities Aid Association. To this day, youth who age out of the nation's foster care system are a population at high risk of having difficulty managing the transition from dependent adolescence to independent adulthood. They experience high rates of educational failure, unemployment, poverty, out-of-wedlock parenting, mental illness, housing instability, and victimization. They are less likely than other youth to be able to rely on the support of kin.

Child welfare agencies are required to make "reasonable efforts" to prevent placement of children in out-of-home care, usually in the form of social services for their families. When the child welfare agency and court deem these efforts unsuccessful and the child enters out-of-home care, the court must approve a "permanency plan" for the child according to time-lines provided in federal law. Most commonly, the initial plan is for the child to return to the care of parents or other family members. Once again, the court generally requires the child welfare agency to make reasonable efforts to preserve the child's family of origin, in this case by providing services intended to help reunite the child with the family.

In many cases, however, children and youth cannot return to the care of their families. In these cases, the child welfare agency and the court attempt to find another permanent family for the child through adoption or legal guardianship. Although the vast majority of children in out-of-home care exit care to what are considered, in the parlance of the child welfare system, "permanent" placements (reunification with family, adoption, and legal guardianship), about twenty thousand exit care each year through legal "emancipation," usually when they reach the age of majority or graduate from high school. In practice, few states allow youth to remain in care beyond their eighteenth birthday, though some will continue to make payments to an out-of-home care provider if the youth in their care is likely to obtain a high school diploma before their nineteenth birthday (Bussey et al., 2000). As a result, of the 513,000 children and youth who were in out-of-home care in the United States on September 30, 2005, fewer than 5 percent, or about 24,000, were eighteen or older. Illinois is the only jurisdiction to discharge a significant number of youth at twenty-one (Bussey et al., 2000). Youth eighteen and older are a unique population in out-of-home care in that the state continues to play a profound parental role in their lives even though they are adults and can choose to leave "the system" at any time.

A recent longitudinal study of the placement trajectories of older foster youth (i.e., those in a position to age out of the foster care system) puts their experience in out-of-home care into perspective. Fred Wulczyn and Kristen Brunner Hislop (2001) analyzed placement histories and discharge outcomes of all youth in twelve states ($n = 119,011$) that were in out-of-home care on their sixteenth birthday. Four findings stand out. First, most of these youth had entered care since their fifteenth birthday, and only 10 percent had entered care as preteens (i.e., twelve or younger). In other words, few of the youth who aged out of care actually grew up in the foster care system. Second, these older youth were less likely to be living with kin and much more likely to be living in congregate care (group homes or children's institutions) than the overall foster care population. Some 42 percent of these youth were living in congregate care, and only 12 percent were living in kinship foster care. Third, nearly one-half (47 percent) of these youth returned to their families when they were discharged from foster care. Finally, more youth experienced "other" exits (21 percent, mainly transfers to other child-serving systems) or ran away from care (19 percent) than were emancipated (12 percent).

These facts raise important issues when one examines the young adult outcomes of older youth leaving the foster care system, the potential role of "permanency" in adult outcomes for this group of youth, and the policy and practice framework established to help them during this transition. Foster children in general face the disadvantages associated with family backgrounds where they have been subjected to maltreatment. Because youth generally enter foster care during adolescence, youth who age out of care have often spent many years in challenging family circumstances before intervention by child protection authorities. Thus, the outcomes experienced by former foster youth during the transition to adulthood may largely be a function of the problems they experienced before they entered foster care.

Support from family is recognized as an important contributor to successful adolescent transitions to adulthood (Furstenburg and Hughes, 1995; Mortimer and Larson, 2002). Yet, placement in out-of-home care, by its very nature, threatens a youth's family relations and can undermine family support. It may be unlikely that a youth's parents will be of much assistance during the youth's transition to adulthood or they may be a potential source of risk to the youth. Members of the extended family, however, may be available for support, but they may not play this role if their relationship to the youth has been negatively affected by the youth's placement in out-of-home care. The potential disturbance in family relations may be particularly likely for youth who age out of foster care. Relatively few of these youth are placed with relatives, the placement setting that is arguably most likely to facilitate continuing relations with extended family. Moreover, a large percentage of these youth live in congregate care settings that are generally staffed by relatively young shift workers who tend to remain in their position for short periods of time. Thus, youth in congregate care may find it difficult to form the kind of lasting relationships with responsible adults associated with the care setting that will help them move toward independence. In addition, congregate care programs are often charged by public child welfare authorities with providing care and supervision of youth but are not expected to play much of a role in family casework associated with youths' placement in out-of-home care. When this is the case, it is likely that congregate care providers will not place a high priority on helping youth maintain their relations with family members. The circumstances of youth who age out of care raise an important question for policymakers and practitioners: How can child welfare policy and practice help maintain supportive family relations for foster youth and build new relationships that can support youth during the transition to adulthood?

In this chapter I describe the challenges facing foster youth as they leave the protection of the child welfare services system. I review the literature on the young adult outcomes of former foster youth and consider the implications of these findings for practice and policy. These implications are framed with recognition that the research conducted to date provides little firm ground to guide policy and practice. Existing research seldom employs the kinds of longitudinal designs needed to make strong inferences about which factors predict later outcomes; the few longitudinal studies conducted to date have seldom made use of appropriate multivariate statistical models to identify predictors of adult outcomes, and there is no rigorous research on the effectiveness of independent living services (Courtney and Bost, 2002). I conclude the chapter with directions for future research.

OUTCOMES FOR FORMER FOSTER YOUTH DURING THE TRANSITION TO ADULTHOOD

In this review I examine the findings from twenty-two studies with samples of youth who had aged out of foster care (see Appendix A). Several limitations of this research literature deserve attention. First, most of the studies are quite dated and do not reflect the significant changes that have taken place since the early 1980s in the nature of the foster care population, including the foster care "baby boom" associated with the crack epidemic of the late 1980s and early 1990s and the rapid growth of kinship foster care. Even fewer studies took place after states had begun implementation of the 1986 federal law that provided funds for independent living services for foster youth, and only one study provides data on outcomes for a representative sample of youth who left out-of-home care since the passage of the Foster Care Independence Act of 1999 (Courtney et al., 2005). Thus, much of the available research may not accurately depict the characteristics of the population that is aging out of care today and the services and supports that are available to them. Second, many of the studies employ rather idiosyncratic samples that may not do a good job of describing the experiences of the general population of former foster youth. Third, most of the studies suffer from high rates of sample attrition because the researchers were often unable to locate many of the former foster youth after they left foster care. The only national study of youth that aged out of foster care, for example, suffered a follow-up attrition rate of more than 50 percent (Cook et al., 1991).

Research findings address several domains of outcomes experienced by former foster youth during the transition to adulthood: education, physical and mental health, substance abuse, criminal justice system involvement, employment and economic self-sufficiency, housing and homelessness, family formation, and family relations. All of these outcomes are important indicators in their own right of the success, or lack thereof, of foster youth in managing the transition to adulthood. In addition, problems in any one domain can make success in another less likely. Indeed, making sense of the outcomes described here is complicated by the fact that research has seldom examined the relationship among these outcomes or the relationship between the outcomes and the experiences of foster youth before and during their stays in out-of-home care. Nevertheless, this review provides sobering evidence of just how difficult the transition to adulthood can be for former foster youth.

Education

Human capital is clearly important for success during the transition to adulthood, but studies of former foster youth find poor levels of educational attainment and that the population fares poorly when compared with its peers. In addition to showing that former foster youth have fewer years of education (Zimmerman, 1982; Jones and Moses, 1984), most studies show that they are less likely to earn a high school diploma or their GED (Zimmerman, 1982; Festinger, 1983; Frost and Jurich, 1983; Jones and Moses, 1984; Barth, 1990; Cook et al., 1991; Courtney et al., 2001, 2005). Ronna Cook et al. (1991), for example, found that 66 percent of the eighteen year olds discharged from care in the United States between July 1, 1987, and June 30, 1988, had not graduated from high school. Only 54 percent of subjects had completed high school 2.5 to 4 years after they were discharged, a low percentage when compared with the 78 percent of the eighteen to twenty-four year olds in the general population with a high school degree. More recently, Mark Courtney et al. (2005) found that roughly 58 percent of their sample of former foster youth had a high school degree at age nineteen compared with 87 percent of a national comparison group (other nineteen year olds in the National Longitudinal Study of Adolescent Health). In contrast, Peter Pecora et al. (2006), in their study of Casey Family Programs alumni and alumni of selected public agency jurisdictions in Oregon and Washington ages eighteen to twenty-nine, found high school completion rates that were comparable with those of the general population. However, they note that over one-third of former foster youth who had completed high school had obtained a GED rather than a high school diploma, a much higher rate than that of the general population.

Not surprisingly, given their low high school graduation rate, most studies find that former foster youth have low rates of college attendance (Zimmerman, 1982; Jones and Moses, 1984; Barth, 1990; Cook et al., 1991; Courtney et al., 2001, 2005; Pecora et al., 2003, 2005, 2006). A study of former foster children in West Virginia, for example, found that only 7 percent of a sample of young adults who had spent at least one year in foster care had accumulated any college credit, though they were twenty years old on average at follow-up; in comparison, over one-quarter of the U.S. population between eighteen and twenty-four years old attended college during the period of the study (Jones and Moses, 1984). More recently, Pecora et al. (2006a, 2006b) found that participation in postsecondary education and bachelor's degree completion rates among former foster youth were much lower than among the general population. Courtney et al. (2005) found the young adults in their study to be much less likely than their age peers to be enrolled in postsecondary education of any kind.

In summary, former foster youth must face the transition to independence with significant deficits in educational attainment, and they do not appear to make up for these deficits during the transition. These educational deficits put them at significant disadvantage in the labor market and likely contribute to some of the other negative outcomes they experience.

Physical and Mental Health

Former foster youth suffer from more mental health problems than the general population (Robins, 1966; Festinger, 1983; Jones and Moses, 1984; Courtney et al., 2005; Pecora et al., 2005). Support for this conclusion comes from data on youth's use of mental health services and research assessments of their mental health. Trudy Festinger (1983), for example, found that subsequent to discharge from care, 47 percent of the sample of former New York foster youth, all of whom had spent at least five years in care, had sought help or advice from a mental health professional, a far higher rate of help seeking than is found in the general population. The Virginia study (Jones and Moses, 1984) reported that 3 percent of their subject population resided in residential or group care facilities after they left the foster care system, an extremely high rate when compared with the 0.3 percent admission rate into psychiatric hospitals in the United States in 1983 (McDonald et al., 1996). Courtney et al (2005) found that nineteen year olds making the transition to adulthood from foster care were more than twice as likely as their peers to receive psychological or emotional counseling. Studies indicate that former foster youth suffer from higher levels of depression than does the general population (Barth, 1990; Cook, 1992). Moreover, Pecora et al. (2005) found that young adults who had been in out-of-home care as adolescents were twice as likely as the general population to have a current mental health problem.

Some research finds little difference between the physical health status of former foster youth and their peers, though this may be largely a function of a lack of attention to this outcome in research to date. Festinger (1983), Jones and Moses (1984), and Cook et al. (1991) found no evidence of abnormal levels of physical health problems in the populations they studied. In contrast, Rosalie Zimmerman (1982) found that the young adults in her sample (nineteen to twenty-nine years old at follow-up), all of whom had spent at least a year in foster care in New Orleans, were more likely to report their health as "fair"' or "poor" than the general population. Among the former foster youth studied by Courtney et al. (2001), Caucasians reported poorer health on a standardized self-report health measure than the general population, whereas African Americans reported health that was comparable with their peers. Courtney et al. (2005) found that the young adults in their sample tended to describe their overall health less favorably, were more likely to report that health conditions limited their ability to engage in moderate activity, and reported more emergency room visits and more hospitalizations during the previous five years than their peers. Although there is mixed evidence that former foster youth experience poor physical health, studies have found that they have difficultly obtaining affordable medical coverage (Barth, 1990; Courtney et al., 2001, 2005; Pecora et al., 2003), leading them to report medical problems that are left untreated (Barth, 1990; Courtney et al., 2001, 2005).

In summary, research is consistent in finding former foster youth to experience mental health problems during the transition to adulthood, but it is less consistent in finding physical health problems. The mental health problems experienced by this population are significant in their own right and raise concerns about the ability of these youth to achieve other important outcomes, such as maintaining healthy relationships and obtaining and maintaining employment.

Substance Abuse

Studies report mixed findings with respect to the use and abuse of alcohol and illicit drugs by former foster youth. In a case control study, Lee Robins (1966) compared male subjects who had been diagnosed as alcoholics with those who had no clinical diagnoses. The alcoholics reported a higher rate of having lived in out-of-home care (76 percent) than those without clinical diagnoses (39 percent). One in eight (13 percent) of subjects in the study by David Fanshel et al. (1990) of young adults (mean age of twenty-four at follow-up) who had been in private agency foster care in the State of Washington reported extreme difficulty with drug abuse in their lives. Richard Barth (1990) found that 19 percent of his convenience sample of youth who had "emancipated" from foster care in northern California (mean age of twenty-one at follow-up) reported drinking once a week or more while in care (comparable with high school students at the time) and that 17 percent had done so since leaving care. In contrast, 56 percent of Barth's (1990) subjects had used "street drugs" since aging out of care. In contrast to studies that suggest a high level of drug and alcohol use among former foster youth, the national study by Cook et al. (1991) found that they used alcohol and other drugs at rates similar to or lower than those found in national surveys of young adults. Pecora et al. (2005) found that the young adults in their study reported drug dependence at a much higher rate than that of the general population but alcohol dependence at a rate similar to that of their peers. Courtney et al. (2005) reported much higher lifetime prevalence of drug (10.9 percent) and alcohol (10.5 percent) abuse than dependence (drug dependence at 3.8 percent; alcohol dependence at 4.3 percent).

In summary, the research literature to date does not provide a very clear picture of the extent of substance use or abuse among former foster youth during the transition to adulthood, although more recent studies suggest that significant percentages of former foster youth suffer from alcohol or drug dependence and abuse.

Involvement with the Criminal Justice System

Former foster youth have a higher rate of involvement with the criminal justice system than the general population (McCord et al., 1960; Zimmerman, 1982; Frost and Jurich, 1983; Jones and Moses, 1984; Fanshel et al., 1990; Barth, 1990; Courtney et al., 2001, 2005). Some 44 percent of the subjects in the Fanshel et al. (1990) study had been picked up by police on charges at one time or another. Among youth participating in the Cambridge-Somerville Youth Study, former foster youth were more likely than youth never in foster care to have had criminal records in adulthood (McCord et al., 1960). Zimmerman (1982) found that 28 percent of her male subjects and 6 percent of her female subjects from New Orleans had been convicted of crimes and served at least six months in prison, a much higher rate than that of the general population. Some 5 percent of the young adults in the West Virginia study were in jail at the time of the study (Jones and Moses, 1984), an extremely high rate compared with the adult imprisonment rate of 1 percent in West Virginia in 1983 (McDonald et al., 1996). Some 27 percent of the males and 10 percent of the females in the study by Courtney et al. (2001) reported having been incarcerated at least once in the twelve to eighteen months since leaving out-of-home care. The young adults in the later study by Courtney et al. (2005) were more likely to have engaged in several forms of delinquent and violent behavior in the past year than their peers. Moreover, 29.8 percent of the males and 10.7 percent of the females reported being incarcerated at least once between the first wave of interviews for the study (at age seventeen to eighteen) and the second wave (age nineteen).

The rates of criminal justice system involvement described in these studies are cause for serious concern about the prospects of former foster youth during the transition to adulthood. Arrest and incarceration are troubling outcomes in their own right. In addition, a criminal record can limit the future employment and housing prospects of these youth.

Employment and Economic Self-Sufficiency

Nearly all studies of former foster youth and all studies done since the late 1980s suggest that these youth face a difficult time achieving financial independence. Availability of national and regional data makes it possible in many cases to compare this population with relevant samples and standards, such as poverty level. Data from several studies show that former foster youth have a higher rate of dependency on public assistance than the general population (Pettiford, 1981; Zimmerman, 1982; Barth, 1990; Jones and Moses, 1984; Cook et al., 1991; Courtney et al., 2001, 2005; Pecora et al., 2005, 2006b). About 30 percent of the young adults in the national study by Cook et al. (1991) were receiving some form of public assistance at the time of the study. One-quarter of the young people in the study by Courtney et al. (2005) were receiving one or more need-based government benefits at age nineteen. Pecora et al (2005) also found a much higher rate of public assistance receipt among the foster care alumni in their study than is typical of the general population.

Former foster youth have a higher unemployment rate than the general population (Zimmerman, 1982; Jones and Moses, 1984; Cook et al., 1991; Goerge et al., 2002; Courtney et al., 2005; Pecora et al., 2005, 2006b). They also have lower wages, which frequently leave them in poverty (Zimmerman, 1982; Festinger, 1983; Barth, 1990; Cook et al., 1991; Dworsky and Courtney, 2000; Goerge et al., 2002; Courtney et al., 2005; Pecora et al., in press). Two relatively recent studies that used unemployment insurance claims data to examine the employment patterns and earnings of former foster youth found that their mean earnings were well below the federal poverty level for up to two years after leaving out-of-home care (Dworsky and Courtney, 2000; Goerge et al., 2002).

Not surprisingly, many former foster youth experience financial difficulties during the transition to independence. Young adults in the study by Courtney et al. (2005) were twice as likely as the nineteen year olds in a nationally representative comparison group to report not having enough money to pay their rent or mortgage (12 percent), twice as likely to report being unable to pay a utility bill (12 percent), and 1.5 times as likely to report having their phone service disconnected (21 percent).

In summary, the research consistently shows former foster youth fair poorly in terms of economic self-sufficiency outcomes during the transition to adulthood. They are less likely to be employed than their peers and more likely to rely on public assistance, and they earn, on average, too little to escape poverty.

Housing and Homelessness

Information on the housing instability experienced by former foster youth comes from research on this population and research on homeless populations. Former foster youth have high rates of mobility and housing instability (Jones and Moses, 1984; Fanshel et al., 1990; Courtney et al., 2001, 2005; Pecora et al., 2005, 2006b). Cook et al. (1991) found that 32 percent of the youth in their study had lived in six or more places in the two-and-one-half to four years since they left foster care. Similarly, Courtney et al. (2001) found that 22 percent of the youth in their sample had lived in four or more places within twelve to eighteen months of exiting care.

Former foster youth also experience high rates of homelessness (Susser et al., 1987, 1991; Sosin et al., 1988, 1990; Mangine et al., 1990; Cook et al., 1991; Courtney et al., 2001, 2005; Pecora et al., 2005, 2006b). Most information comes from studies of adult homeless populations. Researchers have found that when compared with the domiciled population, former residents of out-of-home care are represented at much higher rates across a variety of samples of street homeless populations, shelter residents, and psychiatric facilities that serve homeless populations (Susser et al., 1987, 1991; Sosin et al., 1988, 1990; Mangine et al., 1990). Longitudinal studies of former foster youth also show this population to be at a heightened risk of homelessness. More than one-fifth of the participants (22.2 percent) in the study by Pecora et al. (2005, 2006b) reported having been homeless at least one day within one year of leaving foster care, and 13.8 percent of the participants in the study by Courtney et al. (2005) reported having been homeless at least one night since leaving care.

In summary, former foster youth experience considerable housing instability, including frequent periods of homelessness. Given the limited economic prospects of this group and other problems, such as mental illness and corrections system involvement, it should not be surprising that many former foster youth struggle to maintain stable housing. However, poor housing stability among former foster youth may also be a function of their inability to rely on extended family for housing assistance to the same degree as other young adults.

Family Formation

With regard to family formation issues for former foster youth, studies have examined marriage rates, divorce and separation, marital separation, child bearing, and parenting. With respect to marriage, Elizabeth Meier (1965) and Sandra Cook (1992) found former foster youth were more likely to remain single than their peers. In contrast, Festinger (1983) found no difference between the marital status of her subjects and those of their peers in New York City. Cook et al. (1991) found the marriage rate of former foster youth to be similar to that of poor young adults, though much lower than that of all young adults in the comparable age range. Courtney et al. (2005) found the nineteen year olds in their study to be much less likely than their peers to be married or cohabiting.

Meier (1965) found a higher rate of marital separation and divorce among a sample of former Minnesota foster youth than that in the general population at that time, whereas Festinger (1983) found no difference. Cook (1992) found the former foster children represented in the National Survey of Families and Households to express less marital satisfaction than those in the overall national sample, whereas Festinger (1983) found no difference in marital satisfaction between her sample and national norms. With the exception of the study by Festinger (1983), all studies with data on the subject suggest relatively poor outcomes for this population.

Studies have found that former foster youth have higher rates of out-of-wedlock parenting than their peers (Meier, 1965; Festinger, 1983; Cook et al., 1991; Courtney et al., 2005; Pecora et al., 2003). Some 31 percent of mothers in Festinger's (1983) sample were raising children on their own, and fewer than one-third of the parenting females in the study by Courtney et al. (2001) were married. Zimmerman (1982) found that 46 percent of former foster youth reported that their children had some type of health, education, or behavior problem. Other studies have found that the children of former foster youth become involved in the child welfare system (Meier, 1965; Jones and Moses, 1984). About 19 percent of former foster youth in the West Virginia study reported that they had a child in out-of-home care (Jones and Moses, 1984). In contrast, Courtney et al. (2005) found that while former foster youth were much more likely than the general population to report having children, they were no less likely than their peers to be living with their children.

In summary, research findings are mixed regarding the success of former foster youth in forming their own families. No studies show them to have better outcomes than their peers, and most show less than desirable outcomes.

Family Relations

One finding that is strikingly consistent across studies is the considerable ongoing contact former foster youth have with their families of origin after they leave out-of-home care (Harari, 1980; Zimmerman, 1982; Festinger, 1983; Frost and Jurich, 1983; Jones and Moses, 1984; Barth, 1990; Cook et al., 1991; Courtney et al., 2001, 2005). The studies are not strictly comparable since they reported contact at different points in time after the youth left foster care and measured contact using dissimilar metrics, such as weekly, monthly, or annually. Nevertheless, taken together, the studies suggest that former foster youth report that they are in contact with their mothers and, to a somewhat lesser degree, their fathers well into young adulthood. At least monthly contact between former foster youth and their mothers ranged across studies from one-third to one-half of respondents (Harari, 1980; Zimmerman, 1982; Festinger, 1983; Courtney et al., 2001, 2005), with the same studies finding monthly contact with fathers to range from one-quarter to one-third of respondents. Those with siblings also maintained contact with their siblings over time. Courtney et al. (2001) found 88 percent of former foster youth with at least one sibling to have visited with a sibling at least once since discharge from out-of-home care.

This level of family contact is important because it suggests a possible source of natural support for former foster youth during the transition to adulthood. Indeed, most former foster youth who maintain contact with their family of origin report good relations with their kin. Festinger (1983) found that a majority of her New York respondents who were in contact with their biological families felt "very close" or "somewhat close" to their relatives. Courtney et al. (2005), using the same survey questions as Festinger, found similarly high levels of expressed closeness between former foster youth and their mothers, siblings, and grandparents but less favorable relationships with their fathers. Studies also consistently show that a majority of former foster youth maintain ongoing contact with their former foster families, another potential source of support during the transition (Harari, 1980; Festinger, 1983; Jones and Moses, 1984; Courtney et al., 2001).

Family relations are sufficiently strong for many former foster youth that they live with relatives after they leave care. Cook et al. (1991) found that 54 percent of their respondents had lived in the home of a relative at some point after discharge from out-of-home care, and one-third were living with a relative when interviewed two and a half to four years after leaving care. It should be noted, however, that this rate is much lower than was typical of the general population of young adults at the time of the Cook et al. study. More recently, Courtney et al. (2005) found that the nineteen year olds in their study who had been discharged from out-of-home care were more likely to be living with family than in any other living arrangement: 16.8 percent were living in the home of one or both of their biological parents, and another 17.8 percent were living in the home of a relative. This combined percentage (34.6 percent) is over three times the percentage of youth who were living with a former nonrelative foster parent (10 percent) and higher than the percentage who reported living in their "own place" (28.7 percent). These young people, however, were still about half as likely as their peers to be living with kin; three-fifths of nineteen year olds in the National Longitudinal Study of Adolescent Health were living with family at age nineteen.

As might be expected, given the troubled histories of most of these families, ongoing family relations were not without their problems. Courtney et al. (2001) found that one-quarter of the young adults in their sample reported experiencing problems with their family most or all of the time. Barth (1990) found that 15 percent of his California subjects felt that they had no "psychological parent" or person to turn to for advice. Thus, while the family of origin remains a source of support for many former foster youth during the transition to adulthood, these youth are still less likely to be able to rely on this support than their peers and they also must often weigh the benefits of ongoing family contact against the risks.

Summary

In summary, a review of the outcomes for former foster youth during their transition to adulthood is sobering. On average, they bring to the transition very limited human capital on which to build a career or economic assets. They often suffer from mental health problems that can negatively affect other outcome domains, and these problems are less likely to be treated once they leave care. Although they were placed in out-of-home care as a result of abuse or neglect and not delinquency, the youth often become involved in crime and with the justice and corrections systems after aging out of foster care. Their employment prospects are bleak, and few of them escape poverty during the transition. Many former foster youth experience homelessness and housing instability after leaving care. Interestingly, in spite of court-ordered separation from their families, often for many years, most former foster youth can rely on their families to some extent during the transition to adulthood, though this is not always without risk.

DIRECTIONS FOR POLICY, PRACTICE, AND RESEARCH

Two indisputable facts should guide both policy and practice directed at older youth in foster care and those making the transition to adulthood from care. First, these young people are on average significantly disadvantaged across a number of domains as they approach and later negotiate the transition to adulthood. They also have many strengths, including an optimistic view of the future, high educational aspirations, and generally positive views of the child welfare system, all of which bode well for efforts to engage them in services (Festinger, 1983; Courtney et al., 2001, 2005). Nevertheless, a sober review of the research literature leads inevitably to the conclusion that most young people approaching the point at which they will "age out" of foster care are not ready to be on their own.

Second, youth in foster care are much less likely than their peers to be able to rely on family for support to compensate for their disadvantages during the transition. Research consistently shows the importance of family financial and emotional support and advice to young people during the transition to adulthood. According to the 2001 U.S. Census Bureau Survey of Income and Program Participation, approximately 63 percent of men between eighteen and twenty-four years old and 51 percent of women in that age range were living with one or both of their parents. Former foster youth are much less likely to be living with a parent or any adult member of their family during this time in their lives. They are also less likely to be able to rely on financial support. Parents provide roughly $38,000 in material assistance for food, housing, education, or direct cash assistance throughout the transition to adulthood, or about $2,200 per year (Schoeni and Ross, 2004). Although no comparable data are available on young adults who have left foster care, it seems highly unlikely that they receive support at this level from their parents.

Taken together, these facts suggest that sound social policy would provide state agencies responsible for youth in out-of-home care with the ability to continue to serve as a surrogate parent for these young people during the transition to adulthood. Ongoing parental support during this period has become normative in the United States, and former foster youth are in greater need of this support, on average, than their peers. Recent research comparing outcomes between young people allowed to remain under the care and supervision of child welfare authorities past age eighteen and those who have left care before that provides some evidence that extending care results in improved outcomes in the areas of service access, educational attainment, housing stability, pregnancy, and crime (Courtney et al.,

2005). Similarly, a study of alumni of Casey Family Services—comparing young adult outcomes between Casey alumni that were adopted, exited care prior to age nineteen, or exited care after age nineteen—found that extending services past age nineteen was associated with better self-sufficiency and personal well-being (Kerman et al., 2002). Extended services for Casey Family Services alumni who reached age nineteen while in Casey foster care averaged about $6,000 per year (median of $5,942) between ages nineteen and twenty-four, although the figure was lower when youth who incurred no expenses were taken into account (Kerman et al., 2004). Unfortunately, current federal law does not provide resources to support the work of child welfare agencies that seek to play the parental role after a young person reaches his or her eighteenth birthday:[1]

• The $140 million per year provided to states under the John Chafee Foster Care Independence Program, the primary federal source of funds for independent living services, is woefully inadequate (Courtney and Hughes-Heuring, 2005). This funding is designed to be used by states to prepare foster children and youth of all ages for the transition to adulthood and to support former foster youth between eighteen and twenty-one who have left care. Yet, even if states only used their Chafee Program funds for youth who are sixteen or older and still in care, they would have less than $1,400 per youth per year in Chafee funding to support the wide range of services called for in the enabling legislation.

• Funding has been particularly anemic when it comes to providing housing support for foster youth in transition. In 2008, federal law authorized for the first time federal reimbursement for board and care and associate administrative costs for out-of-home care past age 18 under the Title IV-E Foster Care program of the Social Security Act, the primary federal source of funding for out-of-home care. This state option may prove to be important given the fact that although states can use up to 30 percent of their share of Chafee Program funds to provide housing to current and former foster youth between eighteen and twenty-one, this amounts to less than $150 a month per year for these young people.

• Many states have failed to take up the option of extending Medicaid coverage to former foster youth (Eilertson, 2002). Given the health needs of foster youth, particularly their relatively high rate of mental health problems, and the fact that they are less likely than their peers to be able to rely on their parents' health insurance during the transition to adulthood, it is important that continuity of their access to health care be ensured by extending Medicaid.

- Poor integration and coordination of independent living services for foster youth with the efforts of other public institutions (such as educational institutions, welfare-to-work programs, and housing programs) limit the effectiveness of existing services. The service systems that constitute the "extended family" of formal institutional supports for former foster youth do not communicate with one another very well, leading to duplication of effort and unnecessary gaps in service availability.

There is no solid evidence for the effectiveness of the independent living services that states have chosen as their primary approach to supporting foster youth in transition (U.S. General Accounting Office, 1999; Courtney and Bost, 2002).

- Perhaps the most important limitation of current policy is its target population. Fewer older youth in care actually age out of the child welfare system than exit foster care in other ways, yet this population is the primary focus of federal legislation. Too little attention has been paid to the needs during the transition to adulthood of older youth who exit out-of-home care via other routes, such as family reunification, adoption, guardianship, and running away.

Practitioners are limited in their efforts by the poor policy context and the virtually nonexistent knowledge base regarding effective services for this population. One message that emerges from the research for practitioners, however, is that they must pay more attention to a youth's connections to their family of origin. Although foster youth may not be able to rely on family as much as their peers do, most have strong relations with family, relationships that can be both helpful and harmful. Caseworkers should focus on helping young people maximize the benefits of these relationships while minimizing the potential risks. Although foster parents and other out-of-home care providers do not appear as important as members of the family of origin during the transition to adulthood, they too should be a central focus of practice with foster youth and former foster youth (Courtney et al., 2001).

Research has documented the generally poor outcomes of foster youth making the transition to adulthood, but it provides less guidance regarding what specifically should be done to improve their outcomes. Large-scale longitudinal studies of foster youth making the transition to adulthood can help identify correlates of their successes, thereby providing targets for intervention. Had the outcome monitoring elements of the Foster Care Independence Act of 1999 been implemented in a timely manner, child welfare managers and researchers would have a rich multijurisdictional source of data from which to identify promising policies and practices.[2] In the absence of such data, the field must make do with only a handful of reasonably recent and ongoing studies. Solid evidence for the effectiveness of specific services will only come from experimental evaluations. Funding from the Chafee Program is supporting a few ongoing experimental evaluations of independent living programs, but additional research is needed if the knowledge base for intervention is to advance significantly in the next decade. Finally, qualitative research on foster youth's transitions to adulthood is sorely needed. The voices of the young people themselves will be best heard through this type of research.

One would be hard-pressed to find an adolescent population in greater need during the transition to independence than youth in foster care approaching adulthood. Too often, when the state has stepped in to be these youth's parent, it has failed to do justice to this solemn responsibility. The current federal policy framework is not ideal. The resources devoted to helping youth are inadequate. There may, however, be sufficient support in place in certain jurisdictions to build the political will necessary to make needed changes in federal policy.

APPENDIX A

Studies of Postdischarge Outcomes

See following pages:

No.	Citation	Study Type	Sample	Data Sources	Data Studied	Attrition Rate
1	Theis, Sophie Van Senden (1924). *How Foster Children Turn Out: A Study and Critical Analysis of 910 Children Who Were Placed in Foster Homes by the State Charities Aid Association and Who Are Now Eighteen Years of Age or Over.* New York: State Charities Aid Association.	Retrospective without a comparison group	$N = 797$ adults, ages 18–40, who had been in foster care with the New York State Charities Aid Association during 1898–1922. Of these, 562 had remained in out-of-home care until adulthood, while 235 had been adopted by foster parents.	Observation, interviews, agency records	Self-support, education, criminality	Not reported
2	McCord, J., W. McCord, and E. Thurber (1960). The effects of foster home placement in the prevention of adult antisocial behavior. *Social Service Review* 34: 415–19.	Prospective with a comparison group	$N = 38$ adults in their early 30s, 19 of which had been in out-of-home care. Subjects were those involved in the Cambridge-Somerville Youth Study, a delinquency study of 255 urban boys from lower-class families between 1937 and 1945, when the children were 9–17 years of age. Of 24 who had been in out-of-home care as youths, data were available on 19. A comparison group of 19 others with similar biological family backgrounds was then chosen.	On the basis of direct observations made during the subjects' childhoods and the records of adult deviant behavior, longitudinal analyses of the origins of alcoholism and crime were made.	Criminality, alcoholism, mental health	21%

No.	Citation	Study Type	Sample	Data Sources	Data Studied	Attrition Rate
3	Meier, E. G. (1965). Current circumstances of former foster children. *Child Welfare* 44: 196–206.	Retrospective without a comparison group	*N* = 66 young adults (42 women, 24 men) ages 28–32 who had been in foster care in Minnesota for at least five years and had not been returned home, and who had been discharged between July 1, 1948, and December 31, 1949. This study attempted to use all eligible males and a random sample of eligible females.	Interviews, questionnaires	Homemaking, living arrangements, employment and economic circumstances, health, marriage, parenting, social relationships, sense of well-being and social effectiveness.	20%
4	Allerhand, M .E., R. E. Weber, and M. Haug (1966). *Adaptation and Adaptability: The Bellefaire Follow-Up Study.* New York: Child Welfare League of America.	Retrospective without a comparison group	*N* = 50 boys who had been clients of Bellefaire, a residential treatment center for emotionally disturbed children, in Cleveland for at least 6 months and who had been discharged between January 1958 and June 1961. Subjects were located two years after discharge, at the average age of 18.	Agency records and interviews with the subjects, their parents or parent substitutes, and their therapists if they were still in treatment	Adaptation (behavior, role-fulfillment and role consistency) and adaptability (intrapsychic balance)	4%

No.	Citation	Study Type	Sample	Data Sources	Data Studied	Attrition Rate
5	Heston, L. L., D. D. Denney, and I. B. Pauley (1966). The adult adjustment of persons institutionalized as children. *British Journal of Psychiatry* 112: 1103–10.	Retrospective with a comparison group retrospective with a comparison group	N = 97, 47 former foster youth from Oregon compared with 50 former youth who had never been in care or who had been for less than 3 months. Subjects ranged in age from 21 to 50 when followed up in 1964 and 1965. 25 subjects had been born to schizophrenic mothers in state psychiatric hospitals. All subjects were apparently normal at birth. All subjects were Caucasian.	Agency records, personal interviews, a Minnesota Multiphasic Personality Inventory (MMPI), IQ scores	Socioeconomic station, psychiatric health	27%
6	Robins, L. N. (1966). *Deviant Children Grown Up: A Sociological and Psychiatric Study of Sociopathic Personality.* Baltimore: Williams and Wilkins.	Retrospective with a comparison group	N = 524 child guidance clinic patients, 16% of whom had lived in foster homes and 16% in orphanages for at least 6 months. This sample was then compared with the adult social and psychiatric outcomes of 100 normal school children of the same age, race, sex, neighborhood, and IQ. Subjects were between the ages of 27 and 53 and were chosen from among patients seen at the St. Louis Municipal Psychiatric Clinic between January 1, 1924, and December 30, 1929.	Interviews	School problems and achievement, marital history, adult relationships, military service, job history, history of arrests and imprisonments, financial dependency, geographic moves, history of deviant behavior, physical and psychiatric diseases, alcohol and drug use, intellectual level, cooperativeness, willingness to talk, frankness, and mood	21%

No.	Citation	Study Type	Sample	Data Sources	Data Studied	Attrition Rate
7	Harari, T. (1980). Teenagers exiting from family foster care: A retrospective look. Ph.D. diss., University of California, Berkeley).	Retrospective without a comparison group	$N = 34$ adults between the ages of 17 and 23 (19.8 average) who had exited from foster family care as adolescents and who had not returned to their natural parents upon exit from care. Subjects were interviewed between July 1978 and November 1978. All subjects had exited care as adolescents between January 1974 and June 1978, and all had turned 18 by February 1978. All subjects had to have been in care for a minimum of 1.5 years and had to still be residing in northern California. Subjects with a diagnosis of mental retardation were excluded from the sample.	Questionnaire, interviews	Interpersonal affect and self-esteem scales from the Jackson Personality Inventory (JPI)	60%

No.	Citation	Study Type	Sample	Data Sources	Data Studied	Attrition Rate
8	Pettiford, P. (1981). *Foster Care and Welfare Dependency: A Research Note.* New York: Human Resources Administration, Office of Policy and Program Development.	Retrospective with a comparison group	$N = 614$ (206 on public assistance and 408 not on public assistance) former foster youth, ages 18–21, discharged to their own responsibility between June 1979 and June 1980	Child Welfare Information Service (CWIS) listing of all cases of youth discharged from foster care to their own responsibility between June 1979 and June 1980, public assistance rolls of September 1980	Dependency on public assistance	56%
9	Zimmerman, R. B. (1982). Foster care in retrospect. *Tulane Studies in Social Welfare* 14: 1–119.	Retrospective without a comparison group (limited normative data)	$N = 61$ (29 women, 32 men) young adults, ages 19–29, interviewed between March and April 1980, who were in foster care in New Orleans between 1951 and 1969 for at least 12 months and had not been adopted..	Interviews	Housing status, educational attainment, employment history, income, social support, life satisfaction, family life and relationships, physical and mental health, views regarding foster care experience	64%

No.	Citation	Study Type	Sample	Data Sources	Data Studied	Attrition Rate
10	Festinger, T. (1983). *No One Ever Asked Us: A Postscript to Foster Care.* New York: Columbia University Press.	Retrospective without a comparison group (normative data provided)	N = 277 young adults between the ages of 22–25 (116 women, 161 men) who had been in 30 of 48 private foster care agencies in New York's foster care system for at least five years and were discharged in 1975 when they were 18–21 years old, 76.6% from foster homes, 23.4% from group care settings. Subjects were interviewed between May 1979 and April 1980.	Interviews, questionnaires	Education, employment, welfare dependence, marriage, partnership, children, social support, community participation, health, substance abuse, trouble with the law, and perceptions of well-being	54%
11	Frost, S., and A. P. Jurich (1983). Follow-up study of children residing in the Villages. Topeka, Kans.: The Villages. Unpublished ms.	Retrospective without a comparison group	N = 96 previous residents of The Villages (57 male, 39 female), a long-term residential care center for abused and neglected children from 6 to 18. All subjects had been in care at least 6 months and had "graduated" from the program by October 1, 1982. Ages of subjects at the time of study not explicit. Ages mentioned, however, range from 18 to over 25.	Data from subjects' case files, questionnaires, in-person and phone interviews conducted in 1982 and 1983 with subjects and current and former Villages house staff and office support staff	Educational attainment, employment history and financial stability, relationship formation, criminal behavior, contact with welfare offices, hobbies and other activities, opinion of the care they received	46%

No.	Citation	Study Type	Sample	Data Sources	Data Studied	Attrition Rate
12	Jones, M. A., and B. Moses (1984). *West Virginia's Former Foster Children: Their Experiences in Care and Their Lives as Young Adults.* New York: Child Welfare League of America.	Retrospective without a comparison group (limited normative data)	$N = 328$ adults (157 women and 171 men) between the ages of 17 and 28 (with a mean age of 20 years) who had been in foster care in West Virginia for at least 1 year after October 1, 1977; had been discharged before January 1, 1984; and were at least 19 years old as of that date.	In-person interviews, phone interviews, questionnaires—data collected in 1984	Education, employment, welfare dependence, living arrangements, health, family and social relationships, criminal justice involvement, and experiences in out of home care	48%
13	Fanshel, D., S. J. Finch, and J. F. Grundy (1990). *Foster Children in Life Course Perspective.* New York: Columbia University Press.	Retrospective without a comparison group	$N = 106$ adults (45 women and 61 men) in their 20s and 30s (average age 24) who had been placed in Casey Family foster homes between 1966 and 1984 in Seattle and Yakima, Washington, for a mean of 4.7 years, and who had been discharged by December 31, 1984. Subjects were seen, on average, 7.1 years after leaving care (minimum of 1 year, maximum of 15 years).	Agency records, interviews	Housing, income, education, employment, marriage, parenting, crime, emotional health, social support, and substance abuse	41%

No.	Citation	Study Type	Sample	Data Sources	Data Studied	Attrition Rate
14	Barth, R. (1990). On their own: The experiences of youth after foster care. *Child and Adolescent Social Work* 7: 419–40.	Retrospective without a comparison group	$N = 55$ young adults (29 women, 26 men) between the ages of 17 and 26 (with a mean age of 21) in the San Francisco Bay and Sacramento areas who had been emancipated from foster care between the ages of 16 and 19.5 (time since discharge ranged from 1 to 10 years). Snowball sampling was used to generate this convenience sample.	Interviews conducted in subjects' homes (76%) and over the telephone (24%)	Housing, income, employment, education, criminal activity, contact with foster or birth families, physical and mental health, access to health care, substance abuse, satisfaction with foster care and preparation for independent living	25%
15	Cook, R., E. Fleischman, and V. Grimes (1991). *A National Evaluation of Title IV-E Foster Care Independent Living Programs for Youth in Foster Care: Phase 2, Final Report*. Vol. 1. Rockville, Md.: Westat.	Retrospective without a comparison group (some normative data provided)—this was a multistage, stratified design that used probability sampling	$N = 810$ (356 men, 554 women) former foster youth in 7 states and the District of Columbia, ages 18 to 23, interviewed between November 1990 and March 1991, who had been discharged between January 1987 and July 1988, with a median time in care of 2.5 years.	Interviews	Employment, education, income sources, housing, parenthood, social support, health care, and drug and alcohol use	

No.	Citation	Study Type	Sample	Data Sources	Data Studied	Attrition Rate
16	Cook, S. K. (1992). Long-term consequences of foster care for adult well-being. Ph.D. diss., University of Nebraska, Lincoln.	Retrospective with a comparison group—comparison of survey respondents with and without out-of-home care background	$N = 107$ noninstitutionalized former foster children over the age of 19, with an average age of 37 and an average length in placement of 7 years.	1988 National Survey of Families and Households	Life happiness, self-esteem, depression, marital happiness, parental relations, social isolation	34% overall (not reported for foster care group)
17	Dworsky, A., and M. E. Courtney (2000). *Self-Sufficiency of Former Foster Youth in Wisconsin: Analysis of Unemployment Insurance Wage Data and Public Assistance Data.* Madison, Wisc.: Institute for Research on Poverty. Available at aspe.os.dhhs.gov/hsp/fosteryouthW100/index.htm	Retrospective without a comparison group, using administrative data	$N = 6,274$ former foster youth who were at least 17 years old when they were discharged from Wisconsin's out-of-home care system between January 1, 1992, and December 31, 1998. Subjects were identified using the Substitute Care Module of the state of Wisconsin's Human Services Reporting System (HSRS).	Administrative data from Wisconsin's Unemployment Insurance file, 1995–1999, and from the Client Assistance for Re-employment and Economic Support (CARES) data collection system, January 1995–June 2000	Employment, earnings and public assistance	Not applicable

No.	Citation	Study Type	Sample	Data Sources	Data Studied	Attrition Rate
18	Courtney, M. E., I. Piliavin, A. Grogan-Kaylor, and A. Nesmith (2001). Foster youth transitions to adulthood: A longitudinal view of youth leaving care. *Child Welfare* 6: 685–717.	Prospective without a comparison group (two-wave panel study)	Wave 1: *N* = 141 (80 females, 61 males) foster youth, ages 17–18, who were still in care in 1995 and who had been in care for at least 18 months. Wave 2: *N* = 113 youth (62 females, 41 males) of the former foster youth from Wave 1. Interviews were conducted 12 to 18 months after youth were discharged from foster care. Wave 3: Interviews have been completed with youths approximately 3 years after leaving care, but the results have not yet been published.	Interviews	Wave 1: Demographic characteristics, family background, history of maltreatment and reasons for placement, receipt of mental health or other social services, current health and mental health status, education, employment, delinquency, social support, foster care experiences and preparation for independent living. Wave 2: Living arrangements, income, employment, receipt of public assistance, education, health care needs, mental health, social support, trouble with the law, traumatic events such as physical or sexual assaults, and preparation for independent living	Wave 1: 5%. Wave 2: 20%

No.	Citation	Study Type	Sample	Data Sources	Data Studied	Attrition Rate
19	Goerge, R., L. Bilaver, B. Joo Lee, B. Needell, A. Brookhart, and W. Jackman (2002). *Employment Outcomes for Youth Aging Out of Foster Care.* Chicago: Chapin Hall Center for Children at the University of Chicago. Available at aspe.os.dhhs.gov/hsp/foster-care-agingout02/	Retrospective with a comparison group, using administrative data	$N = 4,213$. Employment and earnings of foster youth who aged out of care in California ($n = 2,824$), Illinois ($n = 1,084$), and South Carolina ($n = 305$) were studied for a total of 13 quarters in 1996–1997 in Illinois and South Carolina and 1995–1996 in California: the four quarters before their 18th birthday, the quarter in which they turned 18, and the 8 quarters after their 18th birthday. Employment and earnings of two comparison groups were used: (1) 5,415 youth in the same three states who were reunified at some point during the four years before their 18th birthday; and (2) 247,295 youth in the same three states who exited an Aid to Families with Dependent Children /Temporary Assistance for Needy Families case at any time after their 14th birthday and reached 18 during the study period. The study population was selected through child welfare information systems in all three states.	Wage data came from Unemployment Insurance (UI) Wage Reporting data in California, Illinois, and South Carolina; AFDC/TANF information came from income maintenance program eligibility and tracking systems in California, Illinois, and South Carolina.	Employment and earnings	Not applicable

No.	Citation	Study Type	Sample	Data Sources	Data Studied	Attrition Rate
20	Pecora, P. J., J. Williams, J. R. C. Kessler, A. C. Downs, K. O'Brien, E. Hiripi, and S. Morello (2003). *Assessing the Effects of Foster Care: Early Results from the Casey National Alumni Study.* Seattle: Casey Family Programs.	Retrospective without a comparison group (some normative data provided)	$N = 1,609$ adults (age 20–51) who had been served by 23 Casey Family Programs (a private not-for-profit foster care agency) field offices between 1966 and 1998, had been placed with a Casey foster family for at least 12 months, and had been out of care for at least 12 months at the time of follow-up interviews. Follow-up data collected on 1,087 members of the sample.	Case record reviews and interviews	Life experiences and services received while in foster care, teenage births, homelessness and home ownership, education, employment	32.4% (26.6% if subjects who had died before follow-up or were in institutions at follow-up were excluded)
21	Pecora, P. J., R. C. Kessler, J. Williams, K. O'Brien, A. C. Downs, D. English, J. White, E. Hiripi, C. Roller White, T. Wiggins, and K. Holmes (2005). *Improving Family Foster Care: Findings from the Northwest Alumni Study.* Seattle: Casey Family Programs.	Retrospective without a comparison group (some normative data provided)	$N = 659$ young adults (ages 20–33) who had been served by Casey Family Programs (a private not-for-profit foster care agency) or selected offices of one of two state agencies (Oregon and Washington) between 1988 and 1998, all of whom had been in care for at least 12 months between the ages of 14 and 18. Follow-up data collected on 479 members of the sample.	Case record reviews and interviews	Mental health, relationships, physical health, social skills, cognitive functioning, employment, education, and housing	27.3% (24.3% if subjects who had died before follow-up or were in institutions at follow-up were excluded)

No.	Citation	Study Type	Sample	Data Sources	Data Studied	Attrition Rate
22	Courtney, M.E., A. Dworsky, G. Ruth, T. Keller, J. Havlicek, and N. Bost (2005). *Midwest Evaluation of the Adult Functioning of Former Foster Youth: Outcomes at Age 19.* Chicago: Chapin Hall Center for Children at the University of Chicago.	Prospective two-wave panel study without a comparison group (some normative data provided)	$N = 732$ young adults in Illinois, Iowa, and Wisconsin who had been in out-of-home care for at least one year after their 16th birthday. Participants were interviewed once when they were 17–18 years old and again at age 19 ($n = 603$).	Interviews and child welfare system administrative data	Relationships, social support, education, employment, economic hardships, health and mental health, sexual behaviors, pregnancy, parenting, and delinquency	4.2% at baseline; 21.4% at follow-up

NOTES

Some of this chapter has been adapted from M. E. Courtney and D. Hughes-Heuring, The transition to adulthood for youth "aging out" of the foster care system, in W. Osgood, C. Flanagan, E. M. Foster, and G. Ruth, eds., *On Your Own Without a Net: The Transition to Adulthood for Vulnerable Populations* (Chicago: University of Chicago Press, 2005).

1. For a more detailed critique of U.S. policy regarding foster youth in transition, see Courtney and Hughes-Heuring (2005).
2. The 1999 law called for states to collect data on all independent living services provided to current and former foster youth and to track outcomes for youth leaving care across a number of important dimensions (e.g., employment, housing, education, and avoidance of risk behaviors). Implementing regulations for this part of the law were only proposed in July 2006, leaving states little choice but to wait for federal guidance in the interim (*Federal Register* 71, no. 135 [July 14, 2006]:40345–382).

REFERENCES

Allerhand, M. E., R. E. Weber, and M. Haug (1966). *Adaptation and Adaptability: The Bellefaire Follow-Up Study*. New York: Child Welfare League of America.

Barth, R. (1990). On their own: The experiences of youth after foster care. *Child and Adolescent Social Work* 7: 419–40.

Bussey, M., L. Feagans, L. Arnold, F. Wulczyn, K. Brunner, R. Nixon, P. DiLorenzo, P. J. Pecora, S. A. Weiss, and A. Winterfeld (2000). *Transition for Foster Care: A State-by-State Data Base Analysis*. Seattle: Casey Family Programs.

Cook, R., E. Fleischman, and V. Grimes (1991). *A National Evaluation of Title IV-E Foster Care Independent Living Programs for Youth in Foster Care: Phase 2, Final Report*. Vol. 1. Rockville, Md.: Westat.

Cook, S. K. (1992). Long-term consequences of foster care for adult well-being. Ph.D. diss., University of Nebraska, Lincoln.

Courtney, M. E., and N. Bost (2002). *Review of Literature on the Effectiveness of Independent Living Services*. Chicago: Chapin Hall Center for Children at the University of Chicago.

Courtney, M. E., and D. Hughes-Heuring (2005). The transition to adulthood for youth "aging out" of the foster care system. In W. Osgood, C. Flanagan, E. M. Foster, and G. Ruth, eds., *On Your Own Without a Net: The Transition to Adulthood for Vulnerable Populations*. Chicago: University of Chicago Press.

Courtney, M. E., I. Piliavin, A. Grogan-Kaylor, and A. Nesmith (2001). Foster youth transitions to adulthood: A longitudinal view of youth leaving care. *Child Welfare* 6: 685–717.

Courtney, M. E., A. Dworsky, G. Ruth, T. Keller, J. Havlicek, and N. Bost (2005). *Midwest Evaluation of the Adult Functioning of Former Foster Youth: Outcomes at Age 19.* Chicago: Chapin Hall Center for Children at the University of Chicago.

Dworsky, A., and M. E. Courtney (2000). *Self-Sufficiency of Former Foster Youth in Wisconsin: Analysis of Unemployment Insurance Wage Data and Public Assistance Data.* Madison, Wisc.: Institute for Research on Poverty. At aspe.os.dhhs.gov/hsp/fosteryouthW100/index.htm.

Eilertson, C. (2002). *Independent Living for Foster Youth.* Washington, D.C.: National Conference of State Legislatures.

Fanshel D., S. J. Finch, and J. F. Grundy (1990). *Foster Children in Life Course Perspective.* New York: Columbia University Press.

Festinger, T. (1983). *No One Ever Asked Us: A Postscript to Foster Care.* New York: Columbia University Press.

Frost, S., and A. P. Jurich (1983). Follow-up study of children residing in the Villages. Topeka, Kans.: The Villages. Unpublished ms.

Furstenburg, F. F., and M. E. Hughes (1995). Social capital and successful development among at-risk youth. *Journal of Marriage and Family* 57: 580–92.

Goerge, R., L. Bilaver, B. Joo Lee, B. Needell, A. Brookhart, and W. Jackman (2002). *Employment Outcomes for Youth Aging Out of Foster Care.* Chicago: Chapin Hall Center for Children at the University of Chicago. At aspe.os.dhhs.gov/hsp/foster-care-agingout02/.

Harari, T. (1980). Teenagers exiting from family foster care: A retrospective look. Ph.D. diss., University of California, Berkeley.

Heston, L. L., D. D. Denney, and I. B. Pauley (1966). The adult adjustment of persons institutionalized as children. *British Journal of Psychiatry* 112: 1103–10.

Jones, M. A., and B. Moses (1984). *West Virginia's Former Foster Children: Their Experiences in Care and Their Lives as Young Adults.* New York: Child Welfare League of America.

Kerman, B., J. Wildfire, and R. P. Barth (2002). Outcomes for young adults who experienced foster care. *Children and Youth Services Review* 24(5): 319–44.

Kerman, B., R. P. Barth, and J. Wildfire (2004). Extending transitional services to former foster children. *Child Welfare* 83(3): 239–62.

Mangine, S., D. Royse, V. Wiehe, and M. Nietzel (1990). Homelessness among adults raised as foster children: A survey of drop-in center users. *Psychological Reports* 67: 739–45.

McCord, J., W. McCord, and E. Thurber (1960). The effects of foster home placement in the prevention of adult antisocial behavior. *Social Service Review* 34: 415–19.

McDonald, T. P., R. I. Allen, A. Westerfelt, and I. Piliavin (1996). *Assessing the Long-Term Effects of Foster Care: A Research Synthesis.* Washington, D.C.: Child Welfare League of America.

Meier, E. G. (1965). Current circumstances of former foster children. *Child Welfare* 44: 196–206.

Mortimer, J. T., and R. W. Larson, eds. (2002). *The Changing Adolescent Experience: Societal Trends and the Transition to Adulthood*. New York: Cambridge University Press.

Pecora, P. J., J. Williams, R. C. Kessler, A. C. Downs, K. O'Brien, E. Hiripi, and S. Morello (2003). *Assessing the Effects of Foster Care: Early Results from the Casey National Alumni Study*. Seattle: Casey Family Programs.

Pecora, P. J., R. C. Kessler, J. Williams, K. O'Brien, A. C. Downs, D. English, J. White, E. Hiripi, C. Roller White, T. Wiggins, and K. Holmes (2005). *Improving Family Foster Care: Findings from the Northwest Alumni Study*. Seattle: Casey Family Programs.

Pecora, P. J., J. Williams, R. C. Kessler, E. Hiripi, K. O'Brien, J. Emerson, M. A. Herrick, and D. Torres (2006a). Assessing the educational achievements of adults who formerly were placed in family foster care. *Child and Family Social Work* 11: 220–31.

Pecora, P. J., R. C. Kessler, K. O'Brien, C. R. White, J. Williams, E. Hiripi, D. English, J. White, and M. A. Herrick (2006b). Educational and employment outcomes of adults formerly placed in foster care: Results from the Northwest Foster Care Alumni Study. *Children and Youth Services Review* 28: 1459–81. At www.sciencedirect.com.

Pettiford, P. (1981). *Foster Care and Welfare Dependency: A Research Note*. New York: Human Resources Administration, Office of Policy and Program Development.

Robins, L. N. (1966). *Deviant Children Grown Up: A Sociological and Psychiatric Study of Sociopathic Personality*. Baltimore: Williams and Wilkins.

Schoeni, R., and K. Ross (2004). *Family Support During the Transition to Adulthood*. Network on Transitions to Adulthood Policy Brief 12. Philadelphia: University of Pennsylvania, Department of Sociology.

Sosin, M., P. Coulson, and S. Grossman (1988). *Homelessness in Chicago: Poverty and Pathology, Social Institutions, and Social Change*. Chicago: University of Chicago, Social Service Administration.

Sosin, M., I. Piliavin, and H. Westerfelt (1990). Toward a longitudinal analysis of homelessness. *Journal of Social Issues* 46(4): 157–74.

Susser, E., E. L. Streuning, and S. Conover (1987). Childhood experiences of homeless men. *American Journal of Psychiatry* 144(12): 1599–1601.

Susser, E., S. Lin, S. Conover, and E. Streuning (1991). Childhood antecedents of homelessness in psychiatric patients. *American Journal of Psychiatry* 148: 1026–30.

Theis, S. V. S. (1924). *How Foster Children Turn Out: A Study and Critical Analysis of 910 Children Who Were Placed in Foster Homes by the State Charities Aid Association and Who Are Now Eighteen Years of Age or Over*. New York: State Charities Aid Association.

U.S. General Accounting Office (1999). *Foster Care: Effectiveness of Independent Living Services Unknown*. GAO/HEHS-00-13. Washington, D.C.: Author.

Wulczyn, F., and K. Brunner Hislop (2001). *Children in Substitute Care at Age 16: Selected Findings from the Multistate Data Archive*. Chicago: Chapin Hall Center for Children at the University of Chicago.

Wulczyn, F. H., K. B. Hislop, and R. M. Goerge (2000). *Foster Care Dynamics 1983–1998: A Report from the Multistate Foster Care Data Archive*. Chicago: Chapin Hall Center for Children at the University of Chicago.

Zimmerman, R. B. (1982). Foster care in retrospect. *Tulane Studies in Social Welfare* 14: 1–119.

Outcomes for Youth Exiting
the Foster Care System

FOUR

Extending What We Know
and What Needs to Be Done
with Selected Data

PETER J. PECORA

Mark Courtney (chapter 3) has written a comprehensive and compelling analysis of the current research regarding outcomes for youth exiting the foster care system and the implications of the research for policy and program design. In this chapter, I highlight two studies to underscore the need to refine services and strengthen community collaborations on behalf of youth exiting from foster care. First I describe the Reilly Nevada study and provide greater detail on the Casey Family Programs longitudinal study of nineteen-year-old, twenty-two-year-old, and twenty-five-year-old foster care alumni. I then discuss policy and program improvements for placement stability, educational remediation, life skills preparation, and mental health services. I conclude with a discussion of needed next steps.

THE DATA: REILLY NEVADA STUDY AND
CASEY FAMILY PROGRAMS SURVEY

Reilly Nevada Study

The Reilly Nevada Study (Reilly, 2001, 2003) examines services in a state that has one of the fastest growing populations in the country but whose foster care population has rarely been studied. Interviews (lasting between sixty and ninety minutes) were conducted with one hundred youth between September 2000 and January 2001. The youth selected had been out of foster care for a minimum of six months. The Division of Child and Family Services produced a computerized list of youth who were discharged at age eighteen (or later, if they had not received a high school diploma or GED) and who had exited in the preceding three years. Although the sample size and response rate (37 percent of the sample, excluding individuals who were deceased or in prison) are modest, the findings provide important information about youth exiting from foster care. The study found that the mean age for this sample of foster care alumni when entering the foster care system was 9.3 years, and the average number of years spent in foster care was 8.3 years. More than 50 percent of the youth had had five or more placements while in foster care (ranging from one to more than fifty). Study highlights include the following.

• *Employment and income:* Most youth (63 percent) were employed at the time of the interview. Some 26 percent, however, had not had regular employment since leaving care, and 55 percent reported that they had been terminated from a job at least once since leaving care. The average hourly wage of the youth who had worked or were working at the time of the interview was $7.25. About 34 percent made less than $5,000 in 1999; 60 percent made less than $10,000. At least 41 percent stated that they did not have enough money to cover basic living expenses.

• *Education:* Some 50 percent of the youth left foster care without a high school degree. But at the time of the interview, the number of young adults who had obtained a high school degree or equivalent rose to 69 percent. Close to one-third of the youth (30 percent) said that they were currently attending or had attended college. Respondents expressed high aspirations regarding education: 75 percent said that they wanted to obtain a college degree.

• *Housing and homelessness:* Since leaving foster care, a startling 36 percent of the youth indicated that there had been times when they did not have a place to live: 19 percent reported living on the streets, and 18 percent said that they has stayed at a homeless shelter. The stability of living arrangements for many youth was questionable: 35 percent reported moving five or more times since leaving foster care.

• *Physical health:* Former foster care youth reported serious health care problems. About 30 percent had a serious health problem since leaving care, and 32 percent reported that they needed health care and could not obtain it. Some 55 percent had no health insurance; the remaining youth were on Medicaid (25 percent) or on other public assistance programs (11 percent), or they had private insurance (9 percent). Only 54 percent of the youth rated their health as very good or excellent.

• *Involvement with the legal system:* Many youth in this study had been involved in the criminal justice system. Four in ten (41 percent) had spent some time in jail; 26 percent had had formal charges filed against them, and 7 percent (not including three additional youth in out-of-state prisons and not interviewed) were incarcerated in a state prison at the time of the interview.

• *Preparedness for adulthood:* Most youth had had some exposure to independent living training programs during their time in care. The most frequently reported types of training that they received were: job seeking (73 percent), housekeeping (72 percent), educational planning (71 percent), money management (67 percent), interpersonal skills (66 percent), food management (65 percent), use of community resources (61 percent), transportation (61 percent), housing (51 percent), job maintenance (59 percent), parenting skills (47 percent), and legal skills (37 percent). Few youth reported receiving concrete assistance for independent living such as assistance in locating housing, the provision of health records, health insurance, or other services upon discharge. Not surprisingly, almost one-third of the youth reported not having a place to live after being discharged, and one-half had $250 or less when they exited foster care (Reilly, 2001, 2003).

Casey Family Program Young Adult Survey

In the 2005 data collection wave, this longitudinal study conducted by Casey Family Programs included interviews with foster care alumni who were served by Casey Family Programs in multiple western states. Eligible participants were age 19, 22, or 25 at the time of interview; currently were receiving or formerly had received foster care, adoption, or guardianship services from a Casey Family Programs field office for 12 months or more;[1] and mentally able to complete the telephone interview.

The response rate was 53.2 percent (n = 193) with a refusal rate of 2.8 percent (N = 10). The majority of the respondents were women (68.4 percent). More than one-half of those interviewed were white (54.9 percent). Other groups represented were African American or black (19.7 percent), American Indian or Alaskan Native (10.9 percent), Hispanic or Latino (8.8 percent), Asian (3.6 percent), and other (2.1 percent). Nineteen year olds made up 29 percent of the sample; twenty-two year olds, 38.9 percent; and twenty-five year olds 32.1 percent. Key findings included the following.

- *Concrete assistance to prepare youth for adulthood:* More than three-quarters (77.1 percent) of the respondents had a copy of their birth certificate. Most youth (94.0 percent) had a driver's license or an identification card. Surprisingly, only 77.1 percent of the young adults reported having a bank account.
- *Housing:* More than one-quarter (26.1 percent) of the respondents had experienced homelessness since leaving care.[2] Almost all of the young adults (93.1 percent) reported that they felt that their current living situation was safe.
- *Physical health:* Slightly more than one-third (36.3 percent) of the young adults did not have health insurance at the time of interview. Several young adults (n = 14), however, reported that they were in the process of obtaining health insurance or anticipated getting it soon through their jobs. Nearly one-half (49.2 percent) of the young adults indicated having "alcohol problems," according to a screener.[3] In the general population, 15.1 percent of eighteen to twenty-five year olds are defined as heavy drinkers (National Center for Health Statistics, 2004).[4] About three in ten respondents (29.4 percent) reported using illegal drugs in the past year, compared with about one in five (20.3 percent) of the eighteen to twenty-five year olds in the general population. Despite elevated alcohol and drug usage, more than one-half (56.3 percent) of young adults reported that their current overall physical health was very good or excellent.
- *Mental health:* When compared with the general population of young adults nineteen to twenty-five years old, a disproportionate number of respondents reported mental health problems. Based on results from the Symptom Checklist-90-R (SCL-90-R) (Derogatis, 1993),[5] almost one-fourth (23.3 percent) of the young adults were experiencing a clinically significant level of mental health symptoms according to a global measure, while over

one-third (36.9 percent) were considered to be a "positive risk or case": that is, they very likely had a psychiatric disorder (White, et al., 2006).

POLICY AND PROGRAM IMPROVEMENTS

The studies reviewed by Courtney, as well as the findings from the Nevada study and the Casey Family Program survey, underscore the need to change policy and programs in many areas. Some of these studies have identified factors that should be addressed in a more focused way in order to improve outcomes for youth exiting foster care. Recent multivariate statistical analyses for the Northwest Alumni Study demonstrate the linkage between placement stability, extracurricular activities, access to education and mental health services, and more comprehensive supports for independent living, on the one hand, and later successful adult functioning, on the other (Pecora et al., 2006b, in press). In this section, I discuss policy and program improvements in four key areas: placement stability; educational remediation; preparation for adulthood; and mental health service access, coverage, and quality.

Placement Stability

Conversations with hundreds of foster care alumni have underscored the pain and anxiety that many alumni felt when their foster care placements disrupted, along with the continuing emotional effect of those experiences on young adults. Researchers in the Northwest Alumni Study found that 23 percent of foster care alumni had a lifetime rate of social phobia, and 20 percent of alumni had generalized anxiety disorder. These findings emphasize the importance of addressing key factors in helping minimize placement disruptions for youth: caseworker stability, strengthening the mental health functioning of youth, and building and sustaining supportive birth family relationships. Much greater attention must be given to ensuring that a child's first placement is his or her last placement. Research is needed to develop a better understanding of the reasons that placement changes occur. It also is important to test cost-effective strategies to lower placement change rates, including benefit-cost analyses that document the benefits from lower school placement change rates, better youth mental health, and greater social support networks for children.

Educational Remediation

Information about the true high school completion rates of youth who have been in foster care is lacking because too few studies have measured this outcome with older alumni. High school completion rates, however, appear to be a concern, particularly given the inordinately high number of youth completing high school with a GED (Pecora et al., 2005). Low rates of vocational and college program completion are equally worrisome (e.g., Davis, 2006; Pecora et al., 2006b). Careful neural-cognitive assessments, ensuring school stability, focused remediation for reading and math, and building on youth strengths could make a huge difference in alumni educational outcomes. With the growing understanding of foster youth's educational challenges, it is time to engage youth, foster parents, birth families, and the education system in collaborations to improve foster youth's educational experiences and outcomes.

Preparation for Adulthood

As the child welfare field considers how to better prepare youth who may emancipate from foster care or spend their later adolescent years in another form of out-of-home care, a broader context of youth's transitions to adulthood needs to be considered. Experts in sociology, economics, psychology, and other fields are examining the societal and economic changes that make it more difficult for all youth to transition to adulthood. Among the factors that need to be considered when policies and programs are planned for youth in foster care are job stability (Does job turnover delay the transition to adulthood?), housing costs (Do housing costs delay the transition to adulthood?), and earnings and wages (Do lower-paying jobs force youth to move back home?) (Danzinger and Rouse, 2007). A key issue is whether youth have supportive families to whom they can return.

There is an untested assumption that independent living services, as currently constructed, are effective. While some youth enter care with pre-existing health conditions and genetic vulnerabilities for mental health disorders that hinder their development, the child welfare and related systems have an obligation to try to improve the life chances of *all* children who are placed for substantial lengths of time.

As Courtney notes, the independent living programs authorized by the Chafee Foster Care Independence Act are grossly underfunded. A related concern is that substantial funds are likely being wasted on inefficient or ineffective strategies to prepare youth for adulthood, when agencies are needing to immediately improve the concrete assistance they provide to youth who are emancipating (Courtney and Bost, 2002; Massinga and Pecora, 2003). The field urgently needs rigorous comparative evaluations of which life skills development approaches work best and which assessment and case planning strategies are most useful.

The stakes are high, not only for helping alumni achieve a good quality of life but also for maintaining a competitive workforce and saving taxpayer dollars. According to a recent economic analysis, for each year that a young adult obtains and retains a job, society gains $10,639 (Plotnick, 2006). Because about one-sixth of emancipated youth received cash public assistance in a typical year (Pecora et al., 2005), the total potential savings to the government could be significant. As noted by Robert Plotnick (2006:2), "If one-sixth of the 23,000 youth who emancipated from foster care nationally every year were able to obtain and retain a living wage job instead of receiving welfare, these alumni would be contributing over 40 million dollars per year ($40,783,000) for every year they were not receiving public assistance."

Specifically, greater emphasis must be placed on each youth having a bank account. One of the Northwest Alumni Study findings was that having concrete resources, such as $250 in cash, contributed significantly to positive outcomes in education and employment or finances for young adults. This set of variables possibly represent more comprehensive independent living preparation—which might begin with an independent living plan (Pecora et al., 2005). Finally, the depth and targeting of housing preparation for youth must be strengthened, including connecting youth with supportive adults, teaching them how to locate reasonable housing, increasing the availability of Section 8 housing designated for foster care alumni, and, perhaps most important, helping alumni obtain and retain living wage jobs.

Mental Health Service Access, Coverage, and Quality

Recent research underscores the urgent need to improve the access and quality of physical health and mental health care services for youths in foster care. David Rubin et al. (2005) compiled the following powerful statistics:

- An estimated one in every two children in foster care has chronic medical problems unrelated to behavioral concerns (Halfon et al., 1995;

Simms, 1989; Takayama et al., 1998; U.S .General Accounting Office, 1995). Evidence suggests that these chronic conditions increase the likelihood of serious emotional problems (Rubin et al., 2004).

• Although children in foster care represent 3 percent of all Medicaid enrollees, they account for 25 percent to 41 percent of mental health expenditures (Halfon et al., 1992; Takayama et al., 1994). In 2001, per capita Medicaid expenditures for children in foster care were more than triple that of nondisabled children covered by Medicaid (Halfon et al., 1992; Takayama et al., 1998), and yet access remains poor and the quality of services remains uneven (U.S. General Accounting Office, 1995).

Research has shown that only one-third of foster youth receive mental health services tailored to their needs (Hurlburt et al., 2004; Burns et al., 2004). Studies suggest that 40 percent to 80 percent of children and adolescents in foster care exhibit a serious behavioral or mental health problem requiring intervention (Clausen et al., 1998; Garland et al., 2000; Glisson, 1994; Halfon et al., 1995; Landsverk et al., 2002; Trupin et al., 1993; Urquiza et al., 1994). Only one-quarter to two-thirds, however, will receive any mental health services (Halfon et al., 1992; Harman et al., 2000; Hurlburt et al., 2004; Burns et al., 2004; Rubin et al., 2004; U.S. General Accounting Office, 1995). Over 50 percent of adults who were placed in foster care as children have mental health problems well into adulthood, and one in four suffer from posttraumatic stress disorder (PTSD) (Pecora et al., 2005).

With their needs often unmet, older children and adolescents in foster care rely increasingly on hospital emergency departments for care, most often in periods around placement changes, for injuries and mental health concerns (Rubin et al., 2004). Additionally, although foster youth generally receive mental health services at a greater rate than the nonfoster population, the specificity and appropriateness of this care may be limited to a small subsection of youth in need of services (Stahmer et al., 2005).

A recent study that included a high proportion of public agency foster care alumni found that, while many of these young adults had recovered from earlier mental health conditions, alarmingly high percentages had mental health disorders, including posttraumatic stress disorder (25 percent), depression (20 percent), modified social phobia (17 percent), and generalized anxiety (12 percent). The study also found that enabling youth in care to remain in one foster care placement, succeed in school, and gain employment experience was linked with higher access to mental health services and better mental health outcomes (Pecora et al., 2006a, in press).

Policy and program improvements are needed in several areas of mental health services. First, we need to better assess and screen youth in care and as they enter care to identify those who need special mental health supports. Second, we must address overmedication of youth in foster care. One approach is to bridge various databases using commonly available strategies and software that links these databases by linking client IDs. Third, evidence-based treatment approaches (EBTs) need to be implemented that are relevant to the ethnic and other unique circumstances of youth in foster care and their families. Fourth, concrete strategies must be identified and implemented to address the most damaging Medicaid changes stemming from the federal Deficit Reduction Act of 2006, especially the provision that limits the use of targeted case management for children and youth in foster care.

Addressing the crucial development needs of children in foster care requires attention to many areas. In addition to those already addressed in this chapter, the following program and policy changes are needed:

1. *States should exercise the federal option to extend foster care to age twenty-one.* The Fostering Connections to Success and Increasing Adoptions Act of 2008 provides states with the option to extend foster care beyond the age of 18 with federal reimbursement. States should exercise this option. It is unrealistic to expect that youth will be ready to live completely on their own at age eighteen. Youth engaged in high school or any type of postsecondary education should be allowed to voluntarily remain in foster care. Youth should have opportunities to integrate themselves into the community through community-based transitional housing while they remain under the state's supervision. This safety net of resources is essential for this population.

2. *More states should extend Medicaid coverage to age twenty-three or twenty-five for young adults who were in foster care, with automatic enrollment in the Medicaid program on their eighteenth birthday.* Recently passed federal legislation allows for this coverage (and federal reimbursement), but state legislators must enact state legislation so that these opportunities are available to youth in their states (National Foster Care Awareness Project, 2000).

3. *Funds should be set aside for room and board for young people ages eighteen to twenty-one who have exited foster care.* Title I of the Foster Care Independence Act allows for 30 percent of newly allocated federal funds for independent living services to be used for this purpose. Chaffee funds can help cover these costs, but they are insufficient. California advocates have proposed legislation to provide special state emancipation funds for

housing, food, and other needs that would be administered by a youth's volunteer guardian (Williams et al., 2005).

4. *Specialized case management services are needed for all older youth in foster care youth to ensure they have a realistic plan of action to live on their own.*

5. *Youth leaving care should be given a portfolio of important documents,* such as their health records and social security cards, along with a list of resources they can access.

6. *The availability of specific after care services should be increased.* After care services include case management and crisis intervention services for youth and for their birth families. These services should be more widely available after youth have been discharged from foster care (Courtney et al., 2005; Reilly, 2001; Williams et al., 2005).

CONCLUSION

With over 500,000 children in care on any given day and over 20,000 emancipating from care as young adults each year, there is an urgent need to improve the outcomes of permanency-oriented foster care services. This chapter reinforces the importance of Courtney's call for stronger research, policy, and practice for permanency planning services for older youth by sharing new research findings and identifying issues that need urgent attention.

NOTES

Parts of this chapter draw from research data collected by the staff of the Casey Family Programs. The author is grateful to and has learned much from youth, parents, child welfare staff, and research colleagues.

1. Service enrollment did not have to be continuous. As an example, a youth could have spent two months in foster care with Casey Family Programs, returned home, and then spent ten more months in foster care with Casey Family Programs.
2. Homelessness was defined broadly as "not having a place to stay."
3. The alcohol screener is widely used in hospital settings as a rapid method for identifying people who might have alcohol problems. As such, it may result in a sizable number of "false positives," that is, people who are falsely screened as having an alcohol problem.

4. Respondents in the general population reported illicit drug use or alcohol use in the preceding thirty days. Heavy use is defined as five or more drinks on each of five or more occasions in the preceding thirty days.

5. This instrument was developed to highlight current psychological symptoms. It is an inventory of ninety psychological symptoms that are categorized in nine primary symptom dimensions (somatization, obsessive-compulsive, interpersonal sensitivity, depression, anxiety, hostility, phobic anxiety, paranoid ideation, and psychoticism) and three global indices (global severity index [GSI], positive symptom distress index, and positive symptom total).

REFERENCES

Burns, B. J., S. D. Phillips, R. H. Wagner, R. P. Barth, D. J. Kolko, Y. Campbell, and J. Landsverk (2004). Mental health need and access to mental health services by youths involved with child welfare: A national survey. *Journal of the American Academy of Child and Adolescent Psychiatry* 43(8): 960–70.

Clausen, J. M., J. Landsverk, W. Ganger, D. Chadwick, and A. Litrownik (1998). Mental health problems of children in foster care. *Journal of Child and Family Studies* 7(3): 283–96.

Courtney, M. E., and N. Bost (2002). *Review of Literature on the Effectiveness of Independent Living Services*. Chicago: Chapin Hall Center for Children at the University of Chicago.

Courtney, M. E., A. Dworsky, G. Ruth, T. Keller, J. Havlicek, and N. Bost (2005). *Midwest Evaluation of the Adult Functioning of Former Foster Youth: Outcomes at Age 19*. Chicago: Chapin Hall Center for Children at the University of Chicago.

Danzinger, S., and C. Rouse (2007). *The Price of Independence: The Economics of Early Adulthood*. New York: Russell Sage.

Davis, R. J. (2006). *College Access, Financial Aid, and College Success for Undergraduates from Foster Care*. Washington, D.C.: National Association of Student Financial Aid Administrators.

Derogatis, L. R. (1993). *Symptom Checklist 90 Revised (SCL-90R) Manual*. Minneapolis: Pearson.

Garland, A. F., R. L. Hough, J. A. Landsverk, K. M. McCabe, M. Yeh, W. C. Ganger, and B. J. Reynolds (2000). *Racial and ethnic variations in mental health care utilization among children in foster care*. Children's Services: Social Policy, Research, and Practice 3(3): 133–46.

Glisson, C. (1994). The effects of services coordination teams on outcomes for children in state custody. *Administration in Social Work* 18: 1–23.

Halfon, N., G. Berkowitz, and L. Klee (1992). Mental health service utilization by children in foster care in California. *Pediatrics* 89: 1238–44.

Halfon, N., A. Mendonca, and G. Berkowitz (1995). Health status of children in foster care: The experience of the Center for the Vulnerable Child. *Archives of Pediatrics and Adolescent Medicine* 149(4): 386–92.

Harman, J. S., G. E. Childs, and K. J. Kelleher (2000). Mental health care utilization and expenditures by children in foster care. *Archives of Pediatrics and Adolescent Medicine* 154(11): 1114–17.

Hurlburt, M., L. Leslie, J. Landsverk, R. P. Barth, B. J. Burns, R. D. Gibbons, D. J. Slymen, and J. Zhang (2004). Contextual predictors of mental health service use among children open to child welfare. *Archives of General Psychiatry* 61: 1217–24.

Landsverk, J. A., A. F. Garland, and L. K. Leslie (2002). *Mental Health Services for Children Reported to Child Protective Services.* Vol. 2. Thousand Oaks, Calif.: Sage.

Massinga, R., and P. J. Pecora (2003). Providing better opportunities for older children in the child welfare system. *Future of Children* 14(1): 151–73. At www.future of children.org.

National Center for Health Statistics (2004). *Health, United States, 2004 with Chartbook on Trends in the Health of Americans.* Hyattsville, Md.: U.S. Government Printing Office.

National Foster Care Awareness Project (NFCAP). (2000). *Frequently Asked Questions II: About the Foster Care Independence Act of 1999 and the John H. Chafee Foster Care Independence Program.* Seattle: Casey Family Programs. At www.casey.org.

Pecora, P. J., R. C. Kessler, J. Williams, K. O'Brien, A. C. Downs, D. English, J. White, E. Hiripi, C. R. White, T. Wiggins, and K. Holmes, K. (2005). *Improving Family Foster Care: Findings from the Northwest Foster Care Alumni Study.* Seattle: Casey Family Programs. At www.casey.org.

Pecora, P. J., Williams, J., Kessler, R. C., Hiripi, E., O'Brien, K., Emerson, J., Herrick, M.A. and Torres, D. (2006a). Assessing the educational achievements of adults who formerly were placed in family foster care. *Child and Family Social Work* 11: 220–31.

Pecora, P. J., R. C. Kessler, K. O'Brien, C. R. White, J. Williams, E. Hiripi, D. English, J. White, and M. A. Herrick (2006b). Educational and employment outcomes of adults formerly placed in foster care: Results from the Northwest Foster Care Alumni Study. *Children and Youth Services Review* 28: 1459–81. At www.sciencedirect.com.

Pecora, P. J., R. C. Kessler, J. Williams, A. C. Downs, D. English, J. White, and K. O'Brien (in press). *What Works in Family Foster Care?* Oxford: Oxford University Press.

Plotnick, R. (2006). *Estimated Public Benefits Received and Taxes Paid in 2005: Foster Care Alumni Receiving Public Assistance Compared to Alumni Not Receiving Public Assistance.* Seattle: Casey Family Programs.

Reilly, T. (2001). *Transition for Care: The Status and Outcomes of Youth Who Have Aged Out of the Foster Care System in Clark County Nevada.* Nevada Kids Count Issue Brief II, March 2001, Center for Business and Economic Research. At kidscount. unlv.edu/2001/transition_fostercare.pdf.

—— (2003). Transition from care: Status and outcomes of youth who age out of foster care. *Child Welfare* 82(6): 727–46.

Rubin, D. M., E. A. Alessandrini, C. Feudtner, D. Mandell, A. R. Localio, and T. Hadley (2004). Placement stability and mental health costs for children in foster care. *Pediatrics* 113(5): 1336–41.

Rubin, D., N. Halfon, R. Raghavan, and S. Rosenbaum (2005). *Protecting Children in Foster Care: Why Proposed Medicaid Cuts Harm Our Nation's Most Vulnerable Children.* Seattle: Casey Family Programs.

Simms, M. D. (1989). The foster care clinic: A community program to identify treatment needs of children in foster care. *Journal of Developmental and Behavioral Pediatrics* 10(3): 121–28.

Stahmer, A. C., L. K. Leslie, M. Hurlburt, R. P. Barth, M. B. Webb, J. Landsverk, and J. Zhang (2005). Developmental and behavioral needs and service use for young children in child welfare. *Pediatrics* 116(4): 891–900.

Takayama, J. I., A. B. Bergman, and F. A. Connell (1994). Children in foster care in the state of Washington: Health care utilization and expenditures. *Journal of the American Medical Association* (JAMA) 271: 1850–55.

Takayama, J. I., E. Wolfe, and K. P. Coulter (1998). Relationship between reason for placement and medical findings among children in foster care. *Pediatrics* 101(2): 201–7.

Trupin, E. W., V. S. Tarico, B. P. Low, R. Jemelka, and J. McClellan (1993). Children on child protective service caseloads: Prevalence and nature of serious emotional disturbance. *Child Abuse and Neglect* 17(3): 345–55.

Urquiza, A. J., S. J. Wirtz, M. S. Peterson, and V. A. Singer (1994). Screening and evaluating abused and neglected children entering protective custody. *Child Welfare* 73(2): 155–71.

U.S. General Accounting Office (1995). *Foster Care: Health Needs of Many Young Children Are Unknown and Unmet.* GAO/HEHS-95-114. Washington, D.C: Author.

White, C., A. Havalchak, K. O'Brien, and P. J. Pecora (2006). *Casey Family Programs Young Adult Survey, 2005: Examining Outcomes for Young Adults Served in Out-of-Home Care.* Seattle: Casey Family Programs.

Williams, J. R., S. M. Pope, E. A. Sirles, and E. M. Lally (2005). *Alaska Foster Care Alumni Study.* Anchorage: University of Alaska.

Permanence and Impermanence for Youth in Out-of-Home Care

FIVE

RICHARD P. BARTH AND LAURA K. CHINTAPALLI

Although research makes clear that many children do not achieve permanency, it offers little detail about these children or their paths to impermanence. Much attention has been focused on youth who never achieve permanence and leave foster care without a "forever family" (e.g., Massinga and Pecora, 2004). But there are also many youth who spend time in out-of-home care in a heightened state of impermanence. These youth include those who are not successfully reunified with their birth families and who experience multiple placements while in foster care and youth who no longer have a legal family because their parents' rights have been terminated.

Permanency is a state of security and attachment involving a parenting relationship that is mutually understood to be a lasting relationship. Permanency achievement is linked to stronger social-emotional development, educational attainment, financial stability, and better health and mental health outcomes (Courtney et al., 2001). Child welfare agencies are expected to achieve permanency for adolescents in foster care by helping them live in families that offer a relationship with a nurturing parent or caretaker and by providing youth with opportunities to establish lifetime relationships and connections with supportive adults.

The child welfare system, however, struggles to find permanent families for children who have reached adolescence. Adolescents in foster care often experience multiple placements and lack connections with significant adults in their lives (Courtney and Barth, 1996; Frey et al., 2005). Permanency attainment may be hindered as a result of youth's behavioral problems (Courtney et al., 2001). Data suggest that reunification and adoption often are not successfully achieved for youth. More than 25 percent of reunifications of adolescents and their parents fail (Wulczyn, 2004). Only a small proportion of adoptions are of adolescents. In FY 2005, only 15 percent of children adopted from foster care were twelve years of age or older (U.S. Department of Health and Human Services, 2006). When adolescents are adopted, they face a greater risk of adoption disruption. Adoption disruptions for adolescents may exceed 20 percent (Berry and Barth, 1990).

Many adolescents are neither reunited with their birth families nor adopted, and they "age out" of the system after turning eighteen years old. Approximately 10 percent of the children who exited care during FY 2005 were eighteen years old or older (U.S. Department of Health and Human Services, 2006). Too many of these youth become homeless, abuse substances, or become involved with crime (Barth, 1990; Courtney and Piliavin, 1998). Runaways also comprise a substantial proportion of all exits from care for older children. In FY 2005, 2 percent (4,445) of the children exiting foster care were listed as runaways (U.S. Department of Health and Human Services, 2006). Frequency of runaway events for youth ages twelve to eighteen in foster care has increased, doubling between 1998 and 2003 (Courtney et al., 2005).

Placement instability while youth are in foster care contributes to the challenges in achieving permanence for adolescents in foster care and the poor outcomes associated with aging out of foster care and running away. Courtney and colleagues (2005) found that increased placement instability while youth are in foster care increased the risk of an adolescent's running away for the first time. Multiple placement moves combine with the absence of caring relationships with adults, sibling separation, and loss of cultural connections to undermine positive outcomes for youth in foster care. Research with California children in foster care indicated that these factors result in negative outcomes for children and youth, including poor educational performance and behavioral problems (Blome, 1997; Newton et al., 2000).

In this chapter, we discuss research findings regarding the reunification of youth with their birth families and reentry rates for youth who are reunified with their birth families. We then consider placement instability and its role in youth impermanence, focusing on the use of congregate care for adolescents and on running away as the method by which some youth leave foster care. We then consider the use of termination of parental of rights that does not result in adoption and the possibility of posttermination reunification and close with a discussion of the implications for research, policy, and practice.

REUNIFICATION OF YOUTH WITH BIRTH FAMILY AND FACTORS ASSOCIATED WITH REENTRY

Data show certain patterns regarding adolescents' exits from foster care. More than one-half of youth who are in foster care at age sixteen entered foster care as adolescents and are in their first spell of foster care (Wulczyn et al., 2005). These youth are more likely to reunify with their birth parents than are youth who enter care at ages seven through twelve, a group that is more likely to leave care by running away (Wulczyn et al., 2000).

Reunification Outcomes

There have been few studies of reunification outcomes for adolescents in foster care, but the studies that have examined these issues suggest that successful reunification is a difficult permanency outcome to achieve for adolescents. In one study that examined planned reunifications involving 149 youth, the researchers found that adolescents were among the groups with the lowest rates of successful reunification (Taussig et al., 2001). Another study of 252 youth ages seventeen or older at time of case closure found that only 10 percent of the adolescents had planned reunifications or permanent placements with relatives; another 10 percent of the adolescents had unplanned reunifications, and 11 percent were runaways (McMillen and Tucker, 1999).

These studies highlight the need to improve reunification efforts for adolescents. More concurrent in-home and out-of-home services are needed, such as combining foster care with the use of Multisystemic Therapy (MST) or Multidimensional Treatment Foster Care (MTFC) that includes individualized behavior therapy and family therapy. MST is a family-centered model focused on goal-oriented treatment designed to enhance a youth's functioning by building stronger family and positive peer relationships while decreasing antisocial behaviors; the goal is to empower families to develop healthy environments through resources and connections (Henggeler et al., 1986). Similar to MST, MTFC is a family-based approach designed to help and support a youth's family in treating troubled youths by decreasing delinquent behaviors and increasing pro-social activities (Chamberlain and Reid, 1998; Fisher and Chamberlain, 2000). Youth typically reside in MTFC homes and then transition back to their birth family home. MTFC interventions are developed and implemented in various environments, including in the MTFC home, at school, and in the community (Fisher and Chamberlain, 2000).

Family connections are important throughout a youth's foster care experience. When adolescents come into care, youth may not maintain connections with family and friends as a result of agency policies and practices. In some cases, for example, visiting may be difficult to arrange because of agency requirements of criminal background checks for each family member or friend. Reducing barriers to family connections can help adolescents maintain consistent contact with family, friends, and community. In addition, at each opportunity during a youth's stay in foster care, the child welfare agency should assess whether the birth family can serve as a permanency resource for the youth and whether reunification is possible. These assessments may be appropriate after parents' rights have been terminated and youth have not been placed with adoptive families. Finally, when youth have been reunified with their families, aftercare services should be provided over a period of more than six months.

Reentry to Foster Care

Information from the National Survey of Child and Adolescent Well-Being (NSCAW) provides a better understanding of reentry to foster care from reunification (Barth et al., 2006). The rate of reentry after reunification is related to the type of placement. Children in congregate care experience the highest reunification rate (nearly 95 percent) and have a reentry rate of 28 percent. Children placed with unrelated foster families experience a reunification rate of almost 88 percent and have a reentry rate of 20.5 percent. The lowest rate of reunification (79.3 percent) is experienced by children in kinship care, and they also have the lowest reentry rate (13.9 percent). Reentry rates also vary in relation to exits from foster care other than through reunification. Some 13 percent of all exits from foster care are to the home of a relative, with a 29 percent rate of reentry to foster care. Among children who run away (about 7 percent of all exits), more than one-half reenter foster care. Though this is not a conventional reentry rate, it is important to recognize that as many as one-half of the children who run away never return to foster care.

Reentry rates differ significantly for children who are placed with unrelated foster parents and those placed with kin. An analysis of NSCAW data revealed that children age seven and older—who were in care for the first time, were placed with unrelated foster parents, and were reunified during the first thirty-six months of care—were more than eight times as likely to reenter foster care than their peers who were placed with kin (Barth et al., 2006). Two explanations for this outcome appear most sensible. First, children who are placed with kin have fewer problems and, as a result, reunifying them with their parents and sustaining those reunifications may be less difficult, resulting in lower reentry rates. Second, children who are likely to have difficulty remaining at home (because of their own difficulties, their parents' difficulties, or an interaction of these factors) may be less likely to be sent home when they live with kin. The child welfare agency and the courts may be more willing to allow additional time to achieve permanency when children live with kin.

The NSCAW analysis (Barth et al., 2006) also found that other factors were associated with reentry to foster care. Previous involvement with child welfare services was strongly associated with reentry across all the types of initial placements. As has nearly universally been shown in other studies (e.g., Courtney, 1994), the analysis found that the length of time that children spent in foster care before the reunification was associated with the success of reunification. Children with shorter stays in foster care were more likely to reenter care (Barth et al., 2006). The data analysis also showed that reentries into foster care increased with the number of prior reentries. Each time a child returns home and then reenters foster care, the child is more likely to have another failed reunification if he or she again returns home. Compared with the 20 percent of all reunifications that fail after the child's first stay in foster care, 39 percent of reunifications fail after a youth's third entry into foster care.

PLACEMENT INSTABILITY AND ITS EFFECT ON PERMANENCY

Placement instability has been defined as three or more moves for a child while in foster care (Webster et al., 2000). Studies suggest that many children in foster care experience placement instability. A California study found that more than 50 percent of children in nonkinship foster care and over 25 percent of children in kinship foster care had experienced at least three moves (Webster et al., 2000). In a study of a large Ohio county, 22 percent of children in foster care had experienced at least three moves (Usher et al., 1999). In Illinois, one study found that over 40 percent of children in foster care had three or more placements (Hartnett et al., 1999). A more recent study in Illinois found that the average number of placement changes for children in their first year of foster rose from 1.7 in 1992 to 2.1 in 2002. This study also found that placement instability was increasing: in 1990, at least 46 percent of children in their first year of foster care had experienced no placement changes compared with fewer than 25 percent of children in their first year of foster care in 2002 (Zinn et al., 2006).

Factors Associated with Placement Instability

Studies have identified two major causes of placement instability: policy-related or system-related issues, such as the use of nonkinship placements and emergency foster home and shelter placements; and difficulties on the part of foster families or the child welfare agency in meeting children's needs. Mary Ann Hartnett and colleagues (1999) found that in Illinois, more than 50 percent of placement changes occurred as a result of policy or system issues. Sigrid James (2004) found that 70 percent of placement moves occurred because of administrative actions—that is, policy or procedural requirements that caused the placement change (including moving children so that they would be placed with siblings or moving to lesser or more restrictive settings). That study found that only 20 percent of placement changes were the result of children's behavior problems (James, 2004).

Other studies, in contrast, have found that children's behavior and emotional problems account for many placement changes. In a recent Illinois study (Zinn et al., 2006), child welfare workers stated that over 75 percent of placement moves were related, in part, to the foster parent's inability or unwillingness to continue to foster the child because of the child's emotional or behavioral problems (27.6 percent) or personal issues affecting the foster parent, such as divorce, marriage, or change in employment (20 percent). In their San Diego study, Rae Newton and colleagues (2000) found that children exhibiting initial problem behaviors, such as aggression or delinquency, were more likely to experience placement changes. In a national probability study of children in out-of-home care, the rate of placement moves during a thirty-six-month period was four times as great for youth with emotional and behavioral problems than for youth without such problems at the time of placement. There was considerable variation, however, in the number of placement moves for youth with emotional and behavioral problems, indicating that the presence of these problems influenced placement moves but did not determine them (Barth et al., 2007).

Placement changes in the first year and age at initial placement also are significant risk factors associated with placement instability. Daniel Webster et al. (2000) found in a California study that children who had more placement changes in the first year of placement were more likely to experience long-term placement instability. Studies also have found that adolescents are more likely than younger children to experience placement changes (Webster et al., 2000; Wulczyn et al., 2003). Andrew Zinn and colleagues (2006) found that each additional year of age at time of placement increased a child's likelihood of a placement change by 4 percent.

Other factors associated with placement changes among children with emotional and behavioral problems are depression and separation from siblings (Wulczyn et al., 2003), uncertainty or hopelessness about reunification, and age of the child (over ten years old) (Barth et al., 2007).

Among children without emotional and behavioral problems, children who are older and who are female (James, 2004; Wulczyn et al., 2003), who report past psychological trauma, and who are involved with the juvenile or criminal justice system are more likely to have placement changes (James, 2004).

Several studies have linked placement instability to negative outcomes for children, including mental health and behavioral problems and increased delinquency. In a longitudinal study of children who entered foster care in San Diego and who had no presenting behavior problems at the time of placement, Newton et al. (2000) found that placement instability contributed to behavioral and emotional problems; they determined that children who experienced more placement changes were at high risk for increased internalizing, externalizing, and total behavioral problems. David Rubin and colleagues (2007) linked children's multiple foster care placements with increasing needs for mental health services. Joseph Ryan and Mark Testa (2005) found that placement instability experiences before the age of fourteen contributed to increases in delinquency charges after that age.

Enhancing Placement Stability

Placement instability is not predestined. Two MTFC-based projects have demonstrated an effect on placement instability and exits. MTFC-P (Multidimensional Treatment Foster Care—for Preschoolers) showed that, for young children, these services can reduce the influence of previous placements on future placements (Fisher et al., 2005). As shown in Figure 5.1, the placement movements for children who were in regular foster care (RFC) were much different than for children who were randomly assigned to and received MTFC-P. For the children in regular foster care, the more placements that children had before entering the study, the more placements they had after entering the study. This finding reflects the predictable pattern of placement instability generating more placement instability. In stark contrast, the children who received MTFC-P had fewer placement moves after entering the study, and those moves were unrelated to their previous moves. For example, a child with four foster care placements before the study and who received MTFC-P did not experience an increased probability of another failed placement as would be expected for children in conventional foster care. Previous placement moves lost their predictive power for children who were in MTFC-P.

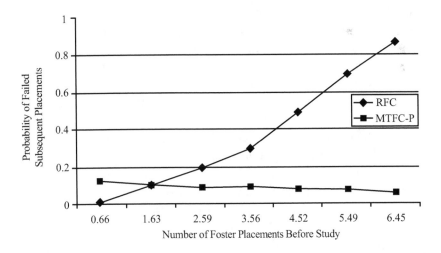

Figure 5.1 Probability of failed placements by prior placements and condition for children in regular foster care (RFC) and in multidimensional treatment foster care for preschoolers (MTFC-P)

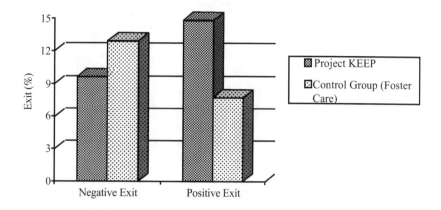

Figure 5.2 Type of exit in Project KEEP and a control foster care group (Chamberlain et al., 2006)

Although some children did experience moves, these moves did not depend on previous instability: the trajectory of placement failure was broken.

Project KEEP is an intervention program that serves children in foster care ages five to twelve years who are in a new foster care placement and their foster parents or relatives. The program is a less intensive form of MTFC with goals of increasing the parenting skills of foster parents, reducing the number of placement changes for children in care, increasing positive placement moves of reunification and adoption, and improving child outcomes in multiple settings (home, school, and community). Foster parents complete a specific parent management training session and receive support from teams of professionals and other foster parents. Daily parent reports provide information on child behavior problems and foster parent stress levels. The evaluation of Project KEEP is the first randomized trial of an MTFC derivative in a child welfare setting. The evaluation shows that children whose foster parents participated in Project KEEP were less likely to run away or have another negative exit from foster care, had fewer incidents of behavior problems, and had fewer planned and unplanned placement changes (Chamberlain et al., 2006). In addition, children participating in Project KEEP were more likely to be reunified, adopted, or placed with a relative. As shown in Figure 5.2, children who participated in Project KEEP were almost twice as likely to leave foster care for reunification or adoption (Chamberlain et al., 2006).

PLAUSIBLE PATHWAYS BETWEEN PLACEMENT
INSTABILITY AND IMPERMANENCE

Preventing or reducing placement instability may reduce youth impermanence. The chain from placement instability to impermanence involves a
sequence of moves, with placement instability likely to contribute to a disconnection between the adolescent and the biological family. Each time a
child moves, the child may be a little further away, both geographically and
psychologically, from family members. With each move, family members
must be contacted and informed of the move, contact information must be
changed, family members must learn new transportation routes to visit the
child, and family must adjust to yet another set of foster parents or group
care providers.

Studies are consistent with this conclusion. Madelyn Freundlich and
Rosemary Avery (2005) completed a qualitative study of interviews with
adolescents and child welfare professionals (seventy-seven total respondents), finding that adolescents in group care have little input into their
own permanency planning and that typical permanency planning for adolescents in group care does not focus on work with families. They found
that the permanency goal of independent living was used far more often
than goals of reunification and adoption for adolescents in group care. The
adolescents interviewed felt their connections to their families were severely hindered by their placement in group care as they typically were located
far from their families of origin. This distance can contribute to a decrease
in visitation and, as a result, present barriers to reunification efforts. Research provides evidence that children who have continued contact with
their families of origin after placement in out-of-home care experience less
placement instability and are more likely to achieve family permanence
(Kupsinel and Dubsky, 1999).

Other studies have found that youth in congregate care settings experience higher levels of placement instability and higher rates of reentry to
foster care. Fred Wulczyn et al. (2003) found that older children in group
care placements lasting longer than 30 months had higher rates of placement instability. In their study of 2,616 children entering congregate care in
1992 and 1993 in Ohio, Kathleen Wells and Shenyang Guo (1999) found that
children whose last placement was a group home reentered care at a faster
rate than children leaving a kinship care placement.

Taken together, the evidence supports a conceptual framework for understanding placement instability that starts with the contribution of youth's

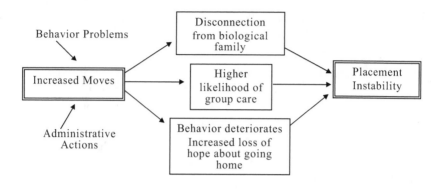

Figure 5.3 A general model of placement instability and placement type

emotional and behavioral problems and administrative decisions; results in disconnection from family and, very often for adolescents, placement into residential care; and then, in turn, results in increasingly poor behavior (which may also cause further estrangement from family) and, ultimately, greater placement instability. These relationships are shown in Figure 5.3. It is likely that the relationships are reciprocal, but the research is too limited to inform an understanding of which reciprocal paths are strong and which are weak. This model appears to offer some opportunities for development of interventions that may have direct and indirect effects on impermanence.

Adolescents in Group Care

Although the use of group care has been declining for much of the last century (Barth, 2005; Wolins and Piliavin, 1964), many adolescents continue to spend time in group homes or residential treatment. Preliminary FY 2005 reports based on AFCARS indicate that 8 percent of children and youth in out-of-home care were in group homes, and an additional 10 percent were in institutions (U.S. Department of Health and Human Services, 2006). These numbers are not disaggregated by age group, but if they were, they would almost certainly indicate that adolescents are the most likely age group to be in group care. In New York City, about one-third of youth ages eleven or older are in group homes or residential treatment centers (New York State Office of Children and Family Services, 2002). In 2001 Wulczyn and Kristen

Hislop (personal communication) found in one study that, among youth in out-of-home care at age sixteen, the percentage of youth in periods of foster care defined as "entry into congregate care" ranged from a high of 65 percent in some states to as low as 14 percent in California, with a mean of 42 percent. At the time these youth exited out-of-home care, a mean of about 50 percent were in congregate care.

Group care is a major reason for youth impermanence. Youth in group care experience greater placement instability (Wulczyn et al., 2003; Wells and Guo, 1999; Oosterman, et al., 2007). Given findings that indicate that group care does not outperform treatment foster care or intensive in-home services (e.g., Chamberlain and Reid, 1991; Hengeller et al., 2003) and the extraordinary expense of group care (some residential facilities now cost nearly $200,000 a year), it is likely that the census of children in group care could be reduced, More extensive use of MST and MTFC services and incentives to recruit foster caregivers for adolescents could result in a reduction in the number of youth in group care.

Reducing the number of youth in group care would likely have the salutary effect of providing these youth with more contact with families who might adopt them. Youth who are adopted recount stories of coaches, bus drivers, shift supervisors, and others who develop a close relationship with youth and then agree to adopt them. Although some residential care providers may become adoptive parents, most of them are too close in age to the youth in their care to make adoption a likely event (NSCAW Research Group, 2005). Foster parents continue to be an excellent resource for adoption. In FY 2005, according to the AFCARS report, 60 percent of the children adopted were adopted by their foster parents (U.S. Department of Health and Human Services, 2006).

EXITING FOSTER CARE THROUGH RUNNING AWAY

Individual, family, and placement factors are associated with high risks of running away. In a recent study, Courtney et al. (2005) found that runaway rates for youth in foster care are higher for females and for older adolescents ages fourteen through sixteen. Adolescents with a history of running away before placement in foster care are at higher risk of running while in care. High levels of family conflict and low levels of family involvement while the youth is in foster care contribute to high rates of running away (Courtney et al., 2005).

The type of placement also is associated with the risk of running away. Placement with a relative caregiver decreases the risk of running away compared with placement with a nonrelative foster family, whereas placement in a residential care facility increases the risk. Other factors associated with running away are repeated foster care placements and the youth's perceptions of the placement setting. When youth consider their placement environments to be warm and caring and when a permanency plan is in place, the risk of running away is reduced (Courtney et al., 2005).

Courtney et al. (2005) found that adolescents typically run to individuals who provide them with a sense of belonging: their family of origin, relatives, friends or romantic partners, or others in their communities of origin. Their reasons for running away vary, from feeling a need to help their parents or siblings to a desire to touch base with their family of origin and know how their family is doing. Some adolescents run at random to the streets or other places. Adolescents who have run away state that running from foster care helps them gain a sense of autonomy and control in their lives, feel "normal," and have the experiences that they believe they are missing because they are in foster care. Youth also talk about using running as a coping behavior to deal with life in foster care (Courtney et al., 2005).

Based on current research, there is a need to study the family-focused treatment implications of various kinds of running. A national study of children running away from foster care should be conducted. Research is needed to deepen the understanding of the extent to which children's placements in more secure facilities keep them from running away. Studies should focus on assessing whether treatment foster care or community group care can prevent running away behaviors.

TERMINATION OF PARENTAL RIGHTS WITHOUT ADOPTION

Youth who remain in foster care after reunification has been ruled out may have adoption as their permanency goal, a goal that involves the termination of their parents' rights. The Adoption and Safe Family Act (ASFA)'s emphasis on termination of parental rights, even when an adoptive family has not been identified for the child, is designed to make it more likely that the child will be adopted. The greater likelihood of adoption is the result of two factors: when a child is free for adoption, the child's need for an adoptive family can be pursued publicly, and prospective adoptive parents who may be reluctant to consider a legal risk adoption (that is, accepting a child when both parents' rights have not yet been terminated) may be more likely to come forward as adoptive family resources. Yet, the extent to which these advantages result in expeditious adoptions for youth is not clear, and growing evidence suggests that this policy may contribute to the impermanence of youth.

The lack of permanency options for older adolescents can result in many youth exiting foster care without connections to family or other supportive adults (Freundlich and Avery, 2005; Frey et al., 2005). As Mark Courtney (chapter 3) and Peter Pecora (chapter 4) point out in this volume, without these connections, youth can be placed in vulnerable positions. Termination of parental rights (TPR) can pose a significant obstacle to permanency for older adolescents who are not adopted because it may prevent possible reunifications between adolescents and their biological parents. Data indicate that a sizable proportion of children whose parents' rights are terminated will not be adopted. NSCAW data indicate that 33 percent of children whose parents' rights have been terminated did not have adoption as a plan at thirty-six months after the TPR occurred (Gibbs et al., 2004). As more adolescents become legally free for adoption but are not adopted, the rise in the number of legal orphans—that is, children who have parents but are legally unattached to them—has risen.

TPR is sought based on a variety of reasons. Table 5.1 provides the results of research with child welfare workers about the reasons that the agency seeks to terminate parents' rights (Gibbs et al., 2004). Although these reasons overlap, they suggest that a sizable proportion of cases result in efforts to terminate parental rights because parents are not actively involved in services, do not change their behavior, or simply run out of time based on legal time frames. The proportion of cases in which TPR was based on abandonment or severe abuse or neglect is less than one-half. These data suggest that many parents permanently lose custody of their children, having done no egregious abusive harm to their children. This finding is consistent with the longstanding evidence that physical abuse and sexual abuse are the least common reasons for child welfare services involvement and continue to become less frequent (U.S. Department of Health and Human Services, 2007).

Interviews with youth who have experienced TPR indicate that these youth may experience a number of difficulties (Gibbs et al., 2004). Some youth report that they were not told about the TPR until after the fact, and other youth report that their parents blame them for requesting the TPR (Gibbs et al., 2004). Youth also report frustration that they may no longer be allowed (by their child welfare worker, the foster parent, or group care-givers) to visit their parents after TPR.

POST-TPR REUNIFICATION

For some older adolescents, an important consideration may be reconnecting them with their birth families despite the legal separation created by termination of parental rights. Although reunification with birth parents after TPR may be an option, it must be carefully considered as it is not appropriate for all adolescents. When assessing this possibility, it is important to recognize that birth parents may be at a different point in their lives than when TPR occurred. A parent, for example, may have addressed a substance abuse problem and can now provide a safe home and care for the adolescent. The adolescent should be assessed in relation to self-care skills and self-preservation abilities. Reconnections of youth and birth parents post-TPR must be based on an established relationship in which the youth and parent verbalize a strong desire to be reunified. Reconnections should be considered after other permanency options have been explored and determined not to be viable options for the adolescent. Finally, both the birth parent and adolescent must be linked to strong support systems and be involved in the planning process of reunification.

Typically, post-TPR placement with a birth parent takes place when an adolescent returns home after running away from foster care or returning home after aging out of the foster care system. When an adolescent under the age of eighteen runs away from foster care to return home, the adolescent is considered on run away status and is not generally allowed to remain in the parent's home. Because the birth parent does not have legal custody after TPR has occurred, the parent is not authorized to register the youth for school or consent to medical treatment. In addition, the adolescent is not entitled to inheritance rights once TPR has occurred.

These difficulties can be overcome by allowing a parent to take legal guardianship with respect to the adolescent after TPR. This legal relationship, however, exists only until the child is eighteen years old. After this time, the child is no longer legally connected to the birth parent, again resulting in the loss of inheritance rights. A second method involves birth parents' pursuit of adoption of their child to regain legal custody. This method reestablishes the legal connection between the adolescent and birth parent, which continues after the adolescent reaches his eighteenth birthday. The

Table 5.1   Reasons for Termination of Parental Rights (TPR)

	RESPONSE (%)
Parent did not participate in services	76
No change in parental behavior	73
Time limits elapsed	62
Abandonment by parent	40
Severity of abuse or neglect	35
Other reason	18
Parent otherwise incapacitated	14
Parent incarcerated for long sentence	11

NOTE: Reasons are not mutually exclusive.

SOURCE: Gibbs et al. (2004).

process of adoption, however, is time consuming and tedious and may not be feasible for all birth parents. Birth parents who adopt their own children are not eligible for adoption assistance benefits.

A third method of family reconnection post-TPR is the court's reversal of the TPR order. When the order is reversed, the birth parent regains all parental rights. Less time consuming than adoption, this method may provide a birth parent and adolescent the best option for maintaining a legal connection before and after the youth turns eighteen. At least two states have enacted laws allowing for TPR reversals: California and New York.

In January 2006, California enacted legislation allowing an adolescent in foster care to petition the court to reinstate her birth parents' legal rights. Under California law, the birth parent's rights must have been terminated at least three years before the adolescent's petition; other permanency options must have been considered and deemed unlikely as options for the adolescent; and sufficient evidence must be presented that reversing TPR is in child's best interests and the birth parent is able and willing to raise the child (Riggs, 2006).

In June 2003, New York passed Section 5015 of the New York Civil Practice Law and Rules to allow for TPR reversals. Unlike California law, there are no established criteria stipulating when reversals can be brought before the court. Similar to California law, however, the motion to vacate the TPR needs to be supported by evidence that it is in the child's best interest; the parent is ready, willing, and able to care for the child again; and others involved in the case (such as the case worker and guardian ad litem) support the decision. If reunification occurs, the family is monitored by the agency for three to six months (Riggs, 2006).

In all, the TPR reversal process is not easy for parents, adolescents, child welfare workers, and the court system to undertake. All parties involved must diligently assess the information and work together to determine what is in the best interest of the adolescent.

IMPLICATIONS

Rates of youth impermanence are high. National estimates of impermanence, however, are not sufficient. The Child and Family Service Reviews (CFSRs) currently monitor replacements into care (reentries) and placement moves (replacements). Two other forms of replacement or reinvolvement with foster care are not counted: replacements of children to other relatives outside of the formal foster care program, and new abuse reports for children who are in care or who have returned home from care (which are not counted unless the new abuse reports trigger a placement move). A national accounting is needed of children in foster care whose parents' rights have been terminated and the proportion of children who emancipate from foster care whose parents' rights have been terminated. More precise measures of permanence will provide child welfare agencies with the information they need to modify or develop new policies and practices to achieve permanency goals for all children and youth in foster care.

Because many youth enter care as youth, child welfare agencies should be required to report CFSR data separately for youth who enter out-of-home care as youth. The CFSR process should include a special set of youth-focused outcome indicators, including re-abuse, running away, reentries to foster care, permanency, and postpermanency indicators. Child welfare agencies should have performance standards regarding the achievement of placement stability, keeping youth in family-like settings, and permanence for youth. They should be allowed to achieve these goals as they see fit and in relation to the best interests of individual youth. In the area of youth services, where there is limited knowledge but there is a clear understanding that youth have different needs and characteristics than younger children, an outcome-informed management approach is needed.

Now ten years old, federal policies and practices regarding TPR must be carefully reexamined. ASFA has specific requirements regarding TPR that states must follow to receive federal funding. For adolescents, the ASFA requirement that proceedings for TPR must be initiated when a child has been in foster care for fifteen of the past twenty-two months may hinder reunification efforts for adolescents in care. One option is that child welfare agencies not be required to move forward with TPR for youth as they do with younger children, terminating parental rights when no adoption resource is available.

The resumption of the federal Title IV E waiver option would allow states to test whether they can increase adoptions without increasing the number of youth who emancipate from foster care as legal orphans. This is a testable question, but it has not been answered. Instead, it has been assumed that the best way for all children to be adopted is to first terminate their parents' rights. This practice belies the ability of youth, regardless of their TPR status, to identify persons who might adopt them. Because youth can be engaged in the decision whether or not to be adopted and can participate in the recruitment of an adoptive parent, they are fundamentally different from younger children. Arguably, youth should be exempt from TPR requirements under ASFA. Adoptions can occur without first requiring TPR by working with youth to help them identify members of their families and broader social networks who might be willing to adopt them and developing those adoption resources before TPR. Other TPR reforms are needed, including the broader institution of policies that permit TPR reversals for youth who have not been adopted and whose parents regain their parental capacity. Adolescents must receive assistance as they prepare to leave care, with independent living services that evolve to address the needs of reunified youth, as well as other youth who leave foster care to other permanent families or to live on their own.

REFERENCES

Barth, R. P. (2005). Residential care: From here to eternity. *International Journal of Social Welfare* 14: 158–62.

Barth, R. P., S. Guo, E. Caplick, and R. L. Green (2006). Exits from out of home care to permanency by 36 months. Unpublished ms.

Barth, R. P., E. C. Lloyd, R. L. Green, S. James, L. K. Leslie, and J. Landsverk (2007). Frequent moving children in foster care: Predictors of placement moves among children with and without emotional and behavioral disorders. *Journal of Emotional and Behavioral Disorders* 15: 46–55.

Berry, M., and R. P. Barth (1990). A study of disrupted adoptive placements of adolescents. *Child Welfare* 69(3): 209–25.

Blome, W. W. (1997). What happens to foster kids: Educational experiences of a random sample of foster care youth and a matched group of non-foster care youth. *Child and Adolescent Social Work Journal* 14: 41–53.

Chamberlain, P., and J. Reid (1991). Using a specialized foster care community treatment model for children and adolescents leaving the state mental hospital. *Journal of Community Psychology* 19(3): 266–76.

—— (1998). Comparison of two community alternatives to incarceration for chronic juvenile offenders. *Journal of Consulting and Clinical Psychology* 66: 624–33.

Chamberlain, P., J. M. Price, J. B. Reid, J. Landsverk, P. A. Fisher, and M. Stoolmiller (2006). Who disrupts from placement in foster and kinship care? *Child Abuse and Neglect* 30: 409–24.

Courtney, M. E. (1994). Factors associated with the reunification of foster children with their families. *Social Service Review* 68: 81–108.

Courtney, M. E., and R. Barth (1996). Pathways of older adolescents out of foster care: Implications for Independent Living Services. *Social Work* 41(1): 75–83.

Courtney, M. E., I. P. Piliavin, and A. Grogan-Kaylor (1998). *Foster Youth Transitions to Adulthood: Outcomes 12 to 18 Months After Leaving Out-of-Home Care.* Madison: University of Wisconsin–Madison, School of Social Work and Institute for Research on Poverty.

Courtney, M. E., I. P. Piliavin, A. Grogan-Kaylor, and A. Nesmith. (2001). Foster youth transitions to childhood: A longitudinal analysis of youth leaving care. *Child Welfare* 80: 685–717.

Courtney, M., E., A. Skyles, G. Miranda, A. Zinn, E. Howard, and R. Goerge (2005). *Youth Who Run Away from Substitute Care.* Chicago: Chapin Hall Center for Children at the University of Chicago.

Fisher, P. A., and P. Chamberlain (2000). Multidimensional treatment foster care: A program for intensive parenting, family support, and skill building. *Journal of Emotional and Behavioral Disorders* 8(3): 155–64.

Fisher, P. A., B. Burraston, and K. Pears (2005). The Early Intervention Foster Care program: Permanent placement outcomes from a randomized trial. *Child Maltreatment* 10: 61–71.

Freundlich, M., and R. J. Avery (2005). Planning for permanency for youth in congregate care. *Children and Youth Services Review* 27: 115–34.

Frey, L. L., S. B. Greenblatt, and J. Brown (2005). *An Integrated Approach to Youth Permanency and Preparation for Adulthood.* New Haven, Conn.: Casey Family Services.

Gibbs, D. A., R. P. Barth, B. T. Dalberth, J. Wildfire, S. R. Hawkins, and S. Harris (2004). *Termination of Parental Rights for Older Foster Children: Exploring Practice and Policy Issues.* Washington, D.C.: U.S. Department of Health and Human Services.

Hartnett, M. A., L. Falconnier, S. Leathers, and M. Testa (1999). *Placement Stability Study*. Urbana-Champaign: University of Illinois, Children and Family Research Center, School of Social Work.

Henggeler, S. W., J. D. Rodick, C. M. Borduin, C. L. Hanson, S. M. Watson, and J. R. Urey (1986). Multisystemic treatment of juvenile offenders: Effects on adolescent behavior and family interactions. *Developmental Psychology* 22: 132–41.

Henggeler, S. W., M. D. Rowland, C. Halliday-Boykins, A. J. Sheidow, D. M. Ward, J. Randall, S. Pickrel, P. Cunningham, and J. Edwards (2003). One-year follow-up of multisystemic therapy as an alternative to the hospitalization of youths in psychiatric crisis. *Journal of the American Academy of Child and Adolescent Psychiatry* 42: 543–51.

James, S. (2004). Why do foster care placements disrupt? An investigation of reasons for placement changes in foster care. *Social Service Review* 78(4): 601–27.

Kupsinel, M. M., and D. D. Dubsky (1999). Behaviorally impaired children in out-of-home care. *Child Welfare* 78(2): 297–310.

Massinga, R., and P. I. Pecora (2004). Providing better opportunities for older children in the child welfare system. *Future of Children* 14(1): 151–73.

McMillen, J. C., and J. Tucker (1999). The status of older adolescents at exit from out-of-home care. *Child Welfare* 78(3): 339–61.

NSCAW Research Group. (2005). *National Survey of Child and Adolescent Well-Being: Baseline Report*. Washington, D.C.: Author.

Newton, R. R., A. J. Litrownik, and J. A. Landsverk (2000). Children and youth in foster care: Disentangling the relationship between problem behaviors and number of placements. *Child Abuse and Neglect* 24(10): 1363–74.

New York State Office of Children and Family Services (2002). *2001 Monitoring and Analysis Profiles with Selected Trend Data*. Albany, N.Y.: Author.

Oosterman, M., C. Schuengel, N. W. Slot, R. A. R. Bullens, and T. A. H. Doreleijers (2007). Disruptions in foster care: A review and meta-analysis. *Children and Youth Services Review* 29(1): 53–76.

Rubin, D. M., A. L. R. O'Reilly, X. Q. Luan, and A. R. Localio (2007). The impact of placement stability on behavioral well-being for children in foster care. *Pediatrics* 119(2): 336–44.

Ryan, J. P., and M. F. Testa (2005). Child maltreatment and juvenile delinquency: Investigating the role of placement and placement instability. *Children and Youth Services Review* 27(3): 227–49.

Taussig, H. N., R. Clyman, and J. Landsverk (2001). Children who return home from foster care: A 6-year prospective study of behavioral health outcomes in adolescence. *Pediatrics* 108(1): 7–14.

U.S. Department of Health and Human Services, Administration for Children and Families (2006). *The AFCARS Report: Preliminary FY 2004 Estimates as of June 2006*. Washington, D.C.: Author.

U.S. Department of Health and Human Services, Administration on Children, Youth and Families (2007). *Child Maltreatment 2005.* Washington, D.C.: U.S. Government Printing Office.

Usher, C. L., J. B. Wildfire, and D. A. Gibbs (1999). Measuring performance in child welfare: Secondary effects of success. *Child Welfare* 78: 31–51.

Webster, D., R. P. Barth, and B. Needell (2000). Placement stability for children in out-of-home care. *Child Welfare* 79(5): 614–31.

Wells, K., and S. Guo (1999). Reunification and reentry of foster children. *Children and Youth Services Review* 21(4): 273–94.

Wolins, M., and I. Piliavin (1964). *Institution and Foster Family: A Century of Debate.* New York: Child Welfare League of America.

Wulczyn, F. H., K. B. Hislop, and R. M. Goerge (2000). *Foster Care Dynamics 1983–1998: A Report from the Multistate Foster Care Data Archive.* Chicago: Chapin Hall Center for Children at the University of Chicago.

Wulczyn, F. H., Kogan, J., and B. J. Harden (2003). Placement stability and movement trajectories. *Social Service Review* 77(2): 212–36.

Wulczyn, F. H., R. P. Barth, Y. Y. Yuan, B. Jones-Harden, and J. Landsverk (2005). *Evidence for Child Welfare Policy Reform.* New York: Transaction De Gruyter.

Zinn, A., J. DeCoursey, R. Goerge, and M. Courtney (2006). *A Study of Placement Stability in Illinois.* Working Paper. Chicago: Chapin Hall Center for Children at the University of Chicago.

Permanence Is a State of Security and Attachment

GRETTA CUSHING
AND BENJAMIN KERMAN

Richard Barth and Laura Chintapalli (chapter 5 in this volume) provide a rich review of recent research documenting the challenges of achieving permanence for adolescents in the child welfare system. They describe evidence that adolescents in foster care are likely to experience "a heightened state of impermanence" as a result of placement instability, failed reunification and reentry, lengthy stays in group care, and termination of parental rights (TPR) without subsequent adoption. Poor outcomes among youth who age out of foster care are viewed as a direct result of the failure to achieve permanence for youth in care. Both interventions and policy changes that could be implemented to enhance permanence for youth are presented.

Barth and Chintapalli provide a definition of permanence that highlights the importance of the emotional quality of the relationship between caregivers and youth. They state, "permanency is a state of security and attachment that involves a parenting relationship that is mutually understood to be a lasting relationship." This child-focused definition spotlights optimal conditions for child development and helps distinguish the greater potential for family connection and nurturing parental relationships present in family-based care but typically absent in institutional placements.

Often, the discourse concerning research, interventions, and policy centers on the more common focus and more conveniently measured outcome of legal permanence. In most research and legislation, achieving "permanence" refers to successful reunification, adoption, or guardianship. This focus obscures the importance of nurturing parental connections that are critically important for youth development, irrespective of whether the relationships are formally recognized with legal sanction. Seminal research in attachment theory has established that children need the opportunity to form personal relationships with select caregivers who provide responsive, sensitive, and continuous parenting over time (Bowlby, 1988; Rutter and O'Connor, 1999). Research further shows that relationships with caring adults and significant others offset the risk of parental impairment and maltreatment (Werner and Johnson, 2004; Werner and Smith, 1982; Feldman et al., 2004).

As researchers and advocates focus on permanency for youth in child welfare, it is essential that the developmental and relational qualities of permanence that underlie legal status and placement characteristics be considered. The qualities of youth's relationships with caregivers and significant others are distinct aspects of permanency that are too often overlooked when agencies focus exclusively on increasing the numbers of youth who achieve legal permanence. Prospects for relationships that provide emotional security and a sense of belonging need to be explored as agencies make efforts to enhance permanence and improve outcomes for youth in foster care. Maintaining a comprehensive notion of permanence opens additional avenues for understanding and improving the experience of foster care for youth who are not legally connected to families and for youth who return home or legally join new families.

PERMANENCE, EMOTIONAL SECURITY, AND BELONGING

Permanency advocates have proposed a conceptualization of permanence that encompasses multiple dimensions and that explicitly acknowledges the importance of the emotional and relational aspects of permanency and connections to culture, family, and tradition in addition to physical stability and legal status. According to Lauren Frey et al. (2005:5), in achieving any of the permanency outcomes, the objective is the optimal balance of physical, emotional and relational, legal, and cultural dimensions of permanency within every child's and youth's array of relationships.

- Physical permanency relates to a safe and stable living environment.
- Emotional and relational permanency relates to the primary attachments, family, and other significant relationships that offer trust and reciprocity.
- Legal permanency relates to the rights and benefits of a secure legal and social family status.
- Cultural permanency relates to a continuous connection to family, tradition, race, ethnicity, culture, language, and religion (Frey et al. 2005:5).

When youth cannot return home to their birth families, it is essential that they be given opportunities to develop relationships with caregivers that are continuous over time and that provide responsive and sensitive care. Recognition of the importance of these relationships is not new in the field of child welfare. Early research in attachment demonstrated the deleterious effects on children when they were maintained in environments that did not allow for the formation of selective and continuous attachment relationships (Bowlby, 1951). This research provided an impetus for communities to discontinue the widespread use of orphanages or group care settings as a first choice for youth who could not live with their birth parents and to rely instead on family foster care (Cliffe and Berridge, 1991). Further research in attachment theory demonstrated that the need for selective attachments is rooted in the biological nature of children and serves the specific purpose of providing emotional security during times of stress (Bowlby, 1982 [1969], 1988; Ainsworth et al., 1978). In addition, the quality of early care that a child receives has an important influence on adjustment and social relatedness (Rutter and O'Connor, 1999). According to attachment theory, early experiences with caregivers are internalized in "working models" of the self in relation to others (Bowlby, 1988). Children who experience sensitive, responsive caregiving are more likely to develop secure attachment relationships with caregivers that increase the likelihood of positive adjustment over time (Simpson et al., 2007; Sroufe et al., 1990; Urban et al., 1991).

Family foster care was intended to provide a better alternative to group care settings for children who could not return home to live with their birth parents. Foster care provides children with the opportunity to receive parenting from only one or two individuals and thus form selective attachments to these specific caregivers within a family setting. It was expected that relationships formed within these family settings would provide a greater continuity of care than group settings (Rutter and O'Connor, 1999). Foster care youth who cannot be reunited with their birth parents have typically experienced early maltreatment, as well as the separation and loss of birth parents as primary caregivers (whether or not parents rights are terminated), and, as a result, they often face challenges in forming secure relationships. By forming attachments to new caregivers, youth can meet their developmental need for an attachment that provides emotional security. They also have an opportunity to internalize new expectations of themselves and others that challenge early expectations learned in the context of relationships characterized by abuse and neglect.

Youth enter foster care with different relational needs depending, in part, on the age at which they enter care. Infants who enter foster care before having developed significant attachment relationships need a sensitive and responsive caregiver who will provide continuity of care over time. This type of care allows children to develop the attachments they need to establish a sense of emotional security and internalize positive expectations of themselves and others. Older youth who enter foster care after having established significant attachments with caregivers and significant others need to maintain these connections whenever feasible. They also need to be afforded opportunities and assistance in forming and maintaining continuous relationships with caregivers that can become significant attachments.

Barth and Chintapalli's review includes several domains of inquiry that suggest the important role of significant attachments, emotional security, and a sense of belonging in the lives of adolescents in the child welfare system. They cite evidence that placement instability is not only the result of emotional and behavioral problems among youth and systemic issues but also can result from uncertainty or hopelessness about reunification and separation from siblings (Barth et al., 2007). Recent evidence from qualitative analyses of youth who run away from foster care (Courtney et al., 2005b) highlights the relational motivations behind this pathway to "impermanence." Youth who enter care between seven and twelve years of age are most likely to exit by running away. In interviews, youth described running away as an attempt to "make connections with family, friends and a community where they sensed (or hoped) they belonged, were cared about and were wanted" (45). Youth most often reported running toward something, to find the family connections, and the significant relationships from which they had been separated (Courtney et al., 2005b). Additional relational precursors to running away included high levels of family conflict and low levels of family involvement in current placements; reduced running away was associated with placement environments considered warm and caring and placement with a relative. Interestingly, some youth described how they created a sense of family through their relationships with caseworkers, caregivers, and other adults when they did not have a connection to their birth family.

These findings highlight the motivational effect on youth of the need to feel a sense of emotional security and belonging. Older children and adolescents come into foster care with a legacy of attachments. When they are not with people to whom they have formed significant attachments, youth are more likely to disrupt their placements by running from otherwise safe environments so that they can be with important people in their lives. This motivation to connect is likely due, in part, to the role that significant attachments play in reducing stress. It highlights the need for youth to remain connected to their significant relationships while in care whenever possible and their needs for opportunities to form new attachments with caregivers who can serve in this role.

For child welfare professionals, practical implications of this work are evident. It seems likely that many episodes of running away can be prevented by providing youth with ongoing safe contact with the important people in their lives. Of particular importance are interventions that proactively support the development of relationships with caregivers and inclusive teaming approaches that reach out to significant others. Through these interventions, it is possible to foster a sense of emotional security and belonging that may help reduce youth's need to run to be with people whom he or she cares about. Teams can implement plans to ensure youth have access to their significant others. In addition, these interventions can transform the diverse perspectives and too often conflicting agendas of the important people in youth's lives into a group effort to facilitate emotional and relational permanence in conjunction with legal, cultural, and physical permanence.

PERMANENCY AND YOUTH OUTCOMES

For youth who cannot return home to live with their birth parents, there is much to be learned regarding how various dimensions of permanence can assist these youth in overcoming multiple risks of early maltreatment and loss so that they can reach adulthood having achieved a sense of well-being and competence. Poor outcomes among youth who "age out" of foster care are often attributed to a failure to achieve legal permanency. Comparisons of outcomes between youth who achieve legal permanence through adoption and those who age out of foster care have been hampered by methodological challenges, yet the limited existing evidence generally indicates that youth who are adopted fare better than those who age out of foster care, particularly with regard to emotional security and a sense of belonging (Triselotis, 2002). There is little research, however, that examines the processes underlying these differences in outcomes.

An understanding of the processes that lead to better outcomes for youth is critical in identifying areas where interventions will be most effective. For example, several differences between youth who are adopted and those who are not may account for the differences in outcomes observed. Youth who are adopted from foster care tend to be younger and have lower levels of emotional and behavioral problems than those who remain in foster care (Connell et al., 2006; Schmidt-Tieszen and McDonald, 1998). Early positive adjustment may result in better outcomes during adolescence and adulthood due to continuity over time, highlighting the need to intervene early to offset the likelihood that problems will develop later. In addition, youth who are adopted are less likely to experience the level of placement instability that is typical among foster youth (Triseliotis, 2002). Given the importance of placement stability in facilitating the continuity of care that is essential for security of attachment to develop, the differences between adopted and foster youth are likely due, in part, to foster youth's lack of opportunity to develop secure attachments with caregivers. Adopted youth also may be more likely to benefit from greater financial support and other resources provided by adoptive families who are particularly invested in their well-being.

Not all youth who age out of foster care without legal permanence fare worse than youth who are adopted. As shown in Figure 6.1, Kerman et al. (2002) examined the outcomes for three groups of alumni from Casey Family Services: youth who had been adopted, youth who remained in foster care for a lengthy period of time (through age nineteen), and youth who had experienced shorter stays (that is, exited before age nineteen). Youth who were adopted and those who stayed for a lengthy period of time had similar outcomes in a variety of domains involving personal well-being and self-sufficiency, including educational attainment, employment, legal involvement, substance abuse, and mental health symptoms. Youth in extended foster care and youth who were adopted fared better than those who experienced shorter stays in foster care.

These findings draw attention to the need to understand the processes involved in achieving positive outcomes for young adults with histories of foster care rather than assuming that permanence defined as a legal status

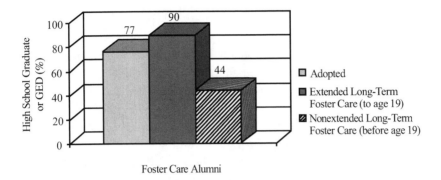

Figure 6.1 A general model of placement instability and placement type

(such as adoption) is the most important element. It is often assumed that foster care is less adequate than adoption in providing placement stability, continuity of relationships, and emotional security, but this assumption may not always be accurate. In some cases, the differences between adoption and long-term foster care may be little more than name and legal status. It is also important to bear in mind that not all adoptions result in stability or emotional security. In the Casey Family Services' alumni study, youth in long-term foster care had a high level of stability of both family placement and social worker and received services from a well-resourced private foster care agency. Each of these factors is a potentially important aspect of promoting positive adjustment among youth.

Youth who do not achieve legal permanence while in foster care often are described as lacking significant relationships with adults, yet there is evidence that some youth form significant attachments to their caregivers or others and create their own families with individuals with whom they do not have biological or legal relationships. As part of an ongoing longitudinal study of foster youth transitioning to early adulthood at Casey Family Services, we asked foster youth if they had someone in their lives who was not their birth parent that they consider a "parent," someone whom they could count on when they needed someone, and someone whom they expected would be there for them in the years to come. Interim results indicate that more than 80 percent report they had someone in their lives who fit the description of "parent," most often a current or former foster parent. These results were obtained for a group of foster youth in a well-resourced private foster care agency, which may account, in part, for these findings. Further research is needed to learn the extent to which youth who are aging out of foster care nationwide may or may not have connections to significant adults and, importantly, what relationship qualities (i.e., emotional security, instrumental support, and financial assistance) may be most beneficial in improving outcomes for youth as they transition to adulthood.

Recent evidence suggests that the quality of youth's relationships with former foster parents has an important effect on their adjustment after leaving care. In an investigation of foster youth five years after leaving care (Cashmore and Paxman, 2006), researchers found that felt security while in foster care, continuity of relationships, and social support were the most robust predictors of positive outcomes. Stability while in care was found to be the means to achieve the more meaningful goals of a sense of security, belonging, and the development of trusting relationships (Cashmore and Paxman, 2006). Similarly, qualitative findings among adults who grew up in foster care highlight the central role that foster families often play in meeting youth's emotional needs for security and belonging (Schofield, 2002).

IMPLICATIONS FOR PREPERMANENCY AND POSTPERMANENCY PRACTICE: A RELATIONAL PERSPECTIVE

A large body of research has documented that youth and families involved with the child welfare system need a range of services and supports, whether youth and families are in need of assistance to maintain and sustain the family unit or are working toward permanency, or whether youth are aging out of foster care. Perceptions that supports and services will not be available for families after adoption pose considerable obstacles to promoting legal permanency (Greenblatt et al., 2003; Kirton et al., 2006), and the frequency of service needs following adoption finalization makes this concern a wise one (Festinger, 2006). A lack of services and supports also has been often cited as a barrier to achieving permanency through guardianship and reunification. As in adoption, the anticipated lack of financial and service supports for guardian families often deters youth's kin and others from moving to a legally permanent guardianship situation (Allen et al., 2003). The supports available to families after reunification are badly needed to increase the number of youth who can be successfully reunified.

A number of practice tools and models supporting preparation for permanency are emerging. Casey Family Services, for example, has developed the Belonging and Emotional Security Tool (BEST: Frey et al., 2008) to assist social workers in conversations with youth and foster parents about youth's sense of emotional security with their foster parents and the extent to which each foster parent has a sense that the youth belongs in the family. Foster parents and youth are asked to respond to thought-provoking sentences about their relationship such as, "I would not kick this youth out of the family, no matter what" (foster parent version) or "My foster parent(s) would not kick me out of the family, no matter what I do" (youth version). Administration of the tool serves to introduce the topic of permanence in a comfortable way. Through processing responses to the items, social workers are able to assess the relationship and facilitate discussions with youth and foster parents that often can lead to a stronger commitment and discussion of legal permanence.

Practice models also have been developed to help prepare youth for permanency. The 3-5-7 model (Henry, 2005), for example, assists children and youth in grieving past losses of their birth families, neighborhoods, schools, and other important aspects of their lives; formulating self-identity; establishing relationships with adults that are characterized by trust and security through attachments; and developing a willingness to permanently join families. This model provides guidelines to assist social workers in working with youth to complete tasks, answer specific questions about their past experiences and future expectations, and use specific skills in the process. Practice frameworks and tools such as the 3-5-7 model and BEST can provide valuable assistance in concretizing potentially ambiguous assessment and intervention work.

Several studies have reported poor outcomes such as high rates of unemployment, homelessness, and mental health problems as foster youth reach young adulthood (e.g., Courtney et al., 2005a; Pecora et al., 2005). Referring back to Figure 6.1, the results of Casey Family Services alumni indicate that youth who spent less time in foster care (exited before age nineteen), compared with youth who spent more time in foster care (exited after age nineteen), did not fare as well (Kerman et al., 2002). Similar results were reported in a recent multistate project (Courtney et al., 2005a). These findings suggest that services and supports provided to adolescents as they transition to young adulthood may confer an advantage.

The implementation of these services, however, often has proved challenging. Benjamin Kerman et al. (2004), for example, reported that when Casey Family Services offered an array of transitional services to youth, only 41 percent accepted the services and received them. This finding is of particular concern given the high level of needs documented among these youth. In efforts to attract more youth to these services, leveraging the motivational impact of significant relationships may be helpful.

With regard to behavioral interventions, a number of evidence-based approaches have proven to be particularly successful with adolescents in recent years. These approaches are family therapies that include, as examples, multisystemic family therapy and functional family therapy (Alexander et al., 2002; Carr, 2000; Thompson et al., 2005). These approaches are based in part on a recognition that adolescents are likely to be more motivated to engage in services when their family members are involved. Family members can help motivate and support youth on an ongoing basis to facilitate their engagement with services and the achievement of positive outcomes. As noted earlier, youth who age out of foster care without a permanent legal family do not necessarily lack significant relationships. These significant relationships can be drawn on when planning for and providing services, providing youth with opportunities to receive the additional support and motivation they need to engage with and follow through on services. Services that respect and involve caregivers who are not legally connected to youth may also serve to assist youth and caregivers in solidifying their bonds and moving toward making a legal commitment.

POLICY IMPLICATIONS

Barth and Chintapalli call for policy changes to better address youth's experiences with impermanence while in foster care. Their recommendations include a national accounting of youth impermanence that extends beyond reentries to foster care and placement moves while in foster care (which are currently monitored by Child and Family Service Reviews) and includes replacements to other relatives outside of the formal foster care program, re-abuse reports for youth who have returned home, and the proportion of children who emancipate from foster care whose parents' rights have been terminated. They also advocate for the separate reporting of Child and Family Service Review data (and with separate indicators) for those who enter foster care as youth, as distinguished from those who enter foster care as children.

In addition to monitoring youth impermanence as measured by placements and the number of youth who age out of foster care, as Barth and Chintapalli recommend, efforts to measure and account for the quality of youth's relationships are needed. Youth who age out of foster care with or without a legal tie to family need relationships with stable adults on whom they can rely. An accounting is needed of the extent to which these relationships are being developed. Many youth may have important relationships with foster parents or relative caregivers who can and should be included in services to assist youth in making a successful transition to adulthood.

RESEARCH IMPLICATIONS

The broadening of any research agenda places a premium on clarified definitions, refined measures, and heuristic frameworks that organize observations and root new work to prior theory and evidence. In order to assess and implement an accounting of permanency as a "state of security and attachment," emotional security, belonging, or other aspects of relationships between youth and caregivers, psychometrically sound measures for these constructs must be developed. This work requires careful attention to existing measures of closely aligned constructs (such as attachment, warmth, and bonding) and empirical assessment of the relationships among the constructs. Challenges in using psychometrically sound measures in applied settings—where they may be viewed as too cumbersome, given the many pressing demands of casework—must be met. Potential solutions may lie in the further engagement of practice leaders in the development and refinement of sound measures that facilitate practice.

Conceptual frameworks, along the line suggested by Barth and Chintapelli, represent another important step in helping to tie child welfare research into allied fields' more extensive basic and applied empirical literature and to catalyze hypothesis testing. Further conceptual work in defining the nonlegal dimensions of permanency and outlining how these dimensions relate to developmental outcomes is needed to facilitate this process. Better definitions and more crystallized hypotheses together will lay the foundation for the development of reliable measures, predictive model testing, and, ultimately, more successful research contributions to practice and policy.

Further research is needed to clarify the processes that lead to better outcomes among youth in the child welfare system, whether they are reunified or adopted, achieve legal guardianships, or age out of foster care as young adults. We need to know more about their relationships with significant adults and how the characteristics of these relationships (such as emotional security, instrumental support, and legal status) contribute to positive adjustment and well-being.

CONCLUSION

Beginning in early childhood and continuing throughout the lifespan, individuals need to form attachments to selective others to develop a sense of emotional security and protect against stress. The quality of the caregiving environment in early childhood and adolescence affects the likelihood of youth achieving positive adjustment and social relatedness. As researchers and advocates focus on permanence, it is critical that permanence be conceptualized in a way that includes the quality of relationships that can provide emotional security for youth across the lifespan and includes connections that are legally sanctioned and those that are not. There is much to be learned about how these relationships may assist youth in achieving positive outcomes in spite of histories of maltreatment and the loss of birthparents as their primary caregivers.

REFERENCES

Ainsworth, M. D. S., M. Blehar, E. Waters, and S. Wall (1978). *Patterns of Attachment.* Hillsdale, N.J.: Erlbaum.

Alexander, J. F., T. L. Sexton, and M. Robbins (2002). The developmental status of family therapy in family psychology intervention science. In H. A. Liddle, D. Santisteban, R. Levant, and J. Bray, eds., *Family Psychology Science-Based Interventions.* Washington, D.C.: American Psychological Association.

Allen, M., M. Bissel, and J. L. Miller (2003). *Expanding Permanency Options for Children: A Guide to Subsidized Guardianship Programs.* Washington, D.C.: Children's Defense Fund and Cornerstone Consulting Group.

Barth, R. P., E. C. Loyd, R. L. Green, S. James, L. K. Leslie, and J. Landsverk (2007). Frequent moving children in foster care: Predictors of placement moves among children with and without emotional and behavioral disorders. *Journal of Emotional and Behavioral Disorders* 15: 46–55.

Bowlby, J. (1951). *Maternal Care and Mental Health.* WHO Monograph Series 2. Geneva: World Health Organization.

—— (1982 [1969]). *Attachment and Loss.* Vol. 1: *Attachment.* New York: Basic Books.

—— (1988). *A Secure Base: Parent-Child Attachment and Healthy Human Development.* New York: Basic Books.

Carr, Alan, ed. (2000). What works with children and adolescents? A critical review of psychological interventions with children, adolescents and their families. In C. Cormack and A. Carr, eds., *Drug Abuse* (pp. 155–77). Florence, Ky.: Taylor and Frances/ Routledge.

Cashmore, J., and M. Paxman (2006). Predicting after-care outcomes: The importance of "felt" security. *Child and Family Social Work* 11: 232–41.

Cliffe, D., and Berridge, D. (1991). *Closing Children's Homes: An End to Residential Childcare?* London: National Children's Bureau.

Connell, C.M., K. H. Katz, L. Saunders, and J. K. Tebes (2006). Leaving foster care: The influence of child and case characteristics on foster care exit rates. *Children and Youth Services Review* 28: 780–98.

Courtney, M. E., A. Dworsky, G. Ruth, T. Keller, J. Havlicek, and N. Bost (2005a). *Midwest Evaluation of the Adult Functioning of Former Foster Youth: Outcomes at Age 19.* Chicago: Chapin Hall Center for Children at the University of Chicago.

Courtney, M. E., A. Skyles, G. Miranda, A. Zinn, E. Howard, and R. M. George (2005b). *Youth Who Run Away from Substitute Care.* Chicago: Chapin Hall Center for Children at the University of Chicago.

Feldman, B.J., R. D. Conger, and R. G. Burzette (2004). Traumatic events, psychiatric disorders, and pathways of risk and resilience during the transition to adulthood. *Research in Human Development* 1: 259–90.

Festinger, T. (2006). Adoption and after: Adoptive parents' service needs. In M. Dore, ed., *The Postadoption Experience* (pp.17–44). Washington, D.C.: Child Welfare League of America.

Frey, L.L., S. B. Greenblatt, and J. Brown (2005). *A Call to Action: An Integrated Approach to Youth Permanency and Preparation for Adulthood.* New Haven, Conn.: Casey Family Services.

Frey, L. L., G. Cushing, M. Freundlich, and E. Brenner (2008). Achieving permanency for youth in foster care: Assessing and strengthening emotional security. *Child and Family Social Work* 13(2): 218–26.

Greenblatt, S.B., G. Cushing, L. L. Frey, and M. Jones (2003). *Recommendations to Increase and Speed Permanency Through Adoption: Summary Report.* New Haven, Conn.: Casey Family Services.

Henry, D.L. (2005). The 3-5-7 model: Preparing children for permanency. *Children and Youth Services Review* 27: 197–212.

Kerman, B.D., J. Wildfire, and R. P. Barth (2002). Outcomes for young adults who experienced foster care. *Children and Youth Services Review* 24: 319–44.

Kerman, B. D., R. P. Barth, and J. Wildfire (2004). Extending transitional services to former foster children. *Child Welfare* 83: 239–61.

Kirton, D., J. Beecham, and K. Ogilvie (2006). Adoption by foster carers: A profile of interest and outcomes. *Child and Family Social Work* 11(2): 139–46.

Pecora, P. J., R. C. Kessler, J. Williams, K. O'Brien, A. C. Downs, D. English, J. White, E. Hiripi, C. R. White, T. Wiggins, and K. E. Holmes (2005). *Improving Family Foster Care: Findings from the Northwest Foster Care Alumni Study.* Seattle: Casey Family Programs.

Rutter, M., and T. G. O'Connor (1999). Implications of attachment theory for child care policies. In J. Cassidy and P. R. Shaver, eds., *Handbook of Attachment: Theory, Research and Clinical Applications* (pp. 823–44). New York: Guilford.

Schmidt-Tieszen, A., and T. McDonald (1998). Children who wait: Long-term foster care or adoption? *Children and Youth Services Review* 20: 13–28.

Schofield, G. (2002). The significance of a secure base: A psychosocial model of long-term foster care. *Child and Family Social Work* 7: 259–72.

Simpson, J. A., W. A. Collins, A. Tran, and K. Haydon (2007). Attachment and the experience and expression of emotions in romantic relationships: A developmental perspective. *Journal of Personality and Social Psychology* 92: 355–67.

Sroufe, L. A., B. Egeland, and T. Kreutzer (1990). The fate of early experience following developmental change: Longitudinal approaches to individual adaptation in childhood. *Child Development* 61: 1363–73.

Thompson, S. J., E. C. Pomeroy, and K. Gober (2005). Family-based treatment models targeting substance use and high-risk behaviors among adolescents: A review. In C. Hilarski, ed., *Addiction, Assessment, and Treatment with Adolescents, Adults, and Families* (pp. 207–33). New York: Haworth Social Work Practice Press.

Triseliotis, J. P. (2002). Long-term foster care or adoption? The evidence examined. *Child and Family Social Work* 7: 23–33.

Urban, J., E. Carlson, B. Egeland, and L. A. Sroufe (1991). Patterns of individual adaptation across childhood. *Development and Psychopathology* 3: 445–60.

Werner, E. E., and J. Johnsons (2004). The role of caring adults in the lives of children of alcoholics. *Substance Use and Misuse* 39: 699–720.

Werner, E. E., and R. Smith (1982). *Vulnerable but Invincible: A Longitudinal Study of Resilient Children and Youth.* New York: McGraw-Hill.

Policy Responses to the Permanency Needs of Youth

PART II

Intervention into a family's life represents one of the most significant intrusions by the state in the private affairs of its citizens. Public child welfare agencies are authorized to investigate reports of child abuse and neglect and, when maltreatment is substantiated and children are at imminent risk of harm, to remove children from their parents' custody and place them into foster care. The state's obligation is twofold: to intervene into families' lives only in cases when it is necessary to protect children from harm and to take on the responsibilities of a parent when the state removes children from their parents' custody. When the state acts in loco parentis, it is expected that it will ensure children's safety and well-being and ensure that children leave foster care to safe, nurturing, permanent families. Just as policy does not embrace the notion that parents may do "as little as possible" in relation to meeting the needs of their children, child welfare policy cannot reasonably accept that the state may do "as little as possible" for children taken into its custody. When the state intervenes to protect children by removing them from their parents, it must act as a responsible parent until the child leaves care to return to her own parents or to new parents through adoption or guardianship. When youth remain in foster care without the benefit of permanent family, the state's obligation, consistent with good parenting, is to ensure that youth leaving foster care are well prepared for adulthood.

The primary levers for system reform are found in law, regulation, and the allocation of resources. These levers define the outcomes to be achieved, the programmatic priorities, and, to some extent, the processes to be used to achieve outcomes and realize priorities. Through the legislative process, funding decisions are made and play significant roles in driving program and practice. In each state, policy decisions shape the provision of foster care services. Child welfare policy at the federal level, however, sets the framework for foster care, including both permanency practice and preparation for adulthood services. Federal child welfare statutes, principally Titles IV-B and Title IV-E of the Social Security Act, establish the goals that state child welfare agencies are to achieve across a spectrum of child welfare services, and they provide federal funding to states to assist them in achieving those goals for children and youth in foster care. Federal child welfare reviews of state child welfare systems, the Child and Family Service Reviews, monitor the performance of states in relation to established goals and benchmarks.

In chapter 7, Madelyn Freundlich focuses on federal child welfare policy, with particular emphasis on new policy directions regarding permanence set by the federal Adoption and Safe Families Act of 1997. Drawing on the small body of research that has informed an understanding of the impact of these federal policies on the successful achievement of permanence for older children and youth, she proposes directions for future research. She makes the case for evidence-based policy that focuses on child well-being and is guided by a development perspective.

In chapter 8, in response, Rosemary Avery points to the absence of attention in "independent living" programs to family and social connections for youth transitioning from foster care to adulthood. She reviews research that has demonstrated the perilous position that federal policy creates for youth as they exit foster care, and she calls for policy that requires that every child have a committed adult who will be in a supportive and personal relationship with the youth before, during, and after the transition to adulthood.

Child welfare policy, like other policy addressing social problems, must consider the social and cultural context within which the strengths and challenges of children, youth, and families emerge. In chapter 9, Robert Hill describes an important aspect of the social and cultural context by focusing on kinship care. He provides a concise but thorough review of the research findings regarding outcomes for children in foster care who are placed with kinship caregivers and those placed with nonkin. Based on findings that suggest positive child safety, well-being and permanence outcomes for children placed with kin, he highlights the benefits of assisted guardianship policies, particularly for older children and youth in foster care.

In response, in chapter 10, Aron Schlonsky provides additional detail on the promising results from evaluations of subsidized guardianship programs for relative caregivers. He cautions against viewing kinship care and subsidized guardianship as panaceas for the many complex problems that confront child welfare systems in appropriately meeting the needs of children and youth in foster care, and he urges attention to the range of services and supports that kin require. Advocating for the further development of kinship and guardianship policy, he raises a number of questions that warrant consideration.

Essential to quality child welfare policy development and implementation is cross-system collaboration. The collaboration between public child welfare agencies and the courts is particularly critical if decisions regarding children's safety, well-being, and permanence are to be effectively made, permanency planning is to proceed in a timely manner, and youth are to be discharged from foster care with the full range of supports and services that they need.

In chapter 11, Karl Ensign, Sabrina Davis, and Elizabeth Lee describe the history of court improvement efforts and the results of a number of evaluations of court reform activities. They examine the effect of court improvement programs that have specifically addressed the needs of youth and broader court reform efforts that have played key roles in promoting permanency for youth in the foster care system. The authors identify several key choice points and system intersections that provide opportunities for greater permanence for older youth. Shirley Dobbin's response, in chapter 12, elaborates on several opportunities for enhancing youth permanence. She describes resources that have been developed to guide dependency courts in strengthening their decision-making processes, lessons learned from the experiences of Model Courts across the United States, and national performance indicators that support dependency court reform. Both chapters describe positive results from court reform efforts and strike an optimistic note regarding the appetite and infrastructure for continuing evaluation of dependency court performance and court-child welfare agency collaboration.

Permanence for
Older Children and Youth

SEVEN

Law, Policy, and Research

MADELYN FREUNDLICH

Policy has long played a pivotal role in shaping child welfare practice in the United States. Beginning with the Indian Child Welfare Act of 1978 (ICWA) and the Adoption Assistance and Child Welfare Act of 1980 (Public Law 96-272) and continuing through the Adoption and Safe Families Act of 1997 (ASFA) and, most recently, the Fostering Connections to Success and Increasing Adoptions Act of 2008, federal law has had a significant role in shaping child welfare practice, in general, and in setting the contours of permanency planning for children and youth in foster care, in particular. At the state level, policy, as articulated by law and driven by class action lawsuits, has shaped permanency planning and practice. There has been only limited research examining the effect of federal child welfare legislation on outcomes for children, youth, and families, and even less attention has been given to the effect of state level policy.

In this chapter, I examine aspects of federal child welfare policy as set forth in Titles IV-B and IV-E of the Social Security Act, with a particular focus on new policy directions set by ASFA. I consider the small body of research that has informed an understanding of the impact of these federal policies on permanence for older children and youth, and I propose directions for future research. I also briefly consider other developments at the federal policy level that relate to child welfare programming and practices that promote permanency for older children and youth. Finally, I examine aspects of state-level policy that affect permanence for older children and youth.

FEDERAL LAW AND POLICY UNDER THE
SOCIAL SECURITY ACT: IMPLICATIONS FOR
PERMANENCE FOR OLDER CHILDREN AND YOUTH

The federal policy framework for child welfare is primarily set forth in Titles IV-B and IV-E of the Social Security Act (U.S.C. 42, secs. 620–679b). Title IV-B provides federal funding for a range of child welfare services without regard to family income. Subpart 1 of Title IV-B provides funding to states for a broad array of child welfare services that may include services designed to promote permanence for older children and youth, though each state has discretion to select the specific services provided. Subpart 2 was added to Title IV-B in 1993 with the enactment of legislation that created and dedicated federal funds to the Family Preservation and Family Support program. This new program, viewed as "renew[ing] the emphasis of the 1980 Congress on preventive services" (Gordon, 1999:646), was subsequently amended by ASFA and renamed the Promoting Safe and Stable Families Program (PSSF). Two additional service areas were added to the two original program areas: time-limited reunification services and adoption promotion and support services (U.S. House of Representatives, 2005).

Title IV-E, also recently amended by ASFA and by the Fostering Connections to Success Act,[1] provides states with open-ended federal matching dollars for the placement and support of some children in foster care, with eligibility criteria that continue to pose challenges. Federal support, for example, is available to cover placement costs for only those children whose families would have been eligible for the now-defunct Aid to Families with Dependent Children program as it existed in 1996 and who meet other eligibility requirements. The income eligibility criteria have not been adjusted for inflation since 1996, resulting in increasingly fewer children qualifying for federal foster care assistance (Kids Are Waiting, 2007). In addition, although the foster care provisions of Title IV-E provide financial supports for out-of-home placements of eligible children, including older children and youth, support is not provided for services designed to promote their well-being or ensure that they exit care to permanent families.

Title IV-E also funds adoption assistance for eligible children with "special needs" who are adopted from foster care. The adoption assistance provisions of Title IV-E provide funding to support the adoptions of children who are determined to have particular challenges that may make adoption more challenging to achieve. Each state defines the conditions that constitute special needs, and they commonly consider older children and youth in foster care as eligible for adoption assistance (U.S. House of Representatives, 2005). Federal funds to support the adoption of children from foster care are otherwise quite limited, requiring that states use state and local dollars primarily to recruit, train and provide services for adoptive families. Research suggests that many families, including children's foster families, have reservations about adopting because of uncertainties regarding ongoing financial and service supports (e.g., Child Welfare League of America, 1991; U.S. Department of Health and Human Services, 2002) State policies regarding adoption subsidies for children who are not eligible for federal adoption assistance and the limited availability of postadoption services appear to influence families' willingness to consider adopting children and youth in foster care (Gibbs et al., 2002). When combined with state policies regarding eligibility to adopt (such as policies that restrict eligibility based on age or sexual orientation), these policies can significantly affect the pool of adoptive families available for older children and youth in foster care.

Child and Family Services to Promote Permanence

Under Subparts 1 and 2 of Title IV-B, federal funding is provided for services that can promote the achievement of permanence for older children and youth through reunification with their parents, permanent placement with relatives, or adoption. Little is known, however, about states' use of funds under Title IV-B, and, consequently, it is difficult to draw conclusions about the effectiveness of these service-dollar investments on permanency outcomes for children and youth. Although states provide Title IV-B plans to the U.S. Department of Health and Human Services (DHHS), minimal reporting requirements make reliable data difficult to obtain on states' use of these dollars (U.S. Government Accountability Office, 2006).

With regard to Subpart 1, there are some data regarding the general categories of services that states provide, but little is known about the specific services provided or who is served with these dollars. A recent Government Accountability Office (GAO) (2006) report found that states primarily use these dollars to operate child welfare programs and serve families whose children are in foster care. The GAO found that the majority of these funds were spent on staff salaries, with the remaining funds fairly evenly split among administration and management, child protective services, and foster care maintenance payments (which accounted for about 11 percent of Subpart 1 funds) (U.S. Government Accountability Office, 2006).

Federal guidelines require that states devote "significant portions" of their Title IV-B, Subpart 2 (PSSF) expenditures to each of the four categories of services that can be provided under that subpart (family support services, family preservation services, time-limited reunification services, and adoption promotion and support services) and that they provide a "strong rationale" for spending less than 20 percent of their allotments on each category (U.S. House of Representatives, 2005). The GAO study (2006) examined states' uses of Subpart 2 funds and found that states spent over 70 percent of these dollars on services to families, with nearly 50 percent used for family support and family preservation services. The remaining Subpart 2 funds were fairly evenly split among family preservation services (nearly 12 percent), adoption support services (over 11 percent), and family reunification services (about 9 percent).

These data suggest that the federal 20 percent rule for expenditures in each category is not being widely implemented. Although federal dollars are available for family reunification and adoption support under Subpart 2, it appears that these services receive support to a lesser degree than the longer-standing family preservation and family support programs. As the GAO (2006) notes, however, there are state-to-state differences in this regard.

The relatively low level of support for family reunification services is of concern, given studies showing that even when states are committed to ensuring that reasonable efforts are made to reunify children and families when children enter care, they often cite the lack of resources to do so. Studies conducted before the enactment of Subpart 2 made clear that most families were not receiving intensive family preservation services designed to prevent the entry of their children into foster care or to reunify families (Barth and Berry, 1994; Courtney, 1994; Fein and Maluccio, 1992). Mark Courtney (1994), for example, found in a sample of children entering foster care between 1988 and 1991 that close to three-quarters (70 percent) received only emergency response services, one-fifth received no services, and only 10 percent received extensive services. These concerns have persisted, despite federal policy that promotes the provision of reunification services (Hutchinson and Sudia, 2002). In particular, studies have highlighted the limited availability of two types of services that frequently are essential to children's safe reunification with their families: mental health and substance abuse treatment services for parents (O'Flynn, 1999; U.S. Department of Health and Human Services, 1999). These findings have important implications for the achievement of permanence through reunification for two groups of children and youth: children who enter foster care at older ages and children who enter care at younger ages but who do not reunify and remain in foster care for extended periods of time.

Because the knowledge base about the use of Title IV-B funds primarily addresses how dollars are generally used and there is little information on who is served with these funds and with what effect, it is not possible to reach conclusions about the role of Title IV-B in supporting and promoting the achievement of permanence for older children and youth. The few studies that have been conducted have focused primarily on family preservation and family support programs and found mixed results (U.S. Department of Health and Human Services, 1997; U.S. House of Representatives, 2005; Washington State Institute for Public Policy, 2006). A better understanding of the impact of Title IV-B in relation to permanence could inform policies regarding the use of funds in both subparts and strengthen future legislative action to enhance the programs funded under this title. Research, for example, is needed to address, among others, the following questions: Are families (birth parents, extended family, adoptive parents) of older children and youth and older children and youth themselves among the primary audiences for the services provided under Title IV-B Subparts 1 and 2? Assuming that data indicate that older children and youth are being served through Subpart 1 and 2 services, what services do they receive? Do these services make permanence more likely for this group of children? Do they speed reunification or permanent placement with relatives? Do they support the timely adoptions for older children and youth who cannot return to their birth families?[2]

Foster Care and Adoption

An assessment of Title IV-E's role in supporting the achievement of permanence for older children and youth necessarily rests on an evaluation of the impact of ASFA. Congress passed ASFA with two key goals in mind: to elevate child safety over preventing the placement of children in foster care and over family reunification and to shorten children's stays in care

(Barth et al., 2005). The median stay in foster care had grown from fifteen months in 1987 to more than two years in 1996 (U.S. House of Representatives, 2005). Many in Congress viewed the child welfare system as having a "reunification-at-all-costs mentality"; adoption was embraced with "fervent bipartisan support" as the principal way to reduce children's long stays in care (Gordon, 1999:646). Within that context, it is not surprising that ASFA, as enacted, addressed safety less than permanency.

Several key provisions of ASFA are relevant in an examination of federal policy responses to the needs of older children and youth in foster care for permanence: (1) limitations in ASFA on the "reasonable efforts" to reunify families requirement, with the resulting use of a "reunification bypass" under certain circumstances; (2) the requirement for permanency hearings within twelve months of the child entering care (in contrast to eighteen months in Public Law 96-272); (3) encouragement of concurrent planning; (4) the requirement that a petition to terminate parental rights be filed once a child has been in care for fifteen of the most recent twenty-two months, unless a specific exception applies;[3] and (5) financial incentives to states for increasing the number of adoptions. In the following discussion, I focus on the implications of these provisions with regard to permanence for older children and youth. I also consider provisions of the Foster Care Independence Act of 1999 in relation to the permanency focus of ASFA.

Reunification Bypass

For the first time in federal law, ASFA limited the application of the "reasonable efforts" provision of Public Law 96-272. ASFA permits a court to determine that "reasonable efforts" to reunify children with their parents are not required if certain circumstances exist: the parent has committed certain acts[4] or the parent's rights previously were terminated to a sibling of the child. ASFA further allows states to develop a set of "aggravated circumstances," which extend beyond the grounds specified in federal law, that can serve as the basis for determining that reasonable efforts do not need to be made to reunify parents and their children in foster care. These provisions have become known as "the reunification bypass" (D'Andrade and Berrick, 2006).

The effect of the reunification bypass—particularly in connection with the "aggravated circumstances" that states have developed as the basis for denying reunification services—is an area on which the knowledge base is only beginning to develop. In 1999, the U.S. General Accounting Office examined the use of the reunification bypass during the early stages of ASFA implementation and concluded that it was not being used to any great extent. Only one study has assessed the use of the reunification bypass in greater depth. Amy D'Andrade et al. (2006) examined its use in six California counties with families whose children were ten or younger upon entry into foster care. They found that although a fairly large number of parents were "eligible" for a reunification bypass under California law (which includes fifteen conditions that are considered "aggravated circumstances"), it was pursued in only a few cases. Of concern, however, was the variability among counties in the use of reunification bypass. The researchers found this variability to be "disconcerting as families' experiences should not be determined principally by geography" (2006:92).

Through their work regarding the implementation of the reunification bypass in California, D'Andrade and Berrick (2006) identified several concerns about the soundness of policies designed to limit reasonable efforts to reunify. First, there is limited research in this area: because the current understanding of families' prospects for reunification is not well developed, it is difficult to know whether all families who fall into statutory categories of "aggravated circumstances" would or would not benefit from reunification services or whether the grounds that are being used necessarily identify the most dangerous parents. Second, many statutes are vague. Some of the grounds for reunification bypass that appear in state laws are not clear and, in some cases, are potentially so broad in scope that there are likely to be wide variations in how the reunification bypass is implemented within a state. Finally, ASFA does not limit the number of aggravated circumstances that states can use to deny reunification services to parents, opening the possibility of ever-expanding criteria to justify the denial of these services (D'Andrade and Berrick, 2006). These issues raise a number of legal and ethical issues about the implementation of the reunification bypass, and they emphasize the importance of ongoing evaluation of this approach, particularly in states that have broadly expanded the bypass grounds.

Adoption as a Primary Permanence Option

In contrast to the limited attention that has focused on ASFA's reunification provisions, efforts to assess the impact of ASFA's adoption provisions began shortly after its enactment. The U.S. General Accounting Office

(1999) examined the ASFA provision mandating that a petition to terminate parental rights (TPR) be filed when a child had been in foster care for fifteen of the most recent twenty-two months. The researchers concluded, two years after ASFA, that the provision was being used appropriately. Stephanie Gendell (2001), observing trend data for the four-year period after ASFA, noted the rise in the number of cases involving termination of parental rights after states implemented ASFA. She raised questions regarding whether children whose parents' rights were being terminated were being adopted, were becoming legal orphans, or were being placed too quickly with adoptive families, thereby risking disruption. She concluded that it was "too early to know the statistical and long-term effects of ASFA" but suggested that it was unclear that the adoption goals of ASFA were being achieved (Gendell, 2001:36).

To date, there have not been rigorous and large-scale evaluations of ASFA (Barth et al., 2005). Data that could be used to assess the impact of ASFA have been limited as a result of two structural features of AFCARS (the Adoption and Foster Care Analysis and Reporting System): the limited number of variables per case and the fact that AFCARS does not allow the longitudinal tracking of cohorts of children over time. Because AFCARS does not lend itself to an examination of changes in child welfare practice, it has been necessary, as noted by Richard Barth et al. (2005), to draw on the findings of local nonexperimental studies and national cross sectional and longitudinal data in order to better understand the law's impact. Even with these sources of information, however, as these researchers note, "the effects of ASFA cannot be fully assessed until enough time has passed that cohorts of children who entered the system after the law's passage have achieved permanency. We are poised at the margins of that time frame" (2005:392).

A few studies have shed light on the effect of ASFA in general and the adoption provisions of ASFA in particular. The Local Agency Survey (LAS) of the National Study of Child and Adolescent Well-Being (NSCAW) administered from 1999 to 2000 provided child welfare administrators' perceptions of ASFA in its early stages of implementation (Mitchell et al., 2005). With respect to the early effects of ASFA in relation to adoption, the LAS found:

- A large majority (93 percent) of child welfare agencies reported that ASFA had shortened time frames for permanency decision-making to less than 12 months.

- More than half of the agencies stated that ASFA had resulted in an increased emphasis on adoption for older children.
- Almost three-quarters of the agencies (74 percent) reported an increased emphasis on adoption for children living with relatives.
- More than one-quarter (28 percent) reported that there had been an increase in the number of families who were precluded from receiving reunification services.

The LAS also found that the impact of federal policy changes was more evident in state-administered child welfare systems, which appeared to have moved more quickly to implement child welfare policy reforms as set forth in ASFA. In particular, state-administered child welfare systems had experienced more success in achieving adoptions than county-administered systems (Mitchell et al., 2005). Differences also were noted between urban and nonurban counties: nonurban counties were more likely to have implemented concurrent planning and to have focused on adoption, particularly of children in kinship care (Mitchell et al., 2005).

The LAS finding that more than one-half of the agencies reported a greater emphasis on adoption of older children and youth is of note. Some have concluded that this emphasis represents a positive direction for this population of children (Charles and Nelson, 2000), but others have expressed concerns about adoption mandates for older children and youth. In their analysis of child welfare data since the enactment of ASFA, Barth et al. (2005) identified several trends that appear to support concerns about the effect of ASFA's adoption provisions on older children and youth. Trend data indicate that since the enactment of ASFA, there has been, simultaneously, a decrease in the number of children reunified with their parents and an increase in the number of adoptions. The number of children who are waiting for adoptive families has not significantly declined even as the number of adoptions has increased. Although there have been meaningful increases in the adoption of young children, the outcomes for older children and youth are not as clear. Trend data also indicate that the number of unadopted older children whose parents' rights have been terminated has been growing substantially (Barth et al., 2005).

These trends in connection with adoption outcomes (or, more precisely, non-outcomes) for older children and youth offer empirical support for concerns that were expressed shortly after the enactment of ASFA and which have continued. Robert Gordon, for example, pointed to the age-insensitivity of ASFA and commented, "If ASFA moves too slowly with regard to young children [taking issue with the fifteen-month time frame for seeking termination of parental rights], it threatens to move too often for older ones" (1999:668). Practitioners and policy observers have continued to call attention to the possibility that ASFA would create a large and growing group of "legal orphans" as parental rights were terminated for older children (Guggenheim, 1995; Wexler, 2002). Barth and colleagues (2005) indicate that these concerns are not unfounded: they found that, when compared with other types of termination of parental rights actions, the termination of parental rights for older children when an adoption resource has not been identified is least likely to lead to adoption.

Adoption Incentive Program

In addition to the provisions that have pressed a growing number of cases toward termination of parental rights, ASFA created financial incentives to reward states for increasing the number of adoptions of children in foster care above baseline numbers. The "first outcome-oriented incentive program in child welfare based solely on the reporting of administrative data" (Maza, 2000:455), the incentive program rewards adoption outcomes but not the achievement of other forms of permanence, specifically reunification and the permanent placement of children with relatives.

The Fostering Connections Act authorizes the adoption incentive program through FY2013. It doubles the incentive amounts states may earn for each increase in the number of older children adopted from foster care (from $4,000 to $8,000) and for children with special needs, under age 9, who are adopted from foster care (from $2,000 to $4,000). The incentive award for any increase in the total number of children adopted from foster care remains at $4,000. The Act also changes the program so that states (even those with declining overall foster care caseloads) continue to have a fiscal incentive to increase adoptions. These changes include fixing each state's baseline adoption numbers at the numbers achieved in FY2007. Specifically, AFCARS data had shown:

- Between FY1998 and FY 2003, the proportion of children ages nine and older in foster care who were waiting to be adopted increased from 39 percent to 49 percent; however, the proportion of children ages nine and older who were adopted remained at one-third.

- Between FY 1998 and FY 2003, the average age of children waiting to be adopted increased from 7.8 to 8.7 years.
- During that same time period, 37 percent of children over the age of nine whose parents' rights had been terminated did not have a plan for adoption but, instead, had a plan for emancipation or long-term foster care.
- Close to 8 percent of all children were emancipated from foster care and did not achieve permanency (U.S. Department of Health and Human Services, 2005b).

The program anticipates that incentive payments will increase the number of adoptions of older children and youth as the original incentive program did for adoptions of children in foster care in general. The resulting absolute numbers of adoptions of children in this age category and the level of adoption incentives that states receive will indicate the general effect of the program. Because there is no independent evaluation of the adoption incentive program (U.S. Office of Management and Budget, 2005), however, it will be difficult to assess the specific factors associated with increased numbers of older child adoptions, if that does indeed occur.

Needed Research on ASFA's Reunification and Adoption Provisions

A number of questions need to be addressed through research to better understand whether and how ASFA provisions have helped achieve permanence for older children and youth. These issues include a fuller understanding of the influence of the reunification bypass: Is the bypass used primarily with families of very young children, or is it being used with families of older children and youth? If it is used with older children and youth, what is the impact—both in terms of expediting permanence and in terms of the psychosocial ramifications for older children and youth?

Research also is needed to deepen the understanding of the effect of ASFA's adoption emphasis for older children and youth. Is the focus on termination of parental rights as appropriate for this group of children as it is for young children? Are different practice approaches called for when considering terminating the rights of parents of older children and youth? Are there effective strategies to increase the prospects of adoption after termination of parental rights? What is the role of adoption incentives in promoting adoption for older children and youth?

Foster Care Independence Act of 1999:
Preparation for Adulthood and Permanence

Since 1986, Title IV-E has provided states with federal funding to provide independent living services to youth between the ages of sixteen and twenty-one in foster care (Title IV-E Independent Living Initiative, Public Law 99-272). In 1999, the Foster Care Independence Act (Public Law 106-169) provided states with greater flexibility and funding to carry out programs to assist youth in making the transition from foster care to adulthood. It is of note that these laws, which are specifically designed to support youth as they move toward adulthood, do not reference family permanency for youth. The recent proposed rule regarding outcomes measures to assess states' performance in operating their independent living programs does not mention "permanency" in any form (*Chafee National Youth in Transition Database*, 2006). With regard to personal connections, it solely references "family support and marriage education" (which focuses on educating youth to maintain their own healthy families through parenting education and child care skills) and "mentoring," which it defines as "programs or services in which the youth regularly meets with a screened trained adult on a one-on-one basis" (*Chafee National Youth in Transition Database*, 2006:40357). The lack of family permanency language in these laws and the absence of expected outcomes on family connections raise important research, policy, and practice issues about the integration of permanency and preparation for adulthood for older children and youth in care.

OTHER KEY ISSUES IN THE INTERSECTION OF FEDERAL
CHILD WELFARE POLICY AND RESEARCH

Additional issues within the context of federal child welfare policy warrant at least a brief mention in connection with permanence for older children and youth: federal child welfare policy in relation to race-based inequities, the Child and Family Service Reviews, and the Title IV-E waiver demonstration program.

Federal Child Welfare Policy and Race-Based Inequities

Since the enactment of ASFA, there has been growing attention to the disproportionate representation of children of color in foster care (Derezotes and Hill, 2006; National Association of Public Child Welfare Administrators, 2006). Concerns have grown that older children and youth of color are particularly disadvantaged in terms of permanent family outcomes (Roberts, 2002). Data indicate that African American and Latino children are less likely to be reunified with their parents and that African American, Latino, and older children not only spend more time in care until the termination of parental rights but also wait longer after parental rights are terminated to be placed with adoptive families (Noonan and Burke, 2005). Nonetheless, the LAS survey found that only 14 percent of the child welfare agencies stated that they had any concerns about the disproportionate representation of children of color in foster care, only 15 percent reported providing training on addressing disproportionality, and only 2 percent reported using performance measures to reduce "racial imbalance in placement" (Mitchell et al., 2005).

Federal child welfare policy does not explicitly address either the disproportionate representation of children of color in foster care or the disparate outcomes that are achieved in relation to permanence for children of color in general and African American children in particular. Whereas the Juvenile Justice Delinquency and Prevention Act addresses Disproportionate Minority Contact (DMC) and directs states to assess DMC and take action to address it when it exists, neither ASFA nor any other federal child welfare statute addresses race- and culture-based inequities for children and youth of color in the child welfare system.

Federal child welfare law speaks to race in two statutes: the Indian Child Welfare Act of 1978 (ICWA) and the Multi-Ethnic Placement Act of 1994 as amended by the Interethnic Placement Act Amendments of 1996 (MEPA-IEPA). The approaches taken in these two federal statutes are distinct: ICWA promotes children's connections with their cultural and tribal communities and requires that Native American children be placed with Native foster and adoptive families, absent a clear showing that such a placement is not in the child's best interest. MEPA-IEPA, which applies to the placement of all non-Native children, prohibits race from being used as a factor in foster care or adoptive family placement decision-making, absent a specific showing that considering race would be in a particular child's best interest.

Given the disparate approaches of the two federal laws, it is unfortunate that an assessment of practice as it has developed in compliance with ICWA and MEPA-IEPA has not been conducted. An assessment is needed of the outcomes achieved when race and culture are given great weight (the ICWA approach) and when they are given virtually no weight (the MEPA-IEP approach) in foster care and adoption decision-making. Such an assessment is particularly important in relation to permanence for older children and youth, for whom it may be expected that racial and cultural identity are particularly salient issues.

Results of the Federal Child and Family Service Reviews

The federal Child and Family Service Reviews (CFSRs) assess the performance of states in connection with three outcomes: safety, permanence, and child and family well-being. Two permanency outcomes have been defined: (1) children have permanency and stability in their living situations, and (2) the continuity of family relationships and connections is preserved for children (U.S. House of Representatives, 2005). The CFSRs provide a snapshot of each state's foster care population based on a review of a small number of cases, generally from thirty to fifty cases. Because many states generally have had only one CFSR, trend data are not available. The CFSR reports, however, provide some qualitative information about ASFA-established processes (Barth et al., 2005).

With regard to older children and youth, the CFSR process has focused more on preparation of youth for independent living than on permanence. In the Child and Family Service Review final reports for a number of states, it was noted that long-term foster care was often being inappropriately used as the plan for older children and youth, either when other options for permanency had not been explored or when neither adoption nor guardianship was being sought for these youth. In states' corresponding Program Improvement Plans, however, activities often focused on strengthening independent living services, on general efforts to provide training on the "special needs" of older children and youth, or on an expansion of placement resources (National Resource Center for Youth Development, 2004). It appears that specific attention to achieving permanency for older children and youth is needed, particularly in Program Improvement Plans. Research can play a viable role in informing the content of these plans and in the evaluation of specific strategies that plans might contain to promote the achievement of permanence for older children and youth.

Title IV-E Demonstration Waiver Projects

An important aspect of federal child welfare policy since 1994 has been the Title IV-E waiver demonstration projects. ASFA expanded the waiver program by authorizing the U.S. Department of Health and Human Services to approve a larger number of waiver demonstration projects (U.S. House of Representatives, 2005). Title IV-E waiver demonstration projects, implemented by twenty-five states since 1997 (Lehman et al., 2005), have permitted states and counties to experiment with and evaluate a range of strategies that flexibly use federal Title IV-E foster care dollars. The funding constraints of Title IV-B and IV-E have consistently been identified by child welfare administrators as "a major source of the lack of available services" (Geen and Tumlin, 1999:5) and a key barrier to tailoring services to the community and to individual child and family needs (Costin et al., 1996).

Several evaluations of Title IV-E demonstration waiver projects have documented benefits for children and families, including greater permanence. In an evaluation of Oregon's Title IV-E waiver project, it was found that flexible funding increased the likelihood of children remaining in their homes, returning home, and establishing permanent placements with relatives within one year of the target maltreatment incident (Lehman et al., 2005). In 2005, the U.S. Department of Health and Human Services released findings and evaluations of the seven state waiver demonstration programs that implemented federally supported guardianship programs. The initial findings reflected that nonrelative guardianship was an effective and viable option for child welfare systems to consider (Congressional Research Service, 2006).

The authority of Department of Health and Human Services to grant Title IV-E demonstration projects expired on March 31, 2006, and was not renewed by Congress (Congressional Research Service, 2006). With the ending of these efforts, there likely will be fewer opportunities to test innovative programs and approaches at the state and county levels. It will be important to consider the implications of this development in relation to creating and evaluating innovative systemic approaches to achieving permanence for older children and youth.

STATE POLICY AND ITS IMPACT ON PERMANENCE FOR OLDER CHILDREN AND YOUTH

In addition to federal policy, policy at the state level plays a significant role in shaping practice designed to achieve and sustain permanence for older children and youth. State policy has a significant role in decisions regarding the removal of children from their birth parents, the circumstances under which "reasonable efforts" can be bypassed (as discussed earlier), and the extent to which ongoing, healthy connections between youth and their birth parents, following termination of parental rights, will be supported. State policy has largely directed the availability of financial and service supports for relatives who assume permanent responsibility for children in foster care. Finally, state law directs much of adoption practice, particularly in terms of who may adopt and the process for adopting children from foster care.

State-level child welfare policy often is also shaped by class action litigation resulting in consent decrees or court orders. In at least thirty-five jurisdictions, class action litigation has brought child welfare systems under the supervision of courts (Child Welfare League of America, 2005). Court orders, consent decrees, and receiverships in these states and counties significantly direct the scope and nature of child welfare programming and practice, often emphasizing permanency outcomes, particularly adoption. Opinions widely diverge as to the results achieved through this strategy (Child Protection Report, 2002; Mezey, 2000), with little empirically based knowledge about the effect of litigation on substantive outcomes for children and families.

CONCLUSION

The successful achievement of permanence for older children and youth is affected by both federal and state child welfare policy. Federal policy is largely set forth in Titles IV-B and IV-E of the Social Security Act, particularly through the new policy directions set by ASFA and the Fostering Connections to Success Act. A relatively small body of research has informed the understanding of the effect of these federal policies, specifically with regard to permanence for older children and youth. Other developments at the federal policy level also affect child welfare programming and practices that promote permanence for older children and youth. At the state level, law and class action litigation shape permanency practice. A broader body of research is needed to assess the effect of current federal and state policies on permanency outcomes for older children and youth and to support the development of new policy. Effective policy should be evidence-based, with a focus on child well-being, of which permanence is a critical component, and should be guided by a development perspective (Wulcyzn, et al., 2005). Through a developmental perspective that recognizes that children entering adolescence and adolescents have unique needs, policy can more effectively support the achievement of permanence for older and children and youth.

NOTES

1. The Fostering Connections to Success and Increasing Adoption Act of 2008 (H.R. 6893) made significant changes in federal child welfare policy, including: new supports and requirements to ensure permanent placements with relatives; increasing resources so that child welfare agencies can more effectively recruit adoptive families for children in foster care who cannot be safely reunified with their birth parents; creating Family Connections Grants to support kinship navigator programs, family group decision-making, intensive family finding efforts, and residential family substance abuse treatment programs; continuing federal support for older youth in foster care; extending federal training to more staff; and allowing Indian tribes direct access to federal foster care and adoption assistance funds.

2. In the arena of family support, the U.S. Department of Health and Human Services recently has devoted federal funds under the Adoption Opportunities Grant program to programs designed to support healthy marriages. Some twenty-six grants have been made to programs designed to disseminate information about the benefits of healthy marriage to children and families and share ideas on marriage strengthening (U.S. Department of Health and Human Services, 2006a). In 2006, grants focused on demonstration projects in postadoption services and marriage education to implement and evaluate programs that help adoptive parents build healthy marriages (U.S. Department of Health and Human Services, 2006b) and similar programs to improve child well-being by removing barriers to form and sustain healthy marriages and strengthen families in Native American communities (U.S. Department of Health and Human Services, 2006c).

3. The exceptions are that the child lives with a relative, services needed by the family have not been provided or offered, or termination of parental rights would not be in the child's best interest.

4. The circumstances are the murder of another child of the parent, voluntary manslaughter of another child of the parent, aiding or abetting in committing such murder or manslaughter, or felony assault resulting in serous bodily injury to the child or another child of the parent.

REFERENCES

Barth, R. P., and M. Berry (1994). Implications of research on the welfare of children under permanency planning. *Child Welfare Research Review* 1: 345–46.

Barth, R. P., F. Wulczyn, and T. Crea (2005). Symposium on the state construction of families: Foster care, termination of parental rights, and adoption. From anticipation to evidence: Research on the Adoption and Safe Families Act. *Virginia Journal of Social Policy and Law* 12: 371–400.

Chafee National Youth in Transition Database: Proposed Rule (2006). *Federal Register* (July 14): 40346–382.

Charles, K., and J. Nelson (2000). *Permanency Planning: Creating Life Long Connections. What Does It Mean for Adolescents?* Tulsa: University of Okalahoma, National Resource Center for Youth Development.

Child Protection Report (2002). *Fixing the Child Welfare System: Do Lawsuits, Court Orders, Reviews and More Regulations Really Help?* Silver Spring, Md.: Business Publishers.

Child Welfare League of America (1991). *Foster Parent Recruitment and Retention Efforts: Summary of Findings.* Washington, D.C.: Author.

—— (2005). *Child Welfare Consent Decrees.* At www.cwla.org/advocacy/consentdecrees .pdf (accessed April 11, 2007).

Congressional Research Service (2006). *Child Welfare: Foster Care and Adoption Assistance Provisions in Budget Reconciliation.* CRS Report for Congress. Washington, D.C.: Author.

Costin, L. B., H. J. Karger and D. Stoesz (1996). *The Politics of Child Abuse in America.* New York: Oxford University Press.

Courtney, M. E. (1994). Factors associated with the reunification of foster children with their families. *Social Services Review* 68: 81–98.

D'Andrade, A., and J. D. Berrick (2006). When policy meets practice: The untested effects of permanency reforms in child welfare. *Journal of Sociology and Social Welfare* 33(1): 31–52.

D'Andrade, A., L. Frame, and J. D. Berrick (2006). Concurrent planning in public child welfare agencies: Oxymoron or work in progress? *Children and Youth Services Review* 28: 78–95.

Derezotes, D., and R. Hill (2006). *Examining the Disproportionate Representation of Children of Color in the Child Welfare System.* At www.racemattersconsortium.org /docs/whopaper3.pdf (accessed May 29, 2006).

Fein, E., and A. N. Maluccio (1992). Permanency planning: Another remedy in jeopardy. *Social Service Review* 66: 335–50.

Geen, R., and K. C. Tumlin (1999). *State Efforts to Remake Child Welfare: Responses to New Challenges and Increased Scrutiny.* Washington, D.C.: Urban Institute.

Gendell, S. (2001). In search of permanency: A reflection on the first three years of the Adoption and Safe Families Act implementation. *Family Court Review* 39: 25–36.

Gibbs, D., K. Siebenaler, K. and R. P. Barth, R.P. (2002). *Assessing the Field of Post-Adoption Services: Family Needs, Program Models, and Evaluation Issues.* At aspe.hhs.gov/HSP /post-adoption01/case-study/index.htm (accessed April 10, 2007).

Gordon, R. M. (1999). Drifting through Byzantium: The promise and failure of the Adoption and Safe Families Act of 1997. *Minnesota Law Review* 83: 637–701.

Guggenheim, M. (1995). The effects of recent trends to accelerate the terminiation of parental rights of children in foster care: An empirical analysis in two states. *Family Law Quarterly* 29: 121–47.

Hutchinson, J. R., and C. E. Sudia (2002). *Failed Child Welfare Policy: Family Preservation and the Orphaning of Child Welfare*. Blue Ridge Summit, Pa.: University Press of America.

Kids Are Waiting (2007). *Time for Reform: Fix the Foster Care Lookback*. At kidsarewaiting .org/reports/files/lookback.pdf (accessed April 10, 2007).

Lehman, C. M., S. Liang, and K. O'Dell (2005). Impact of flexible funds on placement and permanency outcomes for children in child welfare. *Research on Social Work Practice* 15(5): 381–88.

Maza, P. (2000). Using administrative data to reward agency performance: The case of the federal adoption incentive program. *Child Welfare* 79(5): 444–56.

Mitchell, L. B., R. P. Barth, R. Green, A. Wall, P. Biemer, J. D. Berrick, M. B. Webb, and the National Survey of Child and Adolescent Well-Being Research Group (2005). Child welfare reform in the United States: Findings from a Local Agency Survey. *Child Welfare* 84(1): 5–24.

National Association of Public Child Welfare Administrators (2006). *Disproportionate Representation in the Child Welfare System: Emerging Promising Practices Survey*. Washington, D.C.: Author.

National Resource Center for Youth Development (2004). *An Analysis of States' Child and Family Service Reviews and Program Improvement Plans from a Youth Development Perspective*. Tulsa, Okla.: Author.

Noonan, K., and K. Burke (2005). Termination of parental rights: Which foster children are affected? *Social Science Journal* 42: 241–56.

O'Flynn, M. (1999). The Adoption and Safe Families Act of 1997: Changing child welfare policy without addressing parental substance abuse. *Journal of Contemporary Health Law and Policy* 16: 1–19.

Roberts, D. (2002). *Shattered Bonds: The Color of Child Welfare*. New York: Basic Civitas Books.

U.S. Department of Health and Human Services (1997). *National Study of Protective, Preventive and Reunification Services Delivered to Children and Their Families*. Washington, D.C.: Author.

—— (1999). *Mental Health: A Report of the Surgeon General*. Rockville, Md.: U.S. Department of Health and Human Services, National Institute of Mental Health.

—— (2002). *Recruiting Foster Parents*, OEI-07-00-0060. Washington D.C.: Author.

—— (2005a). *Final FY 2005 Annual Performance Plan*. Washington, D.C.: Author.

—— (2005b). *The AFCARS Report.* At www.acf.hhs.gov/programs/cb/stats_research /afcars/trends.htm (accessed June 1, 2006).

—— (2006a). *The Children's Bureau's Programs to Strengthen Healthy Marriages.* At www.acf.hhs.gov/healthymarriage/funding/childrens_bureau.html (accessed July 17, 2006).

—— (2006b). *Demonstration Projects in Post-Adoption Services and Marriage Education.* At www.acf.hhs.gov/grants/open/HHS-2006-ACF-ACYF-CO-0134.html and www.acf.hhs.gov/healthymarriage/funding/childrens_bureau.html (accessed July 17, 2006).

—— (2006c). *Strengthening Marriages and Relationships in Tribal and Native American Communities.* At www.afterschool.ed.gov/healthymarriage/about/strengthening_ marriages.htm (accessed July 17, 2006).

U.S. General Accounting Office (1999). *Foster Care: Early Experiences in Implementing the Adoption and Safe Families Act.* Washington, D.C.: Government Printing Office.

U.S. Government Accountability Office (2006). *Child Welfare: Federal Oversight of State IV-B Activities Could Inform Action Needed to Improve Service to Families and Statutory Compliance.* Washington, D.C.: Author.

U.S. House of Representatives, Committee on Ways and Means (2005). *The Green Book.* Washington, D.C.: Government Printing Office.

U.S. Office of Management and Budget (2005). Adoption Incentive Assessment. At www.whitehouse.gov/omb/expectmore/detail.10003500.2005.html (accessed June 1, 2006).

Washington State Institute for Public Policy (2006). *Intensive Family Preservation Programs: Program Fidelity Influences Effectiveness.* At www.wsipp.wa.gov/rptfiles /06-02-3901.pdf (accessed June 4, 2006).

Wexler, R. (2002). Take the child and run: Tales for the age of ASFA. *New England Law Review* 36(1): 129–52.

Wulcyzn, F., R. P. Barth, Y. Y. Yuan, B. D. Harden, and J. Landsverk (2005). *Beyond Common Sense: Child Welfare, Child Well-Being, and the Evidence for Policy Reform.* Somerset, N.J.: Transaction.

Federal Law and
Child Welfare Reform

EIGHT

The Research-Policy Interface
in Promoting Permanence for
Older Children and Youth

ROSEMARY J. AVERY

In this chapter, I respond to and elaborate on observations made by Madelyn Freundlich in chapter 7 regarding policy issues surrounding youth exiting from care. I discuss independent living programs and the lack of emphasis on family and social connections for youth transitioning from foster care to adulthood, health care coverage and health service access issues for youth who have exited foster care, and service coordination issues. Recent research has focused on the exit end of the foster care system—that is, youth aging out of care—and has well demonstrated the perilous position that federal policy creates for young foster care alumni, both before and after they exit foster care. Of particular concern is the lack of rulemaking requiring every child to have a committed adult willing to be in a supportive and personal (not clinical) relationship with the youth before, during, and after their transition to adulthood. Equally concerning is the inattention that has been given to health care issues that affect this group of youth.

Each year across this country, between twenty thousand and twenty-five thousand youth are discharged from the child welfare system to their own resources (English et al., 2006). In years past, when youth comprised fewer than 25 percent of the child welfare caseload, this group of children in foster care was not such an urgent concern. Caseload demographics, however, have changed radically, and public concern is becoming focused on this vulnerable group of state wards. In 2005, more than 200,000 youth aged thirteen or older were in the foster care system, close to 40 percent of the foster care population; in that same year, 24,407 foster youth exited care to emancipation (U.S. Department of Health and Human Services, 2006). Current policy allows these youth to be discharged from care to "independent living" with no one to rely on but themselves (English et al., 2003; Georgiades, 2005). The majority of these youth have no personal connections to committed adults to help them through this difficult transition period and beyond or to support them when the inevitable adverse circumstances befall, including ill health, victimization, unemployment, unplanned parenthood, or homelessness. Some youth temporarily turn to birth parents or other kin for support and shelter; the majority, however, must learn to navigate the world on their own.

INDEPENDENT LIVING PROGRAMS:
POLICY AND PRACTICE ISSUES

An important question faces policy makers: To what extent is the foster care system preparing these foster care youth for self-sufficiency, independence, and effective community living? An equally important question faces practitioners: What is the best practice to ensure that youth's transition to adulthood is a successful one? With the exception of providing health care, child welfare policy has remained ambivalent about the systems' responsibility for ensuring the safety and well-being of youth after they exit care. Empirical research has not provided evidence as to how best to prepare youth for life after care (Mech, 1994; Voices Issue Brief, 2004), and practice has focused on the importance of providing "life skills" rather than "life connections."

Research since the late 1980s has provided ample evidence that aging out of foster care poses particular problems for youth with tenuous family ties, weak community connections, and poor prospects for stable housing, employment, or support resources. Edmund Mech (1994) found that if youth are not connected with at least one key personal support resource before they leave care, their chances of successful community integration are significantly diminished. Teresa Cooney and Jane Kurz (1996) and Debra Umberson (1992) found that successful functioning after leaving care is inextricably linked to relationships with the family of origin. It is imperative that future policy initiatives address areas of practice that would make it mandatory for caseworkers to vigorously explore ties with biological family, siblings, relatives, former foster families, or other caregivers well before a youth's date of exit from care and to ensure that no youth be discharged from care before age twenty-one without one committed, caring adult connection. Failure to make these connections for youth should be grounds for an extension of foster care past the age of majority.

Great policy strides were made in 1999 for older youth in care with the passing of the Foster Care Independence Act (FCIA), which doubled federal financial support for transitional services and created the John H. Chafee Foster Care Independence Program. The goals of the program are to provide youth with tools that could help them develop better education, vocation, and life skills; prepare youth for education after high school; support youth's personal and emotional needs; provide former foster youth ages eighteen to twenty-one with a variety of supports; and help youth access funds for education and training.

The primary objective of independent living (IL) programs is to prepare foster youth for effective adult living and independence after they exit care, but, to date, we have very little evidence that these programs actually work. Given the short history of IL programs and the traditional lack of federal funding for child welfare systems research, only a few studies have been done on the effectiveness of IL programs, and our knowledge of their effectiveness is limited and conflicting (Georgiades, 2005). Most of the studies that have been completed so far suffer from methodological limitations such as lack of an appropriate comparison group (comparable foster youth who did not participate in independent living programs), limited sample size, limited duration of observation following exit from care, and limited nature of the outcome data studied (for a review of these studies, see Georgiades, 2005).

Studies completed relatively more recently and with fewer methodological limitations indicate that the effect of IL programs on youth outcomes in the medium-term (one to three years) is primarily in domains such as education and employment (Mallon, 1998; Scannapieco et al., 1995), early parenting prevention, anger control, and self-evaluation outcomes (Courtney et al., 2001). A more recent study by Savvas Georgiades (2005) using an appropriate comparison group (foster youth who aged out but did not go through IL training) failed to find a relationship between IL program participation and better social support, better parenting competence, lower

incidence of substance abuse, lower levels of sexually risky behaviors, reduced depression, and increased knowledge in interpersonal, money management, job-seeking, and job-maintenance skills.

A comprehensive evaluation needs to be undertaken to determine the relative merits and costs of these type of "independence" programs compared
with other strategies, such as increasing the discharge age from foster care to
twenty-one for all foster youth who have not been permanently placed with
families and providing services such as postdischarge mentor programs. The
questions for policy makers and researchers are the following: What types
of life skills are successfully taught in a classroom setting? Does IL training
result in youth who are more "functional" as young adults in terms of living
and survival skills, social skills, and economic independence?

HEALTH CARE COVERAGE AFTER FOSTER CARE

Policy strides have been made in the last few years in providing health
care insurance for youth exiting care. The impact of these efforts, however, is still questionable. The bipartisan Foster Care Independence Act
(FCIA) of 1999 provides an important extension to services and supports
for youth making the transition from foster care. Subtitle C of Title I
of the act offers states an important opportunity to provide continued
Medicaid coverage to young people aged eighteen to twenty-one who
have exited care. FCIA established a new optional Medicaid eligibility
group for "independent foster care adolescents," young people who are
are or were in foster care on their eighteenth birthday. States, however, are
responsible for the nonfederal share of Medicaid, and the federal medical
assistance percentage ranges from 50 percent to 76.8 percent, depending
on the state's per capita income. This same cost-sharing rule applies to the
expanded eligibility in FCIA.

If a state takes full advantage of the Medicaid option under FCIA, all foster care youth who are not yet twenty-one could be automatically eligible
for Medicaid without regard to their income status (that is, no income or
resource test would be required for these young adults). However, this full
coverage is optional for states, and, in addition, states have the option to
restrict eligibility to subgroups based on income and other resource tests,
age, or previous foster care eligibility status. In an effort to encourage states
to participate in this federal program, Patricia Montoya (Commissioner

on Children, Youth, and Families in the U.S. Department of Health and Human Services) and Timothy Westmoreland (Director of the Center for Medicaid and State Operations Health Care Financing Administration) (2002), wrote letters to all state child welfare and Medicaid directors urging them to take advantage of the new Medicaid options under the FCIA to ensure that children transitioning from foster care get the physical and mental health care they need.

Automatic enrollment of all youth exiting from foster care in Medicaid or other state-funded health insurance programs would significantly enhance the likelihood that youth would receive essential health care services after exiting foster care. Research indicates that youth exiting care without health insurance are unlikely to obtain medical care when needed (Newacheck et al., 1995). Currently, there are no uniform or comprehensive data available to assess what states are doing to take advantage of health care coverage options for youth exiting care. Abigail English and colleagues (2003) interviewed independent living coordinators in forty-three states to examine how Medicaid and State Children's Health Insurance Programs (SCHIPs) could improve health care access for youth aging out of foster care. The researchers found that when states had not implemented the FCIA Medicaid expansion option, the major reason was budgetary constraints. Budgetary considerations also were cited as the leading obstacle to implementation in the states that had chosen to implement the FCIA Medicaid expansion option. Most states reported that both state budgets and Medicaid budgets were in crisis. In the conclusion to their study, the researchers suggested that it was unacceptable to cite budgetary constraints as a reason for not implementing the FCIA Medicaid expansion option given that the actual number of youth covered under this expansion would be small, the youth are a particularly vulnerable population group, and failure to cover these youth would result in significant social and economic costs in the long run.

Of particular policy concern is the differential access that exiting youths have to continued health care coverage, depending on their state of residence. A youth's access to health care insurance after leaving care should not depend on the state in which they live. To better understand issues of differential access, researchers need to address such questions as the following: What accounts for the significant variation in FCIA Medicaid extension participation patterns among states? What accounts for differences in benefits packages among states? What is the rate of youth utilization of services through this program once they leave foster care?

OTHER BARRIERS TO HEALTH CARE SERVICES
FOR YOUTH EXITING FOSTER CARE

The group of young people who age out of foster care each year is a small but vulnerable population with multiple health concerns, intense health care needs, and few resources for securing health care (English et al., 2003). Eligibility for health insurance coverage, standing alone, will not address the health care problems facing these youth (Allen and Bissell, 2004). Large numbers of former foster youth are homeless, poorly educated, unemployed, and living in poverty. Even when youth have health care coverage through programs such as Medicaid, they often do not have the skills to independently navigate the health care system; they may find that their health care coverage does not fully pay for the services needed, and there is likely to be a dearth of health care providers who can meet the comprehensive and integrated health care service needs of transitioning youth. A number of enrollment and service barriers exist that may be especially problematic for young adults navigating the system on their own for the first time. Specifically, youth may encounter challenges in finding health care providers who will accept Medicaid coverage, given the low reimbursement rates, burdensome administrative requirements, and inefficient payment system; in insuring continuity of care as they move frequently from one living situation to another; and in coordinating wrap-around medical services with mental health and substance abuse treatment services.

J. Curtis McMillen et al. (2005) found that older youths in the foster care system have disproportionately high rates of lifetime and past year psychiatric disorders. Studies have shown that children in foster care suffer more frequent and more serious medical, developmental, and psychological problems than nearly any other group of children (Gollan et al., 2005; Ito et al., 1993, 1998; Perry and Pollard, 1998). Foster youth are undoubtedly at a higher risk for continuing health problems after they exit care because of the circumstance that brought them into care and the ongoing instability they may experience once they enter into care.

HEALTH OUTCOMES FOR YOUTH EXITING FOSTER CARE

Although some smaller studies have documented the health status of youth at the time they exit care and report high rates of physical and mental health problems, no studies have been conducted using nationally representative samples to gauge the true extent of these youth's health problems. Our knowledge of the health status of other at-risk youth (homeless and runaway youth and those living in poverty) is also limited but equally important, as many former foster care youth experience poverty and homelessness soon after leaving care. Courtney and Amy Dworsky (2006) found that a large number of aged-out youth continue to struggle with health and mental health problems, suffer from persistent mental illness or substance use disorders, and find themselves without basic health coverage.

Some states have developed progressive ways to track the health care of children in foster care (such as through electronic "health passports"), and others are making creative use of funds from Medicaid and other state programs to expand access to health services while children are in care. No state tracks the health status of youth leaving foster care, and none has committed to providing support systems for continuity of care after exit. This challenge has yet to be addressed at the national policy level.

It is known that between one-third and one-half of youth aging out of care lose their Medicaid coverage once they transition out of care (Rosenbach, 2001). Concerted efforts are necessary to ensure that youth leaving care are not among the uninsured, for whatever reason. Furthermore, policy makers should closely examine the effect of termination of Medicaid eligibility on young adults after their twenty-first birthday, especially because youth leaving care often obtain low-paying jobs that do not provide health insurance.

SERVICE COORDINATION

A related issue that needs urgent federal policy attention is the coordination of services for parents, children, and youth aging out of care with regard to substance abuse, mental health, and violence. Legislation targeted at this problem has not been enacted, and, as a result, many states have not developed appropriate screening, assessments, and comprehensive treatment options for families and older youth in care. Currently, there are no laws that specifically address the links between child welfare and substance abuse, mental health, and domestic violence, although several laws have been proposed (Allen and Bissell, 2004).[1] Some states, including Connecticut, Delaware, Illinois, and Washington, among others, have used the Title IV-E demonstration waiver authority to respond more creatively to service coordination needs, but others have not, and the authority to grant new waivers has expired. There is currently no comprehensive federal legislative effort in place to address these coordinated service needs.

CONCLUSION

In summary, comparative research is needed on the outcomes for youth aging out of care from various placement settings such as family-based care, kin care, and institutional settings. The need for program evaluation and program impact research on independent living preparation and outcomes is urgent. Furthermore, the research on the postdischarge young adult functioning of former foster youth is insufficient and needs to be federally funded if there is to be an evidence-based foundation for future policy initiatives in child welfare.

NOTE

1. The Child Protection and Alcohol Drug Partnership Act was introduced into the 106th, 107th, and 108th (2003–2004) Congresses. As of this writing, it had not as yet been introduced into the 110th Congress.

REFERENCES

Allen, M., and M. Bissell (2004). Safety and stability for foster children: The policy context. *Future of Children* 14(1): 49–72.

Cooney, T. M., and J. Kurz (1996). Mental health outcomes following recent parental divorce: The case of young adult offspring. *Journal of Family Issues* 17: 495–513.

Courtney, M. E., and A. Dworsky (2006). Early outcomes for young adults transitioning from out-of-home care in the USA. *Child and Family Social Work* 11: 209–19.

Courtney, M. E., I. Piliavin, A. Grogan-Kaylor, and A. Nesmith (2001). Foster youth transitions to adulthood: A longitudinal view of youth leaving care. *Child Welfare* 80: 685–716.

English, A., M. Morreale, and J. Larsen (2003). Access to Health Care for Youth leaving Foster Care: Medicaid and SCHIP. *Journal of Adolescent Health* 23(S): 53–69.

English, A., A. J. Stinnett, and E. Dunn-Georgiou (2006). *Health Care for Adolescents and Young Adults Leaving Foster Care: Policy Options for Improving Access.* Chapel Hill, N.C.: Center for Adolescent Health and the Law, Adolescent and Young Adult Health.

Georgiades, S. (2005). A multi-outcome evaluation of an independent living program. *Child and Adolescent Social Work Journal* 22(5–6): 417–39.

Gollan, J. K., R. Lee, and E. F. Coccaro (2005). Developmental psychopathology and neurobiology of aggression. *Development and Psychopathology* 17: 1151–71.

Ito, Y., M. H. Teicher, C. A. Glod, E. M. Harper, E. Magnus, and H. A. Gelbard (1993). Increased prevalence of electrophysiological abnormalities in children with psychological, physical, and sexual abuse. *Journal of Neuropsychiatry and Clinical Neurosciences* 5(4): 401–8.

Ito, Y., M. H. Teicher, C. A. Glod, and E. Ackerman (1998). Preliminary evidence for aberrant cortical development in abused children: A quantitative EEG study. *Journal of Neuropsychiatry and Clinical Neuroscience* 10(3): 298–307.

Mallon, G. (1998). After care, then where? Outcomes of an independent living program. *Child Welfare* 77: 61–78.

McMillen, J. C., B. T. Zima, L. D. Scott, W. F. Auslander, M. R. Munson, M. T. Ollie, and E. L. Spitznagel (2005). Prevalence of psychiatric disorders among older youths in the foster care system. *Journal of the American Academy of Child and Adolescent Psychiatry* 44(1): 88–95.

Mech, E. V. (1994). Foster youths in transition: Research perspectives on preparation for independent living. *Child Welfare* 73(5): 603–23.

Montoya, P., and T. M. Westmooreland (2000). Letter to State Child Welfare and Medicaid Directors. At www.cms.hhs.gov/smdl/downloads/smd012100.pdf.

Newacheck, P., D. Hughes, and M. Cisternas (1995). Children and health insurance: An overview of recent trends. *Health Affairs* Spring: 244–54.

Perry, B. D., and R. Pollard (1998). Homeostasis, stress, trauma, and adaptation: A neurodevelopmental view of childhood trauma. *Child and Adolescent Psychiatric Clinics of North America* 7: 33–51.

Rosenbach, M. (2001). *Children in Foster Care: Challenges in Meeting Their Health Care Needs Through Medicaid.* Princeton, N.J.: Mathematica Policy Research.

Scannapieco, M., J. Schagrin, and T. Scannapieco (1995). Independent living programs: Do they make a difference? *Child and Adolescent Social Work Journal* 12: 381–89.

Umberson, D. (1992). Relationships between adult children and their parents: Psychological consequences for both generations. *Journal of Marriage and the Family* 54: 664–74.

U.S. Department of Health and Human Services, Administration for Children and Families (2006). *The AFCARS Report: Preliminary FY 2005 Estimates as of September 2006.* Washington, D.C.: Author.

Voices Issue Brief (2004). *Effective Approaches to Supporting Youth Aging out of Foster Care.* Washington, DC: Voices for America's Children. At www.vociesforamericaschildren.org.

Guardianship and
Youth Permanence

NINE

ROBERT B. HILL

Before the 1980s, only a small fraction of children in foster care were in the care of relatives (Hill, 1977). Between 1986 and 2000, however, the proportion of children in foster care living with kin rose from 18 percent to 25 percent (Barbell and Freundlich, 2001). One out of four of the 513,000 foster children in the nation in 2005 were cared for by relatives (U.S. Department of Health and Human Services, 2006). Several factors contributed to the surge in kinship care families. An early factor was the 1979 U.S. Supreme Court decree in *Miller v. Yoakim*, which declared that when kin caregivers of children in foster care meet the state's licensing standards, states must provide them with the same level of foster care stipends provided to non-kin foster parents (O'Laughlin, 1998). As a result of this court decision, the number of licensed relative caregivers in the child welfare systems increased in order to receive the higher foster care stipends rather than the lower payments provided by the Aid to Families with Dependent Children program that had been the only source of support available to them before the Court's decision. Other important factors contributing to the growth in kinship care were the onset of HIV/AIDS and crack cocaine during the 1980s, which disproportionately undermined the parenting capabilities of mothers and fathers in inner-city communities. Increasing numbers of relatives assumed responsibility for rearing children whose birth parents had succumbed to drug addiction or HIV/AIDS (Children's Bureau, 2000).

As growing numbers of kin have assumed responsibility for the temporary care of children in foster care, it has become increasingly important to develop options for kin to become permanent resources for children when they cannot return to their birth parents. Most kin caregivers are reluctant to formally adopt their dependent relatives because they do not want the rights of the birth parents to be terminated (Testa, 2004). As a result, child welfare practitioners and policymakers have turned their attention to guardianship as a permanency option for children in foster care in the care of kin. The Fostering Connections to Success and Increasing Adoptions Act of 2008, for the first time in federal policy, gives states the option to use federal funds for kinship guardianship payments for children cared for by relative foster parents who are committed to caring for their children permanently when they leave foster care. The assistance is available only for some children and relatives, and as a result, guardianship may not be a feasible alternative for all families. Since 1996, however, the federal government has permitted eleven states to institute Title IV-E waiver demonstrations to test the feasibility of providing federally funded guardianship subsidies to kin caregivers for children for whom parental reunification or adoption is not possible (Children's Bureau, 2005).

The interest of child welfare professionals and policymakers in developing other permanent family or "family-like" options for older youth in foster care rests on an understanding that youth should leave foster care with the support of caring committed adults and should not age out of foster care to live on their own (Generations United, 2006; Massinga and Pecora, 2004). Numerous studies have revealed that many youth who age out of foster care are at risk of unemployment, homelessness, single parenting, substance abuse, and involvement with the criminal justice system (Cook, 1991; Goerge et al., 2002; Jonson-Reid and Barth, 2003). Other permanency options are important because many older youth who cannot be reunified with their birth parents reject adoption. They may find adoption unacceptable because of their continuing attachment to their birth parents or because they believe that they are too old to be adopted or that no one would want to adopt a youth of their age (Courtney et al, 2001; Rashid, 2006). The various forms of guardianship that are being explored are designed to provide more permanent or stable living arrangements for youth who are likely to age out of foster care.

In this chapter, I review the research on kinship care in relation to well-being, permanency, and safety. I then examine efforts to make kin guardianship a viable permanency option for many children in foster care and to enhance permanency options for older foster care youth.

KINSHIP CARE

Kinship care, a term coined in the late 1980s as the number of relatives caring for children began to swell, refers to the full-time care, nurturing, and protection of children by relatives, stepparents, godparents, or any other adult—whether blood-related or not—who have a significant relationship with a child. There are two types of kinship care: informal and formal. Informal kinship care refers to situations in which relatives rear children outside the child welfare system with no involvement by the state or county. Formal kinship care describes situations in which the child welfare agency has legal custody of the child and places the child with a relative. Here I focus primarily on youth who are in formal kinship care arrangements and the policy and practice issues associated with relatives becoming permanent resources for them.

There has been much discussion about the quality of care provided to children in kinship care and whether it is inferior to the care offered children by nonkin caregivers (Chipman et al., 2002; Shlonsky and Berrick, 2001). Although many studies have underscored the advantages of kin families, they also have identified many disadvantages (Brown et al., 2002; Children's Bureau, 2000; Chipungu et al., 1998; Cuddeback, 2004; Ehrle et al., 2001; Scannapieco and Jackson, 1996). Here I briefly review research findings that compare kin and nonkin families with respect to key child welfare outcomes: well-being, permanency, and safety. The frequent conflicting findings in these studies are attributable to differences in research design, sampling procedures, geographical location, reliance on administrative records or surveys, and use of cross-sectional or longitudinal data.

Well-Being

Studies regarding the well-being of children in care of kin and nonkin have identified characteristics of both types of families that may affect outcomes for children, the types and levels of services that these families receive, and the characteristics of children who are in the care of kin and nonkin.

Most studies suggest that kin caregivers are more likely than nonkin caregivers to have characteristics that impair their parenting capabilities. Kin caregivers are more likely to be older, single, less educated, and with lower incomes (Altshuler, 1998; Geen, 2003; Grogan-Kaylor, 2000). About one-half of all children in kinship care live with caregivers who are over fifty years old, while children in nonkin families are more likely to live with markedly younger caregivers. Kin are more likely to be in or near poverty, and, as a result, they are more likely than nonkin families to receive benefits for low-income families, such as child-only benefits through the Temporary Assistance for Needy Families (TANF) program, food stamps, free and reduced lunch, Medicaid, Supplemental Security Income (SSI), and public housing (Ehrle and Geen, 2002; Ehrle, Geen and Clark, 2001).[1]

Although nonkin foster parents receive Title IV-E foster care stipends, most kin caregivers, because they are not licensed by the state as foster parents, must rely on the lower TANF benefits (Berrick and Needell, 1999; Leos-Urbel et al., 2002). Urban Institute researchers found that only 12 percent of all public kinship caregivers received foster care payments in 2002, fewer than one-half (45 percent) received TANF payments, 10 percent received Social Security or SSI, and about one-third received no payments at all (Murray et al., 2004).

Research findings are conflicting regarding the employment and health status of kin caregivers. Some studies have found that kin caregivers are more likely to be unemployed or in poorer health than nonkin caregivers, while other research has found no differences (Courtney et al., 2001; Dubowitz et al., 1993; Goerge et al., 2002; Rashid, 2006).

Almost all studies reveal that kin families receive fewer services than nonkin families. Kin families are less likely than nonkin families to receive housing assistance, financial assistance, legal assistance, mental and physical health services, child care, respite care, and support groups (Chipungu et al., 1998; Dubowiz et al., 1993; Freundlich et al., 2003; Geen and Berrick, 2002; Thornton, 1991). Many studies have revealed that kin families are less likely than nonkin families to have frequent contacts with caseworkers, have fewer home visits by caseworkers, and receive less case monitoring (Children's Bureau, 2000; Iglehart, 1994; Peters, 2005). The reasons for this disparity are not clear but may include the lack of motivation of kin caregivers to learn about the availability of services; the refusal of kin caregivers to seek or apply for services; caseworkers' failure to inform kin caregivers about services; or caseworkers' beliefs that kin families are safer than nonkin families and, thus, require fewer contacts from caseworkers and fewer services (Beeman and Boisen, 1999; Gleeson and O'Donnell, 1997).

Research findings about the well-being of children in kin families are mixed. A number of studies have identified positive outcomes for children who are placed with kin. Several studies suggest that children placed in kin families adjust more easily to separation from their birth parents than children placed with nonkin because they have the benefits of continuity of family connections; the sharing of family history and culture; and reduced feelings of self-blame, grief, loss, and stigma (Brown et al., 2002; Cuddeback, 2004; Gebel, 1996; Scannapieco et al., 1997; Shlonsky and Berrick, 2001). Other studies have found that children reared by kin have fewer physical and mental health problems than children reared by nonkin (Benedict et al., 1996; Berrick et al., 1994; Iglehart, 1994). Children in kin care have been found to be less likely than nonkin children to run away, skip school, repeat a grade in school, need special education, or engage in delinquent activities (Children's Bureau, 2000; Keller et al., 2001; Leslie et al., 2000). Other researchers have found that children in kinship care have higher scores on measures of communication skills and lower internalizing, externalizing, and total scores on Child Behavior Checklist 4–18 than children with nonkin (Wulcyzn et al., 2005). One study found that youth in kin care have lower levels of hypertension than youth in nonkin care (Scannapieco, 1999).

In contrast, several studies have found that children in kin families have more behavioral and health problems than children in nonkin families (Berrick et al., 1994; Dubowitz et al., 1993; Zuravin et al., 1993). A study by the U. S. General Accounting Office (1995) found that children in kin families had more health problems as a result of prenatal drug exposure than children in nonkin families. Yet other studies have found no differences between children in kin families and nonkin families with respect to their physical health (including vision, hearing, dental status, obesity, and drug exposure) or emotional well-being (Brooks and Barth, 1998; Dubowitz et al., 1993; Iglehart, 1994; Leslie et al., 2000).

Permanence

Studies consistently reveal that children in kin care have fewer placement moves while in foster care than children in nonkin care (James et al., 2004; Needell, 1996; Wulcyzn and Goerge, 1992; Wulcyzn et al., 2005). A study in California found that children from birth to age five who were placed with nonkin (35 percent) were twice as likely than children placed with kin (18 percent) to have lived in three or more different homes four years later (Berrick et al., 1998). A recent Chapin Hall study of placement moves for children in foster care in Illinois between 1990 and 2004 found the greatest placement stability among children who had been placed with kin at time of entry to foster care; interestingly, this study also found that children with older foster parents (fifty to fifty-nine years old) had fewer placement moves than children with younger foster parents (Zinn et al., 2006). Another study created an index of child stability that was comprised of three measures: different household moves by the child, different school moves by the child, and length of time that the caregiver expected to care for the child. The researchers found that children in kin families had significantly fewer household or school moves than children in nonkin families, and that relative caregivers expected to rear their children for much longer periods of time than the nonrelative caregivers (Westat, 2003).

Studies also suggest that children placed with kin are more likely to maintain connections with their birth families. A study by Nicole LeProhn (1994) found that children placed with kin were more likely than children placed with nonkin to see their birth mothers, fathers, and siblings. A California-based study also found that contact with birth parents was more regularly maintained in kin than nonkin families (Berrick et al., 1994).

Earlier research showed that children in kinship care were more likely than children placed with nonkin to remain in foster care for longer periods of time (Chipungu et al., 1998). These longer stays in care may occur because parents are less intent on regaining custody of their children when they are comfortable with the kinship arrangement, or they may be related to caseworkers' spending less time in permanency planning for children placed with kin families because they believe that they are already with their families (Chipman et al., 2002). More recent research suggests that children placed in kinship care are not remaining in foster care for longer periods of time. Mark Testa (2005) found that in the early 1990s in Illinois, children in kinship care families were 43 percent less likely than children with nonkin families to be adopted or to obtain private guardianship; by 1997, children in kin families were 57 percent more likely to achieve such permanency outcomes than children in nonkin families.

Many studies, however, continue to find that children placed with kin are less likely than children placed in nonkin families to achieve reunification with their birth parents (Courtney, 1994; Freundlich et al., 2003;

Goerge, 1990; Grogan-Kaylor, 2001; Testa, 2005). An Illinois study using multivariate regression models found parental reunification to be strongly related to five predictors: race, age at entry, caregiver job skills, substance abuse problems, and receipt of services (Hill, 2005). These findings suggest that white children who enter foster care under the age of three and who are placed with caregivers who have job skills, do not have substance abuse problems, and receive social services have much higher rates of reunification. Although kinship status was negatively correlated with reunification in a bivariate relationship, it was not significantly related to reunification in combination with these other five predictors. Another study found that children placed with kin were considerably less likely to be reunified during the first year of placement, but the rates of reunification were similar for children in kin and nonkin settings after one year (Courtney, 1994).

Children living with kin are less likely than children living with non-kin to be adopted, an outcome that has been associated with caregivers' concerns related to terminating the rights of the children's birth parents (Gleeson, 1999) and the fact that kin caregivers are less likely to accept unsubsidized guardianship (Testa, 2004).

Evaluations of Title IV-E waiver demonstrations on subsidized guardianship in several states, however, have revealed that offering guardianship subsidies to kin caregivers who do not wish to consider adoption is likely to markedly increase the number of guardianships for children in foster care (Testa, 2005).

Unfortunately, there has been a dearth of studies on the effects of foster care payments on permanency outcomes for children in kin and nonkin families (Courtney, 1994; Gibbs et al., 2006; Needell, 1996). In one of the few analyses of these issues, Jill Berrick and Barbara Needell (1999) systematically tracked a cohort of children entering foster care in California for the first time during the years 1989–1991 who were placed with kin and non-kin. The kinship care families who received the higher foster care stipends had lower rates of reunification (49 percent) than kin families who received the lower AFDC payments (62 percent) and nonkin families receiving the foster care payments (58 percent). Similarly, children in kin families who received the foster care stipends (2 percent) were only somewhat less likely to be adopted than were children in kin families that received AFDC payments (4 percent) but much less likely to be adopted than were children in nonkin families (11 percent). In contrast, regardless of payment levels, children placed with kin (6 percent) were more likely to exit to guardianship than were children placed with nonkin (1 percent). Overall, these findings indicate that children in kinship care families who receive lower AFDC payments have higher rates of reunification and adoption than children in kin and nonkin families receiving the higher foster care stipends. The researchers concluded that higher payment levels may be a disincentive to reunification and adoption. They hypothesized that when families receive higher foster care stipends, they may prolong the child's stay in foster care in order to maximize their income and that families receiving lower AFDC payments have less of a financial incentive to prolong the child's stay in care (Berrick and Needell, 1999).

Safety

Most studies suggest that children placed with kin families are safer than children placed with nonkin families (Children's Bureau, 2000; Testa, 2004). In a five-year study that compared kin and nonkin caregivers with and without substantiated maltreatment reports, Susan Zuravin and colleagues (1993) found that nonkin foster parents were twice as likely to have a confirmed maltreatment report than kin foster parents. Another study found that kin caregivers provided safer home environments than biological parents (Meyer and Link, 1990). These findings must be interpreted with caution, however. Caseworkers may use more lenient standards regarding safety issues with kin than nonkin families. Alternatively, the level of supervision and monitoring of kinship care homes may be less than that provided for nonkin homes (Gebel, 1996; Shlonsky and Berrick, 2001).

A major indicator of children's safety after their exits from foster care is the extent to which children reenter the child welfare system as a result of abuse and neglect. Many researchers have found that children in kinship care are no more or less likely than children in nonkin care to reenter foster care (Courtney, 1995; Wulcyzn et al., 2005). Other studies have found that children who exit to kinship families are less likely than children placed with nonkin families to reenter foster care (Children's Bureau, 2000). Findings based on a cohort of children exiting foster care in the last half of 1989 in California revealed that children placed with kin and subsequently reunified were less likely than children placed with nonkin to reenter foster care (Courtney, 1995). Moreover, when analyzing the net permanence rate (the children who exited foster care to be placed with a family minus those who later reentered care), Needell and colleagues

(1997) found that kin and nonkin homes were essentially equivalent. Although early reunification and adoption rates appear to be greater for children in nonkin care, rates of reentry are lower for children placed with kin (Berrick and Needell, 1999).

SUBSIDIZED GUARDIANSHIP POLICIES

The Title IV-E waiver demonstrations were the most comprehensive initiative to test the feasibility of providing federal funds to assist guardians, most of whom are relatives, to provide permanence for children in foster care. Of the eleven states that have implemented subsidized guardianship waiver demonstrations since 1996, eight states were in the initial phase of the demonstration from 1997 through 2002, and three states were later granted waivers. When the federal government ended the Title IV-E waivers as of March 31, 2006 (Children's Bureau, 2005; Leos-Urbel et al., 2002), there were concerns that many states would lack opportunities to offer subsidized guardianships as a permanency option for thousands of waiting children. However, the Fostering Connections to Success Act gives states the option to use federal funds for kinship guardianship payments for children cared for by relative foster parents who are committed to becoming their guardians.

Although all subsidized guardianship demonstrations were similar in providing financial support for guardians who assumed permanent responsibility for children in foster care, there was some variation in the amount of the subsidies. For example, Illinois provided a guardianship subsidy that equaled the foster care stipend, while most other states provided guardianship subsidies at a level lower than the foster care payments or close to the AFDC/TANF levels. The Fostering Connections to Success Act provides that guardianship subsidies equal the foster care stipend for licensed caregivers.

All states in these demonstrations were required to conduct process and outcome evaluations, as well as a cost analysis. There were wide differences, however, among the states regarding research design, sample sizes, and procedures for assigning cases. Four of the states—Illinois, Maryland, Montana, and New Mexico—used random assignment designs that included experimental treatment and control groups. North Carolina and Oregon conducted a descriptive analysis of their subsidized guardianship programs and examined child welfare outcomes at an aggregate, county-wide level. New Mexico used a comparison group for the small Tribal component of its program, and Delaware relied on a pretest and posttest model to examine differences in outcomes before and after implementation of the waiver (Children's Bureau, 2005).

Illinois was the only state to provide rigorous evidence that subsidized guardianship improves permanency outcomes for children (Children's Bureau, 2005). Its evaluation yielded strong, statistically significant findings that subsidized guardianship increased net permanence (i.e., discharges to reunification, adoption, or guardianship). Moreover, the Illinois evaluation revealed that subsidized guardianship was able to increase overall permanence without lowering the rates of adoption. Results from Illinois suggested that children placed with guardians were at least as safe from repeat maltreatment as children in other permanency settings (Testa, 2004). These findings provided a major impetus for subsidized guardianship recommendations by the Pew Commission on Children in Foster Care (Fostering Results, 2004) and the enactment of the kinship guardianship assistance provisions of the Fostering Connection to Success Act.

A very promising approach to enhance youth permanence is the five-year extension of the original Title IV-E subsidized guardianship waiver in Illinois. Because older youth were found to have the lowest rates of permanence in its demonstration, Illinois focused its second-phase waiver demonstration on enhancing permanence, safety, and well-being outcomes for youth fourteen years and older. The demonstration recognized that a major barrier to obtaining permanence for older youth in foster care was that many of the benefits related to work training, college scholarships, and health benefits are available only to young people with a goal of independent living. In order to provide incentives to achieve permanence for older youth, the new demonstration permits youth to receive these enhanced benefits when they are adopted or are in subsidized guardianship arrangements. Because this new waiver employs randomly assigned treatment and control groups, it will be a rigorous test of the extent to these programmatic changes increase permanency rates for older youth.

An additional thirty-five states, which did not implement Title IV-E demonstrations, have used state funds to provide a wide range of assistance and support to kin guardians, both within and outside the child welfare system. The Kin-Gap program, for example, was implemented in California in 2000 with funds from its TANF grants. It provides kin families with supports and services, including episodic financial assistance, but does not provide kin caregivers with a subsidy beyond the child's TANF grant. Between 1999 and 2003, under this assisted—but unsubsidized—guardianship program, the number of children in formal kinship care for more than twelve months decreased by 65 percent (Generations United, 2006). In 2006, the District of Columbia implemented a pilot unsubsidized guardianship program to provide financial support to low-income grandparents who were caring for their kin children in formal kinship care. Other states that provide unsubsidized financial and social support to both formal and informal kin caregivers include Georgia, Ohio, and Texas. Unfortunately, there are no systematic evaluations of these unsubsidized but financially assisted guardianship programs.

OLDER YOUTH IN FOSTER CARE

Each year, between 18,500 and 25,000 teenagers "age out" of foster care as a result of reaching the age of majority, usually eighteen. In a few states, youth can voluntarily remain in care until the age of twenty-one years, if they are enrolled in some form of postsecondary education (Shirk and Stangler, 2004). Older youth in foster care experience greater placement instability than younger children. Andrew Zinn and colleagues (2006), for example, found that although infants experienced more placement changes than youth between fifteen and seventeen years old during the first month in care, by the end of the first year, adolescents had 75 percent more placement changes than infants. Moreover, older youth are at greater risk than younger children of behavioral and emotional problems (Landsverk and Garland, 1999; Wulcyzn et al., 2005). These behavioral and emotional issues may intensify as youth approach the age at which they will transition from foster care to adulthood. Youth have concerns about establishing viable relationships or connections with their birth parents, extended family members, or significant others (Barth, 1990; Curran and Pecora,1999; Ford and Kroll, 2005).

Achieving permanence for youth must also take into account the disproportionate representation of youth of color, and particularly, Black youth. Disproportionality is manifested in two ways: overrepresentation and disparities. Overrepresentation refers to situations in which the proportion of children in foster care exceeds their proportion in the general census population. Disparities, in contrast, applies to situations in which members of certain groups (usually minorities) receive differential adverse treatment than members of other groups (usually Whites). Blacks are overrepresented in the child welfare system: they are about 2.4 times more likely to be in foster care than in the nation's census population. Whites are underrepresented in the child welfare system: they are less (only 0.76 times) likely to be in foster care than in the census population. Blacks have high racial disparities when compared with Whites: they are three times more likely to be in foster care than White children (Hill, 2006).

Disproportionality in child welfare is strongly related to three factors: race, age at entry, and duration in care. Black children are consistently more overrepresented in child welfare at various stages of child protective services decision-making than White children. Infants and adolescents have the highest placement rates into foster care. An analysis of disproportionality in the State of Tennessee revealed that the age groups with the highest placement rates in foster care were infants (under the age of one) and adolescents between the ages of thirteen and seventeen years old. When age and race were considered together, Black infants had placement rates of 11.6 per 1,000 compared with 8.5 for White infants. Black adolescents had placement rates of 5.4 per 1,000 compared with 3.9 for White teens (Wulczyn et al., 2006).

Children who enter foster care at younger ages are more likely to remain in care longer than children who enter foster care when they are adolescents (Wulczyn et al., 2005), and Black children are more likely to remain in care for longer periods of time than Whites (Hill, 2006). Younger children, because they are more likely to be adopted, tend to have longer placements. Older children, because they are more likely to be reunified, have shorter placements, in general. Older Black youth, however, have longer stays in foster care than older White youth. In addition, because Black children are more likely than White children to enter foster care when young, they are more likely to remain in foster care for longer periods of time and, consequently, are more likely to be overrepresented in the foster care system than White children (Hill, 2006).

In addition to the key factors of race, age at entry, and duration in care, studies also have examined family structure in relation to disproportionality. The Tennessee study (Wulczyn et al., 2006) found that family structure may explain, in part, the overrepresentation of Black children in foster care. Urban areas in Tennessee with limited resources (that is, lower human or social capital) and higher proportions of female-headed families were found to have lower disparities in foster care placement rates between Black and White children, although placement rates for Black children were higher than for White children. The researchers concluded that Black families may be treated differently than White families as a result of their single-parent structures rather than because of race (Wulczyn et al., 2006).

It is also important to note that older Black youth are overrepresented in kinship care families. Federal 2003 data, for example, show that among youth twelve to eighteen years old, 23 percent of Black children were in kin families, compared with only 14 percent of White children (Hill, 2006). This overrepresentation in kin families is important for developing permanency strategies for older minority youth.

IMPLICATIONS FOR RESEARCH, PRACTICE, AND POLICY

Research

Because older youth are overrepresented in kinship care families, more rigorous research is needed on the advantages and disadvantages of rearing older children and youth in kin families. More longitudinal studies, with randomly selected samples, are needed to track the trajectory of adolescents from entry to discharge and after leaving the foster care system. More studies should compare child welfare outcomes (well-being, permanency, and safety) for youth in various settings, such as kin families, nonkin families, and congregate care. These studies must not only rely on administrative records but also incorporate survey data from interviews with the youth, foster parents, birth parents, and caseworkers. Since older youth are more likely to be African American and Latino, these studies must be more sensitive to the diverse cultural patterns (values, languages, nationalities, and parenting styles) of children and families of color. There is also a need for more studies of the protective factors that are correlated with successful experiences of youth while in care and after leaving foster care. Finally, the mixed findings of the many studies examined in this chapter suggest an urgent need for more systematic research designs to enhance understanding of the complex relationships between guardianship and youth permanence. There is a need for more rigorous evaluations of the extent to which subsidized guardianships (whether funded by federal or state governments) promote positive outcomes for adolescents in foster care.

Practice

To improve practice in achieving permanence for youth, several steps need to be taken:

- Concurrent planning should be implemented at the time that the child enters foster care.
- Youth need to be fully involved in futures planning and decision-making.
- Youth must maintain frequent contacts with birth parents while youth are still in care.
- Child welfare agencies must identify maternal and paternal extended family resources early in the youth's stay in foster care.
- Youth must be assisted in developing family connections with nonrelated significant adults.
- The educational, life, and work skills of youth must be enhanced.
- Culturally competent strategies that are responsive to the racial and ethnic diversity of youth of color must be employed.
- More postpermanency support must be provided to youth and their families after youth leave foster care.

Policies

Additional federal and state funding is needed to expedite permanency efforts for youth who are at risk of aging out of foster care. With the newly enacted changes in federal policy regarding Title IV-E funded kinship guardianship assistance, attention must be given to the impact of these resources on expediting the attainment of permanence for youth in foster care through guardianship. In addition to the new federal dollars for kinship navigator programs, federal and state funds should be devoted to providing a wide range of assistance and support to birth parents and informal kin caregivers in order to prevent the unnecessary entry of thousands of children and youth into the child welfare system. In sum, more family-oriented public policies are needed to enhance permanence for older youth in foster care, including through federal and state subsidized guardianships and other family connections, and to produce healthy, resilient and productive citizens in our society.

CONCLUSION

Subsidized guardianship is an alternative permanency option for older youth in foster care. The surge in kin caregivers during the 1980s spurred much discussion about the viability of providing subsidies to relatives who were not interested in adoption but who wanted to be guardians to their kin children. The sharp increase in the number of kin caregivers resulted from several factors: court decisions, which mandated that stipends for kin caregivers equal those for nonkin caregivers, and the simultaneous onset of HIV/AIDs and crack cocaine that disproportionately destabilized families of color, especially in inner-city communities. A debate regarding the advantages and disadvantages of kin families ensued. On the one hand, many studies documented numerous advantages of kinship care families: maintenance of family ties, along with continuity of family history and culture; periodic contact with birth parents and siblings; the lack of trauma or feelings of isolation or stigma among children who were placed with extended family members; and, most of all, the greater stability of placements of children living with kin than among children living with nonkin. On the other hand, many studies identified disadvantages of kinship care families: the older age and lower incomes of many kin caregivers; their receipt of fewer child welfare services than nonkin caregivers; and the higher levels of behavioral and health problems among children in kin families when compared with children in nonkin families.

Most of the five-year Title IV-E waiver demonstrations documented that providing subsidies to kin guardians was a cost-effective strategy for increasing permanency options for thousands of waiting children in foster care. The evaluations of these demonstrations revealed that subsidized guardianship increased permanency outcomes for many youth—without reducing the number of children achieving permanence through adoption or reunification. These evaluations, however, also revealed that more intensive permanency planning efforts were needed to increase the number of older youth achieving permanence through subsidized guardianship.

Older minority youth in foster care continue to experience special barriers: higher placement rates, lower rates of reunification, longer durations in care, and racial disparities in services. Black children are more than twice as likely to be placed in foster care than they are in the general census population, and they are three times more likely than White children to be removed from their families and placed in foster care. Alternatively, Black children are more likely than White children to reside in kinship care families. These placements provide opportunities for many agencies to develop closer connections with extended family members for youth before and after they leave foster care.

In this chapter, I advocate for research, practice, and policy on several fronts:

- More rigorous research on the advantages and disadvantages of raising older youth of any race in kin families
- More systematic evaluations of the innovative unsubsidized financial and social support programs for formal and informal kinship care families in many states
- More culturally competent concurrent planning to make every effort to place children with kin at entry and to develop family connections before youth exit or age out of foster care
- Full implementation of the provisions of the Fostering Connections to Success and Increasing Adoptions Act of 2008 regarding state option to use federal Title IV-E funds for kinship guardianship payments for certain children in foster care and their relative caregivers.

NOTE

1. The child-only Temporary Assistance for Needy Families (TANF) refers to the federal-state welfare program that provides financial support to children who are in the care of relatives and not their biological parents. TANF was created in 1996 and succeeded the Aid to Families with Dependent Children (AFDC) program that had been instituted in the 1930s. Supplemental Security Income (SSI) refers to a federal program that provides financial aid to low-income children and adults with physical or mental disabilities.

REFERENCES

Altshuler, S. (1998). Child well-being in kinship foster care. *Children and Youth Services Review* 20(5): 369–88.

Barbell, K., and M. Freundlich (2001). *Foster Care Today*. Washington, D.C.: Casey Family Programs.

Barth, R. (1990). On their own: The experiences of youth after foster care. *Child and Adolescent Social Work* 7(5): 419–40.

Beeman, S., and L. Boisen (1999). Child welfare professionals' attitudes toward kinship foster care. *Child Welfare* 78(3): 315–37.

Benedict, M., S. Zuravin, and R. Stallings (1996). Adult functioning of children who lived in kin versus nonkin family foster home. *Child Welfare* 75(5): 529–49.

Berrick, J., and B. Needell (1999). Recent trends in kinship care: Public policy, payments and outcomes for children. In P. Curtis, G. Dale, and J. Kendall, eds., *The Foster Care Crisis* (pp. 152–74). Lincoln: University of Nebraska Press.

Berrick, J., R. Barth, and B. Needell (1994). A comparison of kinship foster homes and foster family homes. *Children and Youth Services Review* 16(1–2): 33–64.

Berrick, J., B. Needell, R. Barth, and M. Jonson-Reid (1998). *The Tender Years*. New York: Oxford University Press.

Brooks, D., and R. Barth (1998). Characteristics and outcomes of drug-exposed and non-drug-exposed children in kinship and nonrelative foster care. *Children and Youth Services Review* 20(6): 475–501.

Brown, S., D. Cohon, and R. Wheeler (2002). African American extended families and kinship care: How relevant is the foster care model for kinship care? *Children and Youth Services Review* 24(1–2): 53–77.

Children's Bureau (2000). *Report to the Congress on Kinship Foster Care. Part 1: Research Review*. Washington, D.C.: U.S. Department of Health and Human Services.

—— (2005). *Synthesis of Findings: Assisted Guardianship Child Welfare Waiver Demonstrations*. Washington, D.C.: U.S. Department of Health and Human Services.

Chipman, R., S. Wells, and M. Johnson (2002). The meaning of quality in kinship foster care. *Families in Society* 83(5–6): 508–20.

Chipungu, S., J. Everett, J. Verdick, and J. Jones (1998). *Children Placed in Foster Care with Relatives*. Washington, D.C.: Administration for Children and Families.

Cook, R. (1991). *A National Evaluation of Title IV-E Foster Care Independent Living Programs for Youth: Phase 2 Final Report*. Rockville, Md.: Westat.

Courtney, M. (1994). Factors associated with the reunification of foster children with their families. *Social Service Review* 68(1): 81–108.

—— (1995). Reentry to foster care of children returned to their families. *Social Service Review* 69(2): 226–41.

Courtney, M., I. Piliavin, A. Grogan-Kaylor, and A. Nesmith (2001). Foster youth transitions to adulthood. *Child Welfare* 80(6): 685–717.

Cuddeback, G. (2004). Kinship family foster care: A methodological and substantive synthesis of research. *Children and Youth Services Review* 26(7): 625–39.

Curran, M., and P. Pecora (1999). Incorporating the perspectives of youth placed in family foster care. In P. Curtis, G. Dale, and J. Kendall, eds., *The Foster Care Crisis* (pp. 99–125). Lincoln: University of Nebraska Press.

Dubowitz, H., S. Feigelman, and S. Zuravin (1993). A profile of kinship care. *Child Welfare* 72(2): 153–69.

Ehrle, J., and R. Geen (2002). Kin and non-kin foster care: Findings from a national survey. *Children and Youth Services Review* 24(1–2): 15–35.

Ehrle, J., R. Geen, and R. Clark (2001). *Children Cared For by Relatives.* New Federalism Report, Series B-28. Washington, D.C.: Urban Institute.

Ford, M., and J. Kroll (2005). *A Family for Every Child: Strategies to Achieve Permanence for Older Foster Children and Youth.* Baltimore: North American Council on Adoptable Children and Annie E. Casey Foundation. At http://www.aecf.org /KnowledgeCenter/Publications.aspx?pubguid=%7B104C33ED-5D53-458B-B6AA-C4B645BD273B%7D (accessed 27 July 2008).

Fostering Results (2004). *Family Ties: Supporting Permanence for Children in Safe and Stable Foster Care with Relatives and Other Caregivers.* Champaign: University of Illinois–Champaign/Urbana.

Freundlich, M., L. Morris, and C. Hernandez. (2003). *Kinship Care: Meeting the Needs of Children and Families of Color.* Rockville, Md.: Race Matters Consortium.

Gebel, T. (1996). Kinship care and nonrelative family foster care. *Child Welfare* 75(11): 5–18.

Geen, R., ed. (2003). *Kinship Care.* Washington, D.C.: Urban Institute.

Geen, R., and J. Berrick (2002). Kinship care: An evolving service delivery option. *Children and Youth Services Review* 24(1–2): 1–14.

Generations United (2006). *All Children Deserve a Permanent Home.* Washington, D.C.: Author.

Gibbs, D., J. Kasten, A. Bir, D. Duncan, and S. Hoover (2006). Between two systems: Children in TANF child-only cases with relative caregivers. *Children and Youth Services Review* 28(6): 435–46.

Gleeson, J. (1999). Kinship care as a child welfare service. In J. Gleeson and C. Hairston, eds., *Knship Care* (pp. 3–34). Washington, D.C.: Child Welfare League of America.

Gleeson, J., and J. O'Donnell (1997). Understanding the complexity of practice in kinship foster care. *Child Welfare* 76(6): 801–25.

Goerge, R. (1990). The reunification process in substitute care. *Social Service Review* 64(3): 422–57.

Goerge, R., L. Bilaver, B. Lee, B. Needell, A. Brookhart, and W. Jackman (2002). *Employment Outcomes for Youth Aging Out of Foster Care.* Chicago: Chapin Hall Center for Children at the University of Chicago.

Grogan-Kaylor, A. (2000). Who goes into kinship care? The relationship of child and family characteristics to placement into kinship foster care. *Social Work Research* 24(3): 132–41.

—— (2001). The effect of initial placement into kinship foster care on reunification from foster care. *Journal of Social Services Research* 27: 1–31.

Hill, R. B. (1977). *Informal Adoption Among Black Families.* Washington, D.C.: National Urban League Research Department.

—— (2005). The role of race in parental reunification. In D. Derezotes, J. Poertner, and F. Testa, eds., *Race Matters in Child Welfare* (pp. 215–30). Washington, D.C.: Child Welfare League of America.

—— (2006). *Synthesis of Research on Disproportionality in Child Welfare: An Update*. Seattle: Casey Center for Study of Social Policy Alliance for Racial Equity in the Child Welfare System. At www.caseyfamilyservices.org/pdfs/0226_CC_BobHillPaper_FINAL. pdf (accessed July 27, 2008).

Iglehart, A. (1994). Kinship foster care: Placement, services and outcome issues. *Children and Youth Services Review* 16(1–2): 107–22.

James, S., J. Landsverk, and D. Slymen (2004). Placement movement in out-of-home care. *Children and Youth Service Review* 26(6): 424–40.

Jonson-Reid, M., and R. Barth (2003). Probation foster care as an outcome for children exiting child welfare foster care. *Social Work* 48(3): 348–61.

Keller, T., K. Wetherbee, N. LeProhn, V. Payne, K. Sim, and E. Lamont (2001). Competencies and problem behaviors of children in family foster care. *Children and Youth Services Review* 23(12): 915–40.

Landsverk, J., and A. Garland (1999). Foster care and pathways to mental health services. In P. Curtis, G. Dale, and J. Kendall, eds., *The Foster Care Crisis* (pp. 193–210). Lincoln: University of Nebraska Press.

Leos-Urbel, J., R. Bess, and R. Geen (2002). The evolution of federal and state policies for assessing and supporting kinship caregivers. *Children and Youth Services Review* 24(1–2): 37–52.

LeProhn, N. (1994). The role of kinship foster parents. *Children and Youth Services Review* 16(1–2): 65–84.

Leslie, L. J. Landsverk, M. Horton, W. Ganger, and R. Newton (2000). The heterogeneity of children and their experiences in kinship care. *Child Welfare* 79(3): 315–34.

Massinga, R., and P. Pecora (2004). Providing better opportunities for older children in the child welfare system. *Future of Children* 14(1): 151–73.

Meyer, B., and M. Link (1990). *Kinship Foster Care*. Rochester, N.Y.: Task Force on Permanency Planning for Foster Children.

Murray, J., J. Macomber, and R. Geen (2004). *Estimating Financial Support for Kinship Caregivers*. New Federalism Brief, Series B-63. Washington, D.C.: Urban Institute.

Needell, B. (1996). Placement stability and permanence for children entering foster care as infants. Ph.D. diss., University of California at Berkeley.

Needell, B., D. Webster, R. Barth, M. Armijo, and A. Fox (1997). *Performance Indicators for Child Welfare Services in California: 1996*. Berkeley: University of California at Berkeley.

O'Laughlin, M. (1998). A theory of relativity: Kinship foster care may be the key to stopping the pendulum of termination v. reunification. *Vanderbilt Law Review* 51: 1427–48.

Peters, J. (2005). True ambivalence: Child welfare workers' thoughts, feelings and beliefs about kinship foster care. *Children and Youth Services Review* 27: 595–614.

Rashid, S. (2006). Employment experiences of homeless young adults. *Children and Youth Services Review* 28(3): 235–59.

Scannapieco, M. (1999). Kinship care in the public child welfare system. In R. Hegar and M. Scannapieco, eds., *Kinship Foster Care* (pp. 17–27). New York: Oxford University Press.

Scannapieco, M., and S. Jackson (1996). Kinship care: The African American response to family preservation. *Social Work* 41(2): 190–96.

Scannapieco, M., R. Hegar, and C. McAlpine (1997). Kinship care and foster care: A comparison of characteristics and outcomes. *Families in Society* 78(5): 480–88.

Shirk, M., and G. Stangler (2004). *On Their Own: What Happens to Kids When They Age Out of the Foster Care System.* Boulder, Colo.: Westview.

Shlonsky, A., and J. Berrick (2001). Assessing and promoting quality in kin and nonkin foster care. *Social Service Review* 75(1): 60–83.

Testa, M. (2004). When children cannot return home: Adoption and guardianship. *Future of Children* 14(1): 115–29.

—— (2005). The changing significance of race and kinship for achieving permanence for foster children. In D. Derezotes, J. Poertner, and M. F. Testa, eds., *Race Matters in Child Welfare: The Overrepresentation of African American Children in the System* (pp. 231–41). Washington, D.C.: Child Welfare League of America.

Thornton, J. (1991). Permanency planning for children in kinship foster homes. *Child Welfare* 70(5): 593–601.

U.S. Department of Health and Human Services, Administration for Children and Families (2005). *The AFCARS Report No. 10.* Washington, D.C.: Author.

U.S. General Accounting Office (1995). *Foster Care: Health Needs of Many Young Children Are Unknown and Unmet.* GAO/HEHS-95-114.Washington, D.C.: Author.

Westat (2003). *Evaluation of the Illinois Subsidized Guardianship Waiver Demonstration: Final Report.* Rockville, Md.: Author.

Wulczyn, F., and R. Goerge (1992). Foster care in New York and Illinois. *Social Service Review* 66(2): 278–94.

Wulczyn, F., R. Barth, Y. Yuan, B. Harden, and J. Landsverk (2005). *Beyond Common Sense: Child Welfare, Child Well-Being and the Evidence for Policy Reform.* New Brunswick, N.J.: Aldine Transaction.

Wulczyn, F., B. Lery, and J. Haight (2006). *Entry and Exit Disparities in the Tennessee Foster Care System.* Chicago: Chapin Hall Center for Children at the University of Chicago.

Zinn, A., J. DeCoursey, R. Goerge, and M. Courtney (2006). *A Study of Placement Stability in Illinois.* Chicago: Chapin Hall Center for Children at the University of Chicago.

Zuravin, S., M. Benedict, and M. Somerfield (1993). Child maltreatment in family foster care. *American Journal of Orthopsychiatry* 63(4): 589–96.

A Fine Balancing Act | **TEN**

Kinship Care, Subsidized
Guardianship, and Outcomes

ARON SHLONSKY

Like most helping professions, child welfare struggles with how to minimize harm while taking necessary action. In chapter 9, Robert Hill addresses one of the core and ongoing challenges faced by child welfare professionals: how to safely and effectively provide natural supports in the care of maltreated children. For many of the reasons highlighted by Hill, kinship care has emerged as a key strategy for responding to child maltreatment while helping children maintain important lifelong relationships with their birth families. In general, the field has recognized that families have strengths that can be called on in cases of abuse and neglect, and that good practice dictates that agencies do so. Hill's chapter covers much of the literature to date on kinship care, and in this chapter, I build on his work by providing more detail about the evaluations of subsidized guardianship for relative caregivers and exploring broader policy questions related to this permanency option.

EVALUATIONS OF SUBSIDIZED LEGAL GUARDIANSHIP

In all likelihood, the U.S. child welfare system would be hard-pressed to carry out its mandate without the widespread use of kin as placement resources. As Hill states, the number of children in foster care increased rapidly in the 1980s and 1990s, and much of this increase was accommodated by kinship caregivers. Since then, however, the number of children in care has decreased substantially. Between 1999 and 2005, the number of children in foster care declined from 570,000 to 513,000 (U.S. Department of Health and Human Services, 2006), representing about a 10 percent decrease. This decrease was at least partially driven by the extensive use of subsidized legal guardianship in several states, particularly California and Illinois. In California alone, more than sixteen thousand children living in long-term foster care with their relative caregivers have exited the foster care system into legally permanent homes through the Kinship Guardianship Assistance Payment (Kin-GAP) Program since January 1, 2000 (Shlonsky et al., 2008). Because kinship care is associated with longer stays in out-of-home placement (Goerge et al., 1995; Needell et al., 2006), subsidized guardianship programs have had an important influence on children's lengths of stay in foster care. Children who likely would have remained in long-term foster care with kin, often for years, are able to exit care to legal permanence through subsidized legal guardianship programs. Thus, the tension between the legal permanence of adoption and the familial permanence of family preservation may have found its outlet in the establishment of relative guardianships as the permanent plan. Children, who are already placed in stable, familial homes can be accorded legal permanence by having their adult relatives become their legal guardians.

Title IV-E Waiver Demonstration Evaluations

Results from the first large-scale evaluations of subsidized legal guardianship programs suggest that subsidized guardianship is a viable permanency option in terms of child safety. The most rigorous and comprehensive evaluation of subsidized legal guardianship, a randomized controlled trial conducted in Illinois as part of the Federal Title IV-E Waiver Demonstration Program, found substantial gains in legal permanence (combination of family reunification, legal guardianship, and adoption) for children in both kin and nonkin care (Testa, 2002). Rates of subsequent maltreatment were similar between relatives and nonrelatives (Testa, 2004). Few differences in child well-being were found between guardianship and adopted youth, indicating that the two permanency plans may be more alike than different (Testa and Cook, 2001).

Maryland's subsidized guardianship waiver demonstration also used an experimental design but focused on determining whether offering a lower versus a higher guardianship subsidy for relatives would affect the number of children who exit the foster care system into permanent placements (Mandell et al., 2001). Similar to an earlier cohort study (Simmons, 1997), families that would gain financially were more likely to assume legal guardianship while families that would lose a financial benefit were less likely to make this decision. These findings suggest that for kinship caregivers, financial considerations clearly take precedence over legal permanence, and it is easy to see why. Kinship caregivers tend to have lower incomes than nonrelated caregivers (Berrick et al., 1994); even with a subsidy, they are likely to be hard-pressed to make ends meet. What use is a legally permanent home when a family cannot pay rent?

Though smaller in scale, Oregon's Title IV-E evaluation (Child Welfare Partnership at Portland State University Graduate School of Social Work, 2003) used a quasi-experimental, nonequivalent control group design to examine the performance of subsidized legal guardianship as a permanent plan. Although the permanency findings (i.e., child safety and stability of guardianship) were probably compromised by the small sample size, interviews with caregivers revealed that children exiting to guardianship had high levels of specialized care needs (17 percent), which may have implications for children's future safety, permanence, and well-being.[1]

California's Kin-GAP Program

California's Kin-GAP legislation established a statewide program beginning January 1, 2000, that offers a monthly payment equal to the basic foster care rate to qualified relatives who become legal guardians of children in foster care. These families then exit the foster care system without further child welfare agency or dependency court supervision, and payments continue until the child becomes an adult. Children must have resided with the kinship caregiver for at least one year and be evaluated for guardianship by a social worker before they exit care.

California's Children's Services Data Archive at the University of California at Berkeley, Center for Social Services Research, one of the most highly developed longitudinal child welfare databases in the country, is conducting the ongoing statewide analysis of the Kin-GAP initiative. Though not an experimental design, the California evaluation offers insights into the large-scale rollout of a subsidized guardianship program. Children exiting the foster care system to Kin-GAP have been followed using administrative data from the program's inception on January 1, 2000, to January 1, 2006. During that time, more than 16,000 (N = 16,287) children have exited foster care to legal permanence through the Kin-GAP program. To place this number in perspective, the California foster care population before Kin-GAP implementation (midyear 1999) was about 110,000 and had declined to 80,115 by midyear 2005 (Needell et al., 2006), a more than 25 percent decrease. The point-in-time proportion of children in kinship care also declined between 1999 and 2005, decreasing from 42 percent to 35 percent. In Los Angeles County, one of the largest users of kinship care and Kin-GAP, point-in-time estimates of children in kinship care decreased from 50 percent to 39 percent during that same period. Clearly, the exit of so many children from the foster care system was at least partially responsible for the large decreases in the state's foster care population observed so far in this decade.

The safety and permanency experience of children in subsidized legal guardianship in California also has been exceptional. Children exiting to Kin-GAP are relatively unlikely to experience a subsequent substantiated referral (about 3 percent within one year, 11 percent within four years)[2] or reentry to foster care (about 2 percent within one year, 8 percent within four years).

The reasons for reentry of children from subsidized guardianships are varied, but administrative data are limited in terms of depth of information. An administrative case record review of the more detailed text fields in California's statewide case management system (CWS/CMS) was conducted for a sample of Kin-GAP children who exited and reentered care between January 1, 2000, and February 8, 2002 (N = 97) (Shlonsky, 2002). This more detailed analysis sheds light on the possible reasons for reentry and may provide important information for developing interventions designed to maintain these permanent arrangements. For those children who reentered foster care after exiting to Kin-GAP,[3] the majority returned to care for non-maltreatment-related reasons. In about 12 percent of the cases, caregiver death and health concerns resulted in returns to care; 18 percent reentered due to child behavior problems; 7 percent entered the probation system; and 9 percent reentered foster care to facilitate a reunification. The combination of maltreatment-related categories (neglect, parent contact, physical abuse, school nonattendance, sexual abuse, and sexual abuse by a sibling) comprised 34 percent of the reentries to foster care. Many, although not all, reentries to foster care resulted in a change of caregivers. For the eighty-one children who returned to foster care for whom subsequent placement information was available (four probation cases were missing this information), fifty (59 percent) had a change of caregivers for at least thirty days. More than one-third (37 percent) reentered care without shifting to another out-of-home care provider. For example, some children who returned to foster care for specialized services and/or financial assistance never experienced a change in caregiver.

Preliminary survival analysis of the larger sample ($N = 16,287$) indicate that age is an important factor in reentry to foster care. Children age six to fifteen at the time of exit from care are more likely and older teens are less likely than children under the age of six to experience either a maltreatment recurrence or reentry to foster care. These findings suggest that some caregivers are unable to cope with some of the problems that emerge during adolescence. The increased reentry rates for different groups of children and youth can be attributed to the fact that a larger proportion of children who exited between the ages of six and fifteen would, over the study follow-up period, already be in their teen years or would reach adolescence; youth exiting foster care when they were over fifteen would be in the process of aging out of care; and the youngest children would not yet have reached adolescence.

Evaluation Conclusions

Evaluations of subsidized legal guardianship show great promise. In particular, Illinois and California have safely exited large numbers of children from kinship foster care into legally permanent guardianship homes, with resulting substantial decreases in the overall caseload in these states. Yet Maryland's study and the return of families in California to obtain specialized care rates illustrate the importance of subsidizing legal guardianship at levels that are similar to the basic or, if applicable, specialized foster care rate. In addition, the California and Oregon studies indicate that, similar to adoption, postguardianship services are essential for some families to deal with older children who may be experiencing behavior and other problems in order to maintain the safety and stability of these homes.

CONTEXT OF KINSHIP CARE AND RELATIVE GUARDIANSHIP

Hill (chapter 9) does an excellent job in providing a rationale for the continued use of kinship care as a preferred placement resource. As he states, research findings since the mid-1980s indicate that children growing up in kinship care appear to do at least as well as children growing up in nonrelated foster care across a range of indicators. Nonetheless, kinship care is not a magic bullet. It must be supported to be effective, much like foster care and even adoption. One area that will certainly get attention in the years to come is the ability of the child welfare system to optimize the developmental trajectory of the children it serves (see, for example, Wulczyn et al., 2005). This concern is paramount for all caregivers: birth parents, relative caregivers, nonrelative caregivers, adoptive parents, and guardians alike.

Each type of permanency outcome has its benefits and drawbacks. It is essential that we identify the strengths and challenges of each outcome in relation to the needs of individual children. Rather than attempting to prove that kinship care is good, or the converse, we must identify concerns with each type of placement and work to bolster children in different types of families. For instance, studies of kinship care find that kinship caregivers have high levels of stress and suffer from many health concerns (Minkler et al., 1992; Minkler and Roe, 1996). Compared with nonrelated caregivers, kinship caregivers tend to have lower levels of income and educational attainment (Berrick et al., 1994; Gebel, 1996; Ehrlen et al., 2001), and they may use less-effective parenting techniques (Gaudin and Sutphen, 1993; Gebel, 1996). Children in kinship care have multiple challenges as well, often suffering from substantial health, behavioral, and educational difficulties (Dubowitz et al., 1992, 1994). In terms of subsidized guardianship, the success of the policy with respect to moving older children into legally permanent homes is also one of its challenges, with older children more likely to return to care than younger children.

How are these areas being addressed by the child welfare system and related social service systems? Simply offering subsidized legal guardianship is not the solution to the more complex and pressing issues. Additional supports and services are crucial, particularly with respect to developmental considerations. The newest subsidized guardianship program being evaluated in Illinois as part of the Title IV-E waiver is one example of an intervention that combines child and youth development with legal permanence. Extending support for youth in foster care past age eighteen or nineteen acknowledges that youth are rarely able to support themselves at that age and that extending support through young adulthood may help youth avoid some of the more tragic outcomes commonly associated with emancipation from foster care (Courtney et al., 2005).

Another issue to consider is the association of kinship care with longer stays in out-of-home placement and lower (or at least slower) rates of reunification with birth parents. Although subsidized guardianship has the capacity to move many children out of foster care and into permanent families, there may be a cost in terms of family reunification. That is, some children who may have reunified with their birth parents will, instead, exit the foster care system to the home of their relative with a continued guardianship subsidy (Wulczyn et al., 2002). Even with a "net permanency gain," the cost to the system for maintaining a subsidy, over time, is much greater if the subsidy is equivalent to the foster care board rate (Fluke et al., 1997; Wulczyn et al., 2002). Nevertheless, a proportion of children in the California Kin-GAP evaluation returned to care in order to facilitate a reunification. Some of the less tangible benefits of subsidized guardianship may also translate into improved child well-being, which, in turn, can translate into cost savings.

KINSHIP AND GUARDIANSHIP POLICY: NEW DIRECTIONS AND QUESTIONS

As with any good work, Hill (chapter 9) raises many practice and policy questions about the role of kinship care and subsidized legal guardianship. These issues include the following.

Hill alludes to the much larger number of children in informal (not child welfare involved) kinship care. These caregivers and the children they raise appear to be quite similar to families in more formal child welfare settings. Should subsidized guardianship be offered to all relative caregivers, regardless of whether they are involved with the child protection system? If so, can we afford to do so? What funding streams could be made available? Are there any unintended consequences that we should consider, such as social stigma, lower rates of reunification, and legal and other sanctions when parents reside with caregivers?

Much attention has been paid to adoption decreases in the face of increases in legal guardianship. In their reports, Fred Wulczyn and colleagues (2002) and John Fluke et al. (1997) detail potential cost increases as family reunification rates decrease. These analyses make it readily apparent that financial incentives play a role not only in uptake and maintenance of subsidized legal guardianship but also in other aspects of the child welfare system. How can we make it financially feasible for kinship caregivers to become legal guardians while ensuring that there is not a disincentive to reunify? Are all permanency gains equal, and, if not, should there be a tiered payment structure to reflect the child welfare system's preferred permanency outcome? In the face of little or no differences in child outcomes when comparing adoption and guardianship, should such a payment structure be considered?

Different caregivers bring different strengths and weaknesses to the parenting endeavor. How can we assist caregivers, kin and nonkin alike, to maximize the developmental potential of the children they raise? Like adoptive parents, should relative legal guardians have access to postguardianship services? What might these look like? How would they be funded?

CONCLUSION

Clearly, kinship care is a viable and, in some ways, an optimal placement. Likewise, subsidized guardianship is a relatively safe and stable permanency option. However, neither is a panacea for the many challenges faced by children who have experienced abuse and neglect. Kinship caregivers and the children in their care need additional supports to optimize child safety, permanence, and well-being. The next step for the field is to discover which placement-specific sets of services and funding mixes will result in the greatest good for the largest number of children.

Establishing detailed baseline and ongoing well-being indicators for all children who are investigated for child maltreatment, as well as detailed services information, is key for both clinical and research purposes. Although this effort may appear too costly at the outset, the infrastructure is already present in most Statewide Automated Child Welfare Information Systems (SACWIS). We spend a great deal of money conducting research on youth in care, which often involves collecting information that already exists in child welfare management information systems. If baseline and ongoing data are already present, they can be used to track important service innovations without setting up new data collection infrastructures for each research project. Similarly, if existing information systems are systematically expanded to include detailed services and well-being data, developmentally sensitive service interventions can be more easily developed and evaluated.

On balance, it seems likely that the total cost of subsidized guardianship may exceed the cost of long-term relative care as a result of decreases in the number of reunifications with birth parents. This issue will not go away. As we all know, cost-benefit analyses are notoriously imprecise. We must come to terms with the fact that the cost of providing children with safe, developmentally stimulating, and legally permanent families is exceeded only by the cost of not doing so.

NOTES

1. Although many youth in foster care have specialized care needs, their caregivers are often provided with increased supports and services designed to maintain placement stability and enhance child well-being. Such services would generally be unavailable for children exiting the foster care system to legal guardianship.
2. Substantiated maltreatment is likely an overestimate. Caregivers were not necessarily the subject of the allegation, and rescission of guardianship does not always entail maltreatment though a report might have been filed to establish foster care eligibility (e.g., caregiver death or child placement due to behavior problems).
3. Administrative errors were found in twelve cases, accounting for 12 percent of total reentries to foster care.

REFERENCES

Berrick, J. D., R. P. Barth, and B. Needell (1994). A comparison of kinship foster homes and foster homes: Implications for kinship foster care as family preservation. *Children and Youth Services Review* 16(1–2): 33–64.

Child Welfare Partnership at Portland State University Graduate School of Social Work (2003). *Evaluation of Oregon's Title IV-E Waiver Demonstration Project Final Report.* Portland: U.S. Department of Health and Human Services, Administration for Children and Families.

Courtney, M. E., A. Dworsky, G. Ruth, T. Keller, J. Havlicek, and B. Bost (2005). *Midwest Evaluation of the Adult Functioning of Former Foster Youth.* Chicago: Chapin Hall Center for Children at the University of Chicago.

Dubowitz, H., S. Feigelman, S. Zuravin, V. Tepper, N. Davidson, and R. Lichenstein (1992). Physical health of children in kinship care. *American Journal of Diseases of Children* 146: 603–10.

Dubowitz, H., S. Feigelman, D. Harrington, R. Starr, S. Zuravin, and R. Sawyer (1994). Children in kinship care: How do they fare? *Children and Youth Services Review* 16(1–2): 85–106.

Ehrle, J., R. Geen, and R. L. Clark (2001). *Children Cared For by Relatives: Who Are They and How Are They Faring*. Washington, D.C.: Urban Institute.

Fluke, J.D., C.J. Harper, and C. A. Wahlgren (1997). A fiscal analysis of subsidized guardianship policy in Colorado using simulation modeling. *Protecting Children* 3(13): 10–13.

Gaudin, J., and R. Sutphen (1993). Foster care vs. extended family care for children of incarcerated mothers. *Journal of Offender Rehabilitation* 19(3–4): 129–47.

Gebel, T.J. (1996). Kinship care and nonrelative family foster care: A comparison of caregiver attributes and attitudes. *Child Welfare* 75(1): 5–18.

Goerge, R. M., F. H. Wulczyn, and A. W. Harden (1995). *An Update from the Multistate Foster Care Data Archive*. Chicago: Chapin Hall Center for Children at the University of Chicago.

Mandell, M. B., D. Harrington, and M. Orlin (2001). *The Effect of Subsidized Guardianship on Exits from Kinship Care: Results from Maryland's Guardianship Assistance Demonstration Project*. Washington D.C.: Association for Public Policy and Analysis and Management.

Minkler, M., and K.M. Roe (1996). Grandparents as surrogate parents. *Generations: Journal of the American Society on Aging* 20(1): 34–38.

Minkler, M., K.M. Roe, and M. Price (1992). The physical and emotional health of grandmothers raising grandchildren in the crack cocaine epidemic. *Gerontologist* 32(6): 752–61.

Needell, B., D. Webster, M. Armijo, S. Lee, S. Cuccaro-Alamin, T. Shaw, et al. (2006). *Child Welfare Services Reports for California*. At cssr.berkeley.edu/CWSCMSreports/ (accessed August 31, 2006).

Shlonsky, A. (2002). *Relative Permanence: An Evaluation of California's Subsidized Guardianship Assistance Program for Kinship Caregivers (KinGAP)*. Berkeley: University of California at Berkeley, School of Social Welfare.

Shlonsky, A., D. Webster, J. Magruder, B. Wong, P. Sawh, J. Schmidt, and B. Needell (2008). Relative permanence: An evaluation of Kin-GAP, California's subsidized guardianship program for kinship caregivers. Berkeley, Calif. Unpublished ms.

Simmons, B. (1997). Legal guardianship: analyzing child welfare's alternative to adoption and long-term foster care. Ph.D. diss., University of California at Berkeley.

Testa, M. (2002). Subsidized guardianship: Testing an idea whose time has finally come. *Social Work Research* 26(3): 145–58.

—— (2004). When children cannot return home: Adoption and guardianship. *Future of Children* 14(1): 115–29.

Testa, M. F., and R. Cook (2001). *The Comparative Safety, Attachment, and Well-Being of Children in Kinship Adoption, Guardian, and Foster Homes*. Washington, D.C.: Association for Public Policy and Analysis and Management.

U.S. Department of Health and Human Services, Administration for Children and Families (2006). *The AFCARS Report: Preliminary FY 2004 Estimates as of June 2006.* Washington, D.C.: Author.

Wulczyn, F., E. Zimmerman, and A. Skyles (2002). *Relative Caregivers, Kinship Foster Care, and Subsidized Guardianship: Policy and Programmatic Options.* Chicago: Chapin Hall Center for Children at the University of Chicago.

Wulczyn, F., R. P. Barth, Y. T. Yuan, B. J. Harden, and J. Landsverk (2005). *Beyond Common Sense: Child Welfare, Child Well-Being, and the Evidence for Policy Reform.* New Brunswick, N.J.: Aldine Transaction.

Dependency Court Reform
Addressing the Permanency Needs
of Youth in Foster Care

ELEVEN

National Evaluation of the
Court Improvement Program

KARL ENSIGN, SABRINA A. DAVIS,
AND ELIZABETH LEE

Since the early 1980s, court processes for periodically reviewing plans for children removed from the custody of their parents and approving key decisions made on their behalf have been established and refined. Judicial and public agency officials agree, however, that the delineation of the respective roles of public agencies and the courts and the manner in which courts periodically review and approve decisions made on behalf of children in the care and custody of the state remain a work in progress. Ongoing research in this area is essential. In this chapter, we provide a summary of the sources of dependency court reform. We examine a variety of strategies that address the specific issues facing youth involved in the dependency court process and more general reforms to improve the processing of all dependency cases. Much of the information presented was collected during the ongoing National Evaluation of the Court Improvement Program (CIP) undertaken for the Children's Bureau, U.S. Department of Health and Human Services in 2004 (U.S. Department of Health and Human Services, 2007).

NATIONAL DEPENDENCY COURT REFORM ACTIVITIES

The role of the courts in overseeing dependency cases was formalized in the Adoption Assistance and Child Welfare Act of 1980 (Public Law 96-272). Concerned that children were remaining in foster care indefinitely, this act, for the first time in federal law, mandated that courts (1) assess the "reasonableness" of the child welfare agency's efforts to prevent the need for removal and facilitate the child's reunification with his or her family, (2) adhere to a defined sequence of periodic court hearings for child dependency cases, (3) meet deadlines for permanency planning, and (4) ensure that procedural safeguards be followed regarding out-of-home placement and parental and sibling visitation.

During much of the 1980s, courts struggled to meet the new requirements that they move dependency cases onto their dockets and have them heard in a timely manner. Initially, states routinely failed the federal review elements that states convene a dispositional hearing eighteen months after a child's removal and hold periodic reviews every six months. Although states eventually complied with federal timelines with these requirements, it was readily evident to the field that hearings across the country were too often pro forma and perfunctory (U.S. Senate, Committee on Finance, 1990).

Between 1986 and 1995, there was a 76 percent national increase in the number of children in foster care (Murray and Gesiriech, n.d.). Researchers and practitioners attributed the increase to a variety of factors, including

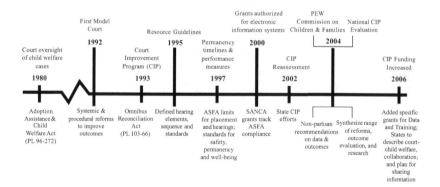

Figure 11.1 Dependency court reform key dates

increases in substance abuse, AIDS, poverty, and homelessness (Administration on Children, Youth and Families [ACYF], 1994; Murray and Gesiriech, n.d.). In addition to higher caseloads, the field noted that court officials often had insufficient training in child welfare issues for judges and attorneys (ACYF, 1994).

In response to these challenges, a number of steps were taken to improve the occurrence and quality of court oversight of dependency cases. Figure 11.1 provides the key events beginning with the enactment of Public Law 96-272. National and state dependency court reforms originate from several sources, including federal funding programs, legislation and directives, multidisciplinary commissions, field-initiated guidelines, and the results of special demonstrations and evaluations.

Federal Funding Programs

In 1993, the Omnibus Budget Reconciliation Act (OBRA) provided new federal funds to state child welfare agencies to establish and expand preventive services, specifically, family preservation and support services; at the same time, Congress recognized that substantive and procedural improvements were needed in the courts that had oversight responsibility of dependency child welfare cases (Chemers, 1995). Consequently, among other provisions, OBRA established the Court Improvement Program (CIP), "the first significant source of federal funding for child welfare–related court activities" (Murray and Gesiriech, n.d.:4).

In the first CIP grant period, FY 1995, $5 million was allocated to states to assess the manner in which their court systems processed child welfare cases. The assessments found inefficiencies within the state laws and judicial processes, as well as barriers to effective decision-making (ACYF, 1994). Funding for FYs 1996–2005 totaled $10 million annually, and states were instructed to use these funds for the implementation and continuing assessment of general court reforms to improve the processing of child welfare cases (ACYF, 1994, 1999, 2003). In FY 2006, CIP funding tripled with the provision of two additional $10 million grants, one for training and one for data collection and analysis (ACYF, 2006).

Although CIP is the principal federal funding source for dependency court reform, there are other discretionary grants available for states and local jurisdictions. For example, the Strengthening Abuse and Neglect Courts in America: Management Information Systems (SANCA

MIS) project awarded two-year grants to six states for the development and implementation of automated information systems in dependency courts to improve tracking of court performance measures (SANCA Project, n.d.).

Federal Legislation and Directives

The Adoption and Safe Families Act of 1997 (ASFA) (Public Law 105-89) established timelines and incentives to move children out of foster care more quickly and led to the development of benchmark outcome measures for timely permanence, safety, and well-being. Although the standards were developed primarily to assess the performance of the state child welfare agencies, courts play important roles in overseeing case management and approving key decisions; as a result, court performance contributes to a state's success or failure. Timely hearings, for example, can speed the permanency process. Access to adequate representation early in the court process can reduce the number of continuances, shorten delays, and decrease the number of appeals. In addition, safety and well-being outcomes can be positively affected by increasing substantive judicial knowledge of child development and adolescent issues, a key to the quality of court oversight in child welfare proceedings.

Subsequent reauthorizations of the basic CIP grant took into account the growing importance of the court in child welfare proceedings. The ACYF Program Instructions emphasized the importance of collaboration between the courts and the child welfare agency (ACYF, 1999, 2003). For example, the Program Instructions require states to give priority to any legal or judicial issues identified in the state's Program Improvement Plans (PIPs) for its Child and Family Services Review (CFSR) or Title IV-E Foster Care Eligibility Review (ACYF, 2003).

Finally, the legislation that established the CIP training and data grants in 2006 also instituted requirements for both state courts and child welfare agencies to demonstrate "meaningful, ongoing collaboration" (ACYF, 2006). For the courts, this demonstration is required as part of the application for any of the three CIP grants; for child welfare agencies, the collaboration must be shown in the development of the PIPs for their CFSRs and Title IV-E Foster Care Eligibility Reviews (ACYF, 2006).

Multidisciplinary Commissions

The Pew Commission on Children in Foster Care, a national nonpartisan panel of experts, recommended that the U.S. Department of Health and Human Services require child welfare agency-court collaboration on federal child welfare reviews, PIPs developed in response to these reviews, and CIP strategic plans. The panel also recommended establishing cross-system, state-level commissions to ensure ongoing collaboration between the courts, child welfare agency, and other relevant public and private entities (Pew Commission on Children in Foster Care, 2004). The ACYF incorporated this recommendation in its June 2006 Program Instruction for CIP grantees, identifying a statewide multidisciplinary task force as the minimal requirement to demonstrate meaningful and ongoing collaboration (ACYF, 2006).

The Pew Commission further recommended, as an essential step in monitoring outcomes for children and youth in foster care, that state and local data from the courts and child welfare agency be synthesized. Beginning with FY 2006, Congress appropriated $10 million in CIP funds for improved data collection, requiring states to describe "how courts and child welfare agencies on the local and State levels will collaborate and jointly plan for the collection and sharing of all relevant data and information to demonstrate how improved case tracking and analysis of child abuse and neglect cases will produce safe and timely permanency decisions" (42 U.S.C. 629h(a)(3), 2006).

Field-Initiated Best-Practice Guidelines

Public interest and professional membership organizations such as the American Bar Association's Center on Children and the Law (ABA), the National Council of Juvenile and Family Court Judges (NCJFCJ), the National Center for State Courts (NCSC), and others frequently provide resources and examples of promising practices in dependency courts. Perhaps the best-known effort is the *Resource Guidelines: Improving Practice in Child Abuse and Neglect Cases* (NCJFCJ, 1995). The *Resource Guidelines* continue to be regarded as the seminal resource for defining the essential elements of properly conducted hearings, including their duration, who should be present, and key decisions and activities that need to take place at each hearing. The *Resource Guidelines* also specify required reports, petitions, and findings.

Special Demonstrations

The two most prominent demonstrations of comprehensive child welfare and court reform are the NCJFCJ Model Courts and the Strengthening Abuse and Neglect in America: Management Information System (SANCA-MIS) grants administered by the Office of Juvenile Justice and Delinquency Prevention (OJJDP). The Model Courts focus on systemic, procedural reforms to improve outcomes for children in foster care (NCJFCJ, 2003). In 2007, there were twenty-five NCJFCJ Model Courts operating under the principles stated in the *Resource Guidelines,* and many more courts had adopted some of its recommendations, such as time-certain docketing, strict no-continuance rules, competent legal representation for all parties, alternative dispute resolution programs, and one judge–one family calendaring (NCJFCJ, 2003, 2006). SANCA grants are used to develop and maintain electronic information systems to track compliance with national court performance standards related to achieving ASFA requirements (OJJDP, 2006b). In 2005, at least twenty-five states were using or developing technology for either case tracking or data management, or both; however, most states seemed to be using these interventions simply to track compliance with deadlines rather than to allocate resources more effectively (Davis and Lee, 2006).

Federal Evaluation

In 2004, a five-year evaluation of CIP began to describe the many paths state courts have followed in the implementation of the program and the outcomes achieved. The National Evaluation of the Court Improvement Program has four interrelated components: (1) reviewing and synthesizing state and local CIP reform activities; (2) reviewing and synthesizing state reassessments of their CIP activities; (3) reviewing and synthesizing existing family court reform evaluations; and (4) conducting in-depth studies of CIP reform models in Connecticut, Delaware, and Texas (U.S. Department of Health and Human Services, 2007).[1]

Court-Specific Evaluations

Many court and state-specific evaluations are conducted on an ongoing basis. The National Evaluation of CIP has identified sixty-one evaluations of juvenile and family court activities and reforms that have been conducted over the past ten years. Of these evaluations, twenty-two focused on alternative dispute resolution, fifteen on systemic and comprehensive court reform, twelve on specialized hearings, and eight on legal representation. The remaining evaluations addressed court-involved parent education and support, case tracking and management, and multidisciplinary training and education. The National Evaluation of CIP produced a synthesis of the collected evaluations in late 2008.

LOCAL DEPENDENCY COURT REFORM ACTIVITIES

A number of activities undertaken by state and local governments to improve dependency case oversight specifically targeted issues affecting youth. A synthesis of the CIP reform activities undertaken by states during 2004–2005 reveals that one-quarter of the states were directly addressing factors that impact youth permanence, including independent living services, truancy, delinquency, and juvenile drug courts.[2] Virtually all states have implemented broader measures that indirectly affect youth permanence, including improving court-agency collaboration, representation for all parties, stakeholder knowledge of child development, and court administration (Davis and Lee, 2006).

Court Reform Activities Specifically Focused on Youth

Independent Living Services

During 2004–2005, five states used CIP resources to provide training to key stakeholders on issues related to "aging out" of the foster care system (Davis and Lee, 2006). Kansas convened an Independent Living Stakeholders Group composed of representatives from both the judiciary and the child welfare agency (State of Kansas, 2005). One Superior Court in Indiana initiated transitional conferencing to assist the youth who are aging out (State of Indiana, 2005). Philadelphia established a court committee that has developed several opportunities for youth to participate in planning their futures (State of Pennsylvania, 2005).

Truancy

Literature indicates that a delinquency record negatively affects a dependent adolescent's permanency prospects, and, as a result, youth attorneys and judges should take preventive measures at the first indication of truancy or substance abuse (Khoury, 2004).

Court-led interventions in response to truancy have taken several forms. Several family court judges in Kentucky, for example, visit schools to discuss the importance of education and other life skills with youth already experiencing attendance problems (Commonwealth of Kentucky, 2005). One judicial district in Colorado implemented a mediation program that assesses family dynamics to determine the cause(s) of truancy; once the cause is identified, a contract is developed among the court, child welfare agency, school, and family to reduce the truancy (State of Colorado, 2005). Rhode Island has established specialized truancy courts that serve over 150 schools; truancy court, which is offered as an alternative to a delinquency hearing, features weekly monitoring by a magistrate who "provides constant supervision of the child and encourages the child to succeed" (Rhode Island Family Court Truancy Court Program [TCP], 2006:1). These weekly sessions provide parents with an opportunity to communicate with teachers and school administrators directly about the child's school problems.

Delinquency

Special challenges exist in dual jurisdiction cases, in which the youth is involved in both the dependency court and delinquency court systems during an overlapping time period. Without proper case management, the complex nature of these cases can result in duplicated efforts, conflicting case goals, and unnecessary depletion of scarce resources (Halemba et al., 2004). One case management suggestion is for dependency court participants to ensure that the delinquency court judge and attorneys are given all pertinent dependency data so that the best decisions are made; additionally, "agencies, courts, and attorneys should work together to design a service plan to address the issues that caused delinquency, impose punishment, and provide permanency" (Khoury, 2004:91). Arizona has devoted much time and energy to studying how to improve dual case management, along with developing plans to implement reforms such as minimizing inappropriate detention placements and combining dependency and delinquency hearings when appropriate (State of Arizona, 2005).

Juvenile Drug Courts

Although not widely addressed by state CIP activities in 2004–2005, juvenile drug courts continue to draw the attention of researchers and practitioners who work with youth. Between 1990 and 1999, the number of youth drug offense cases in juvenile courts increased by 169 percent; in 1999, 11 percent of all juvenile delinquency cases involved drug offenses, and 67 percent of these cases resulted in a delinquent adjudication (Stahl, 2003). Beginning in the mid-1990s, juvenile drug courts were established in response to the growing number of delinquency cases involving drug offenses (National Institute of Justice, 2006). Drug courts for adults had emerged in the 1980s as an effort to reduce court caseloads, but the process had to be adapted to address the particular needs of adolescents (Office of Juvenile Justice and Delinquency Prevention [OJJDP], 2006a). Juvenile drug court programs, for example, recognized that they needed to take into account the possibility of negative peer and family influences and the juvenile's own immaturity and sense of invulnerability (Roberts et al., 1997).

Youth drug courts, in response to the unique needs of youth, incorporated several characteristics of traditional juvenile courts, including comprehensive intake assessments; increased coordination between the court, service providers, and schools; and continuous, active judicial supervision of the case and treatment process (Roberts et al., 1997). As of April 2006, juvenile drug courts were implemented in forty-seven states and the District of Columbia (BJA Drug Court Clearinghouse, 2006). A cross-site, quasi-experimental evaluation of six juvenile courts in Maine identified three key findings regarding the effectiveness of the juvenile drug courts: (1) participants had "significantly lower overall arrest rates than a comparison group … of offenders traditionally adjudicated"; (2) the specialized courts reduced criminal justice-related expenses; and (3) participants were "significantly more likely than non-drug court participants to participate in substance abuse treatment" (Anspach et al., 2003:36).

Broader Court Reform Agenda

In addition to efforts that focus directly on issues that affect dependent youth, broader court reform agendas undertaken within individual courts are relevant to achieving positive outcomes for youth. Improving the quality of court hearings and judicial oversight, along with the timeliness of permanence for all children under the care and custody of the state, is important for youth in care. Dependent adolescents often have the greatest needs, receive the most specialized services, are placed in the most restrictive settings, and are least likely to achieve permanence within a timely fashion. The synthesis of CIP reforms conducted in 2004–2005 found that generalized court reform efforts recently have focused on a number of factors associated with achieving permanence for youth: collaboration between the courts and public agencies; representation for children, dependent youth, parents, and the agency; enhanced knowledge of child development and youth issues within the courts; attention to excessive judicial and attorney caseloads and frequent judicial rotations; and efforts to address other administrative issues such as inconvenient hearing scheduling (Davis and Lee, 2006).

Collaboration

Given the growing importance of courts in child welfare cases, collaboration between state child welfare agencies and court administrators and personnel is essential. Although there are many examples of close working relationships, the two entities are often not on the same page due to localized history and context. By definition, collaboration involves joint problem-solving outside formalized court hearings. Yet, it is important to acknowledge that the relationship is not always one of coequals and that court hearings can be adversarial in nature. Although child welfare agencies are charged with developing and overseeing the child's case plan development and implementation on a daily basis, they are subject to the review and approval of the court on a periodic basis and at key intervals. Some judges may hesitate to work collaboratively with agency personnel outside of the courtroom for fear of allegations of unethical conduct when deciding individual cases.

To address this concern, several states have established laws, court rules, or ethical opinions that allow judges to participate in collaborations to the extent that it does not interfere with their judicial obligations. Furthermore, judges can take steps to minimize the risk that collaborative efforts may be seen as or that actually constitute unethical conduct, such as developing protocol and ground rules for the collaboration that restrict what is discussed (Fiermonte and Salyers, 2005).

Although it can seem to be a daunting task, "aligning disparate goals and practices, ensuring shared responsibility and accountability, building consensus, coordinating resources, facilitating shared leadership, and mutually defining and measuring outcomes are critical components of an effective systems change process" (Dobbin et al., 2004:1). These efforts are particularly important when dealing with the complex issues that are typical for youth in foster care. Initial collaborative efforts may begin small, such as sitting on the same state or local committees, but should increase over time.

The CIP reforms synthesis conducted for the National Evaluation of the Court Improvement Program identified three prevalent forms of collaboration: federally mandated or recommended efforts; voluntary, joint taskforces and workgroups; and electronic data sharing (Davis and Lee, 2006). Government-mandated or recommended collaboration is the most common collaboration type, often a first step for jurisdictions that are less experienced in agency-court collaborations. One recent example of federally mandated collaboration is the requirement that state courts receiving CIP funds establish a statewide multidisciplinary task force that includes, at a minimum, state and local courts and the child welfare agency (ACYF, 2006).

Although voluntary joint task forces have existed for years, more are beginning to appear. At least fifteen states currently have formalized multidisciplinary groups dedicated to improving outcomes for children in the court system, and several other states have less formal arrangements for collaboration, such as placing representatives on subcommittees or forming workgroups for certain projects (Fiermonte and Salyers, 2005; Davis and Lee, 2006). Finally, information sharing is an essential underpinning of true collaboration, systemic problem-solving, and coordinated case management. Data-sharing efforts that funnel data into common Management Information Systems (MIS) have begun among state courts, child welfare agencies, and other agencies. Utah's Court Agency Record Exchange (CARE), for example, allows data sharing among the courts, child welfare agency, Office of the Attorney General, and Office of the Guardian ad Litem (State of Utah, 2005).

Appointment of Counsel

As noted in the *Resource Guidelines,* "each party must be competently and diligently represented in order for juvenile and family courts to function effectively" (NCJFCJ, 1995:22). Competent and diligent representation for children, parents, and the child welfare agency requires mandatory appointments of counsel, manageable attorney caseloads, and substantive and procedural training for all representatives. Although there are several models for providing representation to the child welfare agency, parents, and children, the crucial characteristic of any successful state or local system is the timely provision of quality representation to all parties in a dependency case.

In terms of representing children, federal law requires the appointment of a guardian ad litem (GAL) "in every case involving an abused or neglected child which results in a judicial proceeding." The GAL may be an attorney or a court-appointed special advocate (CASA), and his or her responsibilities are "to obtain first-hand, a clear understanding of the situation and needs of the child … and to make recommendations to the court concerning the best interests of the child" (42 U.S.C. §5106a(b)(2)(A)(ix), 2006).

Although the best interests of children and youth are important, several leading child advocacy organizations promote alternative child representation models. The American Bar Association (ABA) and the National Association of Counsel for Children (NACC) both recommend appointing an attorney that represents the child's wishes when children are able to express their preferences. If the attorney believes that granting the child's preference would be seriously injurious, then he or she may (according to the ABA) or must (according to the NACC) request that a separate guardian ad litem be appointed (Katner et al., 2001).

Some states have addressed concerns about the legal representation of children through legislation. In 2005, for example, New Mexico enacted legislation that requires "the appointment of a client-directed youth attorney for all youth age 14 and over involved in abuse and neglect cases" (State of New Mexico, 2005:15). Similarly, Minnesota, Wisconsin, and Washington have statutes requiring that a traditional attorney be appointed for children of a certain age (First Star, 2006). Some states set a minimum age for consulting the child on whether he or she wants to be adopted; actively engaging adolescents, however, requires that they be consulted at the outset and throughout the duration of the case.

There is no federal requirement for parent representation in abuse and neglect cases, although some states and counties provide representation for indigent parents, particularly in termination of parental rights proceedings (Davis and Lee, 2006). Variation occurs with respect to when in the judicial process the appointment of counsel occurs and how attorneys are provided. The literature recommends appointing representation for all parties as early as possible in the dependency process, preferably by the first hearing and no later than the second (NCJFCJ, 2000). Anecdotal observations from court officials and staff reveal that if parental counsel is not appointed at an early stage, key findings and rulings before the appointment of representation can be appealed and overturned (Davis and Lee, 2006). Therefore, it is in the child's best interest to ensure that parents are represented early in the process to prevent additional delays in achieving permanence.

An analysis of state statutes in 1998 found that thirty-nine states provided for the appointment of counsel to indigent parents (Dobbin et al., 1998). Some jurisdictions, including Connecticut, Delaware, Puerto Rico, and Rhode Island, have used a portion of their CIP funds to hire attorneys to represent parents (Davis and Lee, 2006; Territory of Puerto Rico, 2005; State of Rhode Island, 2005). Washington State implemented a comprehensive pilot, the Parents' Representation Program, in two of its juvenile courts. The program has three objectives: to provide better representation to parents by having attorneys communicate regularly with clients, provide meaningful legal counseling, and be prepared for all proceedings; to decrease court delays by limiting caseloads and not permitting continuances for overscheduling; and to increase compensation for parent attorneys (Bridge and Moore, 2002).

Finally, several states have begun to use CIP funds to address inconsistencies in child welfare agency representation (Davis and Lee, 2006). One notable example is the Prosecution Project in the Texas Panhandle, in which two attorneys, deputized by the state Office of the Attorney General, represent the agency in eighteen mostly rural counties (Texas Court Improvement Project, 2005). Although this approach may not be effective in every jurisdiction, it provides the agency with reliable legal representation through qualified and competent attorneys.

Knowledge of Child Development, Youth Issues, and Services

Broader court reform efforts relevant to youth also include efforts to address the lack of child development knowledge on the part of judges and attorneys. Dependency cases are unique legal proceedings that cannot be conducted in the same manner as criminal or civil cases. Both the people who make important decisions on behalf of children and parents (including with whom a child should live, how often and under what conditions parents are allowed to visit their children, and how long parents are given to complete their court-ordered services) and the people representing the child in court should have a working knowledge of children's physical, mental, emotional, and social development. Adolescents and pre-adolescents have unique needs and problems that require specialized knowledge and treatment. Their age may allow them to remove themselves from placements they do not like and refuse to participate in services, decisions that may stall the permanency process and put the safety and well-being of youth at risk.

Training for key stakeholders on the importance of permanence in child development is frequently incorporated into court improvement efforts (Children's Bureau, 2005). The National Resource Center for Youth Development has emphasized that "in order to effectively advocate for an older youth, a basic understanding of general adolescent behavior patterns is essential" (McNaught and Onkeles, 2004:7). In a 1998 survey, court improvement specialists identified the need for additional training for child representatives in several areas, with child development and child psychology being the most frequently cited areas. The court improvement specialists suggested that training focus on children's and youth's specific needs by age, sex, culture, and race or ethnicity; appropriate psychosocial development; the mental health needs of children and youth; and the effect of maltreatment and parental substance abuse on child and adolescent development and well-being (Dobbin et al., 1998).

In addition to child development training, judges and attorneys should have knowledge of the programs and services available for youth in foster care so that the court can address well-being needs at every hearing. As Kathleen McNaught and Lauren Onkeles note, "education, health, housing, and employment, among others, can have a significant impact on achieving permanency for youth approaching adulthood" (2004:14).

Court improvement programs in several states have begun to offer adolescent-specific trainings to judges and attorneys (Davis and Lee, 2006). Arizona, for example, provides training on adolescent brain development and behaviors and strategies for communicating effectively with teens (State of Arizona, 2005). Wyoming has developed training regarding barriers to permanence, effective advocating, and permanency planning for older teens (Ackerman, 2005). Tennessee and Pennsylvania have presented trainings on independent living and aging out (Kinkead, 2005; State of Pennsylvania, 2005). Oregon has conducted a judicial training covering child welfare agency practices relating to independent living (Oregon Juvenile Court Improvement Project, 2005).

Manageable Caseloads and Judicial Rotations

Broad court reform efforts also have focused on maintaining manageable caseload levels and decreasing judicial rotations in dependency court. High caseloads have multiple negative implications: cases may not be heard as frequently as they should; insufficient time may be allocated to cases, and courts may not be able to thoroughly address all pertinent issues; judges and attorneys may not be prepared for their scheduled hearings; and time may not be available for collaboration with the child welfare agency and other important government offices and service providers (American Bar Association Center on Children and the Law, National Center for State Courts, and National Council of Juvenile and Family Court Judges, 2004).

As with judges and other hearing officers, attorneys must have manageable caseloads in order to be effective. The American Humane Association (AHA) (2004) conducted a dependency attorney caseload study in California that identified discrete actions by attorneys, measured the amount of time that was dedicated to each action, estimated the amount of time attorneys should spend on each action, and developed models to determine caseload standards based on the estimations. The AHA study recommended a maximum caseload of 141 for parent and child dependency attorneys. At the time the report was published, the statewide average for dependency attorneys in California was 273 cases (Nunn et al., 2004).

An alternative to hiring more attorneys is using volunteers. Child representation frequently relies on volunteers, with the most notable example being the CASA program. In addition, a few states use law students to represent children and parents in child abuse and neglect cases. In these programs, law students are supervised by a licensed attorney and typically provide their services in exchange for class credit (Davis and Lee, 2006). Pro bono representation is also a possibility. Georgia, for example, has instituted a "One Child/One Lawyer" program that recruits attorneys from firms to represent one child a year (at no cost) and to remain with the case through permanence (Barclay, 2005). In Maryland, CIP funds provide training to attorneys interested in representing parents in exchange for an agreement to represent at least one parent (Stewart-Jones and Watkins-Tribbitt, 2005).

Another option, implemented in Hawaii's First Judicial Circuit, is to "unbundle" parent representation services. To offset the high cost of attorneys for parents, parent facilitators (usually volunteers) are used to introduce parents to the court process and available resources (State of Hawaii, 2005). The dual effect of this approach is that money is saved and parent attorneys have more time to focus on the legal aspects of their cases. Similarly, Puerto Rico CIP funds have been used to hire a case manager who informs parents of their rights and duties and provides legal referrals (Territory of Puerto Rico, 2005).

The issue of judicial rotation also is important. The Pew Commission recommended that state court procedures be established to "enable and encourage judges proven competent in dependency cases to build careers there" (Pew Commission on Children in Foster Care, 2004:45). This recommendation reflects the *Resource Guidelines*' ideal of employing judges who are "interested in the juvenile court's work and [are] prepared to remain in the court for at least three years" (NCJFCJ, 1995:149). Two closely entwined issues are the movement of judges in and out of the juvenile court and multiple judges hearing different portions of the same dependency case. First, frequent judicial rotation increases the likelihood of having judges unfamiliar with or uninterested in dependency law (U.S. General Accounting Office, 1999). Mandatory judicial rotation, unfortunately, remains a barrier to judicial expertise in some jurisdictions, although the advent of CIP has reduced this practice (Hardin, 2003). Second, having multiple judges hear different aspects of the same case leads to "additional court delays, less efficiency, judges' loss of important information about the children and families, and judges who have less authority and responsibility for their cases" (Hardin, 2003:3).

In Texas, CIP funding was used to establish "cluster courts" that provide the benefit of judicial expertise to rural counties by designating one judge to hear all child abuse and neglect cases for a "cluster" of counties (Texas Court Improvement Project, 2005). The judge travels to his or her designated counties between one and four days a month to hear the child abuse and neglect cases for the entire county. This approach provides the benefits of a single experienced judge per family at a fraction of the cost that would be required if each county were to provide these services.

Other Issues Related to Court Administration

Timely permanence for all children is jeopardized by inefficient court administration. Several interrelated factors contribute to systemic delays in dependency proceedings, including lack of resources and conflicting schedules. Current areas on which CIPs are focusing include the court docketing system and lengthy appeals.

Under the traditional "cattle call" docketing system employed by many courts, multiple cases are assigned the same hearing time, and cases are called before the judge in no particular order. This method is inefficient because all parties, attorneys, and witnesses are required to wait at the court, sometimes for hours, until their case is called (American Bar Association Center on Children and the Law, n.d.). Youth can be required to miss school for an entire day to attend a single hearing, and scheduling conflicts result for attorneys and caseworkers who may have to appear in other courtrooms, increasing the possibility of continuances and delays in permanence.

Some courts have implemented time-certain docketing to address these inefficiencies. Time-certain docketing assigns each case a specific hearing time. The allotted time is based on the average length of time for the type of hearing, but the time allocation can be increased or decreased, depending on individual case circumstances (American Bar Association Center on Children and the Law, n.d.). This method drastically reduces the amount of time the court participants wait to see the judge and can be extremely beneficial in reducing attorney and caseworker scheduling conflicts.

Case managers and other staff can help reduce the number of hearings conducted before the court. The Philadelphia Family Court in Pennsylvania, for example, uses a dependency case manager to conduct pretrial and case management conferences outside of the courtroom (State of Pennsylvania, 2005). At least eighteen jurisdictions use mediation or family group conferencing and decision making practices for some portion of the jurisdiction's dependency cases to reduce the number of contested, and usually lengthy, hearings (Davis and Lee, 2006). Other states use alternative hearing officers for less complex cases if there is a shortage of judges. Some states, such as Massachusetts, have implemented a "judicial recall" in which retired judges are reinstated to reduce the backlog of older cases and expedite the hearings of new cases (Davis and Lee, 2006; Commonwealth of Massachusetts, 2005).

Finally, an increasing number of states are addressing administrative issues by implementing measures to expedite appeals of termination of parental rights. Although appeals are not addressed in federal legislation, they must be taken into account because a child cannot achieve permanence while an appeal is pending. Some methods used to expedite appeals include establishing appellate timeframes; giving priority status to dependency-related appeals; and implementing electronic case tracking, record-keeping, and transcript preparation (Keith, and Flango, 2002). As of December 2004, thirty-eight states and the District of Columbia had procedures, either under statute and/or court rule, that provide for an expedited appeal in cases involving the termination of parental rights (Szymanski, 2005).

CONCLUSION

The vast majority of court reform evaluations have been court-specific, focusing on process outcomes that are directly under their control and purview. Commonly, focus has been on how many hearings are held on time, whether each hearing focuses on the correct content, and perceptions of whether and how the wishes of all parties are queried and explored during the course of the hearing. These measures of court process are important. Courts, however, are an integral part of the child welfare decision-making process, and evaluations must become more comprehensive in scope, measuring child welfare case outcomes that, although they do not fall completely under courts' control, often cannot be achieved without the courts' active engagement.

A number of factors are coalescing to facilitate the role of research and evaluation in improving outcomes for youth in foster care:

• *Field-initiated best practice models have become fairly well defined.* Since the beginning of the twenty-first century, professional membership and advocacy organizations have become actively involved in researching, developing, and disseminating a broad spectrum of best practice guidelines and resources that address nearly every facet of dependency hearings.

• *Federal outcomes have been identified.* Through ASFA, federal legislation has institutionalized child safety, timely permanency, and well-being outcomes and timeframes. Although the courts and child welfare agencies have different and distinct roles for achieving these outcomes, the identification of outcomes and timeframes creates a common ground for collaboration and measuring progress.

• *Courts and child welfare agencies recognize they cannot "go it alone."* They recognize that they must share responsibility for each child's and youth's case planning and decision-making. They realize that they must collaborate at both the systemic and individual case levels in order to ensure that children achieve permanence, while each retains traditional oversight roles for case management and decision making.

• *There is recognition that issues that affect youth in foster care may be especially complex and require collaborative efforts.* Both courts and child welfare agencies recognize that some of the most challenging cases involve children and youth who have spent long periods of time in foster care and whose special needs must be met by multiple agencies. By definition, the complexity of these cases requires collaboration and joint problem-solving.

- *Federal attention is focused on court improvement in dependency cases and the need for rigorous evaluation.* The federal government's sponsorship of the national evaluation of CIP points to a growing federal priority. The Pew Commission's emphasis on court reform and its call for investments in the dependency court system further support federal efforts.

- *Data on children and youth in foster care has improved.* In the past, federal funding for the development of child welfare agency management information systems has been made available through the Statewide Automated Child Welfare System (SACWIS) funding program. Current funding for court case tracking and management information systems development is being made available through CIP. Although these efforts have vastly improved the information available, it is essential that information in child welfare agencies and the courts be integrated as both serve the same families and address the same issues. All too often, however, management information systems for child welfare agencies and state courts are not integrated.

Collectively, these factors point to the need to identify expected outcomes and the problems associated with achieving them and the need for courts and child welfare agencies to work together in order to achieve these outcomes. Absent in the current debate is a clear focus on the developmental perspective specific to the needs and context of youth. Recognition of the different needs of children and youth is critical, yet it remains a missing piece to the research and evaluation puzzle completed to date. All too often, evaluations focus on the factors that remain constant across childhood and adolescence (such as safety) but do not differentiate on the very different needs of children by their age.

As demonstrated in this chapter, the needs of youth can be especially complex, involving multiple agencies and systems. When youth's needs are not sufficiently met, they can be extremely costly to the child welfare and dependency court systems. Failure to meet youth's needs can result in other costs at an individual and societal level, costs that can continue well into adulthood. While youth are in out-of-home care, child welfare agencies and the courts are responsible for their development, well-being, and permanency needs. The knowledge base of "what works," however, is extremely limited. It is critical that research and evaluation focus on this vulnerable population, gaining insights into how to improve immediate and long-term outcomes.

NOTES

1. Connecticut's case management protocol involves a prehearing conference of professionals held early in the dependency court process, coupled with expanded parent representation. Delaware's systemic reforms include one judge/one case assignment practice, a defined sequence of hearings, and increased representation for indigent parents. Texas has instituted a rural reform in which a specially trained judge presides over dependency proceedings in multiple counties.

2. The primary data sources for the synthesis of CIP reform activities were the states' mandatory annual CIP program reports that were submitted to the Children's Bureau in summer and fall 2005. The study size was forty-nine jurisdictions, composed of forty-seven states, the District of Columbia, and Puerto Rico. Reports from Mississippi, Oklahoma, and South Dakota were not received (Davis and Lee, 2006).

REFERENCES

Ackerman, Tara (2005). *Wyoming Supreme Court: Children's Justice Project Progress Report*. Cheyenne: Wyoming Supreme Court.

Administration on Children, Youth and Families (ACYF) (1994). *Implementation of New Legislation: Family Preservation and Support Services, Title IV-B, Subpart 2*. Washington, D.C.: U.S. Department of Health and Human Services.

—— (1999). *The Court Improvement Program: Funding for State Courts to Assess and Improve Handling of Proceedings Relating to Foster Care and Adoption; Instructions for Applying for Fiscal Years (FY) 1999, 2000, and 2001 Funds*. Washington, D.C.: U.S. Department of Health and Human Services.

—— (2003). *Program Instructions for States Applying for Court Improvement Program Funds for Fiscal Years 2003–2006*. Washington, D.C.: U.S. Department of Health and Human Services.

—— (2006). *Instructions for State Courts Applying for New Court Improvement Program Funds for Fiscal Years (FYs) 2006–2010*. Washington, D.C.: U.S. Department of Health and Human Services.

American Bar Association Center on Children and the Law (n.d.). *Using Non-judicial Court Staff to Help Achieve Permanency for Children*. At www.abanet.org/child/courtstaffing.html (accessed May 15, 2006).

American Bar Association Center on Children and the Law, National Center for State Courts, and National Council of Juvenile and Family Court Judges (2004). *Building a Better Court: Measuring and Improving Court Performance and Judicial Workload in Child Abuse and Neglect Cases*. Los Altos, Calif.: David and Lucile Packard Foundation. At www.ncsconline.org/wc/publications/res_ctpers_tcps_packgde4-04pub (accessed June 20, 2006).

American Humane Association (2004). *Dependency Counsel Caseload Study and Service Delivery Model Analysis.* Denver, Colo.: Author.

Anspach, D. F., A. S. Ferguson, and L. L. Phillips (2003). *Evaluation of Maine's Statewide Juvenile Drug Treatment Court Program: Fourth Year Outcome Evaluation Report.* Portland: University of Southern Maine.

Barclay, M. (2005). *Program Report.* Atlanta: Supreme Court of Georgia, Children's Placement Project.

BJA Drug Court Clearinghouse (2006). *Summary of Drug Court Activity by State and County: Juvenile/Family Drug Courts.* Washington, D.C.: American University School of Public Affairs, Justice Programs Office.

Bridge, B. J., and J. I. Moore (2002). Implementing Equal Justice for Parents in Washington: A Dual Approach. *Juvenile and Family Court Journal* 53(4): 31–41.

Chemers, B. M. (1995). *Bridging the Child Welfare and Juvenile Justice Systems.* Washington, D.C.: U.S. Department of Justice, Office of Juvenile Justice and Delinquency Prevention.

Children's Bureau (2005). *A Report to Congress on Adoption and Other Permanency Outcomes for Children in Foster Care: Focus on Older Children.* Washington, D.C.: U.S. Department of Health and Human Services.

Commonwealth of Kentucky (2005). *Court Improvement Program Report.* Frankfort: Kentucky Court of Justice, Administrative Office of the Courts.

Commonwealth of Massachusetts (2005). *Tenth Year Annual Program Report: October 1, 2004–June 30, 2005.* Boston: Supreme Judicial Court.

Davis, S., and E. Lee (2006). *The National Evaluation of the Court Improvement Program: Synthesis of 2005 Court Improvement Program Reforms.* Washington, D.C.: Planning and Learning Technologies.

Dobbin, S. A., S. I. Gatowski, and K. R. Johns (1998). *Child Abuse and Neglect Cases: Representation as a Critical Component of Effective Practice.* Reno: National Council of Juvenile and Family Court Judges, Permanency Planning for Children Department.

Dobbin, S. A., S. I. Gatowski, and D. M. Maxwell (2004). *Building a Better Collaboration: Facilitating Change in the Court and Child Welfare System.* Reno: National Council of Juvenile and Family Court Judges, Permanency Planning for Children Department.

Fiermonte, C., and N. S. Salyers (2005). *Improving Outcomes Together: Court and Child Welfare Collaboration.* Chicago: University of Illinois, Children and Family Research Center.

First Star (2006). *Legal Research: Child Representation in Abuse/Neglect Proceedings.* At www.firststar.org/research/representation.asp (accessed June 19, 2006).

Halemba, G. J., G. C. Siegel, R. D. Lord, and S. Zawacki (2004). *Arizona Dual Jurisdiction Study: Final Report.* Pittsburgh: National Center for Juvenile Justice.

Hardin, M. (2003). *Statement of Mark Hardin on Behalf of the American Bar Association Concerning the Role of the Federal Court Improvement Program in the Implementation of the Adoption and Safe Families Act*. Washington, D.C.: American Bar Association, Governmental Affairs Office.

Katner, D., P. McCarthy Jr., M. Rollin, and M. Ventrell (2001). *NACC Recommendations for Representation of Children in Abuse and Neglect Cases*. Denver: National Association of Counsel for Children.

Keith, A. L., and C. R. Flango (2002). *Expediting Dependency Appeals: Strategies to Reduce Delay*. Willamsburg, Va.: National Center for State Courts.

Khoury, A. (2004). The delinquency factor in permanency planning for adolescents. *Child Law Practice* 23(6): 85, 90–95.

Kinkead, L. B. (2005). *The 2005 Program Report for the Period May 1, 2004–June 30, 2005*. Nashville: Tennessee Supreme Court, Court Improvement Program.

McNaught, K., and L. Onkeles (2004). *Improving Outcomes for Older Youth: What Judges and Attorneys Need to Know*. Tulsa: National Resource Center for Youth Development.

Murray, K. O., and S. Gesiriech (n.d.). *A Brief Legislative History of the Child Welfare System*. Washington, D.C.: Pew Commission on Children in Foster Care.

National Council of Juvenile and Family Court Judges (NCJFCJ) (1995). *Resource Guidelines: Improving Court Practice in Child Abuse and Neglect Cases*. Reno: Author.

—— (2000). *Adoption and Permanency Guidelines: Improving Court Practice in Child Abuse and Neglect Cases*. Reno: Author.

—— (2003). *Model Court Status Report 2003: A Snapshot of the Child Victims Act Model Courts Project*. Reno: Author.

—— (2006). *National Council Model Court Profiles*. At www.ncjfcj.org/content/blogcategory/112/151/ (accessed June 22, 2006).

National Institute of Justice (2006). *Drug Courts: The Second Decade*. Washington, D.C.: U.S. Department of Justice, Office of Justice Programs.

Nunn, D., L. Morhar, and L. Wilson (2004). *Court-Appointed Counsel: Caseload Standards, Service Delivery Models, and Contract Administration*. San Francisco: Center for Families, Children and the Courts.

Office of Juvenile Justice and Delinquency Prevention (OJJDP) (2006a). *OJJDP Model Programs Guide: Drug Court*. At www.dsgonline.com/mpg2.5/drug_court.htm (accessed June 27, 2006).

—— (2006b). *Strengthening Abuse and Neglect Courts in America: Management Information Systems (SANCA-MIS) Project*. At www.ncsconline.org/WC/Publications/KIS_FamJusSANCAProject.pdf (accessed May 15, 2006).

Oregon Juvenile Court Improvement Project (2005). *Year End Report for the Federal FY 2005*. Salem: Oregon Supreme Court.

Pew Commission on Children in Foster Care (2004). *Fostering the Future: Safety, Permanence and Well-Being for Children in Foster Care*. Washington, D.C.: Author.

Rhode Island Family Court Truancy Court Program (TCP) (2006). *About Us*. At www. courts.state.ri.us/truancycourt/aboutus.htm (accessed July 5, 2006).

Roberts, M., J. Brophy, and C. Cooper (1997). *The Juvenile Drug Court Movement*. Washington, D.C.: U.S. Department of Justice, Office of Juvenile Justice and Delinquency Prevention.

SANCA Project (n.d.) *What Is the SANCA Project?* At www.sancaproject.org/sanca. php?doc_type = sancaproject (accessed June 4, 2007).

Stahl, A. L. (2003). *Drug Offense Cases in Juvenile Courts, 1990–1999*. Washington, D.C.: U.S. Department of Justice, Office of Juvenile Justice and Delinquency Prevention.

State of Arizona (2005). *Arizona Court Improvement Program Report Ending 6.30.05*. Phoenix: Supreme Court, State of Arizona, Administrative Office of the Courts.

State of Colorado (2005). *Colorado's Court Improvement Program: Program Report for June 2005*. Denver: Author.

State of Hawaii (2005). *Program report FY 2005*. Honolulu: State of Hawaii Judiciary.

State of Indiana (2005). *Program Report*. Indianapolis: Supreme Court of Indiana.

State of Kansas (2005). *FY 2005 CIP Updates*. Topeka: Supreme Court of Kansas.

State of New Mexico (2005). *Improving Outcomes for Abused and Neglected Children: New Mexico's Court Improvement Project*. Santa Fe: Supreme Court of New Mexico, Administrative Office of the Courts.

State of Pennsylvania (2005). *2005 Project Report*. Mechanicsburg: Administrative Office of Pennsylvania Courts.

State of Rhode Island (2005). *Program Report: June 2005*. Providence: Rhode Island Supreme Court.

State of Utah (2005). *Program Report: Utah's Court Improvement Program, June 2005*. Salt Lake City: Utah Supreme Court, Administrative Office of the Courts.

Stewart-Jones, A. R.and T. Watkins-Tribbitt (2005). *Annual Program Report*. Annapolis: Maryland Judiciary, Administrative Office of the Courts.

Szymanski, L. (2005). *Expedited Appeals in Termination of Parental Rights Cases*. NCJJ Snapshot 10(1). Pittsburgh: National Center for Juvenile Justice.

Territory of Puerto Rico (2005). *Summary Report of Puerto Rico Court Improvement*. San Juan: Oficina de Administración de los Tribunales, Directoria de Programmas Judiciales.

Texas Court Improvement Project (2005). *Program Report: June 30, 2005*. Austin: Texas Center for the Judiciary.

U.S. Department of Health and Human Services (2007). *The National Evaluation of the Court Improvement Program*. At www.pal-tech.com/cip/index.cfm (accessed June 17, 2007).

U.S. General Accounting Office (1999). *Juvenile Courts: Reforms Aim to Better Serve Maltreated Children*. GAO/HEHS-99-13. Washington, D.C.: Author.

U.S. Senate, Committee on Finance (1990). *Foster Care, Adoption Assistance, and Child Welfare Service*. S Prt. 101-118. Washington, D.C.: U.S. Government Printing Office.

Facilitation of   TWELVE
Systems Reform

Learning from Model
Court Jurisdictions

SHIRLEY A. DOBBIN

In chapter 11, Karl Ensign and colleagues outline a number of federal programs, legislation, and directives that have significantly changed court and
child welfare agency expectations, outcomes, and timeframes for processing child welfare cases. After a description of overall judicial reform efforts,
they briefly discuss the development of field-initiated practice guidelines,
various national demonstration projects, and the increasing recognition
of the need for effective collaborations between courts and child welfare
agencies. In this chapter, I add to that discussion by providing additional
information on the *Resource Guidelines* of the National Council of Juvenile and Family Court Judges (NCJFCJ), describing national performance
indicators that are key supports for a reform framework, and discussing the results of research regarding multisystem collaboration in Model
Court sites. I then consider a variety of specific youth-focused activities
undertaken by the NCJFCJ's Model Court jurisdictions across the country.[1] I conclude with an examination of the current state of research on
reform efforts.

RESOURCE GUIDELINES AND MODEL COURTS

Reform is facilitated when there is clear consensus regarding system needs, possible alternatives, how change should take place, and how results will be measured. The *Resource Guidelines: Improving Court Practice in Child Abuse and Neglect Cases* (NCJFCJ, 1995) provides a critical tool in both court and system reform. It details dependency hearing processes, provides options for improved practice, and guides juvenile and family courts in assessing and implementing improvements in their handling of child abuse and neglect cases. At the heart of the *Resource Guidelines* is a philosophy that emphasizes a problem-solving approach to improving court practice—an approach that focuses on judicial leadership and oversight, substantive and timely hearings, and collaboration among all key players in the dependency system.

In chapter 11, the authors note that the *Resource Guidelines* are "regarded as the seminal resource for defining the essential elements of properly conducted hearings, including their duration, who should be present, key decisions and activities that need to take place at each hearing, and required reports, petitions, and findings." Indeed, juvenile and family courts around the nation have looked to the *Resource Guidelines* as a blueprint for court reform. The *Resource Guidelines* also serve as a catalyst for broader systems reform and are not limited to guiding court reform. In Model Court jurisdictions, as well as other juvenile and family courts across the nation, implementation of the *Resource Guidelines* has been a key component in overall systems change initiatives.

The Child Victims Act Model Courts (VAMC) serve as models for how the *Resource Guidelines* can be used as a tool for court and system reform efforts and the implementation of system-wide best practices. Drawing on the best practice principles of the *Resource Guidelines*, as well as the *Adoption and Permanency Guidelines* (NCJFCJ, 2000), Model Courts have assessed current practice, identified strengths and challenges in practice and policy, facilitated a system-wide dialogue, and established priority areas for reform. Model Courts continually assess their child abuse and neglect calendaring practice and case processing and the timeliness and substance of their court hearings. They focus on court and agency barriers to timely permanence and develop and institute plans for court and child welfare reform. Model Courts work collaboratively with child welfare agencies to institute long-term, sustainable systems change and do not focus solely on changes in the court process.

It is important to underscore that the term "Model Court" is somewhat of a misnomer. Model Courts do not model a perfect system, or even the full range of best practices; rather, they model a process of change. Moreover, Model Courts are not only courts; they are court-driven, multisystem reform efforts with strong judicial leadership and involvement of other key stakeholders, including the child welfare agency. In addition to focusing on court performance issues (such as improving timeliness and substance of hearings, calendaring practice, and the clarity and content of court orders and judicial findings), Model Courts address a wide range of issues pertaining to service planning and service delivery, visitation and placement issues, and engagement of the parties in the case planning process. They are involved in initiatives that focus on specific populations of children, such as children from birth to three years of age, youth in foster care, and minority children.

A number of Model Courts have demonstrated the effectiveness of these reforms on the overall court process and timeframes to permanence. Model Courts have achieved shortened timeframes for permanence for children under court supervision and, in some jurisdictions, a significant decrease in the number of children under the supervision of the court.[2] As of yet, however, there has been no comprehensive evaluation that empirically demonstrates the independent or cumulative effectiveness of various practices on the achievement of safe, timely permanence for children and youth in foster care.

NATIONAL COURT PERFORMANCE MEASURES IN CHILD PROTECTION CASES

Experience gained through the Model Courts suggests that court and child welfare reform trend toward an outcome focus. Consistent with Model Court experience, the NCJFCJ, through a collaborative national partnership with the American Bar Association Center on Children and the Law and the National Center for State Courts, has developed national court performance measures for dependency courts to assess safety (to ensure that children are safe from abuse while under court jurisdiction), permanence (to ensure children have permanence and stability in their living situations), due process (to ensure cases are decided impartially and thoroughly, based on evidence before the court), and timeliness (to expedite permanence by minimizing the time from the filing of the petition or shelter care order to the achievement of permanence).[3] Court performance measurement enables courts to determine whether they comply with ASFA timelines; hold substantive, meaningful, and timely hearings; achieve timely permanence for children with minimal disruption in placement; conduct permanency hearings that result in permanence for children; and provide procedural protections for parties, such as notice to parents and foster parents. Two types of measurement activities are vital to court improvement: (1) performance measurement to establish baseline performance, identify areas in need of reform, and chart progress in meeting deadlines and reform goals; and (2) judicial workload measurement to track the resources available to courts and to persuasively argue for what courts need to achieve major gains in their performance. In order to implement and sustain long-term court improvement, courts must have the capacity to engage in ongoing performance measurement and judicial workload assessments.

Data inform reform efforts and hold the court and the broader system accountable for the outcomes they are expected to achieve. Courts that are able to track data and measure court performance are able to establish a baseline against which reform efforts can be measured, target reform initiatives, and assess outcomes. Most dependency courts continue to struggle to develop the capacity to generate data on the national performance measures. Courts that currently are unable to collect the necessary data to measure performance are working toward developing their capacity to collect, manage, report, and ultimately use outcome measurement data. Many courts have developed data-sharing agreements with their child welfare agency in order to gather data on outcomes such as safety and permanence. Although data sharing is an important strategy to enhance systems collaboration and accountability, dependency courts must, at the same time, strive to collect and report data on their own performance.

MULTISYSTEM COLLABORATION AND MODEL COURTS

Collaboration is at the heart of many features of complex reform agendas. In chapter 11, Ensign and colleagues correctly note the increasing focus on the need for effective multisystem collaboration with respect to Court Improvement Project (CIP) reforms, the federal Child and Family Services Review (CFSR) and Program Improvement Plans (PIPs), and overall systems reform. Indeed, as required by the Deficit Reduction Act, the most recent CIP funding requires demonstrated, meaningful collaboration between the court and child welfare agencies and integrated strategic planning. Ideally, CIP Strategic Plans, PIPs developed through the Child and Family Service Review process, and state action should be strategically coordinated to support a common vision and prioritize reform areas that support overall reform efforts. The Pew Commission on Children in Foster Care recommended the development of state commissions on foster care that include membership from the courts, child welfare agencies, and service providers. Many states have developed and implemented such statewide commissions to provide leadership guidance for statewide reform efforts. At the same time, effective multisystem collaboration has been a hallmark of Model Court reforms since the 1990s. As noted, the federal government is increasingly requiring that states demonstrate effective collaboration as a condition of further funding.

There is much discussion in the field about the need to collaborate, but there is little talk of what it actually means to collaborate, how and when to do it, and how to ensure that collaboration is meaningful and sustainable, particularly in complex and highly politicized systems. The Permanency Planning for Children Department of the NCJFCJ conducted a comprehensive study of the collaborative efforts under way in six Model Court sites. The study focused on the collaborative process and structure in each site and found that effective systems reform is (1) driven by strong and effective judicial and system leadership; (2) collaborative and involves all aspects of the system in reform efforts—the court, the child welfare agency, legal advocates, service providers, community representatives, and other key stakeholders; (3) driven by shared, core values around the need for permanence for all children and youth, a shared vision, and common system goals; (4) intentional and planned; and (5) outcome-focused with accountability for all participants. Study results provided the basis for a Technical Assistance Bulletin that outlines different collaborative processes, structures, and strategies that have proven to be successful in facilitating effective multisystem collaborations (Dobbin et al., 2004).

MODEL COURT REFORM ACTIVITIES SPECIFICALLY FOCUSED ON YOUTH

Numerous activities and reforms that are geared toward enhancing outcomes for older youth are emerging from Model Court reform efforts. Model Courts are working with their collaborative partners to develop a shared understanding and shared vision with respect to systemic responses to youth. These shared values serve as the overall framework for multisystem reform efforts and outcomes. They include preserving and supporting permanence in a youth's family of origin when safety can be assured, engagement of youth in the decision-making process and case planning (empowerment of youth), the importance of lifelong connections for youth, and redefining permanence in terms of lifelong connections with caring, committed adults.

Reform efforts implemented by Model Courts include specialized court dockets, specialized service delivery, multidisciplinary training on child and adolescent development, involvement of former foster youth in training programs and reform efforts, having youth represented on multidisciplinary working groups, and involvement of broader community members (including the school, faith-based organizations, and the business community) in reform efforts. Examples of these reform efforts include the following:

• *Judicial benchbooks, checklists, and resource guides.* Several Model Court jurisdictions, such as the Honolulu and New York City Model Courts, have developed benchbooks, checklists, and resource guides that are designed to assist judges in effectively responding to the needs of youth in foster care. Although they differ somewhat in form, these tools outline questions that judges should ask from the bench with respect to the youth's permanent plan and long-term adult relationships, medical and mental health needs, educational goals and achievements, and the youth's aspirations and life goals. They also often include a list of available resources for older youth in the areas of education, health, employment, and housing.

• *Benchmark permanency hearings.* In benchmark permanency hearings, the youth, supportive adults identified by the youth, and the judge sit together in the courtroom to discuss the youth's future plans, educational and career goals, and the steps and skills necessary to facilitate achievement of those goals. Benchmark permanency hearings are being used in a number of Model Court jurisdictions, including Buffalo, Chicago, Newark, and Washington, D.C. In some jurisdictions, a multidisciplinary staff of professionals also participates in benchmark permanency hearings. In some models, only those youth with a goal of another planned permanent living arrangement participate in benchmark permanency hearings. In other models, all youth in foster care participate. The purpose of these hearings is to ensure that all efforts are being made to provide the youth with the support system, skills, and resources necessary to support their long-term goals and to achieve independent and productive lives. Benchmark permanency hearings and associated outcomes have not, as of yet, been evaluated. A comprehensive, longitudinal, quasi-experimental evaluation that measures the effect of these benchmark hearings on long-term youth outcomes (e.g., self-confidence and self-efficacy, sustainable support systems and networks, educational and career achievements) is much needed.

• *Multidisciplinary training programs.* A number of Model Courts sponsor multidisciplinary training programs that focus on child and adolescent development and the specific needs of youth in foster care. In many Model Courts, youth serve on advisory planning committees for training programs or speak at training programs to share their perspectives and insights. Most of these training programs have been evaluated in terms of training components (e.g., quality of faculty and the content of presentations and workshops). However, few have fully evaluated knowledge acquisition and skill development, attitudinal and behavioral changes in participants, or practice and policy changes that have resulted from these training programs. Training programs also have not been evaluated with respect to overall outcomes and whether outcomes for youth improve as a result of training programs.

• *Service provision and mentor programs.* A number of Model Courts—including the courts in Alexandria, Virginia; Cincinnati, Ohio; and Los Angeles, California—have partnered with behavioral and mental health and community service providers to establish mentorship programs designed to support the development of independent living skills and long-term supports for youth in foster care. These programs provide education and mentorship with respect to housing and budgeting, support youth's personal growth and educational achievement, and help youth in developing lifelong social support networks. Again, there is little empirical support for the effect of these programs on long-term, youth-based outcomes.

• *Alternative dispute resolution (ADR) programs.* Many Model Courts have developed alternative dispute resolution (ADR) programs to facilitate the more active involvement of youth in case planning and decision-making. Model Courts—including those in Honolulu, Miami, San Jose, California, and Washington, D.C.—use mediation and family conferencing models. Although many of these programs have been evaluated in terms of permanency outcomes and timeliness, few programs have looked specifically at whether these programs effectively empower youth as decision-makers, although there are some anecdotal findings that support this claim.

STATE OF THE RESEARCH ON REFORM EFFORTS

Although there have been increasing efforts in recent years to link research, practice, and policy, much work is yet to be done in fully integrating research into reform efforts. System professionals and funders lack a clear understanding about what constitutes good research, the time and resources necessary to conduct high-quality research, and the constraints on conclusions that can be drawn. Researchers lack a clear understanding about how to conduct applied research within a highly politicized and complex system and how to make their research findings relevant to practitioners and policy makers.

Taken-for-granted concepts such as "permanence" and "well-being" have not been adequately operationalized, especially with respect to how they may differ for different populations of children. Does permanence mean something different with respect to an older youth than with a young child, and, if so, should permanence be measured differently for youth? In addition to the absence of clear definitions of core principles and system outcomes, there is no clear consensus on how the "effectiveness" of programs, practices, and policies should be measured and against what standards. Are they effective when compared with what and for whom? Adding to these complexities is the growing body of neurological, psychological, and social research specific to adolescents. The research in adolescent development needs to be more fully integrated into practice, programs, and policies that relate to adolescent "permanence" and "well-being."

As with much applied research, there are constraints on research design, particularly with regard to the use of random assignment to control groups and appropriate comparisons. These constraints necessarily limit the conclusions that can be drawn about the effectiveness of programs, practices, and policies and any causal link to child, youth, and family-based outcomes. Challenges encountered in conducting longitudinal studies and long-term studies of programs raise concerns about model drift and sustained, long-term findings and implications. Because of the complexities of conducting applied research, courts and child welfare agencies need to reach out to and involve the research community in designing and implementing meaningful research and evaluation studies. When possible, rigorous methods that allow for appropriate level of controls and generalizability of findings should be employed.

The national court performance measures need to be incorporated into research projects that examine court process and outcomes. Court-related outcomes should be consistent with the operational definitions of the national court performance measures and address the domains of safety, permanence, due process, and timeliness. The inclusion of the national court performance measures in research will facilitate more meaningful comparisons across jurisdictions and contribute to a national understanding of practice, program, and policy effectiveness. In addition, data collection tools should build on and adapt the foundational instruments of the national Toolkit project. The Toolkit project builds on the national court performance measures and outlines a methodology for measurement, suggests data report formats, outlines business rules for management information systems, and discusses strategies to enhance data capacity and obtain buy-in for dependency court performance measures from multisystem professionals and policy-makers.

Although there are many challenges, a shift toward more evidence-based and empirically driven practice and policy development is clearly emerging. There is a strong need to move beyond anecdotal or impressionistic information. Researchers, practitioners, and policy-makers must actively work to build bridges between research, practice, and policy—to share expertise, develop common ground, target appropriate research needs, and effectively translate research findings and data into practical and policy-relevant recommendations.

NOTES

1. More information about the Model Court Project of the NCJFCJ can be found at www.ncjfcj.org.
2. For example, in Chicago, the backlog of children and youth under the court's jurisdiction in out-of-home, long-term foster care was reduced from an estimated 58,000 to fewer than 20,000 in a three-year period. The number is now lower than 16,000 children.
3. The National Dependency Court performance measures were originally developed with funding from the David and Lucile Packard Foundation and was first outlined in the publication Building a Better Court: Measuring and Improving Court Performance in Judicial Workload in Child Abuse and Neglect Cases (American Bar Association, 2004).

REFERENCES

American Bar Association Center on Children and the Law, National Center for State Courts, and National Council of Juvenile and Family Court Judges (2004). *Building a Better Court: Measuring and Improving Court Performance and Judicial Workload in Child Abuse and Neglect Cases.* Los Altos, Calif.: David and Lucile Packard Foundation. At www.ncsconline.org/wc/publications/res_ctpers_tcps_packgde4-04pub (accessed June 20, 2006).

Dobbin, S. A., S. I. Gatowski, and D. M. Maxwell (2004). *Building a Better Collaboration: Facilitating Change in the Court and Child Welfare System.* Technical Assistance Bulletin 8. Reno: National Council of Juvenile and Family Court Judges.

National Council of Juvenile and Family Court Judges (1995). *Resource Guidelines: Improving Court Practice in Child Abuse and Neglect Cases.* Reno: Author.

—— (2000). *Adoption and Permanency Guidelines.* Reno: Author.

Practice Responses to the
Permanency Needs of Youth

PART III

In Parts I and II of this volume, we described the problems related to achieving permanence and preparing youth for adulthood, and we examined some of the policy levers that have shaped and will continue to shape the practice landscape. In this section, we highlight some of the evolving practice responses to the permanency needs of youth in foster care, including their needs for family support into adulthood and beyond. Practitioners provide a critically needed understanding of the needs of the children and families they serve from an "on the ground" perspective. As they strive to meet the permanency needs of youth in foster care, practitioners often must flex and adjust as they work to respond to the immediate needs of youth while, simultaneously, creating new strategies that may more effectively meet the longer-term needs of youth in foster care.

In the first two chapters of this section, the authors consider the practice issues surrounding efforts to promote permanence through reunification and adoption. Taking practice as the starting point, they point to policy supports and additional research that are needed to ensure that youth in foster care have enduring family connections that support them into adulthood and beyond.

In chapter 13, Barbara A. Pine and Robin Spath describe and build on the results of an evaluation of an intensive family reunification program. They identify the features of the program that research has suggested are associated with effective family reunification efforts, and they describe the promising results related to achieving permanence for children, shortening children's foster care stays, and increasing children's chances of remaining at home after reunification. Applying the learning from this evaluation, they suggest a number of ways that family reunification services can be adapted to meet the permanency needs of adolescents, given their unique development needs.

In chapter 14, Ruth G. McRoy and Elissa Madden examine agency practices, programs, and federal policies that affect the likelihood of adoption for youth who are in foster care. They identify a range of continuing practice challenges to adoption for youth despite the many legislative initiatives designed to promote adoption. In addition to providing suggestions regarding future research and policy development to promote adoption for youth in foster care, they discuss a variety of ways to address practice issues, including the recruitment of nonrelated adoptive families for youth in foster care, the provision of adequate postadoption services, and challenging the beliefs of some caseworkers that older youth are "unadoptable."

Practitioners also have sought to expand the effect of their programming through specific strategies that have the potential to improve permanency outcomes for youth in foster care. In the next two chapters of this section, the authors describe two promising strategies. First, they describe family involvement meetings that bring together youth, their birth families, and other important individuals in the youth's life to jointly plan for and with the youth. Second, they describe community involvement strategies that mobilize local resources to prevent the need for youth to enter foster care, support youth and families as they plan for the youth's return to family, and support the youth and family after the youth exits foster care.

In chapter 15, David Crampton and Joan Pennell describe strategies for involving families that embody a number of intuitively and empirically promising practices. They review the common elements of different family involvement practice models and describe research that is beginning to shed light on the effect of family involvement meetings on outcomes for youth and families, family satisfaction, and emotional healing. The authors apply what has been learned about family involvement meetings to work with older youth in foster care, and they make the case for the vital importance of actively engaging youth in family involvement meetings.

In chapter 16, Sandra Stukes Chipungu, Laura G. Daughtery, and Benjamin Kerman discuss community involvement within the context of the need for multilevel solutions for the multilevel problems that youth in foster care and their families face. Considering youth as both vulnerable members of a community, as well as potential resources to the community, they note a variety of opportunities for expanding the ways communities prevent the weakening of family bonds to avert formal involvement with the child welfare system.

In chapter 17, Hewitt B. Clark and Kimberly A. Crosland review the literature on the effectiveness of independent living programs with an eye toward understanding the effect of life skills services and experiences and their relationships to outcomes. They describe innovative strategies at the community and state levels to prepare youth to transition to adulthood, and they present evolving evidence-informed practices and assessment tools that can assist in developing youth's social capital through a network of informal key players who provide supports for youth as they transition to adulthood. Their chapter suggests that youth benefit from extended stays in foster care with continuing services and ongoing efforts to ensure that youth leave care with lifelong family connections.

In chapter 18, the authors present case vignettes illustrating how practice staff in one agency integrate a variety of the practices discussed in the preceding chapters. To help bridge the research-to-practice gap, Madelyn Freundlich, Lauren Frey, Benjamin Kerman, and Sarah B. Greenblatt describe examples from the field at Casey Family Services. Work with the evidence-informed Casey teaming model and community-based family resource centers highlights opportunities for addressing the needs of youth in placement, as well as for supporting fragile families and averting more-intensive, intrusive services.

Permanent Families
for Adolescents

THIRTEEN

*Applying Lessons Learned
from a Family Reunification
Demonstration Program*

BARBARA A. PINE
AND ROBIN SPATH

Family reunification is the primary permanency goal for children in out-of-home care. Although most children in care will eventually be reunified with their families, there is a growing body of research suggesting that many of these children will return to foster care at some point. For these reasons, there has been renewed interest in family reunification practice, particularly with regard to developing a clearer understanding of which programs are most effective with which children and families. In this chapter, we describe a family reunification program that provides intensive family-based and family-centered services. We delineate the features of the program, linking these to existing knowledge about what works in family reunification. We then discuss the findings from a comprehensive evaluation of that program that demonstrated promising results in relation to achieving permanence for children, shortening children's foster care stays, and increasing children's chances of remaining at home once they return. Finally, we discuss key aspects of the program in the context of the developmental needs of adolescents in out-of-home care, and we make recommendations for revising the approach to better meet these needs and achieve permanence for these youth.

THE REUNIFICATION PROGRAM

The family reunification program described in this chapter is an ongoing family reunification program operated by Casey Family Services, a large, nonprofit child welfare agency, in two New England states in conjunction with these states' child welfare agencies. The program, as initially developed, was revised based on evidence about family reunification that was available at the time, including a study that Casey Family Services conducted of the program.

As part of the redesign, the program targeted families who had experienced a first-time removal of their children and developed protocols with the referring state agency to accept families quickly after a child's removal from the family: that is, within five to fifteen days. An additional feature of the redesign was close collaboration with the state agency staff in providing services. Other core program components were:

1. *Intensive family-centered and home-based services.* Studies have demonstrated the value of intensive services in reunifying families (Fraser et al., 1996). A family-centered focus—on the needs of the entire family and not only the child—is critical because the problems that led to placement of the child in out-of-home care are often family-, rather than child-, centered (Fraser et al., 1996). Services that address the needs of the family can include building collaborative relationships with the parents; improving communication, problem-solving, and parenting skills; and meeting concrete needs such as housing, food, job training and employment, and health care. Because many of these activities take place in the home setting, the interventions are best located there as well.

2. *Comprehensive assessment and service planning.* When Peg Hess and colleagues (1992) looked retrospectively at failed reunifications, they found inadequate assessments to be a chief contributor. The comprehensive assessment of families in the program includes a psychosocial history and an examination of the following: current functioning and barriers, parental skills and risks to children, family strengths, readiness and motivation for change, and parent-child relationship and attachment. After the assessment, staff works with the families to develop a service plan.

3. *Regular, frequent, and well-planned parent-child visits with activities linked to the family's service plan.* Well over one dozen studies have documented the relationship between visiting and successful outcomes for families and children (Hess, 1999). Visiting has been called "the heart of family

reunification" (Hess and Proch, 1993:119). I. P. Davis and colleagues (1996) found that visits were key to discharge from care. In the program, parents are helped to practice newly gained parenting skills during visits with their children, such as offering praise, setting limits, and planning activities that are appropriate to their children's age and interests.

4. *Goal-directed services that are both concrete and therapeutic.* A mix of concrete services, supportive counseling, and skills training has been shown to be effective in reuniting families and accelerating the reunification process (Fein and Staff, 1991; Maluccio et al., 1996; Walton et al., 1993).

5. *A strengths-based approach to the work with families.* The competence perspective and strengths approach to practice focus on the capabilities, assets, and positive attributes that can be emphasized in helping families and children grow and develop (Maluccio et al., 2002). With respect to reunification, strengths are seen as "keys to solutions to problems" (Zamosky et al., 1993:157). As Jeanne Zamosky and colleagues point out, "a strengths approach assumes that the very act of adopting this posture will not only enable strengths to be identified, but will enhance the strengths themselves and facilitate their spread throughout the family and its helping network" (157).

6. *Regular service provider team meetings that include foster parents and birth parents whenever possible.* Recognizing the importance of collaborative planning and service delivery, funders of both public and private services, especially in child welfare, are increasingly likely to mandate collaboration as a crucial component for program support. The trend toward privatization and contracting out for services virtually demands effective public/private collaboration (Lewandowski and GlenMaye, 2002). Collaboration and communication were likewise critical in the Casey Family Services' reunification program. Respondents in the study's examination of the collaboration between Casey reunification program staff and the state child welfare agency staff cited good communication as the most important aspect of their collaboration to reunify families. In particular, they found that openness and mutuality in the communication at regular meetings, mutual understanding and respect, and access to the partner provider contributed to successful reunifications. Other contributing factors to success were mutual understanding of goals, clear expectations, valuing the team's work together, and having regular, structured meetings (Pine et al., 2006).

7. *Group work as an integral part of treatment.* Groups can be particularly important as a means of social support for often-isolated parents and

in helping parents gain new skills. They can assist parents in developing an understanding of their situation in relation to child welfare authorities and what they need to do so that their children can return home (Terling, 1999; Wagner, 2003). The goal of reunification programs is not only re-unification but also helping families remain together once children return home. Groups for parents whose children have been removed can help achieve both these ends. Toni Terling (1999) found higher reentry rates for children whose parents could not comprehend or accept the child welfare authority's assessment and expectations of them. Trudy Festinger (1996), in her comparison of children who returned to care with those who did not, cited lower parenting skills and few social supports in families of the returned children.

8. *Reunification within six months.* A study by Mark Courtney and Yin-Ling Irene Wong (1996) showed that the earlier that children exit foster care the more likely they are to reunify. Mark Fraser and colleagues (1996) found that most families were reunified in three months after an intensive intervention; Raymond Kirk (2002) found an average time of nine months to reunification.

9. *An expanded view of success.* Although returning children to their birth families was the primary objective of the reunification program, the program also was designed to help families consider and be involved in developing other permanent plans for their children. As one senior staff member in the reunification program said about one parent whose child could not be returned to her: "This parent is an excellent visiting parent. In the open adoption which she has helped to plan, she can visit her child on a regular basis." An expanded view of family reunification emphasizes the importance of family ties and a more flexible definition of success that aims to "help each child and family to achieve or maintain, at any given time, their optimal level of reconnections—from full reentry of the child into the family system to other forms of contact, such as visiting, that affirm the child's membership in the family" (Maluccio et al., 1993:6).

10. *Use of concurrent planning approaches.* The team approach used in the Casey Family Services reunification program facilitated concurrent planning with open communication about progress, options, responsibilities, and plans. Policy under the Adoption and Safe Families Act now promotes and encourages this approach by clarifying that "reasonable efforts to reunify a child with his or her family and reasonable efforts to secure an adoptive family for a child, if needed, can go on concurrently" (Child Welfare League of America, n.d.).

11. *Competent, professional staff working in teams.* The program used a team of three to deliver services: a masters-level trained social worker, a trained family support worker, and a team leader who provided clinical supervision and oversight on all cases and who managed the collaboration with the partner agency. The team approach enabled staff to work closely with families in the provision of concrete and therapeutic services tailored to each family's needs. Especially noteworthy was the presence of Spanish-speaking staff in the program site serving a large Hispanic population. The Casey Family Services program team worked in concert with its counterpart in the state child welfare agency—a team composed of a caseworker, supervisor, and program supervisor. Strong alliances were built between most families and their helping professionals. Studies show that successful reunification results, in part, from strong worker-family relationships (Fraser et al., 1996).

EVALUATION OF THE REUNIFICATION PROGRAM: AN OVERVIEW

The evaluation of the Casey Family Services reunification program was comprehensive, focusing on both program processes and outcomes.[1] It was conducted by a team of social work researchers at two universities in the region over a period of five years. During the course of the evaluation, a total of 135 families entered the program; 116 families with 274 children consented to be a part of the study.

Process Evaluation

The process evaluation sought to answer the following questions:

- Is the program being implemented as it was designed and within the planned time-frames?
- What factors facilitate or impede implementation?
- Are the interagency collaborative relationships developing as planned?
- What are the characteristics of the families and children who are in the program?
- Are the families being served those whom the program had intended to serve?
- What are the risk factors to child safety and family integrity at case intake?
- What protective factors and strengths are present?
- What aspects of the program need further development?

To answer these questions, the research team used a variety of approaches, including a case study of the program; observation of groups, parent-child visits, and team meetings; focus groups with staff and parent participants; a survey of key informants; and comprehensive reviews of family records at various points during the study. In addition to the overall study of the program as part of the case study, the team examined three components of the program in detail: parent-child visiting, use of groups with parents, and collaboration between the agency and its partner state agencies in the two sites. As each element of the process evaluation was completed, findings were compiled and recommendations based on these findings were made so that staff and administrators might make changes to the program to improve both efficiency and effectiveness.

Outcome Evaluation

The outcome evaluation sought answers to questions about the program's effectiveness, specifically:

- Are families being reunified?
- Are risk factors for families and children reduced?
- Do families remain safe and stable over time?
- Which families are likely to be reunified and stay together?
- What permanent plans are made for children who cannot return home?
- What other positive family connections are made?
- Is the program more effective than standard reunification services offered by state agencies in reunifying families or in achieving permanence for children?

Nine outcomes were measured:

- Improvement in the family's situation
- Improved parenting skills
- Increased child safety
- Child well-being
- Permanency for the child
- Worker-family alliance
- Interagency collaboration
- Family satisfaction with services
- Level of client participation in the program

The study used a number of existing research instruments to measure these outcomes, including the North Carolina Family Assessment Scale for Reunification (NCFAS-R-I), the Adult-Adolescent Parenting Inventory (AAPI-II), and the Worker-Family Alliance (WAI). Several instruments were developed to measure client satisfaction, level of client participation in the program, and child permanence after twenty-four months. In addition, a quantitative descriptive instrument was developed to gather data on child and family characteristics from program files. Another feature of the outcome study was the use of a matched comparison sample of children in out-of-home care and their families drawn from the databases of the two partner state child welfare agencies. Bivariate and multivariate analyses of study data were conducted.

Findings: Process Evaluation

Findings from the case study and other in-depth examinations of the program's components showed that the program was being implemented as planned, with the exception of parent groups that were consistently offered in only one of the two sites. At that site, social support groups were held each week. Staff worked diligently to prepare parents for visits, coach them during the time spent with their children, and evaluate parents' progress with them after the visits were over. With respect to the relationship between the program staff and their partners in the state agencies, respondents indicated the high value that all involved professionals placed on the collaboration and its importance in reunifying families.

The process evaluation also showed that families and children served by the program were typical of those served by child welfare agencies across the country in terms of demographic and other factors. Consistent with national data, fully one-third of the children had diagnosed and chronic health or mental health problems. The children, however, tended to be younger than is the case nationally as a result of the program's intake criterion of first time removal. Parents, as is the case nationally, had multiple problems that brought them to the attention of child welfare authorities, including substance abuse, domestic violence, homelessness, and other correlates of poverty. There were higher numbers of Latino families in the program than on average nationally, owing to the availability of Spanish-speaking staff in one site and the resulting tendency of the state partner to refer their Spanish-speaking families to the program.

Findings: Outcome Evaluation

Were Families Reunified?

The analysis showed that of the 254 children[2] whose families received re-unification services, 197 had a permanent plan in place by the time their family's case with the program was closed and their family was re-referred to the partner state agency. Of the 197 children who achieved permanence, 122 children (61.9 percent) were reunified with their birth parents or the caretaker from whom they had been removed. Moreover, children were re-turned remarkably quickly: 39.1 weeks on average.

Were Other Permanent Families Found for Children Who Could Not Be Reunified?

Of the 197 children who had a permanent plan in place when their families left the program, forty-one (20.8 percent) were placed with an adoptive family, another nineteen (9.6 percent) were placed with a legal guardian, and thirteen (6.6 percent) had a long-term foster home as their permanent plan. The time to permanence for these children was relatively short: 44.2 weeks on average.

Were Risk Factors for Families and Children Reduced?

Results from the *NCFAS-R* were compared over three time points and showed that family strengths increased in five of the seven domains measured by that instrument. Improvements were noted in the family's environment, parental capabilities, family safety, child well-being, and readiness for reunification. Results from the *AAPI* also showed positive changes in parents' attitudes about parental expectations, the use and value of corporal punishment, and parent-child role reversal.

Do Families Remain Safe and Stable Over Time?

The research team obtained information at twenty-four months after intake into the reunification program from forty-two primary caregivers.[3] For families whom the research team was not able to reach, the researchers reviewed the databases of the two state agency partners. This review yielded data on an additional 148 children, resulting in contacts with nearly 60 percent of those who had been served by the program. These results were encouraging. A total of ninety-one children in this group (61.5 percent) had been reunified with and were still living with their parent, thirteen (8.8 percent) were with an adoptive family, three were in a kinship care or legal guardian placement, thirty-six (24.3 percent) were in a planned long-term foster home, and five were in residential treatment.

Return to care after reunification is of major concern in child welfare. Although the scope of the study did not permit a longitudinal examination of families' experiences after their children's return from foster care, the research team was able to review state agency records in both states to determine whether families served through the reunification program or in the comparison group had been re-referred to the child welfare authorities and whether the report of abuse or neglect had been substantiated.[4] Program families fared better than control group families: 25.2 percent of program families were re-referred to the state child welfare agency compared with 32.5 percent of the comparison group families.

Is the Reunification Program More Effective in Achieving Permanency for Children Than Standard Child Welfare Services?

Children served through the reunification program and children in the comparison group experienced high reunification rates: 61.9 percent of program children and 57.2 percent of comparison children. This finding suggests that the program and the two state child welfare agencies (which provided standard services) were successful in achieving permanence for children experiencing their first removal from their parents' custody. Rates of other permanency placements in the two groups were about equal. However, there were significant differences in two dimensions of permanence: length of time in care and the number of placements while in care. Children served through the reunification program achieved permanent placements, on average, in 44.2 weeks compared with an average of 66 weeks for children in the comparison group.[5]

Even more significant were findings regarding placement stability. Most of the program children (64.9 percent) experienced only one placement while in care compared with 40.7 percent of children in the comparison group with only one placement. The difference between the two groups of children experiencing three or more placements was even more significant—only 12.4 percent of program children compared with 35.7 percent of children in the comparison group moved three or more times. In chapter 5 in this volume, Richard P. Barth and Laura K. Chintapalli report on other studies of placement instability that found much higher rates of children experiencing multiple placements and describe the problems associated with such impermanence.

In sum, the reunification program was successful in reunifying children with their families or placing them with another permanent family more quickly than standard services. The program also provided greater placement stability with fewer moves while the children were in care. Finally, permanence for children in the program appeared to be quite stable over time. Their families were less likely than families receiving standard reunification services to experience a re-referral to the child welfare system.

The program approach shows promise for work with adolescents in the child welfare system to connect them with permanent families. In the following section, we discuss how the program's chief features could be modified to achieve this goal.

STRATEGIES FOR ACHIEVING PERMANENCE FOR ADOLESCENTS

Adolescents in Out-of-Home Care

Adolescents—that is, youth from eleven to eighteen years of age—represent nearly one-half of all children in foster care, an estimated 247,645 young people in 2005 (U.S. Department of Health and Human Services, 2007). As Fred Wulczyn reports in this volume (chapter 1), most youth in foster care have not grown up in foster care but, rather, entered care as teens. In 2005, some 38 percent of those entering care were between the ages of eleven and eighteen, a total of 119,311 youths (U.S. Department of Health and Human Services, 2007). Moreover, as many as twenty-five thousand adolescents leave foster care each year as a result of "aging out" of the child welfare system (Frey et al., 2005). Helping these youth achieve permanence has remained elusive, despite almost two decades of attention to the problem. Studies of former foster youth's disproportionate representation among the homeless population, their involvement in criminal behavior, unintended pregnancy, economic dependency, and other problems have sparked wide-ranging policy and practice responses, mainly aimed at helping youth in foster care gain the skills and resources they need to live on their own. Less attention has been given to helping them successfully connect or reconnect with a permanent family. Barth and Chintapalli (chapter 5 in this volume) report on a number of studies that have shown low rates of reunification and adoption for adolescents.

To be sure, adolescents present unique challenges to child welfare practitioners. Many come into care because of their own behavior problems with which their families can no longer cope. As Barth and Chintapalli note, their time in care also can create problems that make it difficult to parent them. Being in foster care can, in itself, be a threat to identity (Hipgrave, 1989). And, adolescence is a time to establish a sense of autonomy from families without compromising connections to them, a delicate balance for all youth that is made even more challenging for troubled youth or those from troubled families (Thompson et al., 2001).

Despite these challenges, adolescents need help in achieve permanence, which has been defined, as cited by Barth and Chintapalli, as a "state of security and attachment" involving a "parenting relationship that is mutually understood to be a lasting relationship." Others have defined permanence as making a physical and psychological connection to a kinship system (Aldgate et al., 1989). Yet others have pointed to the multidimensional nature of permanence, identifying physical, emotional, legal, and cultural dimensions (Frey et al., 2005).

Within the context of the developmental needs and goals of adolescence, permanence may appear quite different from permanence for younger children. Adolescents may develop a variety of attachments to adults and other youth to meet their needs, and birth families may be differently equipped to serve as a resource to an adolescent than they were to parent a younger child—although, as Tony Hipgrave notes, the adolescent needs a "clear understanding of where the present placement fits into a personal past and a personal future" (1989:45). Finally, an important permanency goal is to help youth in out-of-home care develop the skills they need for interdependent living as they move developmentally toward establishing a life outside of the family. Interdependent living is a concept that people are "mutually and constructively dependent" (Maluccio et al., 1990:11). Thus, in helping adolescents achieve interdependence, emphasis should be on essential connections to a significant person or persons, their community, their own history, a system of values, a group, a means of support, a place, and a source of joy (Pine and Krieger, 1990, citing Pasztor, 1988).

Reunification Services for Adolescents and Their Families

The reunification program described in this chapter achieved success in re-unifying children more quickly than standard services and ensured place-ment stability while they were in care. When children could not be reunited with their birth family, permanence was achieved in other ways. Others in this volume address these contributors to children's permanence. In chap-ter 2, Penelope Maza points out that children who come into foster care and stay for long periods are at greatest risk for not achieving permanence in their childhoods. Barth and Chintapalli (chapter 5) cite numerous studies on the effects of placement instability.

The time that children remain in foster care after return home has been ruled out as a permanency option is also important. As of September 2005, there were an estimated 114,000 children awaiting adoptive place-ment nationally. Nearly one-half of these children are nine years of age or older. They have waited an average of 41.6 months, or well over three years (U.S. Department of Health and Human Services, 2007), compared with the average of just over a year (55.7 weeks) for the reunification pro-gram's placement of children with adoptive families. Ruth G. McRoy and Elissa Madden report in this volume (chapter 14) that nearly one-half of all children awaiting adoption nationally are nine years of age or older, a far larger percentage than the 13 percent of children in the reunification program who were ten or older. Nonetheless, the reunification program was successful in achieving permanence for at least two-thirds of these older children. Barth and Chintapalli cite Wulczyn (2005) and point out that approximately one-half of the youth in care at age sixteen entered as older children and were experiencing a first-time removal. These youth, the authors point out, are likely to be reunified. Thus, a program such as the one described in this chapter would appear to have relevance for help-ing adolescents have permanent families.

Adapting the Reunification Program for Adolescents and Their Families

The reunification program provided by Casey Family Services would need to be retooled to comprise a successful reunification program for adoles-cents. In this section, we discuss how the program could be revised to best meet the permanency needs of youth.

Goals and Principles

The purpose of the reunification program was to "safely and permanently return children in foster care to their birth families as soon as possible after initial placement or by six months at the latest" (Casey Family Services, 1999:1). The guiding principles of the program were as follows:

- The safety of the child is paramount.
- Families want the best for their children, and, generally, children grow and develop best in their families of origin.
- Families have strengths that can be enhanced to resolve problems.
- With appropriate supports, most families can provide the love and nurturing environment that are necessary to raise their children.
- The family must be included in and have a major decision-making role in all aspects of services, from initial assessment through service planning to service delivery.
- Services are tailored to meet the individual needs of the family (Casey Family Services, 1999:2).

The program goal and set of principles for the reunification program would need to be revised to guide the development and implementation of a program aimed at permanence for adolescents. An overarching concept for such a program is a youth-driven approach in articulating the program goals and principles. A youth-driven approach would take into account youth's individual developmental needs and strengths, culture, and ethnicity and would view preparation for adulthood as a process that requires mastery of both tangible and intangible skills (Pine et al., 1990). Moreover, ethics demand that adolescents be involved in all aspects of planning for their futures.

In launching a program with a goal to achieve permanence for adolescents in out-of-home care, an important first step is defining what constitutes permanence for these youth. In most cases, the permanency option of choice is reunification with the birth family or the caregiver from whom the youth was removed. However, what is meant by reunification? Should an "either/or" definition apply: either the youth returns home or not? Instead, program designers may wish to consider a broader definition of family reunification that acknowledges that not all parents can provide full-time care for their children but also recognizes that ties to family and family membership have significant benefits for most children and youth.

Family connections and family membership may be especially beneficial as youth reach adolescence and the developmental task of identity formation. The Casey Family Services reunification program was flexible in its consideration of what constituted a successful outcome, as reflected in the following broadened definition of family reunification:

> Family reunification is the planned process of reconnecting children in out-of-home care with their families by means of a variety of services and supports to the children, their families, and their foster parents or other service providers. It aims to help each child and family to achieve and maintain, at any given time, their optimal level of reconnection—from full reentry of the child into the family system to other forms of contact, such as visiting, that affirm the child's membership in the family. (Maluccio et al., 1993:6)

In the case of an adolescent, the permanency goal might be to find (or support) a "stability" family—that is, a family that could provide a flexible home base for a youth approaching adulthood (Aldgate et al., 1989). The "stability" family could be the birth family, a family in the kinship network, or a foster family.

As noted earlier, the reunification program employed a strengths-based approach in its work with families. This approach was articulated in the program design and reflected in the assessment, service planning processes, and day-to-day work with families and the partner state agency. A strengths-based approach is consistent with the youth-driven approach described above.

Competent Staff

In the Casey Family Services reunification program, each family was served by a team of three professionals. The team was composed of a trained social worker with a master's degree and a specially trained family support worker, who, in most cases, had a baccalaureate degree, both of whom were supervised by a team leader. In addition, a state agency child protection worker and his or her supervisor continued to work closely with each family, and each family also worked with a caseworker from the referring state child welfare agency. The evaluation findings on the alliances that these staff members successfully built with their client families and the families with them and the positive program outcomes show that specialized professional training and the development of a wide range of competencies (knowledge, skills, and values) is essential. The findings also make clear that cultural competence is essential. The reunification program resulted in higher success rates of permanence for Latino children than other groups because bilingual and bicultural staff were available to provide both concrete and therapeutic services.

Attention to the needs of adolescents in the child welfare system has resulted in a range of training resources and curricula to prepare competent staff. Examples include Emily McFadden's (1988) *P.U.S.H. for Youth Goals: Leaving Home Again* and Eileen Pasztor's (1988) *Preparing Youth for Interdependent Living.* The National Child Welfare Resource Center for Youth Development at the University of Oklahoma has a regional network of training and technical assistance listed on its website (www.nrcys.ou.edu/yd/resources). These resources can be useful in providing staff with the specialized knowledge, skills, and values that competent practitioners need to work effectively with adolescents on permanency issues.[6]

Early Referral and In-Depth Assessment

The Casey Family Services reunification program featured an early referral of separated families from the partner state child welfare agency and a meeting with the family to determine their willingness to participate in the program. After intake, a comprehensive assessment was conducted to determine the family's strengths and needs with respect to the separation and their potential for reunification. As mentioned earlier, two clinical instruments were used as part of the comprehensive assessment.

Assessment and case planning aimed at establishing permanent connections and achieving reunification for adolescents must assess an individual youth's need for safety, permanence, and well-being (Frey et al., 2005) and take into account their individual developmental needs, their experiences while in out-of-home care, and the strengths they bring to the work at hand. Barbara Pine and Robin Krieger describe a number of instruments and tools that can be used to guide what they call "interdependent living skill assessment" (1990:208). The Ansell-Casey Life Skills Assessment (ACLSA) is another tool currently used to evaluate an adolescent's independent living skills (Casey Family Programs, 2007).

Collaboration and Teamwork in Service Planning

A major distinction in service planning, as implemented in the reunification program and in a retooled program for adolescents, is the involvement of the adolescent in all aspects of the process as a member of the team (Massinga and Pecora, 2004; Frey et al., 2005). There are ethical considerations for involving youth: namely, practice obligations related to client self-determination and informed consent. Youth involvement in service planning also provides adolescents with opportunities to gain critical thinking and decision-making skills when processing the various permanency options with other members of their permanency team. Service planning that involves youth requires that the team be broadened beyond child welfare practitioners, birth parents, and foster parents to include anyone who is significant in the youth's life, such as siblings, other kin such as aunts and uncles and grandparents, teachers and coaches, and former social workers and child care staff (Frey et al., 2005). A collaborative team planning process "strengthens relationships among team members [and] function[s] as the 'safety net' of adults committed to supporting the youth into adulthood" (Frey et al., 2005:9).

In chapter 15 in this volume, David Crampton and Joan Pennell discuss the use of family involvement meetings as an approach consistent with practices that involve youth and their families in planning for their care. They posit that permanence is enhanced through such meetings by stabilizing placements and keeping youth connected to their families and kinship and cultural groups. Family involvement meetings are part of the larger group of family-involvement approaches that have gained recent currency in child welfare (Pennell, 2006). The Casey Family Services reunification program used an approach called family group conferencing to a limited extent in its reunification efforts.

The outcome of planning meetings, whatever form they take, should be a written service plan or agreement. Anthony Maluccio and M. Simm (1989) delineate six characteristics of effective agreements: mutuality, explicitness, honesty, realism, flexibility, and responsiveness. They note that "the agreement can be a tool for involving clients in decision-making and goal planning, using their cognitive powers, taking action on their behalf, and ultimately promoting their competence" (1989:10).

Mix of Concrete and Therapeutic Services

In reunification work, a mix of concrete and therapeutic services has been shown—in both the Casey Family Services' reunification program and elsewhere—to be effective in achieving outcomes (Fraser et al., 1996). Guidelines for the provision of these services abound. For example, the Transition to Independence Process (TIP) model presented in this volume by

Hewitt B. Clark and Kimberley A. Crosland (chapter 17) includes services that focus on social and daily living skills, health, mental health, education, and employment. Barth and Chintapalli (chapter 5) call for the provision of more therapeutic services to youth in out-of-home care such as multisystemic therapy or multidimensional treatment foster care, both of which feature individualized and family behavior therapy. I. Davis (1989) advocates for proactive casework with youth that enhances their growth and development by helping them improve their day-to-day functioning, cope with identity issues, and begin to prepare for adulthood.

Groups for parents were a feature of the Casey Family Services reunification program. Given their identification with peers, adolescents could benefit from a group approach. Groups can provide social support while youth prepare to reunify with their families or move to another permanent family, can offer opportunities for youth learn social skills, and can provide a therapeutic environment focused on assisting youth to deal with loss and grief and the foster care experience.

Since the late 1980s, increased attention to the needs of adolescents in out-of-home care has led to the development of a range of policies, standards, and program models to guide program planning for youth. Among these resources are the *CWLA Standards of Excellence for Transition, Independent Living, and Self-Sufficiency Services* (Child Welfare League of America, 2005); *Independent Living Program Strategies for the 21st Century: Developing a Comprehensive Adolescent Independent Living Program* (Griffen and Carter, 2003); and *Uncertain Futures: Foster Youth in Transition to Adulthood* (Mech, 2003).

Visiting

The most convincing evidence available in the foster care research in the United States is the relationship between parent-child visiting and successful outcomes for children and families. A very positive finding in the study of the Casey Family Services' reunification program was that 90 percent of the families in the program visited their children weekly or participated in most of the planned weekly visits. Nearly all families visited at least one-half of the time that visits with their children were planned. This success undoubtedly resulted from the program's strong emphasis on planning and evaluating visits with parents, as well as coaching them during visits in conjunction with service plan goals for improved parenting skills.

Visiting with significant adults and others in their social network can have enormous benefits for adolescents. Just as for younger children, visits can help adolescents and their families maintain relationships and improve child and family well-being, and they can help youth understand the realities of their and their families' situation, practice new behaviors, provide opportunities to assess change and development, and provide a transition to reunification or another permanent family (Hess and Proch, 1993). Youth and their families should be helped to plan and prepare for visits as well as evaluate them in light of service planning goals.

CONCLUSION

In this chapter, we have tried to make the case that reunifying adolescents in out-of-home care, while requiring some unique approaches and competencies, is not unlike family reunification practice with younger children and their families. We take a broad view of reunification as helping adolescents and their families connect or reconnect at the highest level possible for them. We delineate and discuss components of a family reunification program that has successfully reunified families and found other permanent families for children who cannot return home on a full-time basis. Program approaches that are consistent with the developmental needs of adolescents are considered.

NOTES

1. A more complete discussion of the study and its results can be found in Pine et al. (2007).

2. The potential population of children for the study was 274. Twenty of those children, however, were not removed when their siblings were removed from their parents' custody . As a result, the total number of children who participated in the study was 254.

3. In these cases, the researchers contacted the family with whom the child was residing. When a child was not reunified, the researchers contacted the new, permanent caregiver.

4. A substantiated report does not automatically mean return to care. Follow-up research would be required to determine how many of the children with substantiated reports ultimately returned to care.

5. These averages contrast to the average length of stay nationwide, which is approximately eighty-six weeks (U.S. Department of Health and Human Services, 2006).

6. In addition, recent films such as *Aging Out* by Roger Weisberg and Vanessa Roth (2005) can provide staff with information to assist them in their work with adolescents.

REFERENCES

Aldgate, J., A. Maluccio, and C. Reeves (1989). Adolescents in foster families: An overview. In J. Aldgate, A. Maluccio, and C. Reeves, eds., *Adolescents in Foster Families* (pp.13–31). London: Batsford.

Casey Family Programs (2007). *The Ansell-Casey Life Skills Assessment.* At www.caseylifeskills.org (accessed April 4, 2007).

Casey Family Services (1999). *Family Reunification Program.* Internal planning document. Shelton, Conn.: Author.

Child Welfare League of America (n.d.). *The Adoption and Safe Families Act.* At www.cwla.org/programs/adoption/asfa.htm (accessed June 4, 2007).

—— (2005). *CWLA Standards for Excellence for Transition, Independent Living, and Self-Sufficiency Services.* Washington, D.C.: Author.

Courtney, M. E., and Y. I. Wong (1996). Comparing the timing of exits from substitute care. *Children and Youth Services Review* 68 (1): 81–108.

Davis, I. (1989). Intervention with adolescents in foster family care and their families. In J. Aldgate, A. Maluccio, and C. Reeves, eds., *Adolescents in Foster Families.* London: Batsford.

Davis, I. P., J. Landsverk, R. Newton, and W. Ganger (1996). Parental visiting and foster care reunification. *Children and Youth Services Review* 18(4–5): 363–82.

Fein, E., and I. Staff (1991). Implementing Reunification Services. *Families in Society* 72(6): 335–43.

Festinger, T. (1996). Going home and returning to foster care. *Children and Youth Services Review* 18(4–5): 383–402.

Fraser, M. W., E. Walton, R. E. Lewis, P. J. Pecora, and W. K. Walton (1996). An experiment in family reunification: Correlates of outcomes at one-year follow-up. *Children and Youth Services Review* 18(4–5): 335–61.

Frey, L., S. Greenblatt, and J. Brown (2005). *A Call to Action: An Integrated Approach to Youth Permanency and Preparation for Adulthood.* New Haven, Conn.: Casey Family Services.

Griffin, W. V., and N. Carter (2003). *Independent Living Program Strategies for the 21st Century: Developing a Comprehensive Adolescent Independent Living Program Plan.* Durham, N.C.: Independent Living Resources.

Hess, P. M. (1999). *Visitation: Promoting Positive Visitation Practices for Children and Their Families Through Leadership, Teamwork, and Collaboration*. Harrisburg: Commonwealth of Pennsylvania.

Hess, P. M., and K. Proch (1993) Visiting: The heart of reunification. In B. A. Pine, R. Warsh, and A. N. Maluccio, eds., *Together Again: Family Reunification in Foster Care* (pp. 3–19). Washington, D.C.: Child Welfare League of America.

Hess, P. M., G. Folaron, and A. Jefferson (1992). Effectiveness of family reunification services: An innovative evaluative model. *Social Work* 37(4): 304–11.

Hipgrave, T. (1989). Concepts of parenting and adolescence: Implications for fostering adolescents. In J. Aldgate, A. Maluccio, and C. Reeves, eds., *Adolescents in Foster Families*. London: Batsford.

Kirk, R. (2002). *Final Project Report: Tailoring Intensive Family Preservation Services for Family Reunification Cases*. At www.nfpn.org/tools/articles/files/researchreport.doc (accessed February 20, 2004).

Lewandowski, C. A., and L. F. GlenMaye (2002). Teams in child welfare settings: Interprofessional and collaborative processes. *Families in Society: Journal of Contemporary Human Services* 38(3): 245–56.

Maluccio, A., and M. Simm (1989). The use of agreements in foster family placements. In J. Aldgate, A. Maluccio, and C. Reeves, eds., *Adolescents in Foster Families*. London: Batsford.

Maluccio, A. N., R. Krieger, and B. A. Pine (1990). Adolescents and their preparation for life after foster family care: An overview. In A. N. Maluccio, R. Krieger, and B. A. Pine, eds., *Preparing Adolescents for Life After Foster Care: The Central Role of Foster Parents* (pp. 5–17). Washington, D.C.: Child Welfare League of America.

Maluccio, A. N., R. Warsh, and B. A. Pine (1993). Family reunification: An overview. In B. A. Pine, R. Warsh, and A. N. Maluccio, eds., *Together Again: Family Reunification in Foster Care* (pp. 3–19). Washington, D.C.: Child Welfare League of America.

Maluccio, A. N., L. W. Abramczyk, and B. Thomlison (1996). Family reunification of children in out-of-home care: Research issues and perspectives. *Children and Youth Services Review* 18(4–5): 287–305.

Maluccio, A. N., B. A. Pine, and E. M. Tracy (2002). *Social Work Practice with Families and Children*. New York: Columbia University Press.

Massinga, R., and P. J. Pecora (2004). Providing better opportunities for older children in the child welfare system. *Future of Children* 14(1): 151–73.

McFadden, E. J. (1988). *P.U.S.H. for Youth Goals: Leaving Home Again*. Ypsilanti: Eastern Michigan University, Institute for the Study of Children and Families.

Mech, E. V. (2003). *Uncertain Futures: Foster Youth in Transition to Adulthood*. Washington, D.C.: Child Welfare League of America.

Pasztor, E. M. (1988). *Preparing Youth for Interdependent Living*. West Hartford: University of Connecticut, School of Social Work, Center for the Study of Child Welfare, and Atlanta: Child Welfare Institute.

Pennell, J. (2006). Family involvement meetings with older children in foster care: Intuitive appeal, promising practices and the challenge of child welfare reform. Paper presented at the Research Roundtable, Annie E. Casey Foundation and Casey Family Services. Washington, D.C., September 12.

Pine, B. A., and R. Krieger (1990). Assessing skills for interdependent living. In A. N. Maluccio, R. Krieger, and B. A. Pine, eds., *Preparing Adolescents for Life After Foster Care: The Central Role of Foster Parents*. Washington, D.C.: Child Welfare League of America.

Pine, B. A., R. Krieger, and A. N. Maluccio (1990). Preparing adolescents to leave foster family care: Guidelines for policy and program. In A. N. Maluccio, R. Krieger, and B. A. Pine, eds., *Preparing Adolescents for Life After Foster Care: The Central Role of Foster Parents*. Washington, D.C.: Child Welfare League of America.

Pine, B. A., R. Spath, A. Maguda, G. Werrbach, and C. Jenson (2006). *Collaboration Between the Casey Family Services Family Reunification Program and Its State Agency Partners: Evaluators' Report*. West Hartford: University of Connecticut, School of Social Work.

Pine, B. A., R. Spath, A. Maguda, G. Werrbach, and C. Jenson (2007). *Final Report of the Evaluation of the Casey Family Services Family Reunification Program*. West Hartford: University of Connecticut, School of Social Work.

Terling, T. (1999). The efficacy of family reunification practices: Reentry rates and correlates of reentry for abused and neglected children reunited with their families. *Child Abuse and Neglect* 23(12): 1359–70.

Thompson, S. J., A. W. Safyer, and D. E. Pollio (2001). Differences and predictors of family reunification among subgroups of runaway youths using shelter services. *Social Work Research* 25 (3): 163–72.

U.S. Department of Health and Human Services, Administration for Children and Families (2007). *The AFCARS Report*. At www.acf.hhs.gov/programs/cb/stats_research/afcars/tar/report13.htm (accessed June 4, 2007).

Wagner, M. W. (2003). Families for reunification: A mediating group model for birth parent self-assessment. In J. Lindsay, D. Turcotte, and E. Hopmeyer, eds., *Crossing Boundaries and Developing Alliances Through Group Work* (pp. 147–65). Binghamton, N.Y.: Hayworth.

Walton, E., M. W. Fraser, R. E. Lewis, and P. J. Pecora (1993). In-home family-focused reunification: An experimental study. *Child Welfare* 72(5): 473–87.

Zamosky, J., J. Sparks, R. Hatt, and J. Sharman (1993). Believing in families. In B. A. Pine, R. Warsh, and A. N. Maluccio, eds., *Together Again: Family Reunification in Foster Care* (pp. 155–75). Washington, D.C.: Child Welfare League of America.

Youth Permanence
Through Adoption

FOURTEEN

RUTH G. MCROY
AND ELISSA MADDEN

According to the most recent data, adoption is the permanency goal for 114,000 of the 513,000 children in the nation's foster care system, and almost 50,000 of the children awaiting adoption have been in continuous foster care for three years or more. Although the average age of children in foster care waiting for adoption is 8.6 years old, almost one-third (32 percent) are twelve years of age and older. About 53 percent of these children are males, and the majority of the children are members of ethnic minority groups. Some 55 percent of waiting children live with a foster family, and 19 percent live with a relative; 13 percent are in a pre-adoptive home, and 11 percent live in a group home or institution (U.S. Department of Health and Human Services, 2006a).

Currently, over three-fourths of children adopted from the U.S. public child welfare system meet the criteria for "special needs adoptions" (U.S. General Accounting Office, 2002). The term "special needs adoptions" generally refers to adoption of children who are older; belong to a sibling group; or have physical, mental, or emotional problems. In addition, the term often refers to adoptions of children from ethnic minority groups (Reilly and Platz, 2003; Ryan and Nalavany, 2003).

According to Richard P. Barth and colleagues (2006), youth permanence through adoption can lead to significant cost savings for state and federal governments. Barth et al. compared the costs of adoption subsidies and the costs of foster care over a seven-year period, and they reported that the cost of foster care is significantly higher than the cost of adoption assistance. They concluded that because the costs for adoption are often higher initially and the costs for foster care increase with the child's age, it is likely that governmental savings would prove to be even greater over time.

In recent years, there have been many federal policies and programs that have encouraged adoptions from the public child welfare system. In this chapter, we examine many of the policies, programs, and agency practices that affect the likelihood of adoption for youth who are in foster care. We describe research findings on outcomes for children with special needs and their adoptive families and the preplacement and postplacement service needs of these families. Challenges for achieving permanence for special populations, including African American youth and lesbian, gay, bisexual and transgender (LGBT) youth, are presented. We offer suggestions for future research and specific recommendations to improve adoption practice with older youth and their adoptive families.

OVERVIEW OF RECENT FEDERAL ADOPTION LEGISLATION

Since the early 1980s, several federal legislative initiatives have been instituted in order to increase opportunities for permanence for children in the public child welfare system. In 1980, Congress passed the Adoption Assistance and Child Welfare Act (AACWA). This legislation was designed to help facilitate permanence for children in foster care, either through reunification with the birth family or, in cases where reunification was not possible, placement with an adoptive family. In addition, AACWA provided federal funding to states to provide subsidies on behalf of children with special needs who were adopted from the foster care system.

Despite legislative efforts to facilitate permanence for children more quickly, the number of children in foster care nearly doubled between 1983 and 1995—from 242,000 to almost 500,000—while the number of adoptions from the child welfare system remained relatively stagnant during this period (Maza, 2000). Some researchers have suggested that much of the growth in the foster care population during the mid to late 1980s can be attributed to the onset of the crack-cocaine epidemic, the HIV/AIDS epidemic, and increases in parental incarceration rates (Bass et al., 2004; Hill, 2004; Ruiz, 2000).

Currently, disproportionately high numbers of the children in care are African American: in 2005, African American children accounted for 32 percent (166,482) of the total number of children in foster care (U.S. Department of Health and Human Services, 2006a). Although states vary in the degree to which African American children are overrepresented in the child welfare system, in forty-six states the proportion of African American children in foster care is more than two times the proportion of African American children in the state's total child population (Center for the Study of Social Policy, 2004).

Concerns that "race-matching policies" were resulting in African American children languishing in foster care while caseworkers sought African American adoptive parents led to the passage in 1994 of the Multi-Ethnic Placement Act (MEPA). This legislation prohibited agencies from delaying or denying an adoptive placement on the basis of race, color, or national origin but allowed for race to be "one of a number of factors" in determining a child's adoptive placement (Freundlich, 2000). MEPA also required diligent recruitment of foster and adoptive parents who reflect the racial and ethnic diversity of children needing placement (Hollinger, 1998). In 1996, the Act was amended by the Interethnic Provisions (IEP), which eliminated any consideration of race in child placement and established financial penalties for noncompliance (Hollinger, 1998).

A year later, Congress enacted the Adoption and Safe Families Act of 1997 (ASFA), Public Law 105-89. The act was passed in response to concerns about the growing number of children in the child welfare system, as well as the length of time children were spending in foster care. Provisions of ASFA allowed states to find permanent families for children in the foster care system by clarifying specific circumstances under which states could forgo efforts to reunify families and by establishing strict time frames for states to initiate proceedings to terminate parental rights for children unable to return to their families' care (U.S. General Accounting Office, 2003). More so than any other child welfare policy passed in the past two decades, the enactment of ASFA represented a fundamental shift in thought within the child welfare arena, placing an increased emphasis on child safety and well-being over prevention efforts and family preservation.

Among other mandates, ASFA required states to pursue termination of parental rights if a child had been in foster care for fifteen out of the most recent twenty-two months. Congress also included exceptions that allow states to "fast track" termination of parental rights in extreme cases where the child's safety would likely be endangered. Exceptions to the requirement of reasonable efforts to reunify children and families include when (1) the child has been subjected by the parent to "aggravated circumstances," as defined by each state; (2) the parent has committed or has conspired to commit murder or voluntary manslaughter of one of his or her children in the home; (3) the parent has committed felony assault of one of his or her children in the home; (4) the parent has had parental rights involuntarily terminated for another of his or her children; or (5) the child has been determined by the court to be an abandoned infant (U.S. General Accounting Office, 1999). Under ASFA, states are required to file a petition for termination of parental rights within thirty days of the child's removal from the home in cases where an exception to the reasonable efforts clause has been determined by the court. Although the legislation stipulates that reasonable efforts should be made to preserve and reunify families when possible, the legislation encourages states to concurrently plan for adoption while working toward family reunification so that an adoptive placement can be made quickly should the state pursue termination of parental rights (U.S. General Accounting Office, 1999).

ASFA also established the Adoption Incentive Program to provide fiscal incentives to states to increase the number of adoptions of children from foster care. The Fostering Connections to Success Act of 2008 reauthorizes and expands the program, renewing it for another five years, updating to FY 2007 the adoption baseline above which incentives payments are made, doubles the incentive payments for adoptions of children with special needs and older child adoptions and gives states 24 months to used the adoption incentive payments.[1] Adoption incentives have proved be a powerful motivator for states. In 2005, twenty-one states qualified for incentive funds through the adoption incentive program, with a total of over eleven million dollars awarded to states (U.S. Department of Health and Human Services, 2006b).

The Promoting Safe and Stable Families Amendments of 2001 (Public Law 107-133) expanded the initial Promoting Safe and Stable Families Program, and provides support to states to fund time-limited reunification and post-adoption services and state court improvements to expedite permanence. Another initiative designed to increase adoptions of children from foster care is the Collaboration to AdoptUsKids. Authorized by the Children's Health

Act of 2000 and established by the Children's Bureau in 2002, the collaboration received funding to provide training and consultation on recruitment and retention of foster and adoptive families, maintain an online national photolisting service of children awaiting adoption from foster care, conduct a public awareness campaign to promote adoption of older youth and conduct research on barriers to adoption of children from care and factors associated with successful outcomes (Collaboration to AdoptUsKids, 2007).

In 2003, the Keeping Children and Families Safe Act (Public Law 108-36) reauthorized a number of federal programs, including the Adoption Opportunities Program, which is designed to address barriers to adoption and help find families for children available for adoption, particularly children with special needs. Provisions of the program include federal funding for child-specific recruitment, expanded postadoption services (such as respite care) and mental health day treatment. In addition, this program provides recommendations for removing obstacles to interjurisdictional adoptions.

The Fostering Connections to Success and Increasing Adoptions Act of 2008 included a number of provisions to support child welfare agencies in recruiting, preparing, and supporting families who adopt children from foster care. Among the provisions are federal support for adoption assistance for more children with special needs who are adopted from foster care; expansion of the Adoption Incentive Program to reward states for increasing the number of children adopted from foster care; making older children who exit foster care eligible for additional support; and outreach regarding the adoption tax credit.

These federal policies and federally funded programs have served to increase the number of children adopted from foster care. In the years since ASFA was enacted, the number of adoptions has risen from approximately thirty-one thousand in 1997 to over fifty-one thousand in 2005 (U.S. Department of Health and Human Services, 2005, 2006a). In 2005, some 43 percent of the children adopted were Caucasian-non-Hispanic; 30 percent were African American; 18 percent were Hispanic; and about 2 percent were American Indian, Alaskan Native, and Asian. The majority of children have been adopted by married couples (68 percent), and the next highest proportion of children adopted was by single females (27 percent). Only 3 percent were adopted by single males, and 2 percent of the children were adopted by unmarried couples (U.S. Department of Health and Human Services, 2006a). Barth and Marianne Berry (1988) found that single adopters were more likely than married couples to adopt older children, while James

Rosenthal and Victor Groze (1992) noted that married couples were more likely than single adopters to adopt siblings groups.

In recent years, many states have focused on encouraging foster families and relatives to adopt. Currently, most families who adopt children from the U.S. child welfare system have had a previous relationship with the children (60 percent foster parent adoptions and 25 percent relative adoptions). Only 15 percent of children in foster care in 2005 were adopted by persons previously unknown to them—that is, "general" adopters (U.S. Department of Health and Human Services, 2006a).

CHALLENGES TO ADOPTION: IMPLICATIONS FOR SPECIAL POPULATIONS

Achieving permanence for children of color, as well as children who are gay or lesbian, is often a challenge for many agencies. Cultural sensitivity, knowledge about each group's experiences and placement needs, and knowledge of potential placement resources are necessary to ensure that these children have opportunities for adoption permanence that are equal to the opportunities available for Caucasian and heterosexual children. In the following section, we examine research findings and specific practices and policies that affect adoption for the largest group of children of color needing placement, African American children. This section is followed by a discussion of the unique permanency challenges for gay and lesbian youth in the child welfare system.

Adoption of African American Youth

Despite federal initiatives to increase the number of children in foster care who achieve permanence, more than 100,000 children wait to be adopted, a disproportionate number of whom belong to ethnic minority populations. African American children compose the largest minority group needing adoptive placement. Although African American children represent about 15 percent of the U.S. child population (U.S. Bureau of the Census, 2004), they represent about 36 percent (40,840 children) of the children and youth awaiting adoption (U.S. Department of Health and Human Services, 2006a).

Much of the existing research suggests that African American children historically have received differential treatment in foster care. They are generally in care longer, are less likely to receive mental health services, and are less likely to be reunified with their birth families or to be adopted (Hill, 2004). Barth (1997) found that after controlling for age, African American children were significantly less likely to be adopted than Caucasian children. In 2000, Rosemary Avery found that New York children who waited the longest for permanence (mean = 11.79 years) were more likely to have substantial disabilities and be male, African American, and older when they entered foster care. Avery also reported that caseworker perception of "adoptability" of a foster child influenced recruitment efforts. Similarly, Stephen Kapp and colleagues (2001) reported that in a sample of Kansas families, African American children were overrepresented among children awaiting adoption; in their study, adoption generally took longer for African American children than for other children of color, and Caucasian children were more likely to receive an individual adoption recruitment plan and to be matched with an adoptive family.

More recent data suggest that, although still not equitable, the likelihood of adoption for African American children has steadily increased (Hill, 2006). From their analysis of administrative data from the U.S. Children's Bureau, Mary Hansen and Daniel Pollack (2007) reported that between 1996 and 2003, transracial adoptive placements have expedited adoption for infants and toddlers but not for older youth in care. The authors found that transracial adoptions were finalized, on average, one month more quickly than same race adoptions. However, although it appears that the length of stay differential between African American children and Caucasian children is narrowing for younger children, adoption of older African American adolescents has not kept pace with the adoption of younger children. As Hansen and Pollack (2007) report, the differential gap in adoptive placement increases with the age of the child.

Penny Maza (2002) found that older African American children (61 percent) are much more likely than older Caucasian children (18 percent) to be adopted by single females . Older African American children are also more likely to be adopted by individuals with whom they have had a prior relationship, including foster parents and relatives. According to Maza (2005), 40 percent of older African American children adopted in 2004 were adopted by relatives, compared with 29 percent of Hispanic children and 32 percent of Caucasian children. Hansen and Pollack (2007) also noted that transracial adoptive placements are much less prevalent among African American adolescents than among young children, with over 40 percent of transracial adoptions occurring before the child is three years old.

Devon Brooks and colleagues (1999), Ruth McRoy (2004), and many others have called for a renewed commitment to identifying strategies for recruiting ethnically diverse foster and adoptive families and addressing barriers to retention of recruited families. Tom Gilles and Joe Kroll (1991) found that these barriers include the lack of minority staff, inflexible standards, high fees, and lack of culturally specific recruitment activities. Minority placing agencies have reported significant success in recruiting and retaining families for children of color (McRoy et al., 1997; McRoy, 2004; Hill, 2004).

In 2002, Casey Family Programs launched a breakthrough series collaborative on recruitment and retention of resource families for children in care with teams from twenty-two pilot sites throughout the country. Reports from participating sites demonstrated that many public agencies did not have culturally or linguistically specific recruitment materials or recruitment plans and had not partnered with faith-based organizations to recruit families. Once they recognized the need to alter their approaches, the agencies reported greater success in recruiting families of color for adoption (Casey Family Programs, 2005).

Although MEPA-IEPA called for the elimination of barriers to transracial adoptions, the legislation failed to include a requirement for specialized services and supports that many of these families may need. M. Elizabeth Vonk (2001), Maria de Haymes and Shirley Simon (2003), McRoy (2004), and others have emphasized the need for transracial adoptive parents to be culturally competent and have called on agencies to provide additional support for these families and children. Parents' needs include racial self-awareness and an understanding of the dynamics of racism and discrimination and its impact on their lives as well as their children's; learning about the child's birth culture and finding role models for their children; helping children talk about race and racism openly; and helping the child to recognize, survive, and handle experiences with racism (Vonk, 2001).

Special Permanency Challenges for Gay and Lesbian Youth

Lesbian, gay, bisexual, and transgender (LGBT) youth face particular challenges in relation to permanence. These youth often experience marginalization and often are not placed in safe, supportive environments in which they can acknowledge their sexual orientation if they choose to do so; it is estimated that between twelve thousand and twenty-four thousand LGBT adolescents are in out-of-home care (Lambda Legal Defense and Education Fund, 2001). As adolescents, these youth must cope with their status as a stigmatized minority. Many experience harassment and violence in their homes, schools, and communities, and many of these youth leave foster care through running away and become part of the homeless population (National Center for Lesbian Rights, 2007). LGBT youth who are also members of ethnic minority groups may face additional ostracism from members of their cultural communities who, as a result of religious and cultural beliefs, may be even less accepting of these youth's sexuality and gender identify (Mallon, 1998; Lambda Legal Defense and Education Fund, 2001).

Until recently, there have been few formal policies prohibiting discrimination against LGBT youth in foster care and little training for foster and adoptive parents and child welfare staff regarding gay and lesbian affirming behaviors and practices (Mallon, 1999). In 2002, the Model Standards Project of the Legal Services for Children and the National Center for Lesbian Rights developed professional standards for juvenile justice and child welfare agencies serving LGBT youth (Wilber et al., 2006). In 2003, California passed the first state law, the Foster Care Non-Discrimination Act, calling for fair and equal access to and treatment in all child welfare services and freedom from discrimination on the basis of sexual orientation and gender identity. The law mandates ongoing training for group home administrators, foster parents, and department licensing personnel. In 2006, the Child Welfare League of America published the Best Practice Guidelines for agencies responsible for providing services to LGBT youth in out of home care (Wilber et al., 2006). It is expected that these policies will lead to a greater understanding of the needs of LGBT youth and the development of child welfare programs that are responsive to and affirming of their needs.

Agencies must use gay and lesbian–affirming foster and adoptive family recruitment approaches to increase the likelihood of finding permanence for this population of children and youth. When appropriate foster family placements are not available, many LGBT youth are placed in congregate care settings, where they are much more likely to run away or age out rather than achieve permanence with a family; having experienced discrimination and rejection by peers and sometimes by their birth families, many of these youth fear that they will never be accepted and achieve permanence through adoption (Jacobs and Freundlich, 2006).

To achieve permanence for LGBT youth in foster care, prospective adoptive families need pre-placement training on the effects of social stigma on adolescent development and the challenges that LGBT youth often experience. Adoptive families of LGBT youth should receive ongoing postadoption support to assist them as needs arise (Ford and Kroll, 2005; Wilber, et al., 2006) These youth often struggle with multiple issues, including the loss of their birth families, gender identity and sexual awakening and orientation, harassment at school, stigmatization, low self-esteem, and a sense of worthlessness, and adoptive parents must be able to access services for these youth.

To provide LGBT youth with opportunities for lasting connections to adults and legal permanence, child welfare agencies must make special targeted efforts to find families for them. Agencies should involve these youth in identifying individuals who understand and can meet their individual needs and who may become permanent family resources for them.

ADOPTIVE FAMILIES AND ADOPTED YOUTH: ADJUSTMENT ISSUES AND SERVICE NEEDS

Although many studies have focused on psychological adjustment outcomes, identity, attachment, understanding of adoption, and the overall functioning of children adopted as infants (Brodzinsky, 1987, 1993; Grotevant and McRoy, 1998), relatively limited research has addressed these social and psychological outcomes for children adopted at older ages. The research on older child adoptions has revealed that children who were older when separated from their birth families may have had closer ties to siblings and members of their families (Barth and Miller, 2000; Frasch et al., 2000). Older children and youth often have had more placements while in foster care (Barth and Berry, 1991), may engage in more externalizing behaviors (such as sexual acting out and defiance), and may experience more emotional problems than children adopted as infants or at a young age (Smith and Howard, 1994; Smith et al., 1998). In addition, they may have developmental delays, physical disabilities, educational delays, or mild to severe psychological and behavioral difficulties. Some may have concerns and fears about the possibility of being adopted.

Experiences of traumatic separation from a child's birth family can lead to depression and feelings of powerlessness, as well as identity conflicts for adolescents regarding their relationships with their birth family and how they feel about adoption. The stress of making a permanent attachment to an adoptive family can evoke flashbacks of previous trauma the youth may have experienced. Some youth may express their feelings through denial, anger, and defiant behavior, and they may have fears of intimacy with others after the adoption (Smith and Howard, 1999). Studies suggest that children with behavioral problems are at an increased risk of adoption instability or disruption (McRoy, 1999).

Clinicians and researchers have called for developmentally appropriate pre-placement counseling to aid children and youth in the transition to adoption (Fahlberg, 1991; Barth and Berry, 1988). There is agreement that pre-placement services should include the use of a life story book, good-bye visits with biological parents, pre-placement visits with the prospective adoptive family, counseling, and reading materials, but these services are not consistently offered to youth (Hanna, 2005). As a result, many children are inadequately prepared for adoption (Barth and Berry, 1988; McRoy, 1999; Hanna, 2005). Pre-placement preparation of the adoptive family and the child is a critical component of successful adoptions (Atkinson, 2002).

Adoption Disruption

Although the majority of adoptions are successful (Barth and Miller, 2000), there is evidence that the likelihood of disruption may increase with the age of the child. Rosenthal (1993) reported disruption rates among children adopted at older ages to be between 10 and 15 percent, while Trudy Festinger (2005) indicated that the rate for older children may be as high as 25 percent. With the increase in the number of adoptions since the passage of ASFA, there has been growing concern that adoption disruption rates may increase. Susan Smith and colleagues (2006), however, reviewed administrative data on 15,947 children who had been placed for adoption between 1995 and 2000 and found that, although the overall number of disruptions increased after 1997, there was a greater increase in the number of adoptions. Thus, the rate of disruption was actually 11 percent less for adoptive placements after 1997. These researchers examined risk factors associated with disruption and found that placements at higher risk for disruption involve children who older when they entered care, were African American, were placed with up to four of their siblings, were identified as "handicapped," and were placed with nonrelatives. Jeffrey Haugaard and colleagues (1999) noted that, despite the greater likelihood that children adopted as adolescents would exhibit antisocial, delinquent, and hostile behaviors, the majority of adolescents' adoptions are successful.

Adoption outcome studies indicate that the age of the child at the time of the adoptive placement is a crucial factor that may influence adoption success or disruption (Berry and Barth, 1990; McDonald et al., 2001; Moffatt and Thoburn, 2001; Rosenthal et al., 1988). A child's pre-adoptive history appears to be associated with the child's ability to attach. Children adopted as infants are more likely than children adopted at a later age to develop attachments similar to infants raised in their biological homes (Groze and Rosenthal, 1993), whereas older children and youth often experience greater difficulty forging bonds with their adoptive families. Difficulties with attachment may be attributed to pre-adoption experiences while children are with their birth families or in foster placements. In addition, difficulties with attachment may be attributed to adoption timing factors such as the child's ability to understand and process separation and loss (Berry and Barth, 1990).

Groze and Rosenthal (1993) found that the number of placements a child experiences before the adoption can negatively affect a child's ability to attach and bond with a new adoptive family. The authors caution that children who move multiple times are forced to dissolve attachments to caregivers each time they move, and, over time, repeated moves can undermine a child's ability to attach. Because children adopted when they are older may have stronger ties to siblings and members of their birth family, they may exhibit more difficulty adjusting to and establishing meaningful relationships with their adoptive families (McDonald et al., 2001; McRoy, 1999).

Given the research and practice data on attachment issues in older child adoptions, service providers must prepare families of older youth to both help the child attach and, at the same time, help the child develop autonomy and prepare for the responsibilities and privileges of adulthood. Families must understand the complex "dance" that occurs and help prepare their child for the conflicts and strains of adolescence while adjusting to a new family system (Rosenthal and Groze, 1994).

Postadoption Support Services

Research indicates that many of the problems experienced by adoptive families do not manifest until several years after the adoption is legally finalized (Smith, et al., 1998). There is a growing body of literature that documents the need for postplacement and postadoption services for families who adopt older children (Barth, 1991; Freundlich and Wright, 2003). Jeanne Howard and Smith (2002) report that, with the increase in the number of adoptions of children from foster care and the increased awareness of the challenges that families may encounter after the adoption is finalized, some states have attempted to identify the postadoption services that families need. Although not every adoptive family will require postadoption assistance and support, there is a growing demand for services to help adoptive families address their children's physical, emotional, and developmental needs (Reilly and Platz, 2003). The majority of adoptive families report that many of these postadoption services are helpful (McRoy, 2007) and tend to mitigate the strains in families (Ryan and Nalavany, 2003).

To enhance adoption outcomes, families require adequate preparation and access to postadoption support services. The type and intensity of services provided to adoptive families often varies, depending on the child and family's presenting needs. According to Richard Barth and Julie Miller (2000), the need for postadoption services depends largely on two factors: whether the adopted child has extensive needs and whether the child's needs can be met by existing services in the community. Most adoptive families seek services in four categories:

- Educational and informational services (including information about the child's background, training, and literature to help families learn more about adoption issues)
- Clinical services (such as counseling services for the child and family and support services such as respite care)
- Material services (including adoption subsidies, special education services, and medical assistance)
- Support groups for parents and children (Barth et al., 2001).

Although more research is needed on the elements of postadoption services that are most helpful to families, research suggests that families find self-help or support groups and respite to be very useful (Barth et al., 2001; Rosenthal et al., 1996).

Some adoptive families have reported difficulty accessing postadoption services and dissatisfaction with the services they receive (Lightburn and Pine, 1996; Reilly and Platz, 2003). The most common barriers cited by adoptive parents are lack of information as to how to access services and a general perception that practitioners who provide services do not understand the child's problems (Reilly and Platz, 2003). According to Festinger (2002), the cost of postplacement services not covered by state funds is an additional barrier.

In a study of 912 families referred for postadoption services over a two-year period in Illinois, Smith (2006) found that the most commonly identified emotional and behavioral problems of children for which families sought postadoption assistance were defiance, verbal aggression, lying, and physical aggression. Smith further found that past neglect and physical abuse were significantly related to children's attachment issues. Prior sexual abuse was found to be related to symptoms of posttraumatic stress disorder (PTSD).

The study also identified characteristics of families for whom the risk of dissolving the adoption was greatest: relative adopters, single parents, subsidized guardians, and parents of African American children. These data are particularly valuable to agencies as they design evidence-based postadoption services that reflect the unique service needs of different children and families.

Kathleen Lenerz and colleagues (2006) studied families who sought services through Casey Family Services Postadoption Services located in five New England states. The researchers found that families participated in counseling, support groups, or case advocacy for a median time of just under five months. Families who participated in at least four counseling sessions benefited more than those who participated in fewer sessions. Their findings indicated that services should be responsive to the youth and family's multiple changing needs, should focus on the dynamics of the entire family (not only the most recently adopted child), and should be flexible and funded sufficiently to allow the families to return for services as needed.

Although most research on postadoption services has been conducted from the perspective of adoptive parents, researchers recently have begun to seek the perspectives of youth. In their study, Scott Ryan and Blace Nalavany (2003) asked youth about their concerns related to adoption, and youth reported three primary concerns: fear that others would not understand the experience of being adopted, fear that they might encounter insensitive remarks about their adoptions, and fear of the social stigma that is often associated with adoption. Despite these fears, however, many youth recognized the benefits that can result from adoption.

Cynthia Flynn and colleagues (2004) studied families and youth who were successfully adopted as adolescents. Based on their interviews with both families and youth, these researchers identified four common factors associated with successful adoptions: commitment of both parents and adopted youth; compatible personality traits, including parental flexibility, sense of humor, and positive attitude; the presence of a support system of professionals, family, and friends, as well as spiritual support; and the availability of needed services and willingness of parents to seek postadoption services when problems arise.

YOUTH PERMANENCY RESEARCH NEEDS

Many of the studies on outcomes of adoptions of children and youth with special needs and postadoption services have used small sample sizes, nonrandom samples, and administrative data, and few have included the perspectives of youth and adoptive families. Ryan and Nalavany (2003) have called for more studies that include the voices of youth in order to understand adoption adjustment issues from their perspective. They recommend that studies address the types of activities that youth enjoy with their families, the impact of gender of the child on the type of attention from and relationship with the adoptive parent, and the relationship between the adopted child and the adoptive father. Adoption outcome research with special populations, including minority children and youth placed transracially and inracially and LGBT youth, should also be conducted.

Most research conducted regarding the adoption of children and youth with special needs has focused on nonrelative adoptions. Given the increase in the rate of relative adoptions of African American children, longitudinal outcome studies of these adoptions are needed. Most of the relatives are single females who adopt older youth. If, as research suggests, these adoptions are at greater risk of dissolution (Smith, 2006), further research is needed to identify the factors that may contribute to dissolution and effective interventions to support these families. Motivation for adoption, family dynamics, attachment and identity issues, children's understanding of adoption, and overall family adjustment have been studied in infant adoptions, but more in-depth study is needed to improve our understanding of these dynamics in older child adoptions. Studies of "what works, with whom" (Smith, 2006) are essential in order to develop appropriate interventions that not only maintain intact adoptions but also help adoptive families and children thrive.

Research also is needed on evidence-based practice approaches involving the use of inpatient and outpatient treatment, family therapy, and prevention services with adoptive families (Wulczyn et al., 2005). In addition, studies on the effect of family recruitment and retention initiatives and techniques for matching children with potential adoptive families are needed. As many older youth and their adoptive families have contact through open adoption arrangements with birth family members and foster parents, studies of these relationships and family dynamics are essential.

Finally, it is important to explore caseworkers' attitudes toward adoption for older youth and the attitudes and beliefs of older youth about the meaning of adoption and their perspectives on relationships with adoptive and birth families. Flynn et al. (2004) found that the adolescents' acceptance of the need for adoption was related to their involvement in the adoption process. In order to develop better models to predict successful adoptions of adolescents, there is a need for longitudinal research that explores adolescent attitudes and experiences in adoption.

CONCLUSION

Despite the many legislative initiatives designed to promote adoption, challenges to youth permanence continue, including a shortage of nonrelated families seeking to adopt older children, inadequate postadoption services, youth resistance to adoption, staff issues such as heavy caseloads, and the belief that older youth are unadoptable. A variety of issues have been addressed in the research literature about youth permanence through adoption. Much of the research on older child adoption outcomes has focused on the perspectives of adoptive families about the child's adjustment and on disruption rates, parental satisfaction, parental perspectives on the success of the adoption, and the need for postadoption services (McRoy, 1999).

Studies on factors associated with disruption have been conducted from the perspectives of the child, the family, and adoption agencies. Child factors related to disruption include externalizing behavior problems, sexual acting out, attachment to the child's birthmother, and sexual abuse before adoption. Family factors include lack of a previous relationship to the child, lack of social support from relatives, and unrealistic expectations. Agency factors include inadequate preparation of children and families, lack of ongoing training and support for families, and families having a high number of caseworkers (McRoy, 1999).

Although a great deal of attention has been given to the problems in older child and youth adoptions, most adoptions are successful and parents remain committed to the child and to the adoption (Barth and Miller, 2000). However, in order to promote permanence for older youth, postadoption services, as well as increased financial subsidies, are needed through the child's life cycle in order to address problems as they emerge. Parents and youth could benefit from clinically tested adoption preparation and postadoption interventions that address developmentally appropriate expectations for children's adjustment and behavior; provide an understanding of the experiences of abuse and neglect and adjustment challenges in new familial, school, and community settings; and address family integration issues, experiences of loss, and other developmental adjustments for the family and child. Specialized postadoption services designed for single parents, relative adopters of older youth, and families adopting transracially or adopting LGBT youth and services for adopted youth must also be developed and evaluated.

NOTE

1. The Fostering Connections to Success Act continues, through FY2013, the current annual funding authorization of $43 million for the Adoption Incentive program. It doubles the incentive amounts states may earn for each increase in the number of older children adopted from foster care (from $4,000 to $8,000) and for children with special needs, under age 9, who are adopted from foster care (from $2,000 to $4,000). The incentive award for any increase in the total number of children adopted from foster care remains at $4,000.

REFERENCES

Atkinson, A. J. (2002). *Quality Improvement Center on Adoption: Assessment of Adoption Needs in Virginia and QICA Research Design*. Richmond: Policy Works.

Avery, R. (2000). Perceptions and practice: Agency efforts for the hardest-to-place children. *Children and Youth Services Review* 22(6): 399–420.

Barth, R. P. (1991). Adoption preservation services. In E. M. Tracy, D. A. Haapala, J. Kinney, and P. J. Pecora, eds., *Intensive Family Preservation Services: An Instructional Sourcebook* (pp. 237–49). Cleveland: Case Western Reserve University, Mandel School of Applied Social Sciences.

—— (1997). Family reunification. *Child Welfare Research Review* 2: 109–22.

Barth, R. P., and M. Berry (1988). *Adoption and Disruption: Rates, Risks, and Responses*. Hawthorne, N.Y.: Aldine de Gruyter.

—— (1991). Preventing adoption disruption. *Prevention in Human Services* 9(1): 205–22.

Barth, R. P., and J. M. Miller (2000). Building effective post-adoption services: What is the empirical foundation? *Family Relations* 49: 447–55.

Barth, R. P., D. A. Gibbs, and K. Siebenaler (2001). *Assessing the Field of Post-Adoption Service: Family Needs, Program Models and Evaluation Issues. Literature Review*. Chapel Hill and Research Triangle Park: University of North Carolina School of Social Work, Jordan Institute for Families, and Research Triangle Institute.

Barth, R. P., C. Lee, J. Wildfire, and S. Guo (2006). A comparison of the governmental costs of long-term foster care and adoption. *Social Service Review* 80(4): 127–32.

Bass, S., M. K. Shields, and R. E. Behrman (2004). Children, families, and foster care: Analysis and recommendations. *Future of Children* 14(1): 5–29.

Berry, M., and R. P. Barth (1990). A study of disrupted adoptive placements of adolescents. *Child Welfare* 69(3): 209–25.

Brodzinsky, D. M. (1987). Adjustment to adoption: A psychosocial perspective. *Clinical Psychology Review* 7: 25–47.

——(1993). Long term outcomes in adoption. *Future of Children* 3: 153–66.

Brooks, D., R. P. Barth, A. Bussiere, and G. Patterson (1999). Adoption and race: Implementing the Multiethnic Placement Act and the Interethnic Adoption Provisions. *Social Work* 44(2): 166–78.

Casey Family Programs (2005). *Recruitment and Retention of Resource Families: Promising Practices and Lessons Learned.* Seattle: Author.

Center for the Study of Social Policy (2004). *Fact Sheet 1: Basic Facts on Disproportionate Representation of African Americans in the Foster Care System.* Washington, D.C.: Author.

Child Welfare League of America (2005) *CWLA 2005 Children's Legislative Agenda.* At www.cwla.org/advocacy/2005legagenda01.htm (accessed March 29, 2007).

Collaboration to AdoptUsKids (2007). *About the Collaboration.* At www.adoptuskids. org/about/aboutCollaboration.aspx (accessed March 13, 2007).

deHaymes, M., and S. Simon (2003). Transracial adoptions: Families identity issues and needed support services. *Child Welfare* 82(2): 251–72.

Fahlberg, V. (1991). *A Child's Journey Through Placement.* Indianapolis: Perspectives Press.

Festinger, T. (2002). After adoption: Dissolution or permanence? *Child Welfare* 81(3): 515–33.

——(2005). Adoption disruption: Rates, correlates and service needs. In G. P. Mallon and P. M. Hess, eds., *Child Welfare for the 21st Century: A Handbook of Children, Youth, and Family Services—Practices, Policies, and Programs.* New York: Columbia University Press.

Flynn, C., W. Welch, and K. Paget (2004). *Field-Initiated Research on Successful Adolescent Adoptions: Final Report.* Columbia: University of South Carolina, Center for Child and Family Studies.

Ford, M., and J. Kroll (2005). *A Family for Every Child: Strategies to Achieve Permanence for Older Foster Children and Youth.* Baltimore: North American Council on Adoptable Children and Annie E. Casey Foundation. At http://www.aecf.org/KnowledgeCenter/Publications.aspx?pubguid=%7B104C33ED-5D53-458B-B6AA-C4B645BD273B%7D (accessed July 27, 2008).

Frasch, K. M., D. Brooks, and R. P. Barth (2000). Openness and contact in foster care adoptions: An eight year follow-up. *Family Relations* 49(4): 435–46.

Freundlich, M. (2000). *Adoption and Ethics: The Role of Race, Culture and National Origin in Adoption.* Washington, D.C.: Child Welfare League of America.

Freundlich, M., and L. Wright (2003). *Post Permanency Services.* Washington, D.C.: Casey Family Programs.

Gilles, T., and J. Kroll (1991). *Barriers to Same Race Placement.* St. Paul, Minn.: North American Council on Adoptable Children.

Grotevant, H. D., and R. G. McRoy (1998). *Openness in Adoption: Exploring Family Connections.* Thousand Oaks, Calif.: Sage.

Groze, V. (1996). *Successful Adoptive Families: A Longitudinal Study of Special Needs Adoption.* Westport, Conn.: Praeger.

Groze, V., and J. A. Rosenthal (1993). Attachment theory and the adoption of children with special needs. *Social Work Research and Abstracts* 29(2): 5–13.

Hanna, M. (2005). Preparing school age children for special needs adoption: Perspectives of successful adoptive parents and caseworkers. Ph.D. diss., University of Texas at Austin.

Hansen, M., and D. Pollack (2007). *Transracial Adoption of Black Children: An Economic Analysis.* Berkeley Electronic Press Working Paper. At law.bepress.com/expresso/eps/1942 (accessed February 14, 2007).

Haugaard, J. J., J. C. Wojslawowicz, and M. Palmer (1999). Outcomes in adolescent and older-child adoptions. *Adoption Quarterly* 3(1): 61–70.

Hill, R. B. (2004). Institutional racism in child welfare. In J. E. Everett, S. P. Chipungu, and B. R. Leashore, eds., *Child Welfare Revisited: An Africentric Perspective.* New Bruswick, N.J.: Rutgers University Press.

——(2006). *Synthesis of Research on Disproportionality in Child Welfare: An Update.* Washington, D.C.: Casey-CSSP Alliance for Racial Equity in the Child Welfare System.

Hollinger, J. H. (1998). *A Guide to the Multiethnic Placement Act of 1994 as Amended by the Interethnic Adoption Provisions of 1996.* At www.acf.dhs.gov/programs/cb/pubs/mepa94/mepachpl.htm (accessed August 28, 2006).

Howard, J. A., and S. L. Smith (2002). *Sustaining Adoptive Families: A Qualitative Study of Public Post-Adoption Services.* Washington, D.C.: Association of Administrators of the Interstate Compact on Adoption and Medical Assistance.

Jacobs, J., and M. Freundlich (2006). Achieving permanency for LGBTQ youth. *Child Welfare* 35(2): 299–316.

Kapp, S., T. McDonald, and K. Diamond (2001). The path to adoption for children of color. *Child Abuse and Neglect* 25: 215–29.

Lambda Legal Defense and Education Fund (2001). *Youth in the Margins: A Report on the Unmet Needs of Lesbian, Gay, Bisexual, and Transgender Adolescents in Foster Care.* New York: Author.

Lenerz, K., D. Gibbs, and R. P. Barth (2006). Postadoption services: A study of program participants, services and outcomes. In M. Dore, ed., *The Postadoption Experience.* Washington, D.C.: Child Welfare League of America.

Lightburn, A., and B. A. Pine (1996). Supporting and enhancing the adoption of children with developmental disabilities. *Children and Youth Services Review* 18(1): 139–62.

Mallon, G. (1998). *We Don't Exactly Get the Welcome Wagon: The Experiences of Gay and Lesbian Adolescents in Child Welfare Systems.* New York: Columbia University Press.

—— (1999). *Let's Get This Straight: A Gay and Lesbian-Affirming Approach to Child Welfare.* New York: Columbia University Press.

Maza, P. (2000). Using administrative data to reward agency performance: The case of the Federal Adoption Incentive Program. *Child Welfare* 79(5): 444–56.

—— (2002). Who is adopting older children? *Roundtable* 16(2): 1–7.

—— (2005). Patterns of relative adoption. *Roundtable* 20(1): 1–7.

McDonald, T. P., J. R. Propp, and K. C. Murphy (2001). The postadoption experience: Child, parent, and family predictors of family adjustment to adoption. *Child Welfare* 80(1): 71.

McRoy, R. G. (1999). *Special Needs Adoptions.* New York: Garland.

—— (2004). African American adoptions. In J. Everett, S. Chipungu, and B. Leashore, eds., *Child Welfare Revisited* (pp. 256–74). New Brunswick, N.J.: Rutgers University Press.

—— (2007). *Adoption Success Factors.* Washington, D.C.: U.S. Department of Health and Human Services, Children's Bureau.

McRoy, R. G., Z. Ogelsby, and H. Grape (1997). Achieving same race adoptive placements for African American children. *Child Welfare* 76(1): 85–104.

Moffatt, P. G., and J. Thoburn (2001). Outcomes of permanent family placement for children of minority ethnic origin. *Child and Family Social Work* 6(1): 13–21.

National Center for Lesbian Rights (2007). *LGBTQ Youth in the Foster Care System.* At www.nclrights.org/publications/lgbtqfostercare.htm (accessed February 7, 2007).

Reilly, T., and L. Platz (2003). Characteristics and challenges of families who adopt children with special needs: An empirical study. *Children and Youth Services Review* 25(10): 781–803.

Rosenthal, J. A. (1993). Outcomes of children with special needs. *Future of Children* 3(1): 77–88.

Rosenthal, J. A., and Groze, V. (1992). *Special Needs Adoption: A Study of Intact Families.* New York: Praeger.

—— (1994). A longitudinal study of special needs adoptive families. *Child Welfare* 73(6): 689–706.

Rosenthal, J. A., D. Schmidt, and J. Conner (1988). Predictors of special needs adoption disruption: An exploratory study. *Children and Youth Services Review* 10(2): 101–17.

Rosenthal, J. A., V. Groze, and J. Morgan (1996). Services for families adopting children via public child welfare agencies: Use, helpfulness, and need. *Children and Youth Services Review* 18(1): 163–82.

Ruiz, D. (2000). Guardians and caretakers: African American grandmothers as primary caregivers in intergenerational families. *African American Research Perspectives* 6(1): 1–14.

Ryan, S., and B. Nalavany (2003). Adopted children: Who do they turn to for help and why? *Adoption Quarterly* 7(2): 29–52.

Smith, S. L. (2006). A study of the Illinois Adoption/Guardianship Preservation Program. In M. Dore, ed., *The Postadoption Experience*. Washington, D.C.: Child Welfare League of America.

Smith, S. L., and J. A. Howard (1994). *The Adoption Preservation Project*. Normal: Illinois State University.

—— (1999). *Promoting Successful Adoptions: Practice with Troubled Families*. Thousand Oaks, Calif.: Sage.

Smith, S. L., J. A. Howard, and A. Monroe (1998). An analysis of child behavior problems in adoptions in difficulty. *Journal of Social Service Research* 24(1–2): 61–84.

Smith, S. L., J. A. Howard, and S. Ryan (2006). Where are we now? A post-ASFA examination of adoption disruption. *Adoption Quarterly* 9(4): 19–44.

U.S. Bureau of the Census (2004). *Characteristics of Children Under 18 Years by Age, Race, and Hispanic or Latino Origin, for the United States: 2000*. At www.census.gov /population/cen2000/phc-t30/tab01.pdf (accessed December 1, 2006).

U.S. Department of Health and Human Services (2005). *Adoptions of Children with Public Child Welfare Agency Involvement by State: FY 1995–FY 2003*. Washington D.C.: Author.

—— (2006a). *The AFCARS Report: Preliminary FY 2005 Estimates as of September 2006*. At www.acf.hhs.gov/programs/cb/stats_research/afcars/tar/report13.htm (accessed November 16, 2006).

—— (2006b). *Adoption Incentive Program: Fiscal Year 2005 Earning Year*. At www.acf. hhs.gov/news/press/2006/adoption_incentive_prog.htm (accessed November 17, 2006).

—— (2006c). *Adoption Incentives and AFCARS Penalties: Adoption Promotion Act of 2003 (Public Law 108-145): Information Memorandum*. At www.acf.hhs.gov/programs/cb/laws_policies/policy/im/im0404.htm (accessed November 18, 2006).

U.S. General Accounting Office (1999). *Foster Care: States' Early Experiences Implementing the Adoption and Safe Families Act*. HEHS-00-12. Washington, D.C.: Author.

—— (2002). *Foster Care: Recent Legislation Helps States Focus on Finding Permanent Homes for Children, but Long-Standing Barriers Remain*. GAO-02-585. Washington, D.C.: Author.

—— (2003). *Foster Care: States Focusing on Finding Permanent Homes for Children, but Long-Standing Barriers Remain*. GAO-HEHS-00-1. Washington, D.C.: Author.

Vonk, M. E. (2001). Cultural competence for transracial adoptive parents. *Social Work* 46: 246–55.

Wilber, S., C. Ryan, and J. Marksamer (2006). *CWLA Best Practice Guidelines*. Washington, D.C.: Child Welfare League of America

Wulczyn, F., R. Barth, Y. Yuan, B. Harden, and J. Landsverk (2005). *Beyond Common Sense: Child Welfare, Child Well-Being, and the Evidence for Policy Reform*. New Brunswick, N.J.: Aldine.

Family-Involvement Meetings with
Older Children in Foster Care

FIFTEEN

Promising Practices and the
Challenge of Child Welfare Reform

DAVID CRAMPTON
AND JOAN PENNELL

In the 1980s and 1990s, professionals in child welfare and allied disciplines
around the globe came to a similar realization: decisions about removing
children from their parents should include convening a meeting of the children's family and community and asking for their advice and support. In
locales that included Alabama, New Zealand, Ohio, and Oregon, meetings
of family and community were assembled to help develop a plan for the care
and protection of at-risk youth. Because each community's response was
shaped by its own history and service context, drawing inspiration from different cultures and social service traditions, the specific practices varied.

The overall goal of increasing family and community involvement
in child welfare decision making spread across the United States and in
other countries, fueled by dissatisfaction with conventional child welfare
approaches and positive results from various models of including children,
youth, and families in service planning. Support for family-involvement
practice grew as practitioners observed that family meetings improved
the child welfare agency's decision making by giving caseworkers access
to more information and giving families the opportunity to "buy into" the
process by involving them in developing a plan for the child (DeMuro and

Rideout, 2002). Practitioners saw benefits in family members gaining an opportunity to add their own cultural identity and strengths to plans for children (Pennell and Anderson, 2005).

Nonetheless, balancing the trade-off between rapid decision making and engaging families and communities posed challenges. As Carol Spigner (2005) has written:

> A major challenge for the child welfare system has been striking the right balance between a time-sensitive, child-protective approach and the efforts to engage families in problem solving and resolution of the issues that lead to placement. A second challenge confronting public child welfare agencies is to provide services in a manner that uses cultural and community strengths. (p. ix)

In this chapter, we review the state of family-involvement practice and then specifically relate this practice to working with older youth in foster care. We summarize a growing body of international research which suggests that family-involvement meetings keep children and youth linked with their family and culture without cost to their safety and well-being. While there is promising research regarding these practices, we acknowledge that the international experience has also demonstrated considerable challenges to reforming child welfare systems so that they support and sustain family meeting practice. Here we review the available research on family-involvement practice in relation to outcomes for youth and families, family satisfaction, and emotional healing; we also report on current data-collection efforts in a child welfare reform initiative that includes a family meeting practice called Team Decisionmaking (TDM), which was developed by the Annie E. Casey Foundation as a key component of its Family to Family Initiative (DeMuro and Rideout, 2002). We discuss several issues related to the use of family-involvement meetings with older youth in foster care, including youth and family engagement. We then describe some of the challenges in child welfare reform as they pertain to family involvement. Finally, we offer implications for research and practice.

FAMILY TEAMING PRACTICES

There are a number of approaches to family teaming used in the United States, including family unity meetings, family group conferencing, team decisionmaking, family team meetings, and family team conferencing

(Center for the Study of Social Policy, 2002). For child welfare programs in other countries, the usual term for any family-involvement meeting is family group conferencing (Burford and Hudson, 2000). In New Zealand, which was the first nation to legislate family group conferencing and specify its principles and protocols, the model—as opposed to more informal meetings—is primarily employed in higher-risk situations (Paterson and Harvey, 1991) and has many variations in its application (Walton et al., 2005).

We do not attempt here to describe all the model differences but focus on their common elements, especially the processes that benefit older youth in foster care.

As detailed in a report from the Center for the Study of Social Policy, all family meeting practices include the following:

1. Shared values that emphasize the need for child welfare agencies to interact with children, families, and communities with mutual respect
2. Common expectations that power will shift from being exclusively held by the child welfare system and the courts to being shared with families and communities
3. A broad and inclusive definition of who is included in the "family team" that is making these decisions
4. A meeting place that provides an environment that is supportive of families in the decision-making process
5. A commitment to providing sufficient preparation, coordination, and facilitation of the family meetings in order to balance the needs of all parties while remaining focused on the child's safety and well-being (Center for the Study of Social Policy, 2002)

The meetings are made up of family members, service providers, and other community members who convene to review concerns about the care and protection of a child or children. The professionals present child welfare concerns, these issues are discussed, and the group helps to develop a plan that promotes the safety and well-being of the child(ren) and other family members.

Other aspects of family meeting practices may vary, depending on the model used. To provide a general sense of some of these differences, the components of Family Group Conferencing (FGC) and Team Decision-making (TDM) are provided in Table 15.1. These models were selected because they serve to highlight some significant practice issues, but their selection does not imply that they are more promising than other family-

Table 15.1   Characteristics of Family Meetings

	TEAM DECISION MAKING (TDM)	FAMILY GROUP CONFERENCING (FGC)
Purpose	To make an immediate decision regarding a child's placement	To develop a comprehensive plan for the care and protection of a child
Timing	Before a removal or placement change	Usually two weeks to one month after a referral for a meeting is made
Preparation time	Due to the crisis nature of most meetings, arrangements are made quickly by the assigned social worker.	The preparation for a first-time conference can be 20–30 hours over a 3–4-week period; subsequent conferences usually require less preparation.
Participants	The average number of participants is about five, including the facilitators, a parent, a relative, the social worker assigned to the case, and a community representative or neighbor.	The average number of family group members is 5 to 11, with additional participants, including the coordinator, child welfare worker, other service providers, and anyone else the family identifies as a potential support to them.
Length of meeting	1–2 hours on average	2.5–6 hours on average
Meeting organizer (called facilitator in TDM and coordinator in FGC)	Experienced staff who have demonstrated excellent communication skills are encouraged to become facilitators; once selected, they receive specialized facilitation training	Coordinators whose role is to organize and convene the conference and who do not hold case-carrying responsibility for the children
Group decision making	The public agency shares, but does not delegate, its responsibility to make critical placement decisions.	The family develops a plan on its own during family private time, but agency staff can veto plans they believe are not safe.

SOURCE: Adapted from Crampton and Natarajan (2005) and from Pennell and Anderson (2005).

involvement models. The authors assume that as with any good social work practice, the suitability of the methods depends upon the purpose and context of the intervention and the total configuration of methods applied.

In FGC, the time between a referral and a conference is usually two weeks to one month (Pennell and Anderson, 2005). In contrast, TDM meetings are held when an immediate decision is needed regarding a removal or placement change (DeMuro and Rideout, 2002). The purpose of the meetings also differ: TDM meetings are designed to make an immediate decision regarding a child's placement; FGC meetings are designed to develop a comprehensive plan for the care and protection of the child. The frequency and purpose of the meetings determine many of their other differences. These differences illustrate the tension between rapid decision making and involving family and community in those decisions.

TDM meetings are used for every placement-related decision (i.e., child removals, transfer from one placement to another, and family reunification or other forms of permanence). In the United States, FGC is used in a wide range of circumstances, including decisions about how to support children residing in or returning to their homes and where to place children outside the home. In New Zealand, the family group must be invited to an FGC when a child is considered to be in need of care or protection, and the group must be involved in decision making in situations of involuntary child placements (M. Connolly, Chief Social Worker of New Zealand, personal communication, April 9, 2007).[1] To cover all placement decisions, many TDM programs have limited time for preparation and meeting time, as compared with FGC. These differences can result in a smaller number of participants in TDM and may require more active facilitation of the meeting by a trained facilitator in a TDM compared with an FGC. Both practices encourage the participation of the family group: that is, the immediate family of concern, their relatives, friends, and other close supports. The FGC model refers to the organizer and convener as a "coordinator" rather than a "facilitator," and it stipulates that (to maintain their independence) the coordinators not have case-carrying responsibility, and seeks to engage the family group in creating their own decision-making process. In fact, FGC is expected to include "private family time" when the coordinator and other service providers leave the meeting room and the family group develops a plan on its own. The emphases of the group decision-making process differ in the two approaches. TDM facilitators stress that the public child welfare agency is ultimately responsible for making the final decision. FGC encourages family group members to make their own plan, although child welfare authorities retain veto power.

Denver, Colorado, is an example of a jurisdiction that at one time used a variation on FGC, referred to as Family Group Decision Making (FGDM), and now uses TDM. Prior to using TDM, the public child welfare agency employed ten FGDM coordinators who facilitated approximately five meetings per month, resulting in a maximum capacity of roughly six hundred meetings per year. In 2005, four TDM facilitators in Denver facilitated 1,372 TDM meetings. These data dramatically demonstrate the difference in the number of meetings held under the different approaches: one-half as many TDM facilitators facilitated twice as many meetings as the FGDM coordinators did. However, preparation time for the TDM meetings is necessarily much shorter.

Although no data are available to compare the effect of the processes and outcomes of FGC and TDM, it should be noted that one FGC study found that, during their private time, family group participants were more likely to make decisions in a participatory rather than a manipulative manner after receiving adequate preparation (Pennell, 2006). Thus, if family private time is used, preparation advisably should be undertaken with care. In a review of both outcomes and process in family meetings, David Crampton (2007) noted that preparation time and increased meeting attendance can increase family involvement.

RESEARCH ON FAMILY-INVOLVEMENT MEETINGS

A growing body of international research shows that family-involvement meetings keep children and youth connected with their siblings, families, relatives, and cultural groups without further endangering their safety. So far, few of these outcome studies of family-involvement practices appear in peer-reviewed journals and those available are primarily limited to FGC (Crampton, 2007; Crampton and Jackson, 2007; Pennell and Burford, 2000; Sundell and Vinnerljung, 2004). The studies that have been published indicate that the family meetings show "promising outcomes" (Pennell and Anderson, 2005:4) for families with a wide range of characteristics (Crampton, 2006) and from diverse cultures (Burford and Hudson, 2000).

A persistent finding is that family-involvement meetings appear to advance permanence by stabilizing placements, reconnecting youngsters with their family, or placing them with kin. For instance, an evaluation in Washington, D.C., of children removed from their homes, found that the 454 children whose families participated in family team meetings, as compared with the 335 children whose families did not participate, were placed with kin (as opposed to nonrelative) foster care and returned to their families, both at statistically higher rates (Edwards and Tinworth, 2006). This occurred without greater jeopardy to their safety. Similar findings on permanence were reported in a Texas study: after family group decision making (FGDM, a combination, in this case, of FGC and traditional Hawaiian practices) foster care placements decreased by 54 percent and kin placements increased by 29 percent; compared with children for whom an FGDM was *not* held, the FGDM children were more likely to be reunified with their parents and at a faster rate (Texas Department of Family and Protective Services, 2006). In addition, the Texas evaluation found that although FGDM was associated with family reunification for African American, Hispanic, and Anglo children, this improvement was more evident for the first two groups. This finding underlines the potential of family-involvement meetings to reduce the overrepresentation of racial and ethnic groups in state care. Moreover, communities who are concerned about the disproportionate number of ethnic minority children in foster care often examine key points regarding decisions to investigate, substantiate, and place minority children at higher rates. When a potential bias in decision making is found, a promising remedy is to implement family-involvement meetings at these decision points (Crampton and Jackson, 2007).

The data are more limited regarding well-being. Some studies report benefits (Pennell and Burford, 2000; Texas Department of Family and Protective Services, 2006), and none reveals a pattern that children and young people are worse off because of their meetings.

Family Satisfaction

A consistent finding of the family-involvement research is that families and their workers like the meetings (Pennell and Anderson, 2005; Texas Department of Family and Protective Services, 2006). Family members' satisfaction with the process is noteworthy in itself, given the frequency of strained relationships between the child welfare system and their clientele. Family satisfaction with their level of say also points to a democratizing of child welfare decision making and developing families' efficacy in making decisions (Pennell, 2006). Theorists of civil society will see the implications of family-involvement meetings for creating a civil society with the trust and good will necessary for collaborative endeavors.

It is recognized that client satisfaction alone is not sufficient to demonstrate that family-involvement meetings are effective. Carol Lupton and Paul Nixon (1999), for example, argue that positive family perception is not the same as family empowerment unless the outcomes for children and families served by family-involvement meetings are demonstrably better than the outcomes achieved through the provision of regular services. Nevertheless, a detour into the restorative justice literature points to a further implication of the findings regarding family satisfaction.

Emotional Healing

Feeling good about the deliberations at restorative justice conferences is linked with emotional healing. Retrospective interviews with crime victims in Australia and the United Kingdom found very high levels of satisfaction with restorative justice conferencing, along with substantial levels of emotional recovery (Strang et al., 2006). Emotional recovery included decreases in the victim's fear of and anger against the offender, increases in sympathy toward the offender, and decreases in the victim's sense of being at fault for the crime.

Cognitive behavioral theory also assists in explaining these findings. The face-to-face meeting serves as a form of exposure therapy with the offender and cognitive restructuring by the group as they reassess what happened and make a plan to redress the situation (Angel, 2006). Cognitive behavioral therapy is enhanced by building social supports that offer information, concrete assistance, and emotional relief and that serve as a buffer against developing posttraumatic stress symptoms. In addition, child and adult victims appear likely to benefit from social acknowledgment that they were hurt and validation from the wider community that the harms committed against them are contrary to societal norms (Gal, 2006).

Issues of trauma and posttraumatic stress disorder (PTSD) particularly apply to families served by the child welfare system, given the interaction of poverty and racism with high levels of substance addictions, mental health issues, and domestic violence. Children who are both physically abused and residing in homes with domestic violence tend to have some of the most severe PTSD symptoms (Rossman, 2001). The available information points to the healing potential of family involvement meetings. In a study of FGDM in Newfoundland and Labrador, the crucial importance of having the opportunity to put the pain on the table arose repeatedly, especially among participants with a history of extremely abusive relationships (Burford and Pennell, 1998). A one-year follow-up outcome study showed a decrease in indicators of child maltreatment and domestic violence and increases in child well-being (Pennell and Burford, 2000).

More recently, in a preliminary evaluation of family team meetings (FTMs) in Washington, D.C., caseworkers and magistrates attributed to the meetings a vital role in easing tensions and increasing focus on the issues at hand. A magistrate described parents arriving in court before the establishment of family meetings as in "shell shock," but with family meetings, they came across as less "traumatized" and better able to represent themselves (Edwards and Tinworth, 2005:4). A family meeting coordinator observed the impact of the meetings on the children and young people: "[They] give the children hope that people want them to be with their family members" (4).

Current Data Collection and Analysis Regarding TDM

Although published research on TDM is quite limited, efforts currently are under way to collect more data about the TDM process and its results. Over sixty communities participating in the Family to Family Initiative are using databases to track key TDM meeting characteristics and then link those characteristics to the outcomes of the children they serve. The databases record who attends TDM meetings, meeting time and location, service needs identified at TDMs, and custody and placement recommendations (Usher et al., 2007). When TDM and out-of-home placement data are combined, they can be used to test for correlations between relative attendance at TDMs and increased relative placements, birth parent attendance and increased reunification, and foster parent attendance and fewer foster placement disruptions. Although the data that demonstrate positive correlations between TDM attendance and positive child outcomes do not prove causation, these data can be used by communities to examine the potential benefits of TDM (Crampton, 2004).

The databases also are used to track youth attendance. Many communities have a policy requiring that youth over the age of twelve be invited to participate in TDM meetings with it being their choice on whether to take part. The TDM database can be used to measure compliance with this requirement. TDMs in which youth do not attend can be flagged so that senior managers can explore why youth did not attend and determine what can be done to increase youth attendance. Thus far, many communities that are tracking youth attendance are finding that, despite their best intentions, youth are not consistently attending TDM meetings. These data are getting them to examine what policies and management practices require change, such as mandatory invitations for youth to attend meetings and more stringent protocols for requesting a waiver for mandatory youth invitations to attend meetings. With these baseline data in hand, they can work on increasing their youth attendance statistics.

USE OF FAMILY-INVOLVEMENT MEETINGS WITH OLDER YOUTH IN FOSTER CARE

Given the limited published research on family-involvement meetings, there is even less information about their use with older youth in care. The limited information is partially the result of the fact that one role of family-involvement interventions is to confirm that out-of-home placement is, in fact, the most appropriate way to deal with risks to a child or youth. Because the pool of children initially considered for foster care placement is younger than the children who are in foster care on any given day (Wulczyn et al., 2006), family-involvement practices at the front end of the system are more often used with younger children. The majority of children in the only randomized trial of a family-involvement intervention, for example, were under the age of six, so it is not possible to draw any conclusions about the experiences of the small number of older children in the study (Center for Social Services Research, 2004).

Family meetings, however, are increasingly being used with older youth. TDM, for example, requires the convening of a meeting when older youth are being considered for either legal emancipation or independent living; hence its use puts a spotlight on key issues facing older youth in care. As part of a study of TDM implementation, a TDM facilitator was asked to describe a recent TDM and she provided this example:

The meeting concerned the reunification of a teen mother and her baby with the teen's mother. The meeting included the teen, her mother, her foster parent (who had been caring for the teen and the baby up until this point), three extended family members, the case manager for the foster family, two Guardian at litems, an in-home worker (who would begin working with the family after the reunification), a community advocate (an agency worker from the neighborhood collaborative near where the family lives), the caseworker for the family and the facilitator. This was the fifth TDM in the case and was held to develop and support the reunification plan. The teen had decided that she was not ready to take on a parental role so the plan included ensuring that the teen mother was not left alone with the baby and that the teen succeeded in school. Much of the meeting included talking with the grandmother and the teen about these issues. Unsupervised visits had occurred already so the caseworker felt that the grandmother was ready for the reunification. The in-home worker was there to meet the family and explain how she could support them. This worker speaks Spanish which helps meet the family's needs and the TDM gave the family a chance to meet her. She made arrangements with the family to visit their home the next day. The family members would be providing child care for the baby. The community advocate had been involved in the case since the first TDM and would remain available to help the family meet any community needs. The TDM meeting provided an opportunity for the participants to specifically plan out who will care for the baby when the grandmother is unavailable, what services will be put in place to support the teen's development (support group, classes, etc.) and education (mentor, tutor, etc.), a set schedule with the days and times when the family members will care for the baby, and specific mechanisms for the community advocate to remain a support to the family (weekly visits, phone calls, etc.). The facilitator described this meeting as an ideal TDM. Everyone was there to support a plan that would support successful reunification.

The TDM meeting gave this teen parent an opportunity to express concerns about her new parental role and returning to school so that community and formal supports could be put in place to assist in her return to her mother and the care of her baby. Allowing the youth to take a central role facilitated a more comprehensive plan.

Despite more widespread use of family-involvement meetings with older youth, the field is neither widely nor systematically evaluating their effectiveness with this population. Attention must be given to issues that shape a critical appraisal and application of these techniques to older children and youth and their families: the practices that promote enduring family relationships and permanence and adaptation of these practices to best address the needs of youth of varying cultural, national, and sexual identities.

Child and Family Characteristics That Predict Success

Many family members and youth may initially say there are no relatives available for a family meeting when practitioners ask whether any family members would be willing to raise a child to adulthood. Greater success may be achieved in involving family members when practitioners ask family members and youth to identify people who may be willing to play some role in supporting them and then inviting those potential supporters to come to a meeting. When potential support people are brought together in a meeting and offered services, they may collectively develop a placement or permanency plan that strengthen a youth's transition to adulthood. Before a successful family meeting can take place, there must be a deliberate effort to make sure that the important people in a youth's life are identified and invited to the meeting.

In general, family-involvement practice research suggests that these meetings work well when there are community and extended family members who are willing and able to attend a meeting and help develop a plan for the care and protection of children. Conversely, when there are no community or extended family members to invite to a meeting, this approach is less likely to lead to contributions from the informal network to the plan and its implementation. This commonsense conclusion must be interpreted with some caution as it should not be understood to mean that many families will not benefit from family meetings; rather, it points to the importance of preparation and making sure extended family and community members are invited.

Although the presence of family and community support appears to be important to the success of family-involvement meetings, no child or family characteristics have been identified as predictive of more or less success with family meetings. A study of an Arizona FGDM program that targeted children who had been in out-of-home care for five years or longer or who were free for adoption without an identified adoptive family found no specific child or family characteristics that were predictive of permanence (Velen and Devine, 2005). Similarly, a random assignment study of court mediation with child welfare cases found that no specific case characteristic predicted settlement of the cases (Gatowski et al., 2005). In some communities, there are concerns about using family-involvement practices in cases that include domestic violence or child sexual abuse, but it appears that even in these cases, family meetings can be used with safeguards in place

(Pennell and Anderson, 2005; Pennell and Burford, 2000). If there is a history of violence between two family members, for example, arrangements can be made for them to attend with support persons and for security personnel to be stationed near the family meeting room.

Family and Youth Engagement and Permanency Planning

While the research on the specific use of family meetings with older youth is more limited than the research concerning all children in general, some promising results suggest the potential for using these practices to engage older youth and their families. A Washington State study looked at family group conferences that were held for older youth with high levels of need in group care (Yancey et al., 2005). Despite the lack of family involvement that many youth experience the longer they are in foster care and the challenges of engaging families in many of these cases, the study found that an average of 7.73 family members attended each family group conference. According to the study, attending the conference was beneficial for the youth: "The FGC facilitator and the service providers attending the conferences described looks of surprise, delight and amazement on the faces of the young people as they walked into the room and saw siblings and other family members, many of whom they had not seen for years" (37). The study noted that one of the ways family-involvement meetings promote enduring family relationships is simply by putting the youth and the other family members in a room together and giving them an opportunity to resolve their differences and reestablish connections.

A key element of the process is the attendance of the youth themselves in these meetings. Communities with policies that require any child over the age of twelve to be invited to participate in meetings is consistent with more general recommendations to include older youth in their own permanency planning decisions (Ford and Boo, 2005; Freundlich and Avery, 2004). Youth, however, often are not included in planning and decision-making processes. A review of the Child and Family Service Reviews from twenty-two states noted that in more than one-third of the states, the federal reviewers found that children (when age appropriate) were not regularly involved in developing their case plan (Diaz and Freundlich, 2003). Although there may be circumstances when youth should not attend a meeting as a result of the youth's level of maturity or the emotional nature of the information that will be discussed, it may be possible to allow the youth to attend part of the meeting. In this way, youth can participate in planning decisions but do not necessarily have to hear all the details about the case. For example, if the youth does not want to be present when a perpetrator attends the meeting, they can choose to leave the room for that part of the meeting. As noted earlier, communities using TDM are tracking youth attendance in their databases to better understand when and how youth participation is linked to better youth outcomes.

Family-involvement approaches do not necessarily translate into youth taking part in planning and decision making. The participation of children and young people varies in practice. The Washington State study of FGC for older youth in group care, for example, found that a very high proportion (81 percent) of the youth attended meetings (Yancey et al., 2005). This percentage surpasses those found by an international survey that reports that children and young people are present in only about two-thirds of family group decision-making meetings (Nixon et al., 2005) and may be attributable to the older age of the youth in the Washington State study. The lack of involvement of children in case planning, moreover, was a consistent finding in the Child and Family Service Reviews (U.S. Department of Health and Human Services, 2003).

Equally important, young people's attendance does not ensure genuine participation in the deliberations. Although family-involvement practices promote family relationships and permanence by inviting the youth to the meetings where issues are discussed, simply inviting the youth to the meeting is not sufficient. They must be actively engaged in the process. Agency staff can become uncomfortable with the presence of youth and slip into a parental role, telling the youth what to do rather than listening to them. The result is an adult-focused meeting at which the youth is merely an observer. When meetings become adult-focused, youth report that they do not feel heard, they do not understand the "foreign language" of agency acronyms used in the meeting, and they feel decisions have already been made and they are only invited "for looks" so the agency can say the youth was there (Pat Rideout, personal communication, May 30, 2006; Stacey A. Saunders, personal communication, June 5, 2006). Staff may need special training in techniques to actively engage youth (Ford and Boo, 2005). The training may include observing a skilled facilitator as she actively involves youth in a family meeting or having the skilled facilitator observe the trainee's facilitation skills and then offer constructive suggestions. The Family to Family Initiative is providing youth engagement training to communities that use TDM.

An Arizona study (Velen and Devine, 2005) examined how family group decision making fostered connections between family and young people in care for prolonged periods of time, finding that, at the end of conferences, satisfaction levels on "having a say" were somewhat lower for youth than for adults. Most of the adult participants (95.2 percent) agreed that they had a "real voice in making plans for the future of the child(ren)," compared with 82.9 percent of children and youth who said that they "had a real voice in making plans for my future" (31). On the one hand, these percentages show positive experiences for most participants in a project dedicated to focusing on older foster children; on the other hand, 17 percent of children and youth felt that they had no real voice, indicating the need for strategies of inclusion.

Once youth are invited to family meetings and fully engaged, they should be asked to define what "family" and "permanence" mean to them. Many communities are attempting to reduce the number of older youth in care who are assigned to long-term foster care without making ongoing efforts to ensure that they have permanent families. When a task force in Cuyahoga County (Cleveland) was assembled to address this issue, it implemented a policy that no petition for long-term foster care could be filed without the approval of a TDM. This change, along with others, resulted in a dramatic reduction in the number of youth assigned to long-term foster care (Ford and Boo, 2005). Although older youth may have some reservations about adoption or other permanency outcomes, when they are included in family meetings and engaged in the planning process, they can help find creative solutions that lead to meaningful adult relationships that can help support them into adulthood.

The success of a family meeting should not be judged only by whether it helped identify a new permanent family for a youth. The establishment or reestablishment of family connections through a family meeting may be beneficial for youth long after they leave foster care (Velen and Devine, 2005). Both research and theory suggest that youth who have at least one significant relationship with an adult have greater resilience and a greater chance of successfully transitioning to adulthood (Stein, 2005).

Overall, family-involvement practices promote family relationships by inviting youth to the meetings, engaging them in the discussion, and seeking their ideas about how a plan can be developed. One practice is the use of a youth support person or advocate in a family meeting. A Canadian trial demonstration required that all minors who had been maltreated be accompanied by an adult support to stay by them throughout the proceedings, and most young people readily identified supports such as a relative, foster parent, or guidance counselor (Pennell and Burford, 1995). An English study looked at the efficacy of an independent advocate for children who participated in FGDM meetings. Forty-four meetings were held during the time of the study. Twenty-nine children chose to have an independent advocate, six chose an advocate from their family, four chose not to have an advocate as they felt able to speak for themselves, and five were under the age of four and were apparently not assigned an advocate. Children who had an advocate indicated that their personal position was enhanced, they felt stronger within the family, and they were more able to participate in the professional decision making (Dalrymple, 2002). A Welsh study of children's participation in FGDM also found that those few children who had an advocate were positive about the experience of having one. For example, a fourteen-year-old girl reported that she was happy that an advocate would be with her in the meeting room and that "I was not going to be in the room without her" (Holland and O'Neill, 2006:101).

Whether called an "advocate" or a "support person," these individuals offer a means of fostering youth's safe and effective participation rather than setting up a dichotomy between them and their family group. Most states require that children in state custody have a guardian ad litem (GAL) who is an independent advocate for youth. The TDM model requires that GALs be invited to TDM meetings and, therefore, provides a potential avenue for a youth advocate to strengthen the family meeting process. Training for the independent advocates can assist them in understanding their role in supporting the young person and respecting the family meeting process.

The inclusion of youth in family meetings is consistent with Article 12 of the United Nations 1989 Convention on the Rights of the Child.[2] In accordance with this principle, the New Zealand 1989 FGC legislation views children as entitled members and, thus, having the right to participate unless there are strong reasons to the contrary (Paterson and Harvey, 1991). Outside of New Zealand, policies vary widely on inviting children to meetings, especially those under twelve years of age (Merkel-Holguin, 2003). Exclusion of children may reflect more the worries of adults than the wishes of the children themselves (Marsh and Crow, 1998). Training, reinforced by agency policy and resources, can assist professionals in developing flexible arrangements for how rather than whether to include children and adolescents.

Addressing the Needs of Youth of Varying Cultural, National, and Sexual Identities

Family-involvement practices are often recognized for their potential in developing culturally competent interventions. Proponents of FGC point to the roots of their model in the cultural practices of the Maori people in New Zealand. A North Carolina project conducted focus groups with African American, Cherokee, and Latino/Hispanic North Carolinians and asked how the model could be better adapted to meet the needs of their communities (Waites et al., 2004). The focus group members offered specific suggestions for using location, cultural traditions, facilitators' background, elders, and community education to enhance the use of family meetings in their communities. In a similar way, practitioners of family meetings with older youth should consider how to consult youth and ask them how the meetings can be adapted to best meet the cultural, national, and sexual identity needs of the youth they serve.

Some of the domains identified by Waites et al. (2004) are worth exploring with focus groups of youth: the locations that are best for meetings with youth; how meetings can be more inviting to youth when they must be held in residential treatment centers or detention facilities; the "cultural traditions" that can be incorporated into youth meetings (music, posters, artifacts); the backgrounds that should be sought in facilitators so that they can effectively work with youth; the respected community members and elders who may be brought into the process (including coaches, teachers, and counselors); and community education methods and content that work best for explaining the value and intent of these meetings to youth (such as web pages, PSAs, or flyers).

Practice guidelines for serving LGBT youth in out-of-home care stress that agencies should respond promptly and constructively to problems that arise in placements due to sexual identity issues: "LGBT youth who encounter discrimination, harassment, or other problems in their placements need ready access to agency personnel to initiate a problem-solving process. Likewise, caregivers and staff members need agency support to address issues related to the care of LGBT youth. Well-intentioned caregivers may need help understanding the experiences of LGBT youth, how to apply the agency's nondiscrimination policy, and options for resolving complex questions" (Wilber et al., 2006:44). The guidelines suggest one approach to take when these challenges arise is to convene a meeting with the youth and any other persons who might contribute to collectively identifying a solution that promotes continuity of care and mutual respect and understanding.

Practitioners also should consider the relevance of youth culture to cultural competence. As an example, a youth in a TDM meeting may listen to music on headphones. The adults may become annoyed, thinking the youth cannot possibly hear what is being said with the music on and may conclude that the youth is not interested in being at the meeting. Alternatively, the adults might consider that the youth can hear what the adults are saying, and the music provides some comfort to the youth in a stressful situation (Stacey A. Saunders, TDM trainer, personal communication, June 5, 2006). Practitioners should challenge themselves to consider whether they are working to make meetings youth-friendly by incorporating some of these ideas of youth culture into their practice.

CHALLENGE OF CHILD WELFARE REFORM

Despite the intuitive appeal of family-involvement practice, many communities struggle to implement consistent, engaged meetings with families and older youth in care. Although numerous communities throughout the world have begun family-involvement interventions, it is not known how many of these programs quietly died out as a result of insufficient resources, lack of proven effectiveness, or other reasons. It is clear, however, that many communities have found implementing and sustaining these approaches to be extremely challenging. As noted by Joan Pennell and Gary Anderson (2005):

> Family group conferencing is a method that is simple in terms of its concept, but complex in terms of its implementation. The complexity stems from its divergence in philosophy and practice from the conventional child welfare system in the United States. This system holds parents accountable for their failings without encouraging responsible intervention by the family group and community. (p. xiv)

In addition to undertaking a major philosophical shift, communities that implement these practices must be realistic about the resources that are required to use family meetings effectively. In most cases, planning, training, and policy have not been adequate. New Zealand, unlike most jurisdictions, has legislation that requires family group conferencing. In the United States, federal legislation, the Adoption and Safe Families Act, encourages the involvement of families in planning, and this expectation is further reinforced by the Child and Family Services Reviews (Pennell and Anderson, 2005). The implementation of family-involvement meetings has often gone hand in hand with other child welfare reforms, including instituting differential response systems so that child welfare can respond more flexibly to family situations.

The intuitive appeal of family meetings is a double-edged sword. Why we should use family meetings to engage families and communities is obvious, but how we should do it seems to receive little attention because the concept itself appears self-evident. Moreover, too often we insist on particular protocols rather than on what young people and their families need to participate. For example, FGC proponents often insist that the practice must include extensive preparation time and family alone time. Similarly, TDM requires that every placement decision have a TDM meeting. To engage young people and their families, it is helpful, instead, to focus on what they need to take part safely and effectively in the meetings. This may vary, depending on the youth's social network, the family's situation and culture, the community's resources, the agency's stage of work with the family, and the jurisdictions's legal requirements (Pennell, 2007). For example, if an investigation of child sexual abuse is in process, this is usually not the time to convene a meeting because the alleged offender, the victim, and other family members are typically reluctant to voice their views. In moving forward with a meeting, the facilitator or coordinator needs to be able to answer the following questions in the affirmative: Is there a clear and agreed on reason for holding the meeting? Can the agency use the family's input in developing the service plan (or, conversely, is the plan already preset by court order and agency policy)? Do enough family members agree to take part? Can the family participate safely? (Pennell and Anderson, 2005).

IMPLICATIONS FOR RESEARCH AND PRACTICE

In social services research, a ubiquitous suggestion is that more study is needed. In the case of family-involvement practice, the need for more study is likewise true. There is evidence that these practices are widely used, and there is a growing body of literature on the process used for some models of family involvement. While practitioners sometimes clash over which variation in practice is the best, no camp can point to research that identifies the benefits of their specific approach. Both practitioners and researchers should commit to systematic comparisons of family-involvement practices in order to begin to learn which methods work best for which families in which particular agency, community, and cultural context and how to adapt these practices to meet the unique needs of older youth in foster care.

Research on family-involvement practices to date typically has described the sample of children served, the procedures used, the levels of satisfaction, and, in some cases, the outcomes. Research should compare, at the very least, variations in attendance, maltreatment allegations, and location and services offered with differences in child and youth outcomes. This work has begun with TDM databases in all Family to Family sites, but more sophisticated studies must be developed that examine the utility of preparation time, the requirement of holding meetings for all placement decisions, and encouraging youth to select a support person or advocate to stay by them during the meeting. Studies should explore how to make family-involvement meeting more culturally competent and then test those cultural adjustments in relation to regular practice. In order to answer questions about key practices and cultural adaptation, practitioners and researchers should work together to take the intuitive ideas of family-involvement practices and translate them into specific practice methods that can be compared and evaluated in order to engage young people and their families and achieve the best outcomes.

A persistent finding is that the family meetings promote child and youth permanence without jeopardizing child or youth safety. Because this benefit appears to be particularly pronounced for children and youth from cultural backgrounds that are typically overrepresented in the child welfare system, family-involvement meetings hold the promise of reducing disproportionality in state care. Nevertheless, more research on the outcomes of family-involvement practices is needed to help the field justify the allocation of scarce resources to family meetings and evaluate more thoroughly how family meetings can better promote child and youth safety, permanence, and well-being. In child welfare systems with high caseloads, is it practical to create positions for facilitators who carry no cases so that they can devote their energy to facilitating, organizing, and convening meetings? A decision to do so can be complicated, given that other staff realize that creating a non-case-carrying position may increase their own caseloads in systems that rely on rigid caseload-based staffing formulas.

In fact, scarce resources may provide an opportunity for more study of outcomes. For example, if a community does not have sufficient resources to offer a family meeting in every case and doing so is not a legal requirement, it may be possible to randomly assign cases to family meetings and no family meetings. Analysis of such an experimental design, though, needs to take into account how system-wide changes are needed in order to prepare communities to use family-involvement meeting effectively. For example, family meetings may not be helpful by themselves unless there is a community-wide effort to ensure that family and community members are invited to participate in the meetings and unless there are community-based services and supports ready to sustain the plans that the families develop in their meetings. A recent evaluation of the Family to Family Initiative noted that TDM can be much more effective when there are parallel strategies to recruit resource families and other community partners from the neighborhoods where families served by the child welfare system live (Batterson et al., 2007). These additional strategies help improve TDM attendance and community supports for TDM plans, but these community-wide reforms make it impossible to randomly assign some families to family-involvement practices and other families to conventional practices if they all live in a community that is under reform.

Despite the significant challenges of reforming child welfare systems so they support family-involvement practice and the challenges of evaluating these efforts, there is a growing body of research that suggests that family meetings can improve the lives of the children and young people and their families served by the child welfare system. With additional information about the effectiveness of family meetings and how to make them effective, it may be possible to increase available resources and begin to address the challenges of engaging family and community support for older youth in foster care.

NOTES

This chapter is based on drafts of two separate chapters written by each author. The editors of this volume asked us to combine our chapters into one. Like the numerous communities that are using family involvement practices, our experiences with these practices are different, and, as a result, our perspectives on some of the key issues are also different. Nevertheless, it seemed reasonable to combine our chapters and speak with one voice to highlight both the promise of these practices and the challenges of implementing them in ways that are faithful to the values of family and community empowerment. David would like to thank Pat Rideout, Stacey A. Saunders, and Lynn

Usher for their comments on his previous draft. He is also grateful to Joan for humor, flexibility, and passion for the work. Joan appreciates David's openness to her perspectives, his good will in reshaping the chapter to include both our viewpoints, and his strong commitment to reaching out to youth in care. She also wishes to acknowledge the support of the North Carolina Division of Social Services for her work on family group conferencing and child and family teams.

1. The law is clear that wherever a social worker or a police officer believes a statutory intervention is necessary, an FGC must occur. Thus, the "forming of a belief that there is a need for care or protection" by a social worker is the sole trigger for a Care and Protection FGC. By definition, then, only the more serious cases in relation to child care or protection and young people's offending have a formal FGC, approximately 15–20 percent of cases. A Youth Justice FGC is required wherever the police form a belief that prosecution is warranted or a child or young person is arrested (M. Doolan, former Chief Social Worker of New Zealand, personal communication, April 12, 2007).

2. Article 12 of the U.N. Convention on the Rights of the Child reads: "1. States Parties shall assure to the child who is capable of forming his or her own views the right to express those views freely in all matters affecting the child, the views of the child being given due weight in accordance with the age and maturity of the child; 2. For this purpose, the child shall in particular be provided the opportunity to be heard in any judicial and administrative proceedings affecting the child, either directly or through a representative or an appropriate body, in a manner consistent with the procedural rules of national law" (Office of the United Nations High Commissioner for Human Rights, 1989).

REFERENCES

Angel, C. M. (2006). Restorative justice conceptualized as a cognitive behavioral therapeutic approach: An overview. Unpublished ms., University of Pennsylvania, School of Nursing, Jerry Lee Center of Criminology.

Batterson, M., D. Crampton, T. Crea, F. Harris, A. Madden, L. Usher, and J. Williams (2007). *Implementing Family to Family.* Chapel Hill: University of North Carolina at Chapel Hill.

Burford, G., and J. Hudson, eds. (2000). *Family Group Conferences: New Directions in Community-Centered Child and Family Practice.* Hawthorne, N.Y.: Aldine de Gruyter.

Burford, G., and J. Pennell (1998). *Family Group Decision Making: After the Conference— Progress in Resolving Violence and Promoting Well-Being: Outcome Report.* 2 vols. St. John's: Memorial University of Newfoundland, School of Social Work.

Center for Social Services Research (2004). *The California Title IV-E Child Welfare Waiver Demonstration Study Evaluation: Final Report May 31, 2004*. At cssr.berkeley.edu/childwelfare/researchdetails.asp?name=waiver (accessed February 10, 2005).

Center for the Study of Social Policy (2002). *Bringing Families to the Table: A Comparative Guide to Family Meetings in Child Welfare*. Washington, D.C.: Author.

Crampton, D. (2004). Family involvement interventions in child protection: Learning from contextual integrated strategies. *Journal of Sociology and Social Welfare* 31(1): 175–98.

—— (2006). When do social workers and family members try family group decision making? A process evaluation. *International Journal of Child and Family Welfare* 9(3): 131–43.

—— (2007). Family group decision making: A promising practice in need of more program theory and research. *Child and Family Social Work* 12: 202–9.

Crampton, D., and W. Jackson (2007). Family group decision making and the overrepresentation of children of color in foster care: A case study. *Child Welfare* 86(3): 51–70.

Crampton, D., and A. Natarajan (2005). Connections between group work and family meetings in child welfare practice: What can we learn from each other? *Social Work with Groups* 28(1): 65–79.

Dalrymple, J. (2002). Family group conferences and youth advocacy: The participation of children and young people in family decision making. *European Journal of Social Work* 5(3): 287–99.

DeMuro, P., and P. Rideout (2002). *Team Decisionmaking: Involving the Family and Community in Child Welfare Decisions*. Baltimore: Annie E. Casey Foundation, Family to Family Initiative.

Diaz, P., and M. Freundlich (2003). *Child and Family Service Review Final Reports: An Assessment of States' Success in Involving Children and Families in Case Planning*. New York: Children's Rights.

Edwards, M., and K. Tinworth (with G. Burford, J. Fluke, and J. Pennell) (2005). *Family Team Meeting (FTM) Process, Outcome, and Impact Evaluation*. Englewood, Colo.: American Humane Association. At www.americanhumane.org/site/DocServer/FTM_Report_111605.pdf?docID=3401 (accessed December 15, 2005).

Edwards, M., and K. Tinworth (with G. Burford and J. Pennell) (2006). *Family Team Meeting (FTM) Process, Outcome, and Impact Evaluation: Phase II Report*. Englewood, Colo.: American Humane Association.

Ford, M., and M. Boo (2005). *A Family for Every Child: Strategies to Achieve Permanence for Older Foster Children and Youth*. Baltimore: Annie E. Casey Foundation, Family to Family Initiative.

Freundlich, M., and R. J. Avery (2004). Planning for permanency for youth in congregate care. *Children and Youth Services Review* 27: 115–34.

Gal, T. (2006). Victims to partners: Child victims and restorative justice. Ph.D. diss., Australian National University, Canberra.

Gatowski, S. I., S. A. Dobbin, M. Litchfield, and J. Oetjen (2005). *Mediation in Child Protection Cases: An Evaluation of the Washington, D.C. Family Court Child Protection Mediation Program.* Reno, Nev.: National Council of Juvenile and Family Court Judges.

Holland, S., and S. O'Neill (2006). We had to be there to make sure it was what we wanted: Enabling children's participation in family decision-making through the family group conference. *Childhood* 13(1): 91–111.

Lupton, C., and P. Nixon (1999). *Empowering Practice: A Critical Appraisal of the Family Group Conference Approach.* Bristol: Policy Press

Marsh, P., and G. Crow (1998). *Family Group Conferences in Child Welfare.* Oxford: Blackwell.

Merkel-Holguin, L., ed. (2003). Promising results, potential new directions: International FGDM research and evaluation in child welfare. *Protecting Children*, 18(1–2) [special issue].

Nixon, P., G. Burford, and A. Quinn (with J. Edelbaum) (2005). *A Survey of International Practices, Policy and Research on Family Group Conferencing and Related Practices.* At www.americanhumane.org/site/DocServer/FGDM_www_survey.pdf?docID=2841 (accessed August 26, 2006).

Office of the United Nations High Commissioner for Human Rights (1989). *Convention on the Rights of the Child.* At www.unhchr.ch/html/menu3/b/k2crc.htm (accessed August 26, 2006).

Paterson, K., and M. Harvey (1991). *An Evaluation of the Organisation and Operation of Care and Protection Family Group Conferences.* Wellington, New Zealand: Department of Social Welfare.

Pennell, J. (2006). Restorative practices and child welfare: Toward an inclusive civil society. *Journal of Social Issues* 62(2): 257–77.

—— (2007). Good practices to fit the context of family meetings. Paper presented at the California Family to Family Statewide Convening: Strengthening Our Response to Domestic Violence, Center for Human Services, U.C. Davis Extension, University of California, Sacramento.

Pennell, J., and G. Anderson (2005). *Widening the Circle: The Practice and Evaluation of Family Group Conferencing with Children, Youths and Their Families.* Washington, D.C.: National Association of Social Workers Press

Pennell, J., and G. Burford (1995). *Family Group Decision Making: New Roles for "Old" Partners in Resolving Family Violence: Implementation Report.* 2 vols. St. John's: Memorial University of Newfoundland, School of Social Work.

—— (2000). Family group decision making: Protecting children and women. *Child Welfare* 79(2): 131–58.

Rossman, B. B. R. (2001). Longer term effects of children's exposure to domestic violence. In S. A. Graham-Bermann and J. L. Edleson, eds., *Domestic Violence in the Lives of Children: The Future of Research, Intervention, and Social Policy* (pp. 35–65). Washington, D.C.: American Psychological Association.

Spigner, C. W. (2005). Foreword to Joan Pennell and Gary Anderson, eds., *Widening the Circle: The Practice and Evaluation of Family Group Conferencing with Children, Youths and Their Families*. Washington, D.C.: National Association of Social Workers Press.

Stein, M. (2005). Young people aging out of care: The poverty of theory. *Children and Youth Services Review* 28: 422–34.

Strang, H., L. Sherman, C. M. Angel, D. J. Woods, S. Bennett, D. Newbury-Birch, and N. Inkpen (2006). Victim evaluations of face-to-face restorative justice conferences: A quasi-experimental analysis. *Journal of Social Issues* 62(2): 281–306.

Sundell, K., and B. Vinnerljung (2004). Outcomes of family group conferencing in Sweden: A 3-year follow-up. *Child Abuse and Neglect* 28(3): 267–87.

Texas Department of Family and Protective Services (2006). *Family Group Decision-Making: Final Evaluation*. At www.dfps.state.tx.us/Documents/about/pdf/2006-10-09_FGDM_Evaluation.pdf (accessed December 27, 2006).

U.S. Department of Health and Human Services (2003). *Results of 2001 and 2002 Child and Family Service Reviews*. Administration for Children and Families, Children's Bureau. At www.acf.hhs.gov/programs/cb/cwrp/results/sldoo1.htm (accessed July 2, 2004).

Usher, L., B. Needell, J. Wildfire, and D. Webster (2007). *Evaluation Plan for Family to Family*. Chapel Hill: University of North Carolina at Chapel Hill.

Velen, M., and L. Devine (2005). Use of FGDM with children in care the longest: It's about time. *Protecting Children* 19(4): 25–34.

Waites, C., M. J. Macgowan, J. Pennell, I. Carlton-LaNey, and M. Weil (2004). Increasing the cultural responsiveness of family group conferencing. *Social Work* 49(2): 291–300.

Walton, E., M. McKenzie, and M. Connolly (2005). Private family time: The heart of family group conferencing. *Protecting Children* 19(4): 17–24.

Wilber, S., C. Ryan, and J. Marksamer (2006). *Best Practice Guidelines: Serving LGBT Youth in Out-of-Home Care*. Washington, D.C.: Child Welfare League of America.

Wulczyn, F., R. P. Barth, Y. T. Yuan, B. J. Harden, and J. Landsverk (2006). *Beyond Common Sense: Child Welfare, Child Well-Being, and the Evidence for Policy Reform*. New Brunswick, N.J.: AldineTransaction.

Yancey, B., J. Wirth, and K. Gunderson (2005). *Evaluation of the "Connected and Cared for" Project*. Seattle: University of Washington, Northwest Institute for Children and Families.

Developmentally Appropriate
Community-Based Responses
to the Permanency Needs of
Older Youth Involved in the
Child Welfare System

SIXTEEN

SANDRA STUKES CHIPUNGU,
LAURA G. DAUGHTERY,
AND BENJAMIN KERMAN

The foster care system faces unique challenges in meeting the development needs of youth in out-of-home care. Placement instability, educational interruption, extensive use of congregate care, and discharges to "emancipation" too often describe youth's experiences in foster care (Center for the Study of Social Policy, 2003). These realities are at variance with adolescents' developmental needs for autonomy, structure, continuity of relationship, and extended support—needs that place a premium on a nurturing environment that is created by family, supportive friends, effective and secure schools, and well-resourced communities. Fortunately, philanthropy and state policy are increasingly focusing on the use of preventive and early intervention approaches that may further strengthen the roles that communities play in the lives of youth. These approaches emphasize collaboration and the common interests bridging various service systems, such as child welfare, health care, aging, schools, family services, and mental health (Brookdale Foundation Group, 2006).

Historically, a disproportionate number of youth in foster care have not had the benefit of coordinated community-based service responses. African American and other communities traditionally have responded to families in need by mobilizing resources to provide informal kinship care and avert the need for formal government intervention. Formal support systems, however, have not offered the resources needed to support family-based and community-based responses. Recognizing that there has been little programmatic research on services for youth in foster care, in this chapter we consider the developmental needs of adolescents, theoretical directions, current system priorities, and illustrative preventive and early intervention programs that might be considered to represent the most promising practices.

YOUTH IN FOSTER CARE

Youth enter foster care in two principal ways. Some youth enter foster care at young ages and remain in care until they leave care at the age of majority. Despite public concerns that large numbers of youth are adrift in the foster care system from infancy until they age out of care, relatively few children who enter care at young ages eventually age out (Wulczyn et al., 2002). Children who enter foster care require early, intensive, and effective efforts to connect them with families before they reach adolescence. Approaches to promote reunification and adoption are described elsewhere in the volume. In chapter 13, for example, Barbara A. Pine and Robin Spath describe a reunification program that has demonstrated the value of intensive reunification services for children entering foster care for the first time. In chapter 14, Ruth G. McRoy and Elissa Madden describe effective adoption practices that promote timely adoption when children cannot be safely reunified with their parents.

A second and larger group of youth enters foster care at older ages, including as adolescents. The reunification program described by Pine and Spath and the adoption practices described by McRoy and Madden sustain and build enduring family connections in ways that are relevant for this group of youth. However, these youth may have longer-standing and, in some cases, more ambivalent attachments to their families, having spent more time within them (Wulczyn, 2004; Harden, 2004). Older youth also may have a broader array of extended family relationships, including individuals who are not biologically related to them but who the youth perceives as "family," as well as a history of positive connections with other adults, on which to draw. When these youth exit care, they often return to their birth families or other significant adults in their lives, irrespective of whether these individuals are prepared to meet their needs for transitional support (Courtney and Dworsky, 2006; Pecora et al., 2006).

For both populations of youth—the smaller group of youth who "grow up" in foster care and the larger group of youth who enter foster care at older ages—attention to adolescent development needs is essential. These youth's needs must be met in ways that minimize the barriers to healthy development that the structure of foster care may create. By focusing on healthy adolescent development in the context of family and community development, it is possible to strengthen options for shortening and even preventing out-of-home placement.

ADOLESCENT DEVELOPMENT AND IDENTITY

A recent reconceptualization of adolescent identity development may provide direction for the development of effective interventions with youth and families. Richard Lerner and colleagues (2003) write that these conceptualizations "are predicated on the ideas that every young person has the potential for successful, healthy development and that all youth posses the capacity for positive development." This new understanding of adolescent identity development can contribute to the development of services for adolescents by heightening attention to youth's developmental needs and focusing on adolescents' strengths and successes. Foster care, as currently provided in most communities, reflects an "antithetical theoretical approach" to human development (Lerner et al., 2003). Too often, adolescents in foster care are not seen within the context of normal human development, and programs emphasize deficits and needs instead of strengths and assets. What is lacking is an understanding of the variety of changes essential to developing the physical, emotional, and social assets needed for subsequent success that occur in adolescence.

The identity-related development challenges faced in adolescence are pivotal to successful negotiation of the lifecycle (Erikson, 1968). Formation of an identity includes a sense of psychosocial well-being rooted in "a feeling of being at home in one's body, a sense of 'knowing where one is going,' and an inner assuredness of anticipated recognition from those who count" (Erikson, 1968:165). The social and physical environment in which identity formation takes place is critical. A stable social and physical environment that provides positive supports for the adolescent's efforts at discovering "who he is" or "who he is not" is the optimum environment.

In addition to the growing recognition of stability and continuity as critical factors in supporting identity formation, there is an increased understanding of other resources that youth need. Partly in response to concerns that traditional theories and developmental frameworks have not adequately addressed the needs of minority populations, attention has become more focused on the "moral, cultural, civic and faith" domains of identity (Furrow and Wagener, 2003:116). Each domain points to another slice of the nurturing community that can be enlisted to support developing youth.

FOSTER CARE AND IDENTITY DEVELOPMENT

Most empirical research has focused on adolescent identity development within the context of family. The environment of foster care has been an area of very little research (Kools, 1997, 1999). In one study that examined these issues, African American females in foster care described difficulties in working on identity issues; they reported that they sacrificed a focus on identity in order to accommodate foster care providers, fearing that exploration of identity could compromise the placement and necessitate another move (Daughtery, 2005).

Although there is little relevant research, there has been some examination of the effect of foster care on children's identity development. Joshua Kirven (2000:249) writes that identity development for youth in foster care is compromised by a "crisis of instability" that generates mixed emotions and patterns of negative behavior as a result of the adolescent's removal from friends, schools, neighborhood centers, and communities. Kirven theorizes that "the foster care experience can have serious implications for the social functioning and identity formation of an adolescent in search of safety and a positive sense of self" (p. 249).

Emphasis on removal from communities as a critical factor affecting identity development becomes even more significant in light of research on outcomes for youth exiting foster care. Research indicates that youth often either formally or informally reunite with their birth families. With no sanction or support from child welfare agencies, youth exiting foster care return to their previous homes and communities. These environments often are undergoing developmental challenges of their own that may or may not be supportive to the adolescent as he or she transitions from foster care to adulthood. Both family and community development issues, as discussed in the next section of this chapter, are important considerations.

FAMILY AND COMMUNITY DEVELOPMENT

Family Development

Family development theory posits that families that include adolescents experience a period of intense adjustment. Elizabeth (Betty) Carter and Monica McGoldrick (2005) point out that cultural factors and the sociopolitical context of family life greatly affect the way some families handle their children's adolescence. Cultural factors such as appropriate procreative age and views of the roles of men and women in the family can impact the course of adolescence. The patriarchy of some cultures, for example, may mean that girls who are age thirteen should be concerned about choosing a husband, compared with a thirteen-year-old American middle-class girl who may be more engaged in choosing lipstick. Although they are developmental stressors for any family, discrimination, extreme poverty, and oppression may cause families facing these issues to see their children's adolescence differently than normative middle-class families. These families, for example, may consider the way that a middle-class family handles adolescence to be indulgence. Nonetheless, all families with adolescents prepare for a "qualitative change in the relationship between generations" as the adolescent's demand for more independence "forces structural shifts and the renegotiation of roles within families sometimes going back three generations" (Carter and McGoldrick, 2005:4).

The essential family function as a material and emotional support system for its members is severely taxed to respond to adolescent adjustment. Carter and McGoldrick see a relationship between the ability to successfully navigate and support adolescent development and the availability of responsive community resources. They write that "the availability and access to community resources will have profound implications for the whole family's negotiation of their individual and family life cycles" (Carter and McGoldrick, 2005:44). Families that already are experiencing economic distress and isolation within poor urban and rural neighborhoods and have few available resources are more likely to be profoundly affected during this period (Preto, 2005). Indeed, for some members of our society, there is no adolescent stage—as children may go directly from childhood into adulthood without adolescence's intermediate period of gradually assuming adult responsibilities. Marginalized families may see the "testing and trying out of roles" of middle-class adolescence as a waste of valuable time and support. There is enormous potential for conflict, particularly within new immigrant families where the friction is often cast as both a generational and a cultural conflict.

Given the role of family in adolescent development, kin or other foster families are the placement of choice when youth must enter foster care. Foster care placement disruption studies, however, describe a variety of risks that threaten placement stability and continuity (Connell et al., 2006; Wulczyn et al., 2003). Families that provide foster care for youth may experience considerable stress. The addition of any new member prompts a variety of adjustments in the family roles and routine. These normative adjustments are further complicated when the new member is an adolescent with special needs for supervision, structure, understanding, and flexibility.

Families require extraordinary support in order to survive and launch children prepared to succeed in their environment. Communities that strongly support positive biological and foster parenting and positive adolescent identity development enable these families to begin to achieve some sort of balance (Chipungu and Bent-Goodley, 2004). Some of the kinds of supports and services within these communities are outlined in the next section of this chapter.

Community Development

The developmental needs of youth are best met in a community context. Eco-developmental efforts that maximize the intersection of the social environment and the adolescent's developmental stage contribute to community, family, and individual adolescent functioning (Coatsworth et al., 2002). Understanding the interface between child abuse and neglect and the neighborhood environment has supported the development of practice models that include family preservation services, neighborhood-based foster care, kinship care, and other interventions that support families in crisis (Chahine et al., 2005; Freisthler et al., 2006; Berrick, 2006). The family resource center model, which makes use of multilayered, multileveled support systems including staff trained in community development, has been successfully replicated (O'Donnell and Giovannoni, 2006). Differential response efforts have been implemented in many communities to engage local systems of care in preventing the avoidable separation of children and youth from their families, and these tailored community-based and in-home services and supports have demonstrated success in increasing safety, reducing the need for out-of-home placement, and saving money (Loman and Siegal, 2004, 2005).

John Kretzmann and John McKnight (1993) have argued for a model of community development that focuses on assets and strengths instead of needs. When agencies seek public funding or other government supports, they typically must conduct a needs assessment instead of an asset assessment, a process that tends to list the community failures as opposed to strengths. Listing problems becomes a self-fulfilling prophecy, and the community is forever "deficient." The focus on community needs deepens the cycle of dependence and denigration.

In their call for asset-based community development, Kretzmann and McKnight turn the needs model on its head and construct a capacity strengthening and building model that links individuals, associations, and institutions in order to build communities from the "inside out." Their model suggests that community developers further consider "capturing" institutions such as the local public child welfare agency as a community asset and enlisting them in the process of community development. They specifically mention individuals such as the elderly or adolescents as part of an asset-based community development plan. Children in foster care can easily be seen as a community asset.

Adolescents in Foster Care and the Community

In addition to their role in supporting families, community resources play vital roles in preparing youth in foster care for eventual emancipation from the foster care system by focusing on the acquisition of independent living skills. Independence for youth can be undermined by lack of access to medical care and to affordable housing, residential instability, and victimization (Courtney et al., 1998; Courtney and Barth, 1996; Freundlich, 2003; Pecora et al, 2006; McMillen and Tucker, 1999).

As we consider permanency planning for youth in foster care, program developers need to harness and amplify youth's developmental strengths by crafting a role for inclusive asset-based community development. These young men and women could be the source of a viable asset-rich link between the institution of public child welfare and the communities from which the children come and to which they go when they exit foster care. They may be seen as resources to both the institution and the community.

Public child welfare is in the unique position of linking assets and re-sources from outside the community and building bridges to the communities to and from which adolescents come. Through linkages and bridge building, public child welfare can more effectively address adolescent developmental issues, as well as asset-based community development issues. This approach maximizes the capacity of the social work person-in-environment perspective and, most important, it can support the adolescent's reunification with the birth family. The child or adolescent can return to a well-functioning family that has the opportunity and capacity to maintain a financially stable, secure, child-friendly environment in a safe, thriving community with multiple, easily accessible resources.

RESEARCH ON PROMISING COMMUNITY-BASED PRACTICES

Despite some successful efforts of public child welfare practitioners and policymakers to match child welfare concerns with community concerns, many practices and polices remain focused at the level of the individual child or single family without regard for the neighborhood or community. Although policies and programs acknowledge generally the importance of considering all family relationship assets in permanency planning, some public child welfare practices and policies miss opportunities to provide preventive and early intervention services and maximize the strengths and assets of particular neighborhoods (Everett et al., 1997, 2004).

Child welfare literature is replete with models and policy initiatives that focus on the birth family, the foster family, and the adoptive family in permanency planning. Yet, there are few researched exemplars on how to prevent placement or reunite families that have the opportunity and capacity to maintain financially stable, secure, child-friendly environments in safe, thriving communities with multiple, easily accessible resources. Use of mental health services provides an example of lack of provision of preventive services in the community. J. Curtis McMillen and colleagues (2004) found that only one-quarter of youth received mental health services in the community before they entered the foster care system. Among youth who received residential treatment services, one-half did not receive community-based services before receiving residential services. After the analyses controlled for need, predisposing characteristics, and enabling characteristics, youth of color were less likely to receive outpatient therapy, psychotherapeutic medications, and inpatient services during their stays in residential treatment, and they were more likely to be placed in more restrictive residential treatment. Youth who had been neglected and youth in kinship care were less likely to receive some types of mental health services.

Historically, programs designed to shore up parenting for at-risk families have seen the family in isolation. Parenting education and support programs such as Parents Anonymous have been found useful for motivated self-referring families (Lieber and Baker, 1977). Family preservation programs have been geared to provide intensive home-based interventions for families at imminent risk of the child being placed in foster care. The research on Homebuilders and other variants of the model is addressed elsewhere (e.g., Dagenais et al., 2004; Washington State Institute for Public Policy, 2006). Importantly, one factor that may the limit success of these models has been the lack of attention paid to key community supports and their role in sustaining and restoring the wherewithal of fragile families. Indeed, too often research on successful community-based practices that include an emphasis on family support fails to adequately examine the nature and impact of the intervention on social networks and community supports (Cox, 2005).

Nonetheless, recent trends in child welfare practice recognize the central role of strong family and community networks in promoting a family's capacity to enrich healthy adolescent development. We summarize here recent research and promising programming in two key areas: prevention and early intervention. Following is a list of the specific programs on which this discussion focuses:

Prevention in the community:
Differential response services
Community partnerships for protecting children
Earned income tax credit
Making Connections program

Community early intervention programs for children removed from their families:
Kinship Navigator Program
Relatives as Parents Program
Family to Family Initiative

Prevention Programs

Preventive interventions seek to engage community members and institutions in crafting an alternative response to family crisis that avoids out-of-home placement. These approaches also seek to enhance families' and communities' capacities to meet children's needs before a crisis that may result in a foster care placement. The Center for the Study of Social Policy (2003) reports that leaders of numerous child welfare systems are taking innovative steps to transform the way their agencies work with families and to become more connected to the communities they serve. These significant changes include assigning cases geographically to workers; basing units of staff in local organizations such as schools and family resource centers, along with staff from other agencies; providing support for relative caregivers through subsidized guardianship programs; using some form of family-involvement meetings (such as Team Decisionmaking, family team conferences, and family unity meetings) (see Crampton and Pennell, chapter 15 in this volume) to engage families as partners in making key decisions and designing service plans; and conducting outreach to aid families early on, before maltreatment has occurred.

Since the mid-1990s, an increasing number of states have implemented differential response in child protective services systems. Also referred to as "dual track," "multiple track," or "alternative response," differential response increases the options available in response to accepted reports of child abuse and neglect (Merkel-Holguin, 2005; Schene, 2005; Yuan, 2005). Based on such factors as the type and severity of the alleged maltreatment, the number of previous reports, and the source of the report, the child protective intake system may respond with the conventional investigatory procedure or a more engaging, family-centered service response (Merkel-Holguin, 2005). Although state implementation of differential response varies greatly, these approaches generally provide families who are considered to be low-risk and moderate-risk cases with a family assessment and timely services without formal determination or substantiation of child abuse and neglect. Moving away from an incident-based, adversarial investigation for all reports toward a more family assessment-oriented approach for some reports, differential response offers services without having to investigate or substantiate the allegations (Schene, 2005). It is important to recognize that differential response has not focused principally on cases screened out as inappropriate for child protections services; rather, it has focused on responding differentially to accepted reports of child maltreatment (Schene, 2005).

In two comparative outcome evaluations of differential response, L. Anthony Loman and Gary Siegel (2004, 2005) found strong support in the feedback and outcomes for families for the implementation of careful assessment and community-based differential response. In Minnesota, the researchers compared families served through differential response with families served by counties that used the traditional investigatory approach and found reductions in subsequent reports of child maltreatment and increases in satisfaction in families engaged through differential response. Similar results were seen in Missouri's statewide evaluation.

The use of differential response appears to be increasing, although it is not clear how its use will affect older youth involved with the system. Gila Shusterman and colleagues (2005) found that, in 2002, referrals to alternative response ranged from 20 percent to 71 percent of all accepted maltreatment reports across six states. The researchers noted that trends over five years showed that states were generally maintaining steady levels of alternative response referrals or increasing these referrals. They also found that older children were more likely to receive an alternative response than were younger children. Families receiving differential response appeared to receive services more often than those receiving the investigatory response. Thus, the more welcoming differential response approach may prove to be an important tool to engaging families of youth. It may also help meet youth's pressing concrete and emotional needs and subsequently prevent the dissolution of fragile families, averting the need for some youth to join new families.

Another preventive response is built on the community-based partnership premise that children's safety depends on strong families, and strong families depend on connections with a broad range of people, organizations, and community institutions. The Community Partnerships for Protecting Children (CPPC) was created by the Edna McConnell Clark Foundation and is housed under the auspices of the Center for Community Partnerships in Child Welfare of the Center for the Study of Social Policy. CPPC seeks to reduce child abuse and neglect, increase accessibility of services and supports, increase help-seeking and help-giving among neighbors, and improve performance of the child welfare system. Partnerships engage community members and agencies to reach out and support families before they face crises; intervene more rapidly, comprehensively, and effectively when abuse and neglect occur; and join with the public child welfare agency to improve child protection policy, programs, and practice in ways that more reliably strengthen families and more aggressively safeguard children (Center for the Study of Social Policy, 2003).

According to a recent Chapin Hall evaluation of four partnership communities, the approach strengthens collaboration across community agencies; increases vulnerable families' access to critical services, such as substance abuse treatment, mental health care, and domestic violence services; and improves the quality of the corollary services that sister agencies provide. The most positive outcomes for families were achieved when families participated actively in the development of their own service plans and were connected to services that met their needs, particularly in areas that are pervasive and difficult to change, such as parental depression and parental functioning (Center for the Study of Social Policy, 2006).

Several other programs seek to alleviate the deleterious effects of poverty and weak community networks that undermine the capacity of families to care for their children. These programs include narrow but far-reaching policy responses that seek to put money back into the hands of parents, such as the earned income tax credit (EITC). They also include neighborhood-level approaches that seek to build the workforce and concentrate economic opportunities within given communities. These neighborhood-level programs, exemplified by Making Connections, are grounded in community organizing and inject resources via multitiered approaches to community development.

The EITC is considered the most effective tax policy in history for lifting working families out of poverty. It reduces the tax burden and supplements the wages for low-income and moderate-income households. In 2002, some 4.9 million people, including 2.7 million children, escaped poverty as a result of this credit (Llobrera and Zahradnik, 2004, as cited in Jones, 2006). These benefits play an important asset-building role, contributing to financial stability and making funds available for important family expenses that support healthy child development. In recent years, the federal EITC has provided the model for many state and local EITC programs.

Making Connections, a multiyear initiative of the Annie E. Casey Foundation, represents a multidimensional community-strengthening approach. Located in ten sites around the country, Making Connections joins in full partnership with community residents, community-based organizations, local governments and businesses, social service agencies, community foundations, and other funders. Making Connections sites connect parents with jobs to increase earnings and income, build savings, and accumulate assets. Sites also work with residents to ensure that their children benefit from better health care, quality services, and intensive supports to ensure school readiness and success. Outcome evaluation of Making Connections is currently under way.

Early Intervention Programs

Early intervention programs in foster care services focus on improving the quality and reducing the duration of out-of-home placements. These approaches support formal and informal kinship care and community-based foster care efforts that root support and expectations for caregivers within the network of nurturing social connections that predate the family's formal involvement with the child welfare system. Robert B. Hill, in chapter 9 in this volume, reviews the literature that describes outcomes for youth in kinship care, as well as recent policy innovations to provide financial subsidies to support kin families caring for youth. A number of recent kinship care programs have shown promise, shedding light on keys to practice that successfully achieve positive outcomes for youth.

Commitment to Kin: A Report from Casey Family Programs (Casey Family Programs, 2004) identifies the guiding principles of the optimal kinship care program:

1. Recognition of families as resources
2. Recognition of the strengths and resilience of kinship families
3. Recognition of the importance of children's continued connections with their families
4. Engagement of kinship families, including children, as partners
5. Ensuring that services and supports are provided in a nonstigmatizing way
6. Ensuring that policies are developed and services and supports are provided in a cultural competent way
7. Supporting kin who informally care for children so that children do not have to enter the formal child welfare system
8. Supporting the placement of children and sibling groups with kin, including paternal and maternal kin, initially and when a change in placement must subsequently be made
9. Ensuring that all children in formal kinship care achieve permanence
10. Ensuring that services and supports are fair, responsive, and accountable to informal and formal kinship families and children

Data from a 2005 kinship care services pilot project undertaken by Casey Family Programs suggest the value of providing inexpensive support for kin caregivers who need help in navigating service systems. The Kinship Navigator Program provides services through telephone and face-to-face contacts that offer information about needed supports, referral to specific providers, supportive listening, linkages, linkage to follow-up activities, advocacy for third parties, and education about kinship care. An evaluation of a Kinship Navigator Program (TriWest Group, 2005) found that kin caregivers showed significant and varied needs in several domains and that families who participated for at least three months showed significant improvement in eleven of thirty-one identified domains. These data provide support for the Navigator's change model, which incorporates the provision of information about government agencies, support for caregivers, and referrals for help. A very rough costs/benefits analysis estimated that this relatively inexpensive program averted as many as 690 formal foster care placements and 2,694 months of care.[1]

The Brookdale Foundation Group initiated the Relatives as Parents Program (RAPP) in 1996. RAPP is designed to encourage and promote the creation or expansion of services for grandparents and other relatives who have assumed the role of surrogate parents as a result of parental absence. The program awards seed grants of $10,000 over a two-year period to local agencies and state public agencies. RAPP provides extensive direct services, primarily to relative caregivers caring for children outside the foster care system in forty-four states and the District of Columbia (Brookdale Foundation Group, 2006).

Family to Family, funded by the Annie E. Casey Foundation, is another model that extensively involves the community while acknowledging the importance of extended families and communities to help protect and nurture children. Family to Family provides an opportunity for states and communities to redesign their foster care system to achieve system-wide goals by encouraging the development of a network of family foster care that is neighborhood-based and culturally sensitive. The goals of Family to Family include reducing the number of children placed in foster care; placing children in their own neighborhoods when possible; decreasing the length of stay in foster care; minimizing multiple moves for children in placement; placing siblings together; and reducing any disparities associated with race, ethnicity, gender, or age in pursuing these outcomes. Family to Family also emphasizes reducing the use of congregate care in favor of family placements and aligning funding accordingly.

Family to Family has been implemented in multiple sites. Initial work started in Alabama, Maryland, New Mexico, Ohio, and Pennsylvania. By 2000, sites had been added in California, Colorado, Illinois, Kentucky, Michigan, New York, North Carolina, Oregon, and Tennessee. More recently, sites were added in Alaska, Arizona, and Washington. At this writing, programs operated in seventeen states and eighty individual sites (Annie E. Casey Foundation, 2008). A 1998 evaluation of Family to Family found that it succeeded in sustaining family foster care homes in disadvantaged neighborhoods that are traditionally overlooked as resources; researchers found that "neighborhoods in which child-placement rates are high also are capable of supporting families in which children are at risk of placement" (Center for the Study of Social Policy, 2003:5). Other findings included improved outcomes in the form of increased use of kinship care, improved rates of reunification of children with their parents in some sites, and an overall decrease in number of placement of children in foster care.

Kinship care and community-based supports may prove vital in addressing issues of disproportionality and overrepresentation in the foster care population (Hill, 2004; Carten and Dumpson, 2004). As observed by J. Everett and colleagues:

> Resolving the current crisis in child welfare for African American and all children requires changes in both the policies and the practices of child welfare agencies. These changes should be based on a deliberate and conscious recognition of the cultural patterns of various racial and ethnic groups, particularly as these patterns involve cultural traditions and norms about child rearing and family dynamics so that the approaches used enhance family functioning and the well-being of children. (1997:307)

Families from communities of color—who historically have been significantly affected by the child welfare system—have a particularly rich tradition of extended family members' care of children (Hill, 2004, this volume; Mills and Usher, 2004; McRoy, 2004).

Because many older youth who age out of foster care return to their birth families or extended family members (Courtney and Barth, 1996), efforts should be made to strengthen these bonds, as well as to identify extended kin who are willing and able to make an enduring commitment to these young adults. In FY 2005, some 54 percent of children and youth who left foster care returned to their parents (U.S. Department of Health and Human Services, 2007). These data raise the question of whether some of these youths should have been removed from their families in the first place or, if removed, returned in a timelier manner. Community-based approaches include important features that link and supplement the social and material assets available in the community, while respecting the strengths of the preexisting bonds between youth, family, and community. Connected by 25, for example, is a community initiative that engages youth, public-private partners, and policymakers to improve outcomes for foster youth through investments in services and programs (Connected by 25, 2008).

IMPLICATIONS

Research Agenda

The brief overview of prevention and early intervention programs highlights the strengths of these programs in linking youth, families, and communities. However, further research is clearly needed to support program and policy development, demonstrate cost-effectiveness of prevention and early intervention, and marshal and shape support for needy communities.

As the knowledge base on the transition from childhood to adulthood grows, attention must be given to the transition issues of youth in foster care and must take into account the unique developmental needs of these youth. The research agenda should include the following:

1. *Research that provides a clearer picture of the target population.* Research is needed to develop a clearer understanding of the characteristics of youth served in foster care, including the age of youth at time of entry into foster care and exit from care, the extent to which youth have disabilities and the nature of those disabilities, and the quality of their family relationships and community networks. Research is needed to provide an understanding of these characteristics among subpopulations of youth in foster care, including youth from different racial and ethnic backgrounds and youth of different sexual orientations.

2. *Development of procedures that appropriately address confidentiality issues in relation to research.* Confidentiality laws and regulations often limit researchers' access to state records and prohibit the sharing of data across agencies that serve the same youth. Procedures need to be developed that appropriately address confidentiality concerns while providing access to

data and information that can advance the understanding of youth's needs and the effectiveness of family and community engagement approaches.

3. *Research on the training required for child welfare practitioners who work with youth in foster care.* With the paradigm shift that rebalances the emphasis on physical protection of dependent children with greater consideration for youth, family, and community development, training of caseworkers has become critical. Research is needed to develop effective approaches to training caseworkers in these new skill areas.

4. *Research on kinship care and youth in foster care.* Research is needed to enrich the understanding of how kin networks work, why they work, and when they work and when they do not. Among the key research questions are the institutional and political barriers that impede the implementation of kinship care. Research findings must be coordinated with appropriate policy changes at the federal and state levels.

5. *Research on current community-based interventions and their effect on broader social support networks.* As noted, many of the existing intervention studies paint a limited picture of the results in terms of social network change and growth in available resources, even though the models target these key links as mediators of individual child and family outcomes. The same limitations are evident for microinterventions that address narrower bands of risk factors that contribute to family fragility and child neglect and abuse (for example, EITC and other family economic success programs).

PRACTICE AND POLICY

There are many practice and policy implications for the implementation of a community development approach to serving youth and their families. These implications include the following:

1. *Earlier identification of extended family members and interested adults.* New approaches are needed to ensure that extended family members and interested adults are identified early in the child welfare agency's involvement with the family. Information should be sought from family members and other adults in the youth's life who are most knowledgeable about the youth's life.[2]

2. *Stronger efforts to identify and locate religious institutions in the youth's community that may be able to provide resources for the youth.*

3. *Access to available funds in support of community programming.*

Community supportive programming may be expanded through seeking funds specifically designated to support prevention and family preservation, as well as by exploring currently funded models of care with an eye toward better integration of community networks and resources. Fund managers could convene for creative or best practices solutions to working within child welfare financial systems.

4. *Child welfare agencies' investment in asset maps of their communities.* Asset maps of communities can assist child welfare staff in locating resources for their clients and can provide useful information to plan for future service delivery. Child welfare agencies can serve as the convener of meetings for neighboring jurisdictions and local communities about the services and resources available.

CONCLUSION

This chapter began with a review of the prevention literature in the field of child welfare. Perhaps a reflection of the generally reactive posture in child welfare and child protection services, searches for "prevention" as a child welfare topic did not yield extensive results. Through the thinking presented in this chapter about the scope of the problem, the experience of the field, and the direction of research, we hope that empirical prevention literature will be further catalyzed. As the Community Partnership for Protecting Children recognizes, "no single factor is responsible for child abuse and neglect; therefore no one public agency alone can safeguard children" (Center for the Study of Social Policy, 2003:21). The renewed interest in communities as partners in preventing abuse and neglect of children can also be used to prevent the placement of older teens in foster care. Efforts should be made to maintain youth in their families or extended families if possible and to provide the services and resources to help them transition into adulthood. If youth in foster care return home when they age out of the system, they and their families need help in making this transition as smooth and successful as possible.

NOTES

1. The Fostering Connections to Success and Increasing Adoptions Act of 2008 establishes a new competitive grant program, under Title IV-B, Subpart 1 of the Social Security Act named Family Connection Grants. Under this program, public child welfare agen-

cies and non-profit private organizations may seek federal funding to help children—whether they are in foster care or at-risk of entering foster care—connect (or reconnect) with birth parents or other extended kin. Among the designated uses of these funds are kinship navigator programs, which through information referral systems and other means, assist kinship caregivers in learning about, finding, and using programs and services to meet their own needs and those of the children they are raising.

2. The Fostering Connections to Success and Increasing Adoptions Act of 2008 contains a new child welfare plan requirement under Title IV-E that states must "exercise due diligence" to identify grandparents and other adult relatives of a child, within 30 days of removing the child from the custody of his/her parents; notify those relatives of the child's removal; and provide relatives with options for participating in the care and placement of the child, including information about foster family home licensing and, as applicable, guardianship assistance.

REFERENCES

Annie E. Casey Foundation (2008). *Family to Family: Sites.* At www.aecf.org/MajorInitiatives/Family%20to%20Family/SitesAndContacts.aspx (accessed March 15, 2008).

Berrick, J. D. (2006). Neighborhood-based foster care: A critical examination of location-based placement criteria. *Social Service Review* December: 569–83.

Brookdale Foundation Group (2006). At www.brookdalefoundation.org.

Carten, A. J., and J. R. Dumpson (2004). Family preservation and neighborhood-based services: An africentric perspective. In J. E. Everett, S. S. Chipungu, and B. R. Leashore, eds., *Child Welfare Revisited: An Africentric Perspective* (pp. 225–41). New Brunswick, N.J.: Rutgers University Press.

Carter, B., and M. McGoldrick, eds. (2005). *The Expanded Family Life Cycle: Individual, Family, and Social Perspectives.* 3rd ed. New York: Pearson.

Casey Family Programs (2004). *Commitment to Kin: A Report from Casey Family Programs.* Seattle: Author.

Center for the Study of Social Policy (2003). *Policy Matters: Twenty State Policies to Enhance States' Prosperity and Create Bright Futures for America's Children, Families and Communities.* Washington, D.C: Author.

Chahine, Z., J. Van Straaten, and A. Wiliams-Isom (2005). The New York City neighborhood-based services strategy. *Child Welfare* 84(2): 141–52.

Chipungu, S. S., and T. B. Bent-Goodley (2004). Meeting the challenges of contemporary foster care. *Future of Children* 14(1): 75–93.

Coatsworth, J. D., H. Pantin, and J. Szapocznik (2002). Familias Unidas: A family-centered ecodevelopmental intervention to reduce risk for conduct problems and substance use among Hispanic adolescents. *Clinical Child and Family Psychology Review* 5: 113–32.

Connected by 25 (2008). *About Connected by 25.* Available at www.cby25.org/about.htm (accessed March 15, 2008).

Connell, C. M., J. J. Vanderploeg, P. Flaspholer, K. H. Katz, L. Saunders, and J. K. Tebes (2006). Changes in placement among children in foster care: A longitudinal study of child and case influences. *Social Service Review* September: 398–418.

Courtney, M., and R. Barth (1996). Pathways of older adolescents out of foster care. *Social Work* 41(1): 75–83.

Courtney, M., and A. Dworsky (2006). Early outcomes for young adults transitioning from out-of-home care in the USA. *Child and Family Social Work* 11: 209–18.

Courtney, M., I. Pilavin, A. Grogan-Kaylor, and A. Newsmith (1998). *Foster Youth Transitions to Adulthood: Outcomes 12 to 18 Months After Leaving Out-of-Home Care.* Madison: University of Wisconsin at Madison, School of Social Work and Institute for Research on Poverty.

Cox, K. F. (2005). Examining the role of social network intervention as an integral component of community-based family-focused practice. *Journal of Child and Family Studies* 13(3): 443–54.

Dagenais, C., J. Begin, C. Bouchard, and D. Fortin (2004). Impact of intensive family support programs: A synthesis of evaluation studies. *Children and Youth Services Review* 26: 249–63.

Daughtery, L. (2005). Understanding identity development of African American female adolescents through their foster care experience: "Reachin' landin's, and turnin' corners." Ph.D. diss., Catholic University of America, Washington, D.C.

Erikson, E. H. (1968). *Identity: Youth and Crisis.* New York: Norton.

Everett, J., S. Chipungu, and B. Leashore, eds. (1997). *Child Welfare: An Africentric Perspective.* New Brunswick, N.J.: Rutgers University Press.

——, eds. (2004). *Child Welfare Revisted: An Africentric Perspective.* New Brunswick, N.J.: Rutgers University Press.

Freisthler, B., D. H. Merritt, and E. A. LaScala (2006). Understanding the ecology of child maltreatment: A review of the literature and directions for future research. *Child Maltreatment* 11(3): 263–80.

Freundlich, M., R. Avery, and D. Padgett (2003). Preparation of youth in congregate care for independent living. *Child and Family Social Work* 12: 64–72.

Furrow, J. L., and L. M. Wagener (2003). Identify and transcendence among youth: A view of the issues. *Applied Developmental Science* 7(3): 116–18.

Harden, B. J. (2004). Safety and stability for foster children: A developmental perspective. *Children, Families and Foster Care* 14(1): 30–47.

Hill, R. B. (2004). Institutional racism in child welfare. In J. E. Everett, S. S. Chipungu, and B. R. Leashore, eds., *Child Welfare Revisited: An Africentric Perspective* (pp. 57–76). New Brunswick, N.J.: Rutgers University Press.

Jones, E. (2006). *Places to Watch: Promising Practices to Address Racial Disproportionality in Child Welfare*. Washington, D.C.: Center for the Study of Social Policy.

Kirven, J. (2000). Building on strengths of minority adolescents in foster care: A narrative-holistic approach. *Child and Youth Care Forum* 29(4): 247–63.

Kools, S. M. (1997). Adolescent identity development in foster care. *Family Relations* 46(3): 263–72.

—— (1999). Self-protection in adolescents in foster care. *Journal of Child and Adolescent Psychiatry Nursing* 12(4): 139–52.

Kretzmann, J., and J. L. McKnight (1993). *Building Communities from the Inside Out*. Chicago: ACTA Publications.

Lerner, R. M., E. M. Dowling, and P. M. Anderson (2003). Positive youth development: Thriving as a basis of personhood and civil society. *Applied Developmental Science* 7(3): 172–80.

Lieber, L. L., and J. M. Baker (1977). Parents Anonymous self-help treatment for child abusing parents: A review and an evaluation. *Child Abuse and Neglect* 1: 133–48.

Llobrera, J., and Zahradnik, B. (2004). *A Hand Up: How State Earned Income Tax Credits Help Working Families Escape Poverty in 2004*. Washington, D.C.: Center for the Budget and Policy Priorities.

Loman, L. A., and G. L. Siegel (2004). *Differential Response in Missouri After Five Years*. At www.iarstl.org/papers/MODiffeResp2004a.pdf.

—— (2005). Alternative response in Minnesota: Findings of the program evaluation. *Protecting Children* 20(2–3): 78–92.

McMillen, J. C., and J. Tucker (1999). The status of older adolescents at exit from out-of-home care. *Child Welfare* 78: 339–60.

McMillen, J. C., B. T. Zima, M. T. Ollie, M. R. Munson, and E. Spitznagel (2004). Use of mental health services among older youths in foster care. *Psychiatric Services* 55: 811–17.

McRoy, R. G. (2004). African American adoptions. In J. E. Everett, S. S. Chipungu, and B. R. Leashore, eds., *Child Welfare Revisited: An Africentric Perspective* (pp. 256–74). New Brunswick, N.J.: Rutgers University Press.

Merkel-Holguin, L. (2005). Differential response: A common sense reform in child welfare. *Differential Response in Child Welfare* 20(2–3): 2–3.

Mills, C. S., and D. P. Usher (2004). An Africentric paradigm for child welfare practice. In J. E. Everett, S. S. Chipungu, and B. R. Leashore, eds., *Child Welfare Revisited: An Africentric Perspective* (pp. 214–24). New Brunswick, N.J.: Rutgers University Press.

O'Donnell, J., and J. M. Giovannoni (2006). Consumer perceptions of family resource center delivery strategies. *Families in Society: Journal of Contemporary Social Services* 87(3): 377–84.

Pecora, P. J., J. Williams, R. C. Kessler, E. Hiripi, K. O'Brien, J. Emerson, M. A. Herrick, and D. Torres (2006). Assessing the educational achievement of adults who were formerly placed in family foster care. *Child and Family Social Work* 11: 220–21.

Preto, N. G. (2005). Transformation of the family system during adolescence. In B. Carter and M. McGoldrick, eds., *The Expanded Family Life Cycle: Individual, Family and Social Perspectives* (pp. 274–87), 3rd ed. New York: Pearson.

Schene, P. (2005). The emergence of differential response. *Differential Response in Child Welfare* 20(2–3): 4–7.

Shustermann, G. R., J. D. Fluke, D. M. Hollinshead, and Y. Y. T. Yuan (2005). Alternative responses to child maltreatment: Findings from NCANDS. *Differential Response in Child Welfare* 20(2–3): 32–42.

TriWest Group (2005). *Final Pilot Evaluation Report on the Casey Family Programs Kinship Caregiver Navigator Pilot.* Seattle: Author.

U.S. Department of Health and Human Services, Administration for Children and Families (2007). *The AFCARS Report: Preliminary FY 2005 Estimates as of September 2006.* Washington, D.C.: Author.

Washington State Institute for Public Policy (2006). *Intensive Family Preservation Programs: Program Fidelity Influences Effectiveness—Revised.* Olympia, Wash. At www.wsipp.wa.gov.

Wulczyn, F. (2004). Family reunification. *Future of Children* 14(1): 95–113.

Wulczyn, F., K. B. Hislop, and B. J. Harden (2002). The placement of infants in foster care. *Infant Mental Health Journal* 23(5): 454–75.

Wulczyn, F., J. Kogan, and B. J. Harden (2003). Placement stability and movement trajectories. *Social Service Review* 77: 212–36.

Yuan, Y. Y. T. (2005). Potential policy implications of alternative response. *Differential Response in Child Welfare* 20(2–3): 22–31.

Social and Life Skills Development

SEVENTEEN

Preparing and Facilitating Youth for Transition into Young Adults

HEWITT B. CLARK
AND KIMBERLY A. CROSLAND

All youth find the transition to adult life challenging. Youth who are exiting the foster care system may be particularly challenged as they may be less equipped to handle adult responsibilities. Most youth develop life skills through their family relationships and other long-term relationships marked by continuity (Gutierrez et al., 2001). Unfortunately, the foster care system often hinders the development of life skills. Changes in foster care placement, which many youth in foster care experience, is strongly associated with the development of behavior problems (Newton et al., 2000), which, in turn, may affect life skills development. Youth who lack stable families and relationship continuity are at greater risk. Many youth who "age out" of the foster care system lack strong, positive connections with caring adults on whom they can count (Barth, 1993; Choca et al., 2004) and do not have the skills that are necessary to gain and maintain employment and housing and establish social relationships essential to quality of life (Christenson, 2002; Iglehart, 1994). Leaving the foster care system without a permanent family has been associated with poor outcomes for youth who age out of care, including homelessness, school failure, and criminal involvement (Avery and Freundlich, 2003; Clark et al., 1996; Courtney et al., 2001; Cook, 1992; Dworsky and Courtney, 2000; McMillen and Tucker, 1999).

The phrase "preparation for adulthood" has been used to describe all the social and life skills and support systems necessary for adult life and encompasses both short-term and long-term outcomes for youth (Frey et al., 2005). In general, social life skills preparation enables youth to succeed in the environments in which they live and covers areas such as daily living tasks, self-care, social development, money management, employability skills, housing, self-advocacy, and social problem solving (Bullis et al., 2000; Needell et al., 1998). These skills can be divided into "hard" skills (such as employment-seeking skills, money management, and housing) and "soft" skills (such as communication and problem solving) (Frey et al., 2005).

There are approximately twenty thousand to twenty-five thousand youth who age out of the foster care system each year with the expectation that they will live independently (Allen and Nixon, 2000). In order to aid youth in this transition from foster care to independent living, federal Independent Living Programs (ILPs) were established in 1985 with federal funding made available to states to establish services for youth age sixteen and over (U.S. General Accounting Office [GAO], 1999). Traditional ILPs were intended to provide educational opportunities (including vocational training), counseling and support services, training in daily living skills, outreach services, and a range of other services such as family planning and parenting classes. In general, very little is known about the effectiveness of ILP services and programs, but we do know that child welfare agencies tend to focus on clinical and rehabilitation services for youth, as these services may be easier to find and place less emphasis on social life skill development. Many states have reported an inability to find and sustain appropriate supervised living arrangements and employment opportunities that provide real-life experience needed by youth in foster care (GAO, 1999)

Studies have identified strategies for effective social and life skills development with vulnerable youth and improving their long-term outcomes. Arnold Goldstein and Barry Glick (1994) successfully taught aggressive youth and juvenile delinquents prosocial behaviors using aggression replacement training (ART). ART involves skills training in areas such as anger control and moral reasoning. The curriculum is taught interactively by using modeling, role-playing, performance feedback, and transfer training (Goldstein and Glick, 1994). Initial studies and replication studies on ART have shown significant increases in youth skills and subsequent decreases in problematic behaviors, including reduced recidivism rates for incarceration (Curulla, 1990; Goldstein et al., 1986, 1989).

When social and life skills development is placed in the context of relevant settings and long-term social connections, long-term outcomes for young people are more likely to be more positive. Michael Wald and Tia Martinez (2003) have suggested the importance of youth being "Connected by 25" from both a social and an economic perspective. The majority of young adults develop network systems to include family, friends, and other community members that provide guidance and support, both financially and socially. Young people in the foster care system, however, have fewer opportunities to learn necessary social and cognitive skills as fewer resources are available to help them become connected and develop adequate social and economic relationships.

This reality is of concern in light of the growing understanding of the importance of social capital. As defined by James Coleman (1988), social capital is the set of complex social mechanisms that parents use to advance their children's chances of success. Social capital may be important in determining which youth are successful despite being at risk of long-term disadvantage (Furstenberg and Hughes, 1995). Pedro Carneiro and James Heckman (2003) have suggested that social capital in the form of social skills, attitudes, and cognitive abilities that are learned in childhood and adolescence may be the predicting variables for success in school and life. They have suggested that future policies or programs that increase cognitive and social skills early in a child's life may be more effective in increasing college attendance rates than current incentive programs such as tuition assistance.

Recently, based on the experience of several innovative programs, it has been possible to identify the programmatic features that are necessary for promoting social and economic development in youth. Two of these programs are described in detail in this chapter. One of these approaches, developed by Casey Family Services (Frey et al., 2005), was created specifically for the foster care population. A second approach, called the Transition to Independence Process (TIP) model, was developed for transition-age young people (age fourteen through twenty-five) to assist them in achieving their transition-to-adulthood goals, irrespective of their current setting (Clark and Davis, 2000).

In addition to discussing these programs, in this chapter we describe the federal foster care independence program and discuss early and more recent studies that have attempted to evaluate the effectiveness of these independent living programs. We provide examples of innovative strategies at community and state levels to prepare youth to transition to adulthood. We then discuss evolving evidence-informed practices and assessment tools and conclude with a discussion of the implications for research and practice.

FEDERAL FOSTER CARE INDEPENDENCE PROGRAM

The Title IV-E Independent Living Initiative, also known as the Foster Care Independent Initiative Act of 1999 and now known as the Chafee Act, provides funding for services to prepare adolescents in foster care to live independently. With the enactment of the 1999 law, states received an increase in overall federal funding and new flexibility in the use of federal funds to assist youth in foster care in such areas as education, housing, and employment (Child Welfare League of America [CWLA], 1999). In addition, under the Chafee program, states may use up to 30 percent of their funds to assist with room and board for former foster youth (ages eighteen to twenty-one), and they may provide extended Medicaid coverage for these youth. Through a reauthorization of funds for this program in 2001, a tuition voucher program was created to assist youth in foster care pursue postsecondary education (CWLA, 1999). These funds are allocated under the same formula as general Chafee funds.

Currently, states have flexibility in deciding how to use Chafee funds, and in many cases, states do not draw down the maximum in allocated Chafee funds (Massinga and Pecora, 2004). As a result, the services provided to youth vary widely from state to state. A recent GAO report (2004) attempted to assess the impact of the increased federal funding provided by the Foster Care Independence Act of 1999. Most states reported increased services for older youth and expanded services for younger youth. Despite these efforts, however, the GAO found that states were not making full use of available resources. At the same time, it has been difficult to determine which programs are successful since few have been evaluated with any methodological rigor (Collins, 2001). Further, little is known about the extent to which independent living services actually reach young people in foster care or how well these services are tailored to the individual needs of youth. It is not clear, for example, whether services are being provided to young people with emotional and behavioral difficulties or who have experienced trauma (Vander Stoep et al., 2000). Despite additional federal funding and expansion in programs offered, adolescents who leave care at the age of majority continue to experience substantial social and life skill deficits (Shirk and Stangler, 2004).

EVALUATION OF INDEPENDENT LIVING PROGRAMS

Early Studies

Only a few studies have attempted to evaluate the effect of life skills training on the functioning level of youth leaving foster care at age eighteen to live on their own. These studies have focused on outcomes such as employment, housing, and education after youth leave care. Three studies conducted in the early 1990s showed varying results on the effects of independent living programs (Cook, 1991; Shippensburg University Center for Juvenile Justice Training and Research, 1993; Center on Children, Families, and the Law, 1994). The Westat Project (Cook, 1991, 1992, 1994) used record data and interview data with youth aging out of foster care. The researchers compared these youth with youth in the general population and with youth living below the poverty level on several indicators, including employment, education, and social networks. Results based on follow-up over a period of up to four years after the youth were discharged from foster care showed no differences between youth who had received no ILP services and youth who had received some ILP services. Results, however, showed that youth who had been trained in multiple skill areas had more positive outcomes in five core areas (budgeting, obtaining credit, consumer credit, education, and employment) and greater overall self-sufficiency.

The Nebraska study (Center on Children, Families, and the Law, 1994) surveyed youth one year after discharge from foster care at age eighteen regarding their current functioning in eight core areas: employment, money, family planning, health, education, housing, community resources, and household management. No significant differences were found between youth who did and did not receive ILP training or among youth who received varying levels of ILP training. The study concluded that the Nebraska youth were functioning better than those who were interviewed in Cook's study (1991, 1992, 1994): educational levels and employment outcomes were better, and the rate of teen pregnancy was lower.

The third study (Shippensburg University Center for Juvenile Justice Training and Research, 1993) evaluated Pennsylvania's ILP by surveying youth one year after leaving foster care through emancipation. This study compared youth who had participated in ILP services with youth who had not participated. The study used outcome measures similar to those in the Westat and Nebraska studies (use of public assistance, educational completion, employment status, living arrangements, youth's perception of the importance of life skills, and involvement in social organizations and activities) and created a composite index of independence. Only two of seven outcome measures showed differences between ILP participants and nonparticipants. ILP participants were more likely to maintain housing (that is, they were living alone or living with their own children, spouse, partner, friends, or other nonrelated persons), and they were more likely to participate in social organizations. This study also found that youth who exited foster care after age eighteen, regardless of participation in an ILP, were more likely to have completed high school and to have independent housing arrangements. Older youth (ages nineteen to twenty-one) and male youth were more likely to be employed when they exited foster care and at follow-up one year later.

It is difficult to draw definitive conclusions from these studies as a result of methodological limitations and measurement, design, and data collection issues. None of the studies was controlled in terms of randomization of participants, and one study did not use a comparison group. Two studies used comparison groups that were based on self-reports that the youth had not received independent living services. The survey response rates in two studies were low: 48 percent for the Nebraska study and 24 percent for ILP participants in the Pennsylvania study. Interpretation is also made difficult by the lack of information about the ILP participants' experiences while in care, which may have been quite varied. The actual acquisition of skills by ILP participants was not evaluated in these studies. It is recognized that many factors can affect the acquisition of both social and life skills. The incidence of behavioral, emotional, academic, and developmental problems, for example, appears to have a negative effect on the acquisition of these skills, as well as on placement instability and length of time in care (Klee and Halfon, 1987; Cooper et al., 1987; Proch and Taber, 1985). The foster care system itself, given its reliance on group homes and shelters and the frequent placement changes for many youth, may contribute to the emotional trauma many youth experience, which, in turn, may affect their skill acquisition. Studies suggest that placement with foster families may improve skill acquisition because foster parents may offer more individualized attention and support than group and residential care staff (Reddy and Pfeiffer, 1997).

Recent Studies

Several outcome evaluations of former foster care youth have been made since the beginning of the twenty-first century. Three of these studies are described here: the North Carolina independent living program (ILP) evaluation (Lindsey and Ahmed, 1999), the Chapin Hall Midwest evaluation (Courtney and Dworsky, 2005), and the Northwest alumni study (Pecora et al., 2005).

The effectiveness of North Carolina's county-administered ILP programs was evaluated in a study that compared outcomes for participants and nonparticipants in four core areas: housing, education, employment, and financial self-sufficiency. The only state requirements for the ILPs were that all eligible youth be assessed to determine need for services and that each youth's case plan include an independent living component. Each county had the latitude to decide how the ILP program was developed. Some counties offered structured monthly meetings and other group activities, and other counties provided services on an individual basis. For the study, "ILP participants" were defined as those who received services beyond the required initial assessment; "nonparticipants" were defined as youth who did not receive services after the initial ILP assessment. Survey questionnaires were mailed to ILP participants and nonparticipants who had exited care at the age of majority over a three-year period (Lindsey and Ahmed, 1999).

The study found that ILP participants, when compared with nonparticipants, were more likely to live independently or pay all of their housing expenses while living with others. ILP participants reported higher educational levels and a greater desire for increased educational attainment. No significant differences were found with respect to employment or financial outcomes. The study had several limitations. First, the response rate to the surveys was low (32 percent for ILP participants and 23 percent for nonparticipants). Second, given the range of ILP services that were delivered in different counties, it was not possible to determine who had received different types of services (group meeting versus individual services, for example). Third, although there were no significant differences between the two groups with regard to gender or race, the ILP participants were slightly older (mean of nineteen years of age versus eighteen years of age). It is unclear whether this factor or other possible factors that were not evaluated (such as behavioral and emotional characteristics) might have affected the results.

The Chapin Hall Midwest evaluation (Courtney and Dworsky, 2005) and the Northwest alumni study (Pecora et al., 2005) did not make distinctions between those who received and those who did not receive ILP services. In the Chapin Hall study, two waves of interviews were conducted, one wave at seventeen or eighteen years of age and a second wave at nineteen years of age. The study compared the outcomes of youth who were still in foster care at the time of the second interview with the outcomes for youth who had left foster care by the second interview. One of the states in the Midwest evaluation (Illinois) allowed youth to remain under the supervision of the child welfare agency through their twenty-first birthday. Most of the youth surveyed at the time of the second interview were nineteen years old (95 percent). Females (54 percent) slightly outnumbered males (46 percent). Approximately 70 percent of the youth identified themselves as belonging to a racial or ethnic group, mostly African American. The interviews focused on a variety of domains, including education, employment, physical and mental health, social supports, delinquency, relationships with family, substance abuse, sexual behavior, and receipt of independent living services.

Results showed that almost one-third of the young adults were neither working nor in school, twice that of a nationally representative peer group their age (the Add Health sample). Almost one-third of the youth had neither a high school diploma nor a GED, compared with about 10 percent of their peers. Only 46 percent of the youth in the study had a savings or checking account, compared with 82 percent of their peers nationally, and nearly one-half of the women in the study received housing or economic assistance, such as food stamps. Another key finding of this study, like the Pennsylvania study, was that young adults who remained in care after the age of eighteen were more than twice as likely to be enrolled in a school or training program. Those youth who remained in care and who had a high school diploma or GED were more than three times as likely to be enrolled in a two-year or four-year college than those who left care at age eighteen (37 percent versus 12 percent). Youth who left care at the age of eighteen were nearly three times more likely than a national sample of their peers to be disconnected from work or school. The potential effects of independent living services on these outcomes were not evaluated in this study. Researchers plan to conduct a third round of interviews with study participants when they reach twenty-one years of age (Courtney and Dworsky, 2005).

The Northwest alumni study examined the outcomes for adults between the ages of twenty and thirty-three who had been placed as a youth in family foster care within one of three agencies: Casey Family Programs; the Oregon Department of Human Services, Division of Children, Adults, and Families; and the Washington Department of Social and Health Services, Children's Administration, Division of Children and Family Services. The study examined outcome variables related to mental health functioning, education, employment, and finances. Response rates to the survey were high, at approximately 75 percent.

Results indicated that much higher percentages of these young adults were doing better on outcome measures than the youth in the North Carolina and Midwest studies. Approximately 85 percent of the young adults had completed high school or their GED, and approximately 80 percent were employed (after adjusting for those not in the workforce such as full-time students and homemakers). One-third (33 percent) of the young adults, however, had incomes at or below the poverty level, three times the national poverty rate. High levels of mental health problems were reported. Over 50 percent had clinical levels of at least one mental health problem such as depression, social phobia, panic disorder, posttraumatic stress disorder, or drug dependency. Racial and gender differences were not reported in this study, but researchers indicated that these differences will be analyzed during the next phase of the study. Although independent living skills were not specifically analyzed, several questions were asked regarding youth's receipt of services and knowledge of life skills. Approximately 84 percent reported that they had access to employment training, 68 percent reported access to independent living training groups, and 57 percent reported they were somewhat or very prepared for independent living. Although more than one-half of young adults reported they were prepared to some extent for independent living, only 33 percent had a driver's license, only 38 percent had at least $250 in cash, and only 23 percent reported having dishes and utensils. These findings suggest a discrepancy between young adults' perceptions of their readiness to assume adult roles and their actual ability to successfully live independently (Pecora et al., 2005).

INNOVATIVE STRATEGIES

Several community-level and state-level programs employ innovative strategies for serving youth who are transitioning from foster care. Because the shared goal of these programs is for youth to be "Connected by 25," each program focuses on improving youth connections to important social networks or economic opportunities.

The Jim Casey Youth Opportunities Initiative (JCYOI) is a national foundation created specifically to support youth in foster care to successfully transition to adulthood. One component of this initiative is the "Opportunity Passport," an innovative tool developed by JCYOI to provide youth with direct experience in money management; enable youth to gain monetary assets; and improve outcomes for youth in the areas of employment, housing, and community life. Available to youth ages fourteen to twenty-three who were in foster care at the age of fourteen or older, the Opportunity Passport is comprised of a personal debit account for short-term expenses, a matched individual development account to be used for medium-term and long-term asset building, and additional benefits that are designed and negotiated at the local level. Being piloted in twelve sites nationwide at time of this writing, this program is new and most participants are in the saving phase. As a result, no long-term data on effectiveness are available. Initial case studies, however, show promise. Young adults who have withdrawn money use it mainly for business, housing, and educational purposes. In addition to the Opportunity Passport, JCYOI actively engages youth through youth leadership boards that empower them to plan for their own futures and become their own advocates. This feature is unique as very few foster care systems involve youth in making decisions for themselves and in system design.

The UPS School to Career Program is a partnership between the Maryland Department of Human Resources, which provides the state's independent living program, the United Parcel Service (UPS), the Living Classrooms Foundation, and the Annie E. Casey Foundation. Typically, job readiness programs offer such services as workshops, internships, job banks, job shadows, and job training. The UPS program provides all of these services but with a goal of teaching employability skills to foster youth ages sixteen to twenty-four in a relevant work environment that includes UPS and several other participating employers. The program provides retention services at the job site to help youth maintain a consistent work ethic, health benefits, and reimbursement for college. The Living Classrooms Foundation, a nonprofit organization in Maryland, provides transportation to the youth.

Two innovative features of the School to Career Program are the dual customer model of sustainability that seeks to ensure that the respective needs of youth and employers are met and the attention to data and self-evaluation. In relation to the dual customer model of sustainability, the program provides job coaches to help youth both improve job-related skills and work toward long-term career goals such as continuing their education. In turn, youth provide UPS with the benefit of higher retention rates, resulting in cost savings related to hiring and training. Outcome data show that more than three hundred foster youth who participated in the program while in foster care have found employment with UPS or other employers within the competitive marketplace. The retention rate is significantly higher for these youth employees than other employees who are not connected to the program. UPS and the Annie E. Casey Foundation are currently replicating this program in seven other cities (Annie E. Casey Foundation, 2006).

NC LINKS is North Carolina's state independent living program designed to assist youth in foster care make a successful transition to adulthood (North Carolina Division of Social Services, 2000). Established in 2000, the program currently has a budget of $2.1 million in federal and state funds and provides services for all foster youth between the ages of sixteen and twenty-one years, including youth who have aged out of foster care. The young adults must be willing and active participants in the assessment, planning, and services process. Caseworkers complete an objective assessment of each youth, identifying the youth's strengths and current resources. Youth are provided targeted services based on assessment results. Services, for example, might help the youth obtain sufficient income to meet their daily needs, safe and stable housing, sufficient academic or vocational training, and connections to relevant individuals outside of the child welfare system. Trust funds may be established for important costs such as auto repair, furniture, and insurance. Scholarship and conference funds also are available to youth as educational incentives for them to remain in school. Because this program is relatively new, little outcome data are available.

One common denominator of these programs is the use of individualized assessment and planning strategies. Initial outcome data for these programs are promising, although the effects of these programs are not entirely clear because little attention has been given to the application or fidelity of any of the programs—that is, randomized controlled studies have not been conducted. Because these programs are new and continue to expand, it is hoped that future fidelity and outcome measures will provide more empirical information to help determine the functional components of each program and possible common elements. In addition, the funding for each program differs. States and counties have limited funding mechanisms for these types of services. The NC LINKS' use of a mixture of Chafee and state funds is an approach that other states may choose to implement.

EVOLVING EVIDENCE-INFORMED PRACTICES

In addition to the relatively new programs discussed earlier, some empirically validated transition-to-adulthood programs have incorporated life skill development strategies that can support positive outcomes for youth as they move into young adulthood and beyond. Although only one of these programs (Casey Family Services) was developed specifically for youth in foster care (Frey et al., 2005), all programs encompass similar individually tailored strategies for preparing and supporting young people in transition into adulthood roles. The other three programs, Project RENEW (Hagner et al., 1999), Project ARIES (Bullis, 1999), and the TIP model (Clark and Foster-Johnson, 1996; Clark and Davis, 2000)] were developed for youth with emotional or behavioral difficulties. These programs appear to have relevance for youth in foster care because many older youth within the foster care system experience behavioral and emotional difficulties (Newton et al., 2000).

Casey Family Services

Casey Family Services, a nonprofit child welfare agency operating in seven states, provides a broad array of programs to meet the needs of children and youth in foster care. Historically, the Casey Family Services transition program has helped youth complete school, find affordable housing, and make connections to colleges and universities. Recent program redesign has further emphasized the integration of life skills work with a permanency teaming approach that aims to promote enduring family connections alongside safety and well-being. A team of individuals composed of key people in the youth's life join with the youth in an individualized planning process to address problems and goals in relation to the youth's strengths and needs. There are six components to the Casey Family Services practice approach:

- Partnering with youth as the central player in their own integrated planning process and engaging them in identifying essential team members
- Including parents, family members, caregivers, significant adults, professionals, and community members in the team process to improve relationships, inform shared decision making, and expand permanency and life skills resources
- Exploring each adult's level of commitment to a youth over time
- Engaging youth in a collaborative casework process that prepares them to actively and meaningfully participate in team planning
- Developing a youth-centered, family-focused integrated plan that addresses the critical dimensions of safety, permanence, and well-being
- Facilitating an ongoing collaborative team planning process (Frey et al., 2005)

Continuing evaluations of this approach and its forerunner have shown that youth transitioning from Casey Family Services foster care can achieve better outcomes than youth who participate in traditional programs. Outcome data from foster care alumni who were served between 1966 and 1998 showed that approximately 73 percent of the Casey alumni graduated from high school compared with 60 percent of foster care youth in comparable studies (Kerman et al., 2002). A significantly higher percentage of female Casey Family Services foster youth (87.8 percent) were employed full or part time when compared with the national female average (76.3 percent). These findings are encouraging but call out for more research to move the program toward the criteria of an evidence-based practice.

Project RENEW

David Hagner et al. (1999) studied career-related outcomes for students attending a demonstration project titled Project RENEW (Rehabilitation, Empowerment, Natural Supports, Education, and Work) located at the New Hampshire Community and Technical College. Study participants were eighteen young people, ages sixteen to twenty-two years, with emotional and behavioral difficulties who were served by three career education specialists (Cheney et al., 1998). Project components included personal futures planning, flexible secondary and postsecondary curricula, support for employment, interagency collaboration, mentoring, developing social skills, and access to flexible funding resources in order to address young persons' critical needs (such as housing) or to support a career or educational goal (such as tuition fees for career training).

After two years of program participation, 67 percent of the eighteen youth had completed high school, 83 percent were employed, and 50 percent were pursuing postsecondary education. The percentage of participants involved with the Department of Corrections declined from 72 percent to 17 percent by the end of the program. There were statistically significant increases in participants' satisfaction with school, employment, handling of life problems, and progress toward personal goals. The graduation and employment outcomes were comparable with or well beyond national survey rates reported for similar individuals. Results of this study indicated that person-centered planning and support for transition goals was a viable strategy to enhance employment and other positive postsecondary outcomes. Results also indicated that collaboration across transition-related agencies such as vocational rehabilitation, schools, and adult mental health agencies was a key factor in achieving better postsecondary outcomes for young people with disabilities. Finally, social skills training was found to be central to successful transition to adulthood roles.

ARIES Program

The ARIES program (Achieving Rehabilitation, Individualized Education, and Employment Success) was implemented as a community-based transition program serving students ages sixteen years and older with emotional and behavioral difficulties (Bullis, 1999). During the period 1995 to 1999, the ARIES program provided services to eighty-five students from several high schools in a suburban Oregon school district. Services were provided in the school and in the community. Michael Bullis et al. (2002) studied the quantitative and qualitative impact of the ARIES program. Of the eighty-five adolescents, sixty-one exited the program through graduation, terminating their involvement, or leaving the immediate area. Of the sixty-one exiters, thirty-six graduated from secondary school. Of the eighty-five participants who entered the project, 55 percent were employed at the time of the evaluation, and 65 percent were "successfully engaged," meaning they were employed or enrolled and/or completed school, and were not arrested during the time they participated in the project. Qualitative analysis revealed that person-centered planning, individualized educational placement and support, competitive job placement, and service coordination were central to higher positive outcomes at the end of the program for the participating young adults.

Transition to Independence Process (TIP)

The Transition to Independence Process (TIP) model (Clark and Davis, 2000; Clark and Foster-Johnson, 1996) encompasses the best practices of transition programs for young adults with behavioral or emotional difficulties (Bullis, 1999; Cheney et al., 1998; Clark and Foster-Johnson, 1996; Clark and Stewart, 1992; Clark et al., 1993; Davis and Vander Stoep, 1996, 1997; Hagner et al., 1999; Modrcin and Rutland, 1989). The TIP model was developed to engage youth and young adults in their own futures planning process and provide them with developmentally appropriate services and supports. It involves youth, their families, and other informal key players in a process that prepares youth for and facilitates greater self-sufficiency and the successful achievement of goals in each of the transition domains. Those domains are employment, career-oriented education, living situation, personal-effectiveness and quality of life, and community-life functioning. Seven guidelines operationally define the TIP model:

- Engage young people through relationship development, person-centered planning, and a focus on their futures
- Tailor services and supports to be accessible, coordinated, developmentally-appropriate, and built on strengths to enable young people to pursue their goals across all the transition domains
- Acknowledge and develop personal choice and social responsibility with young people
- Ensure a safety net of support by involving a young person's parents, family members, and other informal and formal key players
- Enhance the young person's competencies to assist him or her in achieving greater self-sufficiency and confidence
- Maintain an outcome focus at the young person, program, and community levels
- Involve young people, parents, and other community partners in the TIP system at the practice, program, and community levels

Each guideline has either empirical support or broad professional consensus indicating that it reflects promising practices for use with young people with emotional and behavioral difficulties and their families (Bullis and Fredericks, 2002; Bullis et al., 2002; Karpur et al., 2005; Hagner et al., 1999; Fitzgibbon et al., 2000; Clark et al., 2004). Research findings regarding best practices in promising transition programs across the country are consistent with the TIP model and its guidelines. For example, studies have reported improved postsecondary progress and outcomes for the young people who were served using the TIP model or most of the TIP practices (Clark et al., 2008b).

Two studies illustrate the types of outcome studies that support the TIP model. First, an evaluation of the effectiveness of a TIP-type program in Vermont that operates in nine communities in the state (Clark et al., 2004) analyzed progress for participating youth. The study found substantial improvements in the outcomes for young people with emotional and behavioral difficulties, including: (a) an increased percentages of young people who were employed and completed educational goals; (b) quadrupling of the average wage received by youth; (c) decreased percentages of young people involvement in the criminal justice system; (d) decreased use of "intensive" mental health and substance abuse services such as inpatient treatment; and (e) decreased use of public assistance such as welfare benefits and Supplemental Security Income. A cost-avoidance analysis showed substantial savings as a function of the community-based TIP-type program.

Second, Arun Karpur et al. (2005) conducted a study that examined the postsecondary outcomes of exiters from one of the Florida sites that used the TIP model. This site had operated for a sufficiently long period of time to permit an assessment of outcomes for a substantial number of young adults with emotional and behavioral disturbances (EBD) who participated in the program. Existing state databases were used to compare postsecondary outcomes of program exiters and match comparison groups of former students from the same urban school district. The comparison groups were matched on age, gender, and ethnicity and were composed of two groups: former students with EBD classifications who had not had specialized transition services and former students with no previous disability classifications. Outcomes for the TIP program exiter group with regard to postsecondary indicators of education or vocational training (as well as incarceration rates) were statistically better than the outcomes for the comparison group with EBD. There was not a statistically significant difference between these two groups on the percentage of young adults employed. On most of the postsecondary outcome indicators, the TIP program exiter group percentages more closely approached the percentages for the comparison group of young adults with no disability classifications than the matched comparison group with EBD. An implication of these findings is that the TIP program exiter group may have a higher likelihood of achieving future employment that provides a livable wage as a result of higher percentages of young adults who continued into postsecondary education.

A current cross-site study involves the implementation of the TIP model, or a slight variation of it, at five community sites across the nation. The preliminary findings show statistically significant improvements on youth progress indicators across the transition domains related to employment and education. They also show reductions in interference of mental health/substance use on daily-life functioning (Clark et al., 2008a).

The TIP model is designed to serve youth and young adults with EBD in the community, irrespective of the settings in which they are located. They may be in or out of school; they may reside in crisis units, foster care settings, group homes, or homes of family of origin or relatives; or they may be incarcerated. The studies summarized above did not focus exclusively on young people in foster care, but because many youth in foster care have EBD, these studies involved some youth in care. The results from these and other TIP-related studies are very encouraging. The TIP model is considered an "evidence-informed practice" for improving the progress and outcomes of transition-age youth and young adults with serious challenges.

ASSESSMENT INSTRUMENTS

Personnel working with transition-age youth often seek instruments to assist them in assessing young people's life skills and tracking their progress across transition domains. A variety of assessment instruments can be of some assistance in assessing young people's life skill development (Bullis, 2002; Karpur et al., 2006; Daniel Memorial Institute, 1988; Nollan et al., 2002). Two of the instruments, the Ansell-Casey Social Skills Assessment and the Transition to Adulthood Program Information System are described here.

The Ansell-Casey Life Skills Assessment (ACLSA) (Nollan et al., 2002), a standardized measure used to evaluate youth independent living skills, can be completed and analyzed online. It consists of statements regarding youth's knowledge base of specific life skills. It is designed to facilitate conversations and deepen rapport with the youth. Six life skill areas are included: daily living tasks, housing and community resources, money management, self-care, social development (communication, relationships, and community values), and work and study habits (career planning, decision-making, and study skills). Four versions of the ACLSA have been developed to be completed with youth in different age ranges. It is appropriate for youths from all gender, ethnic, and cultural backgrounds, and living circumstances (whether the youth lives with parent[s], in foster family care, in a group home, or in other settings).

The Transition to Adulthood Program Information System (TAPIS) Progress Tracker is a third-generation instrument that has been pilot-tested and is currently being programmed to be integrated into an internet-based system for collecting individual data on a quarterly basis. The TAPIS Progress Tracker will provide information that assists in assessing and tracking a young person's progress and outcomes. The Progress Tracker will be used to collect data at time of program intake and then every ninety days thereafter. Data relate to the young person's progress and difficulty across the transition domains of employment, education, living situation, personal adjustment, and community-life functioning. Each transition domain consists of objective information on the indicators of the young person's progress and difficulty and an assessment of overall levels of functioning within each domain. The TAPIS Progress Tracker is to be completed by personnel who are most knowledgeable about the young person's recent experiences or the personnel who are working with the young person on transition-based issues. This individual draws on all available sources, including, but not limited to, the youth, parents, foster parents, agency records, school reports, and other informal and formal key players in the life of the young person. The TAPIS Program Tracker also will provide program effectiveness data for continuing quality improvement of transition programs.

The ACLSA and the TAPIS Progress Tracker vary in two respects. First, they differ in relation to standardization. The ACLSA versions for children and adolescents (under sixteen years of age) are standardized. Although both the ACLSA for youth over sixteen years of age and the TAPIS Progress Tracker have an empirical base, neither has full standardization. Second, the youth or young adult and caregiver typically complete the ACLSA; the TAPIS Progress Tracker is completed by a transition facilitator or other personnel who are most knowledgeable about the young person's experiences and needs.

Each instrument has advantages and disadvantages. Both can provide important information on the youth's knowledge of life skills and how the youth is managing the transition to adult life, and both provide opportunities to discuss these perspectives with the young person. The ACLSA seeks to secure both the youth's and caregiver's perspectives on the youth's knowledge of life skills. Comparing the similarities and differences in the two resulting profiles may provide an occasion for a valuable learning discussion between the caregiver and young person. The benefits of using the ACLSA will be limited if the youth's caregiver is not familiar with the youth (such as in cases when the youth has recently been placed with the caregiver) or the youth is not available or is unwilling to complete the assessment. The TAPIS Progress Tracker collects data from an adult who knows the youth, and data collection is not affected by the youth's unavailability or unwillingness to participate in the process. But it does not ask the youth about his or her perspectives. Both instruments can assist a transition site in working more effectively with youth and young adults. Both, however, require that staff be committed to actively using the assessment information with the youth and their families in ways that create a dialog for understanding a youth's transition progress toward greater self-sufficiency, personal adjustment, and community-life functioning.

CONCLUSION AND FUTURE RECOMMENDATIONS

Young people exiting foster care are often ill prepared to assume young adult life roles. It is encouraging that both the Casey Family Services program and the TIP model outline many of the same practices and strategies to improve outcomes for youth who are being prepared for and supported in their transitions into adulthood roles. Ruth Massinga and Peter Pecora (2004) have suggested the importance of four main strategies for preparing youth to succeed as adults: systematic skills assessment, independent living skills training, involvement of caregivers as teachers, and developing connections with birth families and the community. Both the Casey Family Services program and the TIP model emphasize these features, with an overriding goal of developing youth's social capital through a network of informal key players who provide supports for youth as they transition to adulthood. Both programs also incorporate a major emphasis on competency development of interpersonal and community-life skills.

Although the research findings from the Casey Family Services program and the TIP model are promising, there clearly needs to be a much greater understanding of how to most effectively deliver services and supports to youth as they transition into adulthood roles and functioning and how to develop economic capital with these young people (such as through the JCYOI Opportunity Passport). Qualitative and quantitative studies are needed to provide a fuller understanding of the effect of the functional aspects of programs for transition-age youth and an evaluation of the cost and cost-benefits of serving these young people effectively. Future studies might also benefit greatly by having young adults assist in the design of methods and instrumentation to ensure that programs are youth-friendly and relevant to their lives.

REFERENCES

Allen, M. L., and R. Nixon (2000). The foster care independence act and John H. Chafee foster care independence program: New catalysts for reform for young people aging out of foster care. *Journal of Poverty Law and Policy* 7(2): 197–216.

Annie E. Casey Foundation (2006). *School to Career Partnerships.* At aecf.org/Child-FamilyServices/SchooltoCareer.aspx (accessed April 17, 2007).

Avery, R., and M. Freundlich (2003). *Deleterious Consequences of Aging Out of Foster Care.* Summary Report. Washington, D.C.: National Convening on Youth Permanence.

Barth, R. P. (1993). On their own: The experiences of youth after foster care. *Child and Adolescent Social Work Journal* 7: 419–40.

Bullis, M. (1999). *Achieving Rehabilitation, Individualized Education, and Employment Success Project for Adolescents with Emotional Disturbance: Final Report on the ARIES Project.* Eugene: University of Oregon, Institute on Violence and Destructive Behavior.

—— (2002). Gathering information on transition adjustment. In M. Bullis and H. D. Fredericks, eds., *Vocational and Transition Services for Adolescents with Emotional and Behavioral Disorders: Strategies and Best Practices* (pp.185–97). Champaign, Ill.: Research Press.

Bullis, M., and H. D. Fredericks (2002). *Vocational and Transition Services for Adolescents with Emotional and Behavioral Disorders: Strategies and Best Practices.* Champaign, Ill.: Research Press.

Bullis, M., C. J. Tehan, and H. B. Clark (2000). Teaching and developing improved community life competencies. In H.B. Clark and M. Davis, eds., *Transition for Youth and Young Adults with Emotional and Behavioral Difficulties into Adulthood: Handbook for Practitioners, Educators, Parents, and Administrators* (pp. 107–31). Baltimore: Paul H. Brookes.

Bullis, M., T. Morgan, M. Benz, B. Todis, and M. D. Johnson (2002). Description and evaluation of the ARIES Project: Achieving rehabilitation, individualized education, and employment success for adolescents with emotional disturbance. *Career Development for Exceptional Individuals* 25: 41–58.

Carneiro, P. M., and J. J. Heckman (2003). *Human Capital Policy.* IZA Discussion Paper No. 821. At ssrn.com/abstract=434544.

Center on Children, Families, and the Law (1994). *Independent Living Skills Evaluation: Former State Wards—Baseline Report.* Lincoln, Neb.: Author.

Cheney, D., D. Hagner, J. Malloy, G. Cormier, and S. Bernstein (1998). Transition services for youth and young adults with emotional disturbance: Description of initial results of Project RENEW. *Career Development for Exceptional Individuals* 21: 17–32.

Child Welfare League of America (CWLA) (1999). *CWLA Standards of Excellence for Services for Abused or Neglected Children and Their Families.* Washington, D.C.: Author.

Choca, M. J., J. Minoff, L. Angene, M. Byrnes, L. Kenneally, D. Norris, D. Pearn, and M. M. Rivers (2004). Can't do it alone: Housing collaborations to improve foster youth outcomes. *Child Welfare* 83(5): 469–92.

Christenson, B. L. (2002) *Youth Exiting Foster Care: Efficacy of Independent Living Services in the State of Idaho.* Cheney: Eastern Washington University.

Clark, H. B., and M. Davis, eds. (2000). *Transition for Youth and Young Adults with Emotional and Behavioral Difficulties into Adulthood: Handbook for Practitioners, Educators, Parents, and Administrators.* Baltimore: Paul H. Brookes.

Clark, H. B., and L. Foster-Johnson (1996). Serving youth in transition to adulthood. In B. Stroul, ed., *Children's Mental Health: Creating Systems of Care in a Changing Society.* Baltimore: Paul H. Brookes.

Clark, H. B., and E. S. Stewart (1992). Transition into employment, education, and independent living: A survey of programs serving youth and young adults with emotional /behavioral disorders. In K. Kutash, C. J. Liberton, A. Algarin, and R. Friedman, eds., *Proceedings of the Fifth Annual Conference: A System of Care for Children's Mental Health—Expanding the Research Base* (pp. 189–98). Tampa: University of South Florida, Louis de la Parte Florida Mental Health Institute.

Clark, H. B., K. Unger, and E. S. Stewart (1993). Transition of youth and young adults with emotional/behavioral disorders into employment, education and independent living. *Community Alternatives International Journal of Family Care* 5: 20–46.

Clark, H. B., B. Lee, M. E. Prange, and B. A. McDonald (1996). Children lost within the foster care system: Can wraparound service strategies improve placement outcomes? *Journal of Child and Family Studies* 5(1): 39–54.

Clark, H. B., O. Pschorr, P. Wells, M. Curtis, and T. Tighe (2004). Transition into community roles for young people with emotional/behavioral difficulties: Collaborative systems and program outcomes. In D. Cheney, ed., *Transition Issues and Strategies for Youth and Young Adults with Emotional and/or Behavioral Difficulties to Facilitate Movement into Community Life* (pp. 201–25). Washington, D.C.: Council for Exceptional Children.

Clark, H. B., N. Deschenes, D. Sieler, M. Green, G. White, and D. Sondheimer (2008a). Services for youth in transition to adulthood in systems of care. In B. A. Stroul and G. M. Blau, eds., *The System of Care Handbook: Transforming Mental Health Services for Children, Youth, and Families.* Baltimore: Paul H. Brookes.

Clark, H. B., A. Karpur, N. Deschenes, P. Gamache, and M. Haber (2008b). Partnerships for Youth Transition (PYT): Overview of community initiatives and preliminary findings on transition to adulthood for youth and young adults with mental health challenges. In C. Newman, C. Liberton, K. Kutash, and R. M. Friedman, eds., *The 20th Annual Research Conference Proceedings: A System of Care for Children's Mental Health—Expanding the Research Base* (pp. 329–32). Tampa: University of South Florida, Louis de la Parte Florida Mental Health Institute.

Coleman, J. S. (1988). Social capital in the creation of human capital. *American Journal of Sociology* 94 (Suppl. 95): S95–S120.

Collins, M. E. (2001). Transition to adulthood for vulnerable youths: A review of research and implications for policy. *Social Service Review* 75(2): 271–91.

Cook, R. A. (1991). *A National Evaluation of Title IV-E Foster Care Independent Living Programs for Youth: Phase 2.* Rockville, Md.: Westat.

—— (1992). *A National Evaluation of Title IV-E Foster Care: Independent Living Programs for Youth Phase 2 Final Report*. Rockville, Md.: Westat.

—— (1994). Are we helping foster care youth prepare for their future? *Children and Youth Services Review* 16: 213–29.

Cooper, C. S., N. L. Peterson, and J. H. Meier (1987). Variables associated with disrupted placement in a select sample of abused and neglected children. *Child Abuse and Neglect* 11: 75–86.

Courtney, M. E., and A. Dworsky (2005). *Midwest Evaluation of the Adult Functioning of Former Foster Youth: Outcomes at Age 19*. Chicago: Chapin Hall Center for Children at the University of Chicago.

Courtney, M. E., I. Piliavin, A. Grogan-Kaylor, and A. Nesmith (2001). Foster youth transitions to adulthood: A longitudinal view of youth leaving care. *Child Welfare* 80(6): 685–717.

Curulla, V. L. (1990). Aggression replacement training in the community for adult learning disabled offenders. Unpublished ms., University of Washington, Special Education.

Daniel Memorial Institute (1988). *Daniel Memorial Independent Living Skills System*. At danielkids.org.

Davis, M., and A. Vander Stoep (1996). *The Transition to Adulthood Among Adolescents Who Have Emotional Disturbance*. Delmar, N.Y.: National Resource Center on Homelessness and Mental Illness Policy Research Associated.

—— (1997). The transition to adulthood for youth who have serious emotional disturbance: Development transition and young adult outcomes. *Journal of Mental Health Administration* 24: 400–427.

Dworsky, A., and Courtney, M. E. (2000). *Self-Sufficiency of Former Foster Youth in Wisconsin: Analysis of Unemployment Insurance Wage Data and Public Assistance Data*. Madison, Wisc.: Institute for Research on Poverty.

Fitzgibbon, G., J. A. Cook, and L. Falcon (2000). Vocational rehabilitation approaches for youth. In H. B. Clark and M. Davis, eds., *Transition to Adulthood: A Resource Assisting Young People with Emotional or Behavioral Difficulties* (pp. 75–89). Baltimore: Paul H. Brookes.

Frey, L. L., S. B. Greenbelt, and J. Brown (2005). *A Call to Action: An Integrated Approach to Youth Permanency and Preparation for Adulthood*. New Haven, Conn.: Casey Family Services.

Furstenberg, F. F., and M. E. Hughes (1995). Social capital and successful development among at-risk youth. *Journal of Marriage and the Family* 57: 580–92.

Goldstein, A. P., and B. Glick (1994). Aggression replacement training: Curriculum and evaluation. *Simulation and Gaming* 25(1): 9–26.

Goldstein, A. P., B. Glick, S. Reiner, D. Zimmerman, and T. Coultry (1986). *Aggression Replacement Training*. Champaign, Ill.: Research Press.

Goldstein, A. R., B. Glick, M. J. Irwin, C. McCartney, and I. Rubama (1989). *Reducing Delinquency: Intervention in the Community*. New York: Pergamon.

Gutierrez, M., M. Berkey, and A. Bergson-Shilcock (2001). *Strengthening Families to Promote Youth Development*. Baltimore: Annie E. Casey Foundation.

Hagner, D., D. Cheney, and J. Malloy (1999). Career-related outcomes of a model transition demonstration for young adults with emotional disturbance. *Rehabilitation Counseling Bulletin* 42: 228–43.

Iglehart, A. P. (1994). Adolescents in foster care: Predicting readiness for independent living. *Children and Youth Services Review* 16: 159–69.

Karpur, A., H. B. Clark, P. Caproni, and H. Sterner (2005). Transition to adult roles for students with emotional/behavioral disturbances: A follow-up study of student exiters from Steps-to-Success. *Career Development for Exceptional Individuals* 28(1): 36–46.

Karpur, A., H. B. Clark, J. Knab, and N. Deschenes (2006). Transition to Adulthood Program Information System (TAPIS). In C. Newman, C. Liberton, K. Kutash, and R. M. Friedman, eds., *The 19th Annual Research Conference Proceedings: A System of Care for Children's Mental Health—Expanding the Research Base*. Tampa: University of South Florida, Louis de la Parte Florida Mental Health Institute.

Kerman, B., J. Wildfire, and R. P. Barth (2002). Outcomes for young adults who experienced foster care. *Children and Youth Services Review* 24: 79–104.

Klee, L., and N. Halfon (1987). Communicating health information in the California Foster Care System: Problems and recommendations. *Children and Youth Services Review* 9: 171–85.

Lindsey, E. W., and F. U. Ahmed (1999). The North Carolina independent living program: A comparison of outcomes for participants and nonparticipants. *Children and Youth Services Review* 2: 389–412.

Massinga, R., and P. J. Pecora (2004). Providing better opportunities for older children in the child welfare system. *Future of Children, Families, and Foster Care* 14(1): 151–73.

McMillen, J. C., and J. Tucker (1999). The status of older adolescents at exit from out-of-home care. *Child Welfare* 78(3): 339–60.

Modrcin, M. J., and A. C. Rutland (1989). Youth in transition: A summary of service components. *Psychosocial Rehabilitation Journal* 12: 3–13.

Needell, B. J., R. P. Barth, and M. Johnson-Reid (1998). *The Tender Years: Toward Developmentally Sensitive Child Welfare Services for Very Young Children*. New York: Oxford University Press.

Newton, R. R., A. J. Litrownik, and J. A. Landsverk (2000). Children and youth in foster care: Distangling the relationship between problem behaviors and number of placements. *Child Abuse and Neglect* 24(10): 1363–74.

Nollan, K. A., M. Horn, A. C. Downs, and P. J. Pecora (2002). *Ansell-Casey Life Skills Assessment (ACLSA) and Life Skills Guidebook Manual*. Seattle: Casey Family Programs.

North Carolina Division of Social Services (2000). *NC LINKS: Helping Teens Make a Successful Transition from Foster Care to Self-Sufficiency.* At www. dhhs.state.nc.us/ dss/c_srv/cserv_ind.htm.

Pecora, P. J., R. C. Kessler, J. Williams, K. O'Brien, A. C. Downs, D. English, J. White, E. Hiripi, C. R. White, T. Wiggins, and K. Holmes (2005). *Improving Family Foster Care: Findings from the Northwest Foster Care Alumni Study.* Seattle: Casey Family Programs.

Proch, K., and M. Taber (1985). Placement disruption: A review of research. *Children and Youth Services Review* 7: 309–20.

Reddy, L. A., and S. I. Pfeiffer (1997). Effectiveness of treatment foster care with children and adolescents: A review of outcome studies. *Journal of the American Academy of Child and Adolescent Psychiatry* 36: 581–88.

Shippensburg University Center for Juvenile Justice Training and Research. (1993). *An Evaluation of Pennsylvania's Independent Living Program for Youth.* Shippensburg, Pa.: Author.

Shirk, M., and G. Stangler (2004). *On Their Own: What Happens to Kids When They Age Out of the Foster Care System.* Boulder, Colo.: Westview.

U.S. General Accounting Office (1999). *Foster Care Effectiveness of Independent Living Services Unknown.* GAO/HEHS-00-13. Washington, D.C.: U.S. Government Printing Office.

—— (2004). *HHS Actions Could Improve Coordination of Services and Monitoring of States' Independent Living Programs.* GAO-05-25. Washington, D.C.: U.S. Government Printing Office.

Vander Stoep, A., M. Davis, and D. Collins (2000). Transition: A time of developmental and institutional clashes. In H. B. Clark and M. Davis, eds., *Transition for Youth and Young Adults with Emotional and Behavioral Difficulties into Adulthood: Handbook for Practitioners, Educators, Parents, and Administrators* (pp. 3–28). Baltimore: Paul H. Brookes.

Wald, M., and T. Martinez (2003). *Connected by 25: Improving the Life Chances of the Country's Most Vulnerable 14–24 Year Olds.* Menlo Park, Calif.: William and Flora Hewlett Foundation.

From Research to Practice   **EIGHTEEN**

Improving Permanency Outcomes
for Youth in Foster Care

MADELYN FREUNDLICH,
LAUREN FREY, BENJAMIN KERMAN,
AND SARAH B. GREENBLATT

As the chapters in this volume demonstrate, much has been learned from the research that can inform youth permanence practice and result in improved permanency outcomes for youth. In chapter 15, David Crampton and Joan Pennell describe the growing body of research on family involvement models that can support the achievement of permanence outcomes for youth. Other authors focus on research that has illuminated effective approaches to achieving and sustaining youth permanence in different ways. In chapter 13, Barbara Pine and Robin Spath provide information on the positive outcomes of a family reunification program that offers intensive family-based and family-centered services, and they consider how key aspects of this program could be adapted in the context of the developmental needs of adolescents in out-of-home care. In chapter 14, Ruth G. McRoy and Elissa Madden discuss the research base for achieving positive outcomes through adoption for youth in care. Adding to this knowledge base is research, as Hewitt Clark and Kimberly Crosland describe in chapter 17, which provides a greater understanding of effective approaches to integrating permanence and preparation for adulthood, thereby meeting the holistic needs of youth for family relationships and life skills. In chapter 16, Sandra Stukes Chipungu, Laura G. Daughtery, and Benjamin Kerman contribute an additional perspective by describing research on the role of community in supporting youth and families and sustaining healthy family relationships.

In this chapter, we draw on these authors' work and illustrate ways in which one agency, Casey Family Services, is applying empirically based knowledge in practice to improve permanency and well-being outcomes for youth in foster care. Through the use of case studies, we describe ways in which Casey is translating research into youth permanency practice in specific areas:

1. Youth-centered, family-focused teaming, with an emphasis on the permanency teaming model of Casey Family Services
2. Identification and engagement of family resources for youth in care
3. The concurrent planning framework of the Casey teaming process that facilitates the achievement of permanence
4. Role of teaming in preparing youth for adoption
5. Integration of permanence and preparation for adulthood practice
6. Community-based preventive services to support youth and strengthen and preserve families

COLLABORATIVE PERMANENCY TEAMING: THE CASEY FAMILY SERVICES MODEL

Casey Family Services developed its collaborative permanency teaming model based on the agency's ongoing commitment to achieve family permanency outcomes for all children and youth, involve consumers in planning, and maintain birth family connections. Consistent with research cited in chapter 13, Casey's permanency teaming model involves youth in all aspects of the process as a member of the team. The Casey permanency teaming model likewise embeds the rationale for family involvement offered in chapter 15: Casey practice embodies values that emphasize the importance of interacting with children, families, and communities with mutual respect; expectations that power will shift from being exclusively held by the child welfare system and the courts to being shared with youth, families, and communities; an inclusive definition and broad composition of the "family team" that makes decisions with youth; a meeting place that provides an environment that is supportive of youth and families; and a commitment to providing sufficient preparation, coordination, and facilitation of team meetings in order to balance the needs of all parties while remaining focused on the youth's safety, permanence, and well-being.

In the Casey permanency teaming model, the permanency planning social worker engages in a range of activities that include preparing the youth for permanent family relationships; identifying and recruiting a permanent parent, as well as lifelong family connections; preparing the parent(s) to make and sustain a lifetime commitment; transitioning the youth to the permanent family (if necessary); achieving a legal permanency outcome; and designing and implementing postpermanency supports. The social worker's roles include advocating for family permanency; facilitating the collabora-

Case Example 1: Kenton

Kenton, age fifteen, entered foster care when he was eleven. An honor student and athlete, he lives with a foster family who is deeply committed to him. After his birth mother's death, Kenton was parented by his father, Derek, until Derek's mental illness undermined his capacity to parent safely. Kenton is very protective of him. Kenton's five older siblings aged out of foster care, and he is aware of how they struggle to make a good life for themselves. He feels a strong sense of loyalty to them while, at the same time, wanting a different life for himself.

When Kenton was asked about identifying a permanency team to help him plan for his future, he was uncertain that his father should be included. He worried that other team members may have difficulty relating to him, given his mental illness. Through a series of individual meetings in which his social worker helped him clarify his concerns and consider his options, Kenton decided to include his father. The social worker met with Derek several times to help him understand how he could contribute to Kenton's team in ways that only a father could. The social worker developed a strong working relationship with him that has supported Derek's participation on Kenton's team.

Kenton also identified as team members two women who had played important roles in his life. Rhonda is the neighbor of a former foster family and works in the social services field. When contacted about being a member of Kenton's team, she expressed great interest in helping with the planning for Kenton. Serena is a friend of Kenton's birth father. Having lived near the family when Kenton was growing up, she is very aware of the birth father's struggles. When contacted, Serena readily agreed to be a member of Kenton's team and now supervises visits between Kenton and his birth father. Kenton's foster parents are also important members of his team. During a recent crisis in which Kenton was unfairly accused of wrongdoing by a neighbor, Kenton was able to see them as "parents," standing up for him in a difficult time and claiming him as their son.

tive teaming process; preparing the youth to engage in and embrace family relationships, and preparing all family members to make informed decisions and sustain lifelong commitments to a youth; using the social work relationship with youth as a "bridge" to family relationships, connecting or reconnecting them to family; and supporting the youth to exit foster care to a permanent family safely, securely, and as quickly as possible.

As Kenton's case illustrates, Casey's collaborative planning and decision-making process extends beyond child welfare practitioners, birth parents, and foster parents to include important adults in the youth's life. Kenton identified his own team members, a first step in his active and meaningful engagement in his own permanency planning and decision making. His case further shows how birth family and other significant adults are engaged in active and meaningful roles. As reported in chapter 15, research has found that the active engagement of parents and extended family, as well as other significant "family like" adults, can be key to achieving positive outcomes for children and youth in foster care.

Kenton's case also illustrates the benefits highlighted in chapter 15 when youth and families are actively engaged together in the planning and decision-making process. By bringing together adults who know and are committed to the youth, collaborative planning and decision making provides opportunities for emotional healing, a greater commitment on the part of family and youth to mutually develop plans, the greater probability that mutually developed plans will be implemented, and higher levels of youth and family satisfaction.

Kenton's case is an example of the initial work that provides the foundation for Casey's permanency teaming process. Rather than episodic team meetings that focus on particular decisions or crises, this model reflects an ongoing relationship-building process, beginning with individual meetings, like those described in Kenton's case, and continuing until the youth achieves permanence. The social worker facilitates three types of team meetings to nurture participant relationships, culminating in a productive large team: individual sessions with each team member, joint sessions with two or more team members, and large team meetings with all team members or large subgroups as appropriate (e.g., a "core group" of birth parents, extended family, and youth). The social worker applies all three types of meetings flexibly and strategically throughout the entire permanency planning process. In the individual and joint meetings, the social worker may orient new team members to the teaming process, prepare or debrief large team meeting participants, explore and implement permanency-readiness activities with various constellations of participants (e.g., with the youth alone or together with family members or the youth's therapist), facilitate difficult conversations, discuss the youth's needs with potential permanent parents in more depth, and explore and define adult commitments to the youth. At each step, preparatory contacts allow the social worker to identify areas of agreement to build consensus, as well as any differences of opinion or potential conflicts between team members that may undermine teamwork. The social worker can then use additional individual or joint sessions to address these differences before the large team meeting. The social worker generally brings the core team together in a large team meeting approximately eight to ten weeks after case assignment, and every four to six weeks thereafter.

In Kenton's case, individual meeting have established the groundwork for effective large team meetings. As a next step in preparing for the large team meeting, the social worker will work individually with Kenton to prepare a meeting agenda and discuss how he will participate and what support he may need to participate as fully as possible. The social worker also will meet individually with Kenton's father, Derek, and with Kenton's foster parents to discuss possible agenda items, how they will participate, and what support they may need to fully participate. In addition, the social worker will meet individually with Rhonda and Serena to discuss potential agenda items and what they wish to contribute to the meeting.

IDENTIFICATION AND ENGAGEMENT OF POTENTIAL FAMILY RESOURCES

Case Example 2: Justine

Justine, fourteen years old, has been in foster care for eight years. She lived with a number of foster families before being referred to Casey. Her current foster parent wants to help Justine find a permanent family but cannot be a permanent resource herself. Justine's team initially was composed of her Casey social worker, her state social worker, her therapist, and her current foster parent. Through conversations about important people in her life, Justine told her social worker that she would like very much to have a former foster mother, Tanya, join the team. Her social worker learned that Justine maintained contact with Tanya long after Tanya withdrew from foster parenting after she relocated to a nearby state. Before these conversations with Justine, no one was aware of this important relationship in Justine's life. Tanya joined Justine's team, first by phone and eventually in person. Adoption by Tanya is being explored, with the hearty support of the rest of the team.

Case Example 3: Drew

Drew, age sixteen, has been in foster care since he was eight years old. He lost contact with his siblings and half-siblings over the years. When his team initially explored reconnection, Drew grew very negative, stating, "if they wanted to find me, they would have!" With members of his team, Drew spent more time talking about his siblings, and, after these conversations, he decided that he wanted efforts to be made to find them. His social worker was able to locate information in Drew's case record about an uncle in another state. She reached his uncle by letter and then by phone. The uncle was able to connect Drew with all of his siblings, as well as with his maternal grandmother. Drew's foster mother is now facilitating phone calls and visits with these family members. Drew is delighted to be reconnected and advised his team that when working with other youth, social workers should "do this quickly. For me, it should have happened eight years ago."

Case Example 4: Maria

Six-year-old Maria entered foster care at age two and now lives with a Casey foster family. She recalls little about any family members, and there has been no subsequent family involvement. Her Casey social worker, Wanda, "mined" Maria's case record and found that she had paternal relatives in Florida. Wanda contacted these relatives and learned that Maria's birth father resided in Texas. The relatives, however, did not have any contact information for him. Using the information that the relatives could provide, Wanda used the internet and found Maria's father. When reached, Maria's father was very interested in being involved in planning for Maria and stated that he would like Maria to live with him. He knew that Maria was in foster care but explained that he was not certain how to connect with the public child welfare agency, fearing that if he appeared "pushy," he would lose all chance to regain custody of Maria. He had been waiting for the agency to contact him.

Justine's, Drew's, and Maria's cases illustrate key steps in achieving permanency for many youth who apparently have been disconnected from family and significant adults in their lives. Youth who have been in foster care for extended periods of time, have little or no birth family involved in their lives, or who entered foster care at an early age and have few memories of family members may need intensive support to kindle family connections.

The identification of potential family resources for youth among the adults previously or currently in youth's lives, as these cases show, can be a multifaceted process. A vital first step involves fully engaging youth in a discussion of the important adults in the youth's life, as emphasized in chapter 13. In Justine's case, the social worker explored with her the important adults in her life and learned about Tanya as a result of these conversations. These types of conversations with youth often yield new information about the youth's emotional connections with birth family members and other important adults within the youth's natural network of relationships, such as foster parents, mentors, coaches, teachers, godparents, and older siblings.

Drew's case provides an example of case mining to locate family members about whom the youth has no information. Through the teaming process, Drew was able to reconsider his refusal to allow efforts to find his siblings, with highly successful results in reconnecting him to them via information about his uncle that the social worker found in Drew's case record. Maria's case illustrates "family finding" for a child who has lost contact with all important adults formerly in her life and who was so young at the time of her entry to foster care that she has little recall of her family. Her social worker reached out to relatives identified through case mining (as did Drew's social worker), supplementing official records with internet search technologies, to find Maria's birth father. Casey's case mining activities are similar to those used in Texas, which has developed procedures for thorough case file review to gather identifying information regarding possible birth family or kin resources. Through case mining, the social worker collects names, social security numbers, birthdates, and any other identifying information that can facilitate a search for the child's family. Priority is placed on relatives who have made efforts to contact the youth's social worker in the past and relatives with whom the youth indicates that he or she wants contact.

At Casey, case mining prioritizes the gathering of information about relationships from the past and those with potential for the future. Internet searches complement case mining when one or more of the following situations exist: (1) the youth has no connection to his or her birth family or information about birth and family history; (2) the youth expresses a longing to be reconnected to birth relatives, and information on these relatives is not otherwise available; (3) the youth feels hopeless and is grieving the loss of relationships; (4) the youth is unable to accept legal permanence because of ambivalence and loyalty conflict related to family of origin issues and relationships; (5) the youth has only professionals as part of his or her permanency team; and (6) there has been no success in identifying or recruiting a potential permanent parent(s).

CONCURRENT PLANNING:
TEAMING TO ACHIEVE PERMANENCY

Case Example 5: Jaime and Lara

Jaime, age fifteen, and his sister, Lara, age fourteen, entered foster care together eight years ago. Both now live in the same residential treatment center, where Jaime has been for three years and Lara for two years. A permanency team was brought together for both young people; it includes their state social worker; the Casey social worker; their therapists at the residential treatment center; a former foster mother for both children, who continues to want to maintain connections with them; the children's birth father, Carlos; and a birth aunt on their father's side, Stella. Efforts to involve the children's mother and maternal relatives have not been successful to date.

Through the teaming process, the team explored Carlos's interest in and ability to parent Jaime and Lara. The team also discussed alternatives for permanence, including adoption, based on the outcome of exploratory discussions with Carlos. Carlos has had regular visits with both children. He has admitted that he continues to abuse drugs and that, while he would like to be a parent, he realizes that he cannot take on this responsibility. He wants very much to remain a presence in his children's lives. Stella also wants to be in Jaime's and Lara's lives. She is not able to commit to being a permanent family resource for them now but states that when they reach age eighteen, they are welcome to come and live with her. Jaime and Lara are heartened by the reconnections with their father and aunt and wish to maintain these relationships.

The team is implementing the concurrent plan and has begun to explore adoption with Jaime and Lara with the goal of recruiting an adoptive family who would adopt the two siblings together, be able to meet their mental health needs, embrace their reconnections with their father and aunt, and understand and appreciate their Latino heritage, of which both young people are very proud. Jaime and Lara are open to the opportunity to have a new family and to have lives as teenagers outside the residential care setting. They share what they would want in an adoptive family. The permanency social worker begins the adoptive family recruitment process.

Jamie and Lara's case illustrates the concurrent planning approach described in chapter 13 as critical in permanency planning for children and youth in foster care. Pine and Spath highlight the benefits of a team approach in facilitating concurrent planning with open conversations about progress, options, responsibilities, plans, and back-up plans. In this case, the Casey social worker employs a concurrent planning approach to identify a permanent parenting relationship for Jaime and Lara. The social worker uses a youth-driven approach (highlighted by Pine and Spath) that takes into account the individual developmental needs and strengths, culture, and ethnic identity of both youths.

Consistent with a concurrent planning framework, Jaime and Lara's team begins by exploring the possibility of reunification with their father. The work undertaken with Carlos finds strong support in the research which, as Pine and Spath describe in their chapter, has demonstrated the value of intensive services in reunifying families. The team uses the research-based foundations of effective reunification practice: comprehensive assessment and service planning and goal-directed services that are both concrete and therapeutic. The social worker's focus on regular, frequent, and well-planned visits between the youth and Carlos is based on a solid body of research that documents the relationship between visitation and successful reunification outcomes.

When their father and aunt each prove to be important family resources in Jaime's and Lara's lives but conclude that they are not able to be a consistent full-time parent, the social worker continues the concurrent permanency planning process. She explores adoption with Jamie and Lara, their birth father and aunt, and other members of the team, facilitating an open dialogue about how adoption can meet their needs for a permanent parent while supporting their ongoing connections with birth family members.

As the social worker begins to recruit an adoptive parent(s) for Jamie and Lara, she will likely use the approaches described in chapter 14. She may recruit prospective adoptive families from within the wider community through ongoing agency efforts and through collaborations with other specialized recruitment agencies or community partners. She will involve Jaime and Lara actively in the process, assisting them in developing a description of their likes, dislikes, personality traits, strengths, skills, attitudes, and wishes about being part of a family. The social worker will involve all members of their permanency team in recruitment, identifying potential permanent parents within their own family and community and faith-based networks, as well as contacting other organizations and groups that might assist in recruitment. Working closely with Jaime and Lara, their social worker may use child-specific recruitment strategies, including media marketing resources such as newspaper or television features, flyers, videotapes, or other promotional materials that use their photographs and stories. Team members, as part of the teaming process, will discuss and refine all of these activities. Once a potential permanent parent is identified, the social worker will include that person on the permanency team and begin the process of building the relationships between birth family members and the newly recruited permanent parent.

Case Example 6: Barb

Barb, age ten, was in residential treatment when her team was assembled. The initial plan was to work toward reunification with Barb's father (Peter), her stepmother, and their new baby. Progress was being made toward reunification when during a weekend visit, Barb's stepmother, who has a history of substance abuse, physically assaulted Peter. Barb called a neighbor for help, and the neighbor called the protective services hotline. The police arrested her stepmother and, because of previous incidents of domestic violence, she was sentenced to prison. Peter, faced with managing on his own with a new baby, began to question his ability to parent Barb, particularly given Barb's mental health needs. Barb's aunt and uncle (Peter's sister and her husband) were members of her team throughout the permanency planning process and supported reunification with the understanding that they were willing to become Barb's legal guardians if this plan became appropriate. When events placed unmanageable pressures on Peter, the team—at the urging of Peter and other family members—moved forward with the alternative permanent plan. Barb went to live with her aunt and uncle while maintaining frequent contact with her father. Barb has been thriving with her aunt and uncle for the past six months. The legal guardianship will be finalized soon.

Barb's case also illustrates the concurrent planning framework of Casey's permanency teaming model. In Barb's case, reunification was the primary permanency goal, well supported by Barb's aunt and uncle, who were members of her team, and other team members. When the change in Peter's circumstances raised questions for all team members, including Peter, about the appropriateness of a reunification plan, Barb's aunt and uncle, who were actively engaged in the planning process, were able to propose legal guardianship with them. The benefits of guardianship with relatives have been well documented, as described by Robert Hill (chapter 9) and Aron Shlonsky (chapter 10) in their discussions of kinship care and subsidized guardianship. Through guardianship with her aunt and uncle, Barb will be able to have the love and support of caring relatives who are committed to her safety and well-being, remain within her family of origin, and have regular contact with her father and sister.

THE TEAMING PROCESS:
PREPARING YOUTH FOR ADOPTION

Case Example 7: Rangsey

Rangsey, age fifteen, entered foster care at age twelve as a result of serious physical abuse. He has had six different foster care placements since entering care. At one point, he and his older brother were placed together with a foster family. His brother, Bourey, has since aged out of foster care. Rangsey remains close with his brother. Rangsey struggles at school and requires special education services. Rangsey is proud of his Cambodian heritage.

Currently, Rangsey's permanency team is composed of Thomas (his Casey social worker), the state social worker, Frank (his coach at school) and Mary (the coach's wife), his therapist, and his attorney. The team is exploring the possibility of Rangsey's adoption by Frank and Mary. Rangsey's therapist has helped all team members understand the many issues that Rangsey brings to this exploration, given his history and experiences in foster care, an understanding that has helped shape Thomas's life book work with Rangsey. This work has included taking Rangsey to a number of the houses and apartments where he lived before he and his brother entered foster care. Rangsey's brother has accompanied them on these visits, and Rangsey and Bourey have shared memories from each place. Thomas took Rangsey to one of the schools that he attended as a child, where a teacher whom Rangsey especially liked continues to teach. Rangsey and the teacher talked about his school experiences, shared memories, and posed for photographs as one way of preserving this reconnection. The outing to the school included a lunch at a Cambodian restaurant that Rangsey remembered from his childhood.

In chapter 14, Ruth G. McRoy and Elissa Madden describe research regarding the characteristics of older children and youth who are adopted from foster care and the critical importance of adoption preparation and postplacement and postlegalization adoption services for these children and youth. Rangsey shares some of the characteristics that McRoy and Madden identify: he was at an older age when separated from his birth family, he has ties to his sibling, he has had multiple placements while in foster care, and he has educational delays. The teaming process for Rangsey addresses many of the issues identified as critical to the successful adoption of older children and youth in foster care. His social worker has provided him with developmentally appropriate preplacement life book services to assist him in clarifying his past life as he explores the possibility of a new life with an adoptive family. As part of the ongoing work, his social worker also works with Frank and Mary to prepare them as they consider adopting Rangsey. The social worker will use joint sessions to involve Frank and Mary in the life book work with Rangsey and help them understand, share, and integrate his personal history into their newly developing shared family history.

The growing body of literature that documents the need for postplacement and postadoption services for families who adopt older children and youth in foster care is described in chapter 14. This chapter reports on studies that suggest that most adoptive families seek services in four categories: educational and informational services (including information about the child's background, adoptive parent training, and referral to adoption literature to help families learn more about adoption issues); clinical services (such as counseling services for the child and family and support services such as respite care); material services (including adoption subsidies, special education services, and medical assistance); and support groups for parents and children, particularly services that address their children's physical, emotional, and developmental needs. The social worker will use individual meetings with Frank and Mary to help them further define their commitment as Rangsey's adoptive parents. Once that commitment is finalized, team members will work together to locate the services that Rangsey, Frank, and Mary identify as essential to support them as a family. Relevant services may include advocacy and consultation to help Frank and Mary meet Rangsey's special education and other needs, subsidy support to assist the family with his range of needs, counseling for Rangsey as he makes the transition from foster care to membership in his new adoptive family, and supports for the inclusion of Rangsey in the family's life. Rather then being passive recipients of the professionals' postpermanency service prescription, Frank, Mary, and Rangsey act as a family with team support to carefully identify the services that are most meaningful and responsive to their perceived needs.

INTEGRATING PERMANENCY AND PREPARATION FOR ADULTHOOD PRACTICES

Case Example: 8: Caleb

Caleb, age seventeen, most recently reentered foster care at the age of fourteen. His mother left him in his father's care when he was young, but she has maintained some contact over the years. His father, who raised him as a single parent, was incarcerated for grand larceny and possession of narcotics Caleb has two half-sisters on his mother's side with whom he has had only a sporadic relationship. Caleb has lived with three foster families since returning to foster care. He is currently living with Mr. Dunn, a single father who raised a nephew who is now an adult and living on his own.

The permanency teaming process for Caleb began in February 2006. His team members include Mr. Dunn; a former foster mother, Benita, who remains committed to being involved in Caleb's life; Caleb's attorney; the state agency social worker; the private agency social worker; and Caleb's therapist. Caleb's two half-sisters, who work long hours on second shift, participate by telephone in the team meetings. The teaming process addresses permanence and preparation for adulthood needs in an integrated way.

Key to the team's permanency work are Caleb's reconnections with his half-sisters and with his mother, an assessment of the appropriate level of connection with his father, and an exploration of the relationship between Caleb and Mr. Dunn and the possibilities for deepening that relationship emotionally and legally. An essential role for the social worker as team facilitator has been to introduce these important members of Caleb's family network to each other and to facilitate the development and strengthening of the relationships. Family members have joined together to support Caleb by taking on responsibility for tasks that will help Caleb prepare for adulthood. Mr. Dunn helped him develop a list of life goals on which Caleb included dates and locations for the SAT and a list of colleges that are of interest to him. His former foster mother, Benita, provided him with the pretest manual for the SAT and volunteered to drive him to the tests, as well as to visit two local colleges. One of his half-sisters has offered to assist with transportation as well. Mr. Dunn and the school guidance counselor are assisting Caleb in completing financial aid applications for college. The state social worker has located funds to pay for driver education so Caleb can obtain his driver's license.

Caleb's case illustrates how both permanency and preparation for adulthood practices can be effectively integrated in the teaming process. Research that supports this integrated approach, underscoring the importance of developing and strengthening youth connections to important social networks and economic opportunities is described in chapter 17. In preparing for the team meetings, Caleb's social worker has worked closely with Caleb to develop the agenda for each meeting, an agenda that consistently focuses on both permanence and preparation for adulthood. Caleb's needs for permanent family relationships, both within his family of origin and, potentially, with his foster father, are prioritized. These relationships form the basis for the development of plans that will prepare Caleb for his initial steps into the adult world and that will encourage and support him throughout his adult life. As Caleb's case illustrates, the teaming approach can help develop individually tailored strategies to support youth as they prepare to transition into adulthood roles. Caring family team members support Caleb's college plans and life skill development in different ways, while the team continues simultaneously to clarify, define, and strengthen permanent family relationships.

The Casey model incorporates the programmatic elements that Hewitt B. Clark and Kimberly A. Crosland (chapter 17) identify in their research: the active engagement of youth in the assessment, planning, and services process; individualized assessment and planning strategies; and customized services that respond to the youth's strengths and needs. At the core, the integration is achieved through purposeful partnering with youth to help them assume the role of the central player in their own integrated planning process. The social worker engages the youth in identifying essential team members, including parents, family members, caregivers, significant adults, professionals, and community members in the team process. The team focuses on strengthening family relationships, sharing decision making, and expanding the youth's life skills resources in all transition domains (e.g., employment, career-oriented education, living situation, personal effectiveness and quality of life, and community-life functioning). These approaches are consistent with the work that is being implemented by the California Permanency for Youth Project, California Youth Connections, and the National Governors' Association Policy Academy for Youth in Transition.

Moreover, Casey is finding that, through teaming, the integration of family permanence and life skills preparation can be facilitated even in the face of significant child and family risk factors. Caleb, who had already reached the age of seventeen when his team was assembled, had experienced multiple family placements. His father's incarceration impeded his ability to plan with Caleb. Through the teaming process, however, family members and other significant adults in Caleb's life were able to marshal their joint resources to explore opportunities for family permanence and to prepare Caleb for his initial steps into adulthood. As a result of the extended team network and the evolving trust among members, participants shared information to support a thorough assessment of Caleb's needs and a full exploration of options. It can be expected that the teaming process will support the achievement of family-based permanence for Caleb, as opposed to leading to Another Planned Permanency Living Arrangement (APPLA) as the outcome. APPLA is not likely to be appropriate for Caleb, given the types of situations recognized by federal regulations as warranting the use of APPLA: a young person specifically has requested that emancipation be his or her permanency goal; the young person's parent has a bond with the youth but the parent has a physical or emotional disability, and the youth's foster parents have agreed to raise the youth to the age of majority and facilitate the youth's contact with the parent; or the youth's tribe has identified another permanent living arrangement for the child (Code of Federal Regulations, 2008).

Though these are not issues in Caleb's case, some cases involve family members' active domestic violence or active substance abuse. In these cases, the safety of all team meeting participants is paramount. Responsible preparation and contingency planning anticipates the potential for compromised judgment or behavioral controls. The input of all family members is essential, and those members who pose a safety risk may need to be included in the teaming process in ways that take the safety risks into consideration. These approaches include holding separate team meetings if the parties are not able to be in the same room together or using individual meetings with each party to develop a safety plan that will structure the meetings they attend together. Known safety concerns provide an opportunity for family members to have honest and direct conversations, thereby improving the likelihood of realistic permanency planning and a safe and successful permanency decision on behalf of the child or youth.

COMMUNITY-BASED FAMILY PRESERVATION AND SUPPORT

In chapter 16 in this volume, Sandra Stukes Chipungu, Laura G. Daughtery, and Benjamin Kerman spotlight a number of community-based child welfare practices to preserve safe and strong connections between vulnerable children and families, as well as to strengthen the environments that surround them. As they point out, many parents experience stressors in their lives and have limited access to supportive community resources. And as noted in chapter 9, the parents of many children who are unable to care for them informally place their children with relatives. Other children come to the attention of child welfare authorities and are placed with relatives who are licensed as foster families. In both situations, many of these relatives are older, have limited incomes, and require services and supports as they assume responsibility for raising their grandchildren or nieces and nephews. Family strengthening, however, need not wait until a child is formally placed in foster care. Practitioners, program directors, and researchers are developing and evaluating evidenced-based and cost-effective family support and placement prevention services to avert the need for more intrusive, traumatic, and costly protective service and removal responses.

In addition to teaming with families whose children are in foster care, Casey also has explored the application of teaming, family-strengthening services, and other community-based strategies to preserve family relationships under strain. Operating in eight sites, Casey has developed Family Resource Centers that strengthen fragile families and support both the family's capacity to meet their children's developmental needs and the community's capacity to support resident families. These hybrid early-intervention and prevention models aim to create a welcoming and engaging family support environment, share planning and direction with community residents to foster leadership development and capacity building, and promote the availability of culturally sensitive services and supports.

Several key family strengthening processes and their results unify the work within these diverse sites. Family Resource Center staff engage families by joining with them in family and community-strengthening activities that families themselves identify and prioritize, irrespective of their involvement with the child welfare system. Drop-in and enrollment-based activities provide a range of activities and supports with goals of improving access to services, including information and referral and advocacy training; parenting classes, homework clubs, and after-school programming to enhance child and family well-being; programs that increase family economic stability, such as English for speakers of other languages, job readiness, and earned income tax credit preparation; and strategies that develop local leadership and community resources through collaboration, such as parent and youth advisory committees, leadership training, and co-location of services.

Using many of the components of a differential response system (which provides community supports and services for families who are assessed as low risk and averts the need for their formal involvement with the child welfare system), the Family Resource Centers seek to engage families who otherwise might not have access to—or be open to accepting—the supports they need. Common obstacles to service use are removed through placing the family support centers within the neighborhoods where families live, welcoming families in collaboration with local parent aides, and avoiding some of the trappings of formal services that tend to stigmatize families in need of assistance. Moreover, the more flexible boundaries of family support settings respond to the episodic ebb and flow of many families' needs for support over time.

Two case descriptions illustrate both the diversity of this community-based work and the potential for flexible community-based family support to strengthen and preserve families. In the first case, a caregiving grand-mother has assumed responsibility for her teenage granddaughter after the teen's mother was incarcerated.

Case Example 9: Gladys

Seeing an advertisement for a kin care provider support group in the local newspaper, Gladys contacted the Casey Family Resource Center. Several months earlier, Gladys's thirteen-year-old granddaughter, Miriam, came to live with her after Miriam's mother (and Gladys's daughter) was imprisoned. Although she was committed to caring for her granddaughter "no matter what," Gladys was unsure that she would have the emotional and financial ability to do the job well or forever.

Gladys reached out to the support group because she felt that she needed someone to talk to regarding the difficulties managing her granddaughter and their household. After attending only a few support group sessions, Gladys began to cherish the support of her peers who shared their experiences and tips. As her trust of the staff facilitating the group grew, she sought out additional psychoeducational information about Miriam's needs as she enters adolescence. Gladys successfully found healthy after-school activities for her granddaughter, yielding both talent development experiences for Miriam and needed respite for herself.

Over time, Gladys became involved with a number of additional center activities that helped with her family's financial challenges. Gladys participated in budgeting and financial planning classes. To help with chronic transportation problems, she began an individual development account to save for a car. With some of the more immediate economic and social challenges well addressed, Gladys has been increasingly confident and optimistic about her family. She is considering taking legal guardianship of Miriam.

Gladys's case illustrates the benefits that families find in community-based services designed to meet families "where they are" without judgment and structured to connect families with the expertise of other families whose wisdom comes from their own experiences and successes. The Family Resource Center provides families with a range of opportunities that support adolescent development and family development, as highlighted in chapter 16.

In the second case, the Family Resource Center helps a mother whose mental illness has compromised her parenting, resulting in her child's foster care placement. With the return home of the child, the Center uses collaborative teaming to engage a range of supportive and caring resources who can help maximize the success of the family's reunification.

Case Example 10: Jan

Jan has been reported to child protective services on multiple occasions, principally when she becomes symptomatic as a result of a bipolar disorder and is unable to care for her son. After the most recent report, Jake, age fifteen, was placed with his maternal grandmother in another community. At this point, Jake has returned home and will now attend his original school and reconnect with important people in the community. Jake has expressed an interest in continuing to play basketball and getting involved in school plays as he was when he lived with his grandmother.

Jan has approached staff at the Family Resource Center's after-school program at a local school, looking for help with Jake now that he has returned home. This contact is one of several that Jan has made with the Center, often reaching out to staff around various "issues of the moment." The responsiveness of the staff at each contact has helped support the development of a trusting relationship between Jan and the staff.

With Jake's return home, the Family Resource Center staff work with Jan to put together a team who can assist her. Her team consists of her mother (who had cared for Jake), her sister, her therapist, Jake, Jake's social worker at the Center's after-school program, and the guidance counselor at Jake's new school. Through the teaming process, Jan has developed stronger skills in effectively navigating the mental health system, particularly with her therapist's assistance; reached agreements with her mother and sister to be respite resources when she is struggling to parent Jake; and enrolled Jake in two after-school activities that match his sports and theater interests. The involvement of her mother and sister on the team has proven to be particularly helpful. Their participation in team meetings has helped them overcome their suspicions about Jan's commitment to Jake and has helped them develop greater trust in the service providers who are working with the family. The team, as a whole, is now on the "family's side" in all planning and decision making.

As Jan's case illustrates, the use of teaming in a community-based setting can effectively strengthen vulnerable families and preserve family permanence for children who previously needed foster care placement. The family members in this case have an opportunity to make the most of their relationships, strengthen their own ability to problem solve, and support one another during the periods when Jan is less able to care for Jake on her own. The work with Jan's mother and sister in preparation for team meetings proved very helpful in expanding their ability to recognize and serve Jake's best interests as the core purpose of their collaborative work together, as opposed to their being caught up in emotions related to long histories of family dysfunction and unresolved anger and disappointment.

Jan's and Jake's team, over time, increasingly will focus on longer-term supports and back-up planning, rather than addressing crisis situations related to Jan's mental health issues. As pointed out in chapter 16, these types of processes provide parents with opportunities to become more empowered each time they initiate their own support plans, and they effectively preserve and strengthen the family and community connections that are vital to success. Equally important, Casey has found that these community-based processes help youth feel a greater sense of stability, emotional security, and self-confidence in being a part of the team planning and decision making with their family members.

CONCLUSION

Several applications of empirically based knowledge to improve permanency and well-being outcomes for youth in foster care are presented in this chapter. We demonstrate how Casey Family Services has drawn on research as it has developed and implemented its youth-centered, family-focused teaming model. This approach represents one of the agency's applications of the growing body of youth permanency research to practice, applications that may vary from those that other agencies are developing and implementing. We illustrate how Casey's applications effectively work to identify family resources for and with youth in care, how the concurrent planning framework of the Casey teaming process is used to facilitate the achievement of family permanence for youth, how teaming effectively prepares youth for adoption, the integration of permanency and preparation for adulthood practice through the teaming process, and the use of community-based prevention services to support and strengthen youth and families. Through the use of its teaming approach, Casey has been able to translate research into effective practice and achieve family permanence for youth whose previous experiences may have suggested that permanence was not a realistic goal. The case examples provided in this chapter, drawn from actual cases and revised to protect the privacy of the clients, show that research can be translated into practice with successful results for youth.

REFERENCES

Code of Federal Regulations (2008). 45 CFR section 1356.21(h)(i), (ii), and (iii).

Afterword

Making Families Permanent and Cases Closed—Concluding Thoughts and Recommendations

With growing attention to permanence as a primary goal for all children in foster care, attention has begun to focus on the needs of youth for lifelong families, as well as safety and well-being. Historically, the child welfare system did not work to ensure that youth in foster care had enduring family relationships that would last a lifetime. Instead, child welfare agencies focused their efforts on preparing them to leave foster care to live "independently." In both policy and practice, the emphasis was on providing youth with a range of social and life skills with the expectation that they would leave foster care well equipped to assume their roles in the adult world. As youth aged out of foster care to live on their own, their cases were closed.

The wisdom of that approach has come into doubt with recent research documenting the troubling outcomes for youth who age out of foster care without the benefit of permanent family relationships. Research makes clear that the majority of youth who age out of foster care at age eighteen or older, like others in their late teens, are not prepared to assume adult roles. Research also demonstrates that youth who leave foster care, like other youth, need the ongoing support and guidance of family members and other caring, committed adults as they transition into the adult world. These studies have added to the sense of urgency. Policy and practice must recognize and more effectively address the needs of young people in foster care by ensuring that they have enduring family relationships to support them as they move into adulthood and beyond. Allowing youth to age out of foster care to live on their own, with the closure of their cases and the termination of the child welfare system's involvement, can no longer be accepted practice.

To achieve positive outcomes for youth, research, policy, and practice must be grounded in a clear understanding of *permanence*. As defined by Casey Family Services (2005), permanence means having an enduring family relationship that is safe and meant to last a lifetime; that offers the legal rights and social status of full family membership; that provides for physical, emotional, social, cognitive, and spiritual well-being; and that assures lifelong connections to extended family, siblings, other significant adults, family history and traditions, race and ethnicity, culture, religion, and language. In achieving permanency outcomes, the objective is the optimal balance of physical, emotional and relational, legal, and cultural dimensions within every child's and youth's array of relationships.

Here we identify some of the most important themes regarding permanence for youth in foster care that emerge from this volume's chapters. We consider five key areas: the permanency needs of youth in foster care; permanence and preparation for adulthood; policy to support system reform initiatives; essential practice strategies; and research, policy, and practice collaborations. Within each of these key areas, we discuss some of the major cross-cutting themes and the resulting implications for research, policy, and practice.

PERMANENCY NEEDS OF YOUTH IN FOSTER CARE

Family permanence for youth is a complex concept that encompasses legal status, geographic location, and social connections. In research, policy, and practice, the primary emphasis with regard to permanence has been on legal arrangements—principally through adoption and guardianship—and physical stability. As the authors in this volume consistently make clear, for youth in foster care whose developmental status and needs differ from younger children in care, greater attention must also be given to issues of emotional security and the social aspects of permanence.

As work proceeds toward achieving the optimal mix of physical, legal, relational, and cultural permanence for young people in foster care, challenges remain in developing data systems that can provide information on their permanency needs and the extent to which permanence is being achieved and sustained for them. Because of their limitations, national child welfare databases currently do not permit a determination of whether youth have actually achieved and sustained legal permanence or have in place a network of supportive family or family-like relationships. At the same time, there is a limited understanding of the permanency needs of different populations of young people in foster care and the strengths that they can bring to planning, achieving, and sustaining permanence. These issues have important implications for research, policy, and practice.

Implications for Research

To improve the understanding of youth's permanency needs, research is required to enhance the understanding of their emotional connections within relationships and to examine the implications of the foster care experience for social functioning and identity formation, particularly as these processes affect permanence. Research is also needed to explore and describe the strengths of youth in planning for—and meeting—their permanency needs, including the factors associated with resilience. Studies must enrich the understanding of the permanence experiences of different populations of youth in foster care, including those of color; gay, lesbian, bisexual, and transgender (GLBT) youth; and youth involved in both the child welfare and the juvenile justice systems.

In addition, researchers must test new approaches to the collection of national data so that data on permanency outcomes (as well as other outcomes) are available. In particular, such data systems must capture information on whether youth have achieved legal permanence or have in place a network of supportive family or family-like relationships.

Implications for Policy

These themes have important implications for policy, which must prioritize permanence as an outcome. Policy can make permanence for youth in foster care a key priority by explicitly recognizing and providing incentives to achieve the emotional and social dimensions of permanence in individualized assessment and service planning.

Policy should recognize and support the different permanency needs of different youths in foster care, particularly those who may be at greatest risk of leaving care without a permanent family (for example, older youth who have been in care for more than two years and who may be poor candidates for reunification). Policy also must recognize the strengths of youth in planning for and meeting their permanency needs, including the factors associated with resilience. Policy further plays a critical role in funding the research that is needed to enhance the understanding of the process and experience of permanence.

Implications for Practice

Because practitioners are the professionals who work directly with youth and their families, they play critical roles in recognizing and addressing permanency needs. Specifically, practitioners must recognize and address the emotional and social dimensions of permanency through individualized assessment and service planning. They need to develop a clear understanding of emotional security and the variety of connections that young persons establish through the range of their relationships. In order to understand and meet youth's permanency needs, practice needs to incorporate assessments of the implications of the foster care experience for adolescents' social functioning and identity formation, particularly as these processes affect their motivation and capacity to expand family connections. Finally, practice must use concurrent planning from the time that each youth enters foster care.

PERMANENCE AND PREPARATION FOR ADULTHOOD

A number of critical themes regarding permanence and the preparation of youth in foster care for adulthood emerge from the chapters in this volume. Among the most important ones that research, policy, and practice must address are the following:

- The need to fully integrate permanence and preparation for adulthood so that family permanence is sought for all youth in foster care and they are prepared for adulthood, irrespective of permanency goal.
- The importance of actively involving youth in permanency planning and preparation for adulthood.

- The development and provision of permanence and preparation for adulthood services with an understanding of the disproportionate representation of children and youth of color in foster care and the disparate outcomes that historically have been achieved for them.
- The need to develop a better understanding of the experiences of gay, lesbian, bisexual, and transgender youth in relation to permanence or preparation for adulthood services.
- The provision of quality training for the child welfare workforce to ensure that young persons achieve and sustain family permanence and are well prepared for adulthood.

Research can contribute significantly to practice and policy in permanence and preparation for adulthood by broadening the understanding of the specific organizational, programmatic, practice, and policy factors that support the full integration of permanence and preparation for adulthood; by testing youth engagement strategies in order to identify the most effective approaches; and by identifying culturally appropriate services in response to the needs and strengths of African American, Latino, Native American, and GLBT youth.

Policy and practice likewise play important roles in ensuring that permanence is sought for all youth in foster care and that efforts continue to be made to identify and support potential enduring relationships, irrespective of the youth's permanency goal. Policy and practice can promote positive outcomes by recognizing and supporting family connections as pivotal to the preparation of youth in foster care for adulthood and by requiring that a caring, committed adult be identified for each young person who leaves foster care without the benefit of legal permanence.

From both policy and practice perspectives, a key issue is the ongoing use of "Another Planned Permanent Living Arrangement" (APPLA) as a permanency goal for many children who may benefit from pursuing permanent family connections. APPLA can be used appropriately and effectively by simultaneously focusing on preparing each young person for adulthood through skills development and by either supporting existing family connections or forging new ones. From a policy perspective, two other issues must be addressed to promote the integration of permanence and preparation for adulthood: first, a stronger policy interface between the Adoption and Safe Families Act and the Fostering Connections Act, on the one hand, and the Chafee Foster Care Independence Act on the other hand, so that family permanence and preparation for adulthood services are recognized as complementary; second, the elimination of policies that penalize youth who achieve permanency (such as policies that render youth ineligible for services or educational benefits if they return home or are adopted at a younger age).

In addition to these themes, the chapters in this volume include discussions of other important issues related to two key areas: post–foster care outcomes for youth and family permanence.

Post–Foster Care Outcomes for Youth

As is made clear in this volume, much remains to be learned about the effect of current services designed to prepare youth in foster care for adulthood. There is no conclusive systematic evidence of the effectiveness of independent living programs. To the extent that these programs have been evaluated, the primary focus has been on skill development, with mixed results, and little attention has been given to a young person's development of networks of supportive family or family-like relationships. Similarly, little is known about the effect of the Chafee Foster Care Independence Act. The act made resources available to serve youth preparing to leave foster care, but little is known about the impact of these resources on the level and effectiveness of services made available. Fortunately, federal efforts to expand the Chafee evaluation are currently under way.

Research has demonstrated very poor outcomes for many youth who age out of foster care. Recent outcomes studies identify an elevated risk for a variety of health, mental health, housing, financial, and other problems, coupled with a decreased likelihood of having adequate health insurance. More, however, needs to be understood about the longer-term outcomes for those who leave care through emancipation or aging out. In addition, little is known about those who exit foster care to other service systems, including mental health and criminal and juvenile justice. Finally, many youth leave care by running away, but there is a limited understanding of the characteristics of those youth, the reasons they run, or ways to reduce running behavior. Research suggests that many youth who run away reunify with their parents on their own at some point, but more needs to be understood about these family relationships.

Implications for Research

Research is needed in a number of areas to enhance the understanding of post–foster care outcomes for youth. Among those are rigorous evaluations of independent living program to identify effective components, including programmatic elements designed to connect youth with family and other committed adults, support their connections with key adults, and emphasize skills teaching in the context of family relationships. Studies are needed to provide a better understanding of the use of federal independent living funds and the effectiveness of those services in improving outcomes for youth. Finally, ongoing longitudinal studies are needed of the outcomes for youth following their exits from foster care, with a focus on the factors that predict success or lack of success for foster care alumni, particularly the results of having connections to family and other key resource people in the youth's life.

Implications for Policy and Practice

Policy and practice must reexamine the concept of "independence" for youth at the age of eighteen and the acceptability of "aging out" as an appropriate option. Both must reframe the concept of "independent living preparation" to "preparation for adulthood" and reconceptualize the goal for youth as "interdependent living" as opposed to "independent living." A body of knowledge regarding evidence-based practices must be developed to ensure that youth have both social and economic capital as they prepare for—and enter—adulthood. Attention must be given to the resources available through the Chafee Foster Care Independence Program, as well as other transitional services that can support family involvement and provide concrete services for youth.

Family Permanence for Youth

Several key themes emerge from the authors' contributions regarding achieving and sustaining family permanence for youth. First, placement factors appear to play key roles in undermining family permanence for youth. Two factors, in particular, have been identified: multiple changes in placement settings and an overreliance on congregate care. From research, policy, and practice perspectives, it is essential to identify, assess, and provide evidence-based services that stabilize youth's placements while they are in foster care. Through understanding and implementing evidence-based practices that promote placement stability, young people's opportunities for family permanence will be enhanced. In addition, research, policy, and practice must focus on identifying and addressing the factors that are associated with the appropriate and inappropriate use of congregate care as a placement resource. Family-based care, with its potential to provide opportunities for long-term family relationships, should be used for youth who do not need structured group settings. It also is critical to identify and implement practices and approaches that can promote the achievement of family permanence for those who are appropriately placed in congregate care settings.

A second theme is that family permanence through reunification with parents and relatives is not well understood. Despite the fact that reunification is the most common permanency exit for older children and youth in foster care, few studies have focused on the reunification of youth with their birth parents. Much more needs to be understood about successful reunification approaches, in terms of both planned reunification and unplanned (self-initiated) reunifications and the factors associated with re-entry to foster care from reunification. Research, policy, and practice must give significantly greater attention to reunification and contribute to the building of a knowledge base of evidence-based practices. Although little attention has been given to reunification with parents, there has been greater research, policy, and practice interest in kinship care. Research suggests significant benefits for youth when permanence is achieved through kinship care, particularly when subsidized guardianship is available to kin families. More needs to be understood, however, about permanence with relatives. In particular, research, policy, and practice must focus on subsidized guardianship as a strong permanency option for youth and their kin caregivers. Finally, the importance of siblings as key family connections and potential lifelong supports, regardless of reunification with caregivers, is only beginning to be realized. Research, policy, and practice must focus on supporting and strengthening youth's connections with their siblings.

Third, the significant role of foster parents as permanency resources for many older children and youth in foster care has become better understood. Research, policy, and practice, however, must address the services and supports that foster parents need to provide legal and social permanence for older children and youth, including financial supports that facilitate giving serious consideration to adoption or guardianship for those in their care.

Fourth, family permanence through adoption is an area in which much more needs to be understood. For example, questions remain as to how termination of parental rights and adoption can be most effectively used in achieving permanence for youth in foster care. Research, policy, and practice must recognize that adoption practices and policies for youth are necessarily different from adoption practices and policies for younger children. In addition, little attention has been given to the experiences and needs of youth whose parents' rights have been terminated but who have not been adopted. There should be focus on processes that support a reconsideration of these youth's birth family relationships, as well as other relationships with caring, committed adults.

Finally, sustaining permanence is an issue that requires greater attention. For many youth, permanence is "impermanent": that is, they return to foster care after reunification or their placements with kin or adoptive families disrupt. Research, policy, and practice must focus on the effectiveness of ongoing permanency planning efforts with youth for whom initial permanency efforts have not been successful. The effectiveness and cost-benefit of postpermanency services must also be carefully examined.

POLICY TO SUPPORT SYSTEM REFORM INITIATIVES

A consistent theme in this volume's chapters is that key levers of required policy change in the child welfare arena are legislative reform, class action litigation and court mandates, and approaches that provide for the testing of innovative policies and programs. A second key theme is that adequate and flexible funding is essential to achieving and sustaining permanence for youth.

Information is limited on the broad effect of federal policy reforms on efforts to achieve and sustain family permanence for youth. Although data indicate that since the enactment of the Adoption and Safe Families Act, the total number of adoptions has increased and the number of children being reunified with their families has declined slightly, little more regarding permanency outcomes for youth in foster care is known. It is essential that a clear understanding be developed of how federal funds are being used for services that support and strengthen families—that is, services that prevent the need for children and youth to enter foster care and that support the safe reunification of children and youth with their families after they enter foster care. Research, policy, and practice need to use child and family services reviews more fully to learn about permanency outcomes for older children and youth in foster care. Particular emphasis needs to be placed on permanency outcomes for those of color.

Equally limited is information about the impact of court reform efforts on improving permanency outcomes. Research, policy, and practice must find ways to promote strong collaboration between the courts and child welfare agencies in planning for and achieving permanence for youth in foster care. Two key approaches to strengthening the court-agency collaboration are (1) requiring and supporting data sharing between courts and child welfare agencies (in accordance with appropriate protections) and (2) implementing cross-training for court and child welfare staff.

ESSENTIAL PRACTICE STRATEGIES

Three essential practice strategies emerge from the volume's chapters: (1) front end services to prevent children from entering foster care whenever possible; (2) family involvement meetings that support permanency planning and the preparation of youth for adulthood; and (3) the development and use of community supports and services on behalf of youth and their families. The importance of preventive services has long been recognized, but resources for these services generally have been limited. Key to the provision of effective preventive services are policies that place priority on—and fund—evidence-based programs that are successful in lowering the incidence of child abuse and neglect and reducing the need for children to enter foster care.

As reported in this volume, studies indicate that family involvement meetings are viewed favorably by families and practitioners. The evidence, however, is not yet sufficient to validate the intuitive understanding that these meetings contribute to better permanency outcomes. Researchers, practitioners, and policymakers need to collaborate in the development and implementation of ongoing studies of family involvement models and the outcomes that these approaches achieve, particularly with youth in foster care and their families. A better understanding is needed of the benefits and challenges of team decision-making models that involve youth, parents, other supportive adults, and community partners in meetings with child welfare professionals.

Experience suggests that better outcomes for youth are achieved when child welfare agencies have strong relationships with the communities from which youth come. Greater attention needs to be paid to developing community supports and services for parents and informal kin caregivers so that foster care entry can be avoided whenever possible. Stronger collaborations are needed between child welfare agencies and communities to strengthen prevention services and supports and to meet the needs of parents and kin caregivers when children and youth leave foster care to return to their families. Research, policy, and practice must encourage the development of strong working relationships between child welfare agencies and community services and supports.

RESEARCH, POLICY, AND PRACTICE COLLABORATIONS

The collaboration of research, policy, and practice is essential to achieving and sustaining permanence for youth in foster care. As the authors of the chapters in this volume consistently demonstrate, research is needed to explore innovative models to move toward evidence-based practice and provide the foundation for sound child welfare policy. Collaboration among researchers, policymakers, and practitioners is needed to promote the design of mixed research methods that include both quantitative research and qualitative research featuring the voices of youth.

Researchers, policymakers, and practitioners also must be partners in developing and using the results of research and evaluations to inform policies and practices that advance successful and sustained family connections for youth in foster care. Through ongoing communication with researchers, practitioners and policymakers can use research-based knowledge to evaluate and strengthen current practices and policies and develop future approaches that are evidence-based.

Research, policy, and practice collaboration is also critical to the development of data systems that provide aggregate information on youth outcomes: whether youth have achieved and sustained legal and social permanence; how well youth fare as they enter adulthood and take on adult roles; and the experiences of those who exit foster care not to family but to other systems, through "aging out" or through running away. Through such collaborations, accountability in child welfare can be increased by measuring system performance more aggressively and collecting better and more relevant data.

CONCLUSION

As demonstrated in this volume, there are evidence-based policies and practices that support family permanence for youth. These policies and practices can inform how administrative decision makers and frontline providers move forward. Additional research, however, is needed in many critical areas to expand the understanding of what works in achieving and sustaining family permanence and preparing youth for adulthood with the support of family. Research plays a vital role in addressing key child welfare policy and practice issues. Through the development of a greater understanding of what works and the implementation of evidence-based policies and practices, it will be possible ensure that youth leave foster care to permanent families. Their child welfare cases will be closed with the assurance that they have the support of family and other caring, committed adults in their lives. It is hoped that this volume provides the foundation for a strong research agenda to achieve these critical goals for all children and youth in foster care.

REFERENCES

Casey Family Services (2005). *A Call to Action: An Integrated Approach to Youth Permanency and Preparation for Adulthood.* New Haven, Conn.: Author.

Contributors

Rosemary J. Avery is Professor and Chairman of the Department of Policy Analysis and Management at Cornell University. Her research program focuses on national child welfare issues, particularly permanence for adolescents exiting foster care. She serves as evaluator on two federal grants focusing on permanence for youth living in congregate care settings.

Richard P. Barth is Professor and Dean of the School of Social Work at the University of Maryland School of Social Work. He has helped develop and evaluate innovations in child abuse prevention, foster care, school social work, adolescent parenting services, adoption, and independent living services.

Laura K. Chintapalli has served as a case manager at the Safe Children Coalition in Sarasota County, Florida, as a research assistant and associate at the University of North Carolina at Chapel Hill School of Social Work, and currently as a foster care licensing social worker in Chatham County, North Carolina.

Sandra Stukes Chipungu is an Associate Professor at Morgan State University Department of Social Work. She received her doctorate and two masters degrees from the University of Michigan and her undergraduate degree from Morgan State University. Her areas of research are child welfare, foster care and kinship care, African American families and children, social policies, substance abuse prevention, and program evaluation.

Hewitt B. (Rusty) Clark is the Director of the National Center on Youth Transition for Behavioral Health and is a Professor in the Department of Child and Family Studies at the Florida Mental Health Institute, University of South Florida. He has developed and researched innovative programs concerning individualized planning and interventions for children, youth, and families with emotional/behavioral difficulties and transition to employment, educational opportunities, and independent living.

Mark E. Courtney is Executive Director of Partners for Our Children, a public-private partnership housed at the University of Washington and devoted to improving child welfare services. He is also the Ballmer Chair for Child Well-Being in the School of Social Work at the University of Washington, as well as fellow and former director at Chapin Hall Center for Children.

David Crampton is an Assistant Professor of Social Work at the Mandel School of Applied Social Sciences, Case Western Reserve University in Cleveland, Ohio. His work explores the use of family meetings and other community-based child welfare practices.

Kimberly A. Crosland is a board-certified behavior analyst and Assistant Professor at the University of South Florida. She is the research director for the Behavior Analysis Services Program, a statewide initiative for foster children and families funded through the Department of Children and Families.

Gretta Cushing is a Senior Research Associate at Casey Family Services. She is currently the lead investigator of the Casey Longitudinal Study of Foster Youth Development, a study designed to examine outcomes and developmental trajectories of youth with a history of foster care as they transition to young adulthood.

Sabrina A. Davis of Planning and Learning Technologies, Inc., is responsible for multiple aspects of the National Evaluation of the Court Improvement Program. She has represented children in abuse and neglect proceedings as a student attorney and as a volunteer court-appointed special advocate. She is currently licensed to practice law in Arizona and Washington, D.C.

Laura G. Daughtery is Assistant Professor at the National Catholic School of Social Service, Catholic University of America. A licensed social worker in the District of Columbia and Maryland, she spent nearly ten years in public child welfare. Her areas of research interest include adolescents in foster care and African American children in child welfare.

Shirley A. Dobbin is an Assistant Director of the Permanency Planning for Children Department of the National Council of Juvenile and Family Court Judges. She is involved in a number of research and evaluation projects involving permanency planning at the local, state, and national levels. She has coauthored a number of technical assistance bulletins and articles about child welfare practice and systems change.

Karl Ensign, Director, Evaluation for Children, Youth, and Families, at Planning and Learning Technologies, Inc., has twenty years experience in policy development and evaluation of children and family services. He was previously employed in the Office of the Assistant Secretary for Planning and Evaluation, U.S. Department of Health and Human Services. He is currently leading the National Evaluation of the Court Improvement Program for the Children's Bureau.

Madelyn Freundlich is a child welfare consultant at Excal Consulting Partners LLC. She formerly served as General Counsel and Director of Child Welfare Services for the Child Welfare League of America, as Executive Director for the Evan B. Donaldson Adoption Institute, and as Policy Director for Children's Rights. She holds graduate degrees in social work, public health, and law.

Lauren Frey has twenty-five years experience in permanency planning, child welfare system reform, foster care, and adoption. As Project Director of Permanency Services at Casey Family Services, she assists direct practice divisions in implementing permanency practice. She is a national trainer, consultant, and speaker.

Sarah B. Greenblatt has worked throughout her career with and on behalf of vulnerable children, families, and their communities. Since 2001 she has coordinated national technical assistance as the Director of the Casey Center for Effective Child Welfare Practice at Casey Family Services in New Haven, Connecticut. She previously served as Director of the National Resource Center for Foster Care and Permanency Planning at Hunter College.

Robert B. Hill is a senior researcher at Westat, a research firm based in Rockville, Maryland. His current work focuses on the overrepresentation of children of color in the child welfare system and on the well-being of kinship care families. He has a doctorate in sociology from Columbia University.

Benjamin Kerman has been conducting program evaluation and child welfare research at Casey Family Services since 1997. As Director of Research and Evaluation, his current activities focus on foster care, family preservation, and family support. A licensed psychologist, he serves on the adjunct faculty of the Yale Child Study Center.

Elizabeth Lee is Senior Project Analyst, Planning and Learning Technologies, Inc. She has over fifteen years experience conducting policy, cost, and program research and evaluation in a variety of human service fields, including child welfare, Head Start, substance abuse, court reform, and community-based services.

Elissa Madden is currently pursuing a doctoral degree in social work at the University of Texas at Austin. She holds both a bachelor's and a master's in social work from Baylor University. Her research interests are primarily in the area of permanence for children in care and the use of mediation in child protection cases.

Anthony N. Maluccio is Professor Emeritus, University of Connecticut, Graduate School of Social Work, and Professor (Retired), Boston College, Graduate School of Social Work. He has been Visiting Professor at Universita' di Padova and Fondazione Zancan, as well as Melbourne University. His research spans child welfare, including permanency and reunification services.

Penelope L. (Penny) Maza is the Senior Policy Research Analyst in the U.S. Children's Bureau in the Department of Health and Human Services. She conducts statistical analyses on data from the Adoption and Foster Care Analysis and Reporting System, which informs the development of federal policy in child welfare. She is the author of numerous articles in the child welfare field.

Ruth G. McRoy is a Research Professor and the Ruby Lee Piester Centennial Professor Emerita at the University of Texas at Austin School of Social Work. Interests include family preservation; open, youth, and transracial adoptions; and postadoption services. In collaboration with AdoptUsKids, she leads a team at the University of Texas examining barriers to adoption and factors associated with successful adoptions of children with special needs.

Peter J. Pecora is the Senior Director of Research Services for Casey Family Programs and Professor, School of Social Work, University of Washington, Seattle. He has worked with agencies in the United States and abroad to refine foster care programs, develop evaluation strategies, and implement intensive home-based services, training, and risk assessment systems.

Joan Pennell is Professor and Head, Department of Social Work, North Carolina State University. She is the principal investigator of the North Carolina Family-Centered Meetings Project, which receives funding for work in child welfare from the North Carolina Department of Health and Human Services and work in schools from the North Carolina Department of Public Instruction.

Barbara A. Pine is Professor Emerita at the University of Connecticut where her teaching and research were in three main areas: social work administration, child welfare, and professional ethics. She has consulted and published extensively in child welfare policy, programs, and practice.

Aron Shlonsky is Associate Professor at the University of Toronto and Director of the Bell Canada Child Welfare Research Unit. Before entering academia, he served as a protective services worker, sexual abuse therapist, and substance abuse counselor. Professional interests include actuarial risk assessment in child welfare, kinship foster care, sibling relationships in out-of-home care, subsidized guardianship, and evidence-based practice and evaluation research.

Robin Spath is Assistant Professor and Chair of the Women and Children Substantive Area at the University of Connecticut School of Social Work. She has given presentations and authored and coauthored a number of publications on topics related to child welfare, family violence, and research methodology.

Fred Wulczyn is a research fellow at Chapin Hall Center for Children at the University of Chicago. He is the recipient of the National Association of Public Child Welfare Administrators' Peter Forsythe Award for leadership in public child welfare. He is director of the Center for State Foster Care and Adoption Data, which focuses on using information technology to bridge the worlds of research and management.

Index

overview, 41–43; reentry to foster care, 91–92; reunification, 90–91
—studies: alumni (19–25) (*see* Casey Family Programs, young adult survey; Casey Family Services, alumni study; Reilly Nevada study); summary of, 58–70
disproportionality, 167. *See also* racial disparity
dispute resolution programs, 192
divorce rates, after aging out of the system, 50–51
DMC (Disproportionate Minority Contact), 139
docketing system, 192, 202–203
Downs, A. C., 69
drug abuse. *See* substance abuse
duration of foster care. *See* time in foster care
Dworsky, A., 66, 70

earnings. *See* employment; income
economic self sufficiency, after aging out of the system, 48–49
Edna McConnell Clark Foundation, 301
education, former foster children: after aging out of the system, 44–45; bachelor's degrees, 45; GED rates, 45; high school completion rates, 45; post-secondary, 45; Reilly Nevada study of discharge outcomes, 76; West Virginia, 45
educational remediation, policy direction, 80
EITC (earned income tax credit), 302
electronic data sharing, 197
emancipation, as case goal, 13
emotional healing, family meetings, 273–74

emotional permanence, 111
emotional problems: adopted children, 256–57; evidence-informed practices, 328; factor in placement instability, 93–94
employment, after foster care: aging out of the system, 48–49; income levels, 49, 76; JCYOI (Jim Casey Youth Opportunities Initiative), 322; Reilly Nevada study of discharge outcomes, 76
English, D., 69
entering foster care: admission rate, by race or ethnicity, 19–21; placement type, by age at admission, 21–22
ethnic identity, family meetings, 282–83
evidence-informed practices: ARIES program, 326; Casey Family Services, 324–25; handling emotional and behavioral disturbances, 328; overview, 323–24; Project RENEW, 325–26; TIP (Transition to Independence Process), 326–29
extended services, discharge outcomes, 55

family-based care: age at first admission, 21–22; MST (Multisystemic Therapy), 90–91; MTFC (Multidimensional Treatment Foster Care), 90–91. *See also* out-of-home care; placement types
family development theory, 295–96
family formation, after aging out of the system, 50–51
Family Group Conferencing (FGC), 203, 268–71
Family Group Decision Making (FGDM), 271